AMERICAN
ROCK'N'ROLL
THE UK TOURS
1956-72

AMERICAN ROCK'N'ROLL
THE UK TOURS
1956-72

Ian Wallis

MUSIC MENTOR BOOKS
York, England

British Library Cataloguing-in-Publication Data
A catalogue record for this book is available from the British Library.

ISBN 0 9519888 6 7

Published worldwide by Music Mentor Books *(Proprietor: G.R. Groom-White)*
69 Station Road, Upper Poppleton, York YO26 6PZ, North Yorkshire, England.
Telephone/Fax: +44 (0)1904 330308   *email:* music.mentor@lineone.net

Technical support by PJP Information Systems, Bradford, West Yorkshire.

Cover by It's Great To Be Rich, York.

Printed and bound in Great Britain by Antony Rowe Ltd, Eastbourne, East Sussex.

Acknowledgments

This book could never have been written without the assistance, enthusiasm and encouragement of a very important band of friends, acquaintances and rock'n'roll enthusiasts. May I therefore offer a big thank you to this star-studded list of names: Graham Barker, Julian Barker, Paul Barrett, Bill Beard, John Beecher, Freddie Bell, Rick Biddle, Terry Biddle, Dave Booth, David Bowell, Peter Burns, Donna Cade, Trevor Cajiao, Terry Clemson, Breathless Dan Coffey, James Cullinan, Bob Dunham, Jim Elliott, Rob Finnis, John Firminger, John Garodkin, Jim Grant, Ronnie Hawkins, Derek Henderson, John Ingman, Willie Jeffery, Terry Kay, Geoff Kember, Val Kember, Peter Koers, Frankie Jean Lewis, Peter Lewry, Ken Major, John McPhee, Bill Millar, Arthur Moir, Bob Naylor, Colin Phillips, John Poole, Marvin Rainwater, Morten Reff, Steve Richards, Brian Smith, Keith Stanley, Tez Stokes, Dave Travis, Tony Warran, Tony Wilkinson, Chas White, George White and Terry Young.

My research commenced with the weekly music press and extended out through countless specialist magazines and fanzines, the most important of which were *Melody Maker*, *Record Mirror*, *Disc*, *New Musical Express*, *Sounds*, *Now Dig This* (the greatest rock'n'roll magazine in the world, ever), *The Boppin' News*, *Crickets File*, *Haley News*, *Gene Vincent Fan Club Magazine*, *Penniman News*, *The Shaking Keyboard*, *Kentucky*, *Sun Sound Special*, *Rock'n'Roll Collector*, *Fireball Mail*, *R'n'B Monthly*, *Not Fade Away*, *Shout*, *Country Music People*, *New Kommotion*, *Shindig*, *Lonely Blue Boy News*, *Lewis Scene*, *Soul Music Monthly*, *Memphis*, *Strictly Cash*, *Twangsville*, *Opry*, *Rock'n'Roll Scene*, *Camel Walker*, *Texan Star* and *Jazz Monthly*.

When rock'n'roll was relegated from the theatres to the clubs and ballrooms during the Sixties, it became increasingly difficult to unravel the complexities of each tour. Mixed in with all the bogus Drifters and Platters were the genuine rock'n'roll tours, details of which were poorly advertised, if at all. My research became more intense, and many hundreds of hours were spent at the British Newspaper Library in Colindale examining local papers from all across the United Kingdom in the hope of locating show adverts, which would gradually bring together the various pieces of the jigsaw. So obsessive did this become that every little clue was followed up, until one day, while avidly tracking up into Scotland one of Gene Vincent's many tours and seeking clarification of a possible date in the extreme north at Wick, my efforts were temporarily halted by the realisation that the Wick local paper was not printed during the Herring Fishing season! When was that? I paused and then laughed out loud at the absurdity of the situation, picturing those grizzled fishermen in their oilskins putting aside their nets and heading to the local dance hall to catch a Gene Vincent rock'n'roll show. This crazy music that nobody wanted got everywhere in the end and it is still out there if you want to find it.

For Mum and Dad

Contents

Introduction

Many excellent books have been written about rock'n'roll music including countless biographies, chart listings and record company histories. However, until now, there has been no serious attempt to make a close study of live rock'n'roll. This is a startling omission, as nothing can compare with the energy and excitement of a live rock'n'roll show. All the great performers had wonderful stage acts, and if you were ever fortunate enough to see Little Richard, Gene Vincent or Bill Haley in their prime then I wager that you can still close your eyes and vividly recall the frantic vocals, the pumping piano and the honking saxophone. Indeed, if truth be known, the whole fantastic experience is still indelibly branded on your soul.

I believe the research for this book to be totally original. Commencing in 1956, it traces the rise of rock'n'roll as a live music in Britain and documents every UK tour by an American (or Canadian) performer. It details every show played in every town or city, listing the dates, the venues and wherever possible the identities of the backing groups, the supporting acts, the names of the promoters and even a summary of British television appearances. Each tour is described at length, the information having been extracted from contemporary reports.

The defining basis for inclusion is artists who have been classed as rock'n'roll. Some, like Clyde McPhatter or Bo Diddley, would also feature in a book on R&B, while other such as Johnny Cash (country), Ben E. King (soul) or Bobby Vee (pop) could just as easily be reclassified elsewhere, but as rock'n'roll is not an exact science, I have made the definition a reasonably wide one. In any case, no two people are likely to agree, so I have made the rules!

Inevitably, there will be some errors and omissions in the listings. Shows were sometimes booked or cancelled at the last moment and the music press were notoriously unreliable with their information. Nevertheless, an enormous amount of detailed research has been carried out and I am confident that there is an acceptable level of accuracy.

On several occasions, American performers visited Britain solely to play for US troops at their military bases. The general public were excluded from these shows and they are therefore not featured in this study. However, gigs at US bases which were played as part of a public tour are included where known.

For those who remember the golden era of rock'n'roll, this book will re-awaken some wonderful memories and for those too young to have experienced it first time round, I hope that I have adequately conveyed the excitement and intensity of the period. Those of us who were teenagers in the Fifties and early Sixties were lucky to live through such an exhilarating period of change and have the opportunity to hear fresh and new the greatest music in the world.

CHAPTER ONE

1955-56

We're Gonna Teach You To Rock

It now seems extraordinary to reflect that, until the summer of 1956 there was nowhere in Britain to hear live rock'n'roll music. The name of Bill Haley had regularly featured in the British charts since December 1954, and in the twenty months since then classic hits by Elvis Presley, Carl Perkins, Gene Vincent, Frankie Lymon & The Teenagers and Pat Boone had established the new music despite negligible coverage on television and distinctly limited exposure on the radio. Even the music press ignored rock'n'roll for as long as possible, and, in the case of the jazz-fixated *Melody Maker*, hated it with a passion. The British teenager could sit at home and spin 78 rpm records of 'Blue Suede Shoes' or 'Heartbreak Hotel', or possibly catch the *Rock Around The Clock* movie at the local cinema, but there was nowhere to hear the music performed live.

During 1955, American stars Guy Mitchell and Johnnie Ray had toured the UK amidst a blaze of publicity with acts which were not rock'n'roll, but which did nevertheless generate much of the same primitive excitement. The Canadian vocal group, the Crew Cuts, arrived in September for three months and their shows did include a small segment of their own sanitised rock'n'roll. They sang 'Ko Ko Mo', 'Don't Be Angry', 'Earth Angel' and 'Sh-Boom', but only as part of a traditional hat-and-cane variety act. More interesting would have been Cab Calloway performing his 'Minnie The Moocher' to British audiences also in September, but his tour was a low-key affair and received very little publicity.

In February 1956, country star Slim Whitman made his first British tour, while the Ink Spots featuring Bill Kenny spent almost half a year playing the variety theatres and music halls, also taking in a television appearance from the London Palladium. Both the Deep River Boys and the Golden Gate Quartet played shows during September, and the latter even included 'Rock Around The Clock' during their appearance at the Manchester Hippodrome. British teenagers were ready for rock'n'roll. Now it was time for the real thing.

BILL HALEY & HIS COMETS

The first abortive attempt at a rock'n'roll tour of Britain was announced by promoters Lew and Leslie Grade in February 1956. They were proposing a two week season for Bill Haley at the London Palladium in April to be followed by six provincial dates. His US commitments made the plan impossible, but by May the Grades were reportedly attempting to reschedule the tour for February 1957.

TONY CROMBIE & HIS ROCK'N'ROLL ROCKETS

It was announced at the beginning of August that jazz drummer Tony Crombie was leaving Ronnie Scott's Orchestra to form Britain's first rock'n'roll band. A theatre tour was promoted by top impresario Bernard Delfont and commenced on 11 September 1956 with a week-long residency at the Theatre Royal, Portsmouth supported by Maxine Daniels and Don Fox. Crombie and the Rockets, featuring vocalist Clyde Ray, performed eight songs in a twenty-minute act, opening with 'We're Gonna Teach You To Rock' and closing with 'The Saints Rock'n'Roll'. The Theatre Royal was in the midst of its centenary celebrations, but despite fears that marauding teddy boys might disrupt the proceedings, it was reported that Crombie's act '*produced a tumultuous surge of excitement, greater than had been seen for one act before*'. Live rock'n'roll had finally arrived in Britain.

Crombie's tour had barely got under way when London's Studio 51 opened for regular Thursday and Saturday sessions by Rory Blackwell's Rock'n'Rollers, and on Monday, 18 September nineteen year old singer and guitarist Tommy Steele made his professional debut in London at Al Burnett's Stork Room. Later that month, former Ronnie Scott vocalist Art Baxter formed a six-piece rock'n'roll band, the Rockin' Sinners, in preparation for a tour of theatres and dance halls for promoter Jeff Kruger.

Before the end of 1956, other pioneering British rock'n'roll acts including Don Sollash's Rockin' Horses, Leon Bell's Bellcats, the Rock'n'Roll All Stars and the Kirchins had entered the fray, but for the purposes of this text we will henceforth concentrate solely on the American and Canadian performers who played live in the UK.

R.B. SHAW & HIS MELODY MOUNTAINEERS

September 1956	
29-31 Clacton Butlin's Holiday Camp	
Promoter unknown	

Since the Seventies many of the biggest rock'n'roll shows in Britain have been held at holiday camps, so it is a curious coincidence that the first-ever stage performance by an American rock'n'roller should have taken place at Butlin's in Clacton as part of the *Jazz Festival Weekend* of 1956.

An ambitious project, it featured fourteen acts including the orchestras of Johnny Dankworth, Ted Heath and Eric Delaney, as well as

Shirley Bassey, Ronnie Scott and the Tubby Hayes Band. Rock'n'roll was presented by Tony Crombie's Rockets, the Kirchins, and — as a late addition to the bill — the American act, R.B. Shaw & His Melody Mountaineers, who were secured from a nearby USAF base.

The weekend was not a great success. Only eight hundred turned up instead of the anticipated four thousand, and, although the majority were well-behaved, there was considerable tension between the jazz buffs and the small but vociferous group of rock'n'roll fans. There were complaints of heckling during Ted Heath's set (*'Morons at the back of the hall kept calling out "Go! Go! Go!" and shouting for rock and roll with pathetic attempts at wit'*), while some fans who wanted rock'n'roll all the time were reduced to organising a jam session in one of the chalets. Even this caused problems as there were repeated complaints about the noise. Rock'n'roll had started the way it meant to carry on.

LIONEL HAMPTON & HIS ORCHESTRA

October 1956			5	Sheffield	City Hall
21	London	Empress Hall	6	Wolverhampton	Civic Hall
22	Preston	Public Hall	7	Glasgow	St. Andrew's Hall
23	Leicester	De Montfort Hall	8	Edinburgh	Usher Hall
24	Birmingham	Town Hall	9	Newcastle	City Hall
25	Cardiff	Sophia Gardens	10	Bradford	St. George's Hall
26	London	Royal Albert Hall	11	Lewisham	Gaumont
27	Ramsgate	Coronation	13	Luton	Cresta
29	Bristol	Colston Hall	14	London	Royal Festival Hall
30	Norwich	St. Andrew's Hall	15	Sheffield	City Hall
31	Bournemouth	Winter Gardens	16	Birmingham	Town Hall
November 1956			17	Leicester	De Montfort Hall
2	Hanley	Victoria Hall	18	Edmonton	Regal
3	York	Rialto			
4	Liverpool	Empire *(matinée)*			
	Manchester	Kings Hall			
Promoter — Harold Davison					

Not strictly a rock'n'roll tour, the visit of much-respected jazz musician Lionel Hampton had been eagerly awaited by his British fans. The first hint that all was not well came with a report from the States that Hampton would be slanting his act to cash in on the current craze, and that rock'n'roll vocalist Mamie Watts had been added to his band. Early reviews of the tour were very positive, but as the days passed the jazz connoisseurs became increasingly unhappy. *Melody Maker* published letters of protest under the banner headline *'Spare Us This Trash, Hampton'* and, with few teenage fans attending the concerts, his attempts to perform rock'n'roll were largely unappreciated by the older audience.

By the time the tour reached the Royal Festival Hall, the situation had become critical. Promises that this, at least, would be an 'all jazz' show were not kept and British bandleader Johnny Dankworth led the protest, storming out of the concert and demanding his money back. Early rock'n'roll in Britain was nothing if not controversial.

PAT BOONE

December 1956			January 1957		
26	Tooting	Granada	3	Leicester	De Montfort Hall
28	Birmingham	Town Hall	4	Manchester	Free Trade Hall
29	Sheffield	City Hall	5	Newcastle	City Hall
			6	Kilburn	Gaumont State
Promoters — Lew and Leslie Grade					

Pat Boone was the first major rock'n'roll star to appear in Britain, and at the time his tour was very big news indeed. If Elvis represented a threat to the Establishment, Pat was strictly the acceptable face of rock'n'roll. The media loved to compare the two singers and to speculate as to which was the more popular.

Boone was keen to explain his views on the new music: 'Rock'n'roll is a good outlet for tension and emotion, and it will stay popular as long as people are not ashamed to like it, but I condemn those who perform it on stage in a distasteful way. There are people who have made a name for themselves by arousing their audience sensually. Let's admit it, I try to make my performance exciting: I move around the stage, I snap my fingers and I stamp my feet, but I refuse to do anything to offend anybody. True, the teenagers get excited over me. They scream and try to touch me. They are aroused by the presence of a personality they have only known through records or TV. I can understand this, but I try to make sure that they wake up in the morning with a good clean taste in their mouths — I don't want them to feel ashamed of anything they have done.'

Boone underlined his clean-cut image when he opened his tour at the Granada, Tooting, smartly dressed in a light sports jacket, dark grey pants, white shirt, pastel tie and white shoes that emphasised his college boy appeal. His act included versions of 'Rock Around The Clock', 'Money Honey' and a medley of rock'n'roll favourites aimed strictly at the under-21's. Snapping his fingers and stomping his feet, he always managed to stay well within the bounds of accepted good taste. Pelvic gestures were definitely out, and any teenagers who did become aroused, did so only in the best possible taste.

Jack Parnell and his orchestra provided both support and backing for Pat throughout his short tour, and other numbers performed included 'Tutti Frutti', 'Ain't That a Shame', 'I'll Be Home', and 'Long Tall Sally'. England's own hit sensation, Alma Cogan — 'the girl with the giggle in her voice' — was added to the bill at Kilburn.

TV appearances
Sunday Night At The London Palladium   30 December 1956
Val Parnell's New Year Star Time   1 January 1957

CHAPTER TWO

1957

Everybody Razzle Dazzle

By the beginning of 1957, rock'n'roll fever had taken a grip in Britain. Tony Crombie's first tours had been an overwhelming success, and agent Jeff Kruger reported that his office income had trebled during the last three months thanks to the combined efforts of Crombie, Art Baxter and Don Sollash. Teenagers were showing an insatiable appetite for rock'n'roll, though the music business itself was still not taking it seriously, merely tolerating it as a passing fad that would soon be forgotten along with the Davy Crockett hat and the yo-yo. Probably more out of wishful thinking than anything else, the music press confidently predicted that rock'n'roll was about to give way to the calypso.

Tommy Steele, Britain's first rock'n'roll star, started the year at the top of the Hit Parade with 'Singing The Blues', but even while riding high on the charts he was already publicly distancing himself from rock'n'roll and laying the groundwork for his later career as an all-round entertainer. Before too long his popularity would be challenged by Terry Dene, an altogether more dedicated rock'n'roller, but sadly a much less stable character.

There were several major stories occupying the front pages of the newspapers during January. Prime Minister Sir Anthony Eden resigned through ill health and was succeeded by Harold Macmillan. In Monaco, former actress Grace Kelly gave birth to Princess Caroline, while closer to home Prince Charles attended school for the first time at the age of eight. A story which ran for several days involved the escape and subsequent recapture of two dangerous inmates from Rampton Mental Hospital. One of them, axeman Frank Mitchell, would later become infamous as one of the victims of the Kray twins.

But for *Daily Mirror* readers at least, one story totally eclipsed all other news during the early part of 1957. Their build-up to and coverage of the British tour by Bill Haley & His Comets was unbelievable, and it is doubtful whether any subsequent showbusiness story — not even the Beatles, nor the Spice Girls — has come anywhere close to equalling it.

On 23 January, the *Mirror*'s front page was dominated by the announcement of Haley's tour, relegating to a minor role the story of royal polio injections for Charles and Anne. The following day, almost a full page was devoted to a detailed listing of the tour itinerary and the launch of a competition enabling readers to win Haley show tickets.

Leading up to the ensemble's arrival in Britain, details of the tour were considered sufficiently important to rate as front page news on six separate days, with coverage elsewhere in the *Mirror* on a further six occasions, sometimes spilling over two or even three pages. Bill may have been kept off the front page on 2 February by the revelation that the celebrity temptress Sabrina was insuring her 41-inch bust for £100,000 at Lloyd's, but otherwise he seemed to enjoy a free run.

Thirteen ballrooms around the country were holding competitions with show tickets as prizes. The *Mirror* chartered a special train, *The Rock'n'Roll Choo Choo*, to collect Bill and the Comets when they alighted from the SS *Queen Elizabeth* at Southampton and to transport them into London. Seats on the train were greatly coveted and one hundred were offered as prizes in another competition. *Mirror* journalist Noel 'He's No Square' Whitcomb flew out to New York to meet the Comets after their Australian tour and he re-crossed the Atlantic on the *Queen Elizabeth* ghost-writing Bill's daily diary for avid *Mirror* readers as the build-up to the UK tour reached fever pitch. One lucky Surrey teenager, Madge Macbeth, won yet another competition and was flown with her mother to Cherbourg to join Bill on the *Queen Elizabeth* for the last leg of his journey. The *Mirror* even bought up all four thousand tickets for the matinée performance at Kilburn on 24 February, and duly sold the lot through coupons in the newspaper.

In the face of such incredible hype, Bill Haley was probably on a hiding to nothing, but at least the hysteria demonstrated the extraordinary rise of interest in rock'n'roll within Britain. Along with Elvis, he was the biggest act in rock'n'roll, but contrary to popular belief he was not the first American to perform in Britain in 1957.

LITTLE ABNER

February 1957			March 1957	
4-9	Brighton	Hippodrome	1-2 Edinburgh	Empire
11-16	Finsbury Park	Empire		
18-23	Chiswick	Empire		
25-28	Edinburgh	Empire		
Promoter — Bernard Delfont				

The success of Tony Crombie's rock'n'roll variety package prompted impresario Bernard Delfont to launch a new rock'n'roll venture. Billed as the '(S)cool For Cats' tour, it promised to bring together 'a top-line American Negro artist' and a British skiffle group.

Little Abner, whose real name was Abner Kenon, was touted as 'Harlem's King of Rock'n'Roll', and had been signed by Billy Marsh of the Delfont office after hearing him in West End cabaret.

The skiffle contribution came from Russell Quay & His City Ramblers, while the billing was completed by Suzi Miller, Maria Pavlou, Dolores Ventura and Billy 'Uke' Scott, with Dickie Dawson acting as compere. It was far from a star-studded line-up, but did garner quite a lot of pre-tour publicity. It seems unlikely that Little Abner's ability as a rock'n'roller made much impact, as — significantly — no reviews of the tour were printed, and Abner did not later pursue this aspect of his career. He was, however, offered a part as a rock'n'roll singer in a proposed movie starring Diana Dors and Victor Mature.

BILL HALEY & HIS COMETS

February 1957					
6-9	London	Dominion	22	Plymouth	Odeon
10	Coventry	Gaumont	23	Southampton	Gaumont
11	Nottingham	Odeon	24-26	Kilburn	Gaumont State
12	Birmingham	Odeon	**March 1957**		
13	Manchester	Odeon	1-2	Belfast	Hippodrome
14	Leeds	Odeon	3	Edmonton	Regal
15	Sunderland	Odeon	4-5	Croydon	Davis
16	Newcastle	Odeon	6	Norwich	Carlton
17	Bradford	Odeon	7	Doncaster	Gaumont
18-19	Glasgow	Odeon	8	Wolverhampton	Gaumont
20	Liverpool	Odeon	9	Cheltenham	Gaumont
21	Cardiff	Capitol	10	London	Dominion

Promoters — Lew and Leslie Grade

Bill Haley & His Comets sailed into Southampton on the morning of 5 February. There were no fewer than seventeen in the party including Bill's wife, Cuppy, the six Comets — namely Billy Williamson (steel guitar), Rudy Pompilli (tenor sax), Ralph Jones (drums), Franny Beecher (guitar), Al Rex (double bass) and Johnny Grande (piano and accordion) — and Bill's manager, the eccentric Lord Jim Ferguson, who was accompanied by his 77-year old mother, Charlotte. Grande and Jones brought along their wives, and Williamson both his wife and little Billy Junior. Others in the entourage included Haley's agent, Jolly Joyce, and their bandboy, Vince 'Catfish' Broomall, whose job it was to look after all the instruments and luggage. They had nearly been stranded back in New York, as, just prior to the *Queen Elizabeth* setting sail, it transpired that Haley had mislaid his passport. It took a frantic call to the State Department in Washington to specially authorise his departure. Ironically, the missing passport was found a short while later among his luggage.

An enormous crowd of people was waiting at Southampton and Haley was visibly moved by the enthusiastic reception. The special train had travelled down from London packed full both with fans and a healthy contingent from TV, radio and the press. British rock'n'rollers Rory Blackwell & His Blackjacks performed on the platform at Waterloo Station and again during the train journey. Bill even joined them for a rousing version of 'See You Later, Alligator' as they hurtled though the English countryside.

When the train finally reached its destination, they were confronted by a mob scene as no fewer than ninety police officers tried to escort them through the crowd. Bill and Cuppy did make it to a waiting car only to be surrounded by hundreds of girls plastering lipstick kisses on the windows and beating against the roof and the bodywork. After twenty minutes and with police riding both on the bonnet and the roof of the car they were able to escape to the safety of the Savoy Hotel. Haley was shaken by the ferocity displayed by his fans, but noted in his diary that *'this is the greatest welcome ever given to an American artist'*.

The tour opened at the Dominion Theatre in London, where a packed audience erupted with a roar of delight as the curtain slid open to reveal seven men splendidly attired in tartan tuxedos and rocking their way into

The Comets rehearse at the Dominion Theatre, London.

'Razzle Dazzle'. The atmosphere was supercharged and the physical antics of the Comets left the crowd breathless. Nothing like this had ever been seen on a British stage. During the instrumental 'Rudy's Rock', Al Rex swung his giant bass high into the air and Rudy Pompilli lay flat on his back feverishly blowing into his sax. Haley knelt beside him strumming his acoustic guitar while Ralph Jones attacked his drum kit like a man possessed. The whole stage was a blur of colour and frantic movement. The fans went wild with delight. Guitarist Franny Beecher added a touch of comedy to the proceedings with a falsetto parody of 'You Made Me Love You', and Billy Williamson took his share of the vocal duties on 'I'm In Love Again'. As the act moved towards its conclusion, Haley increased the temperature with 'Shake, Rattle And Roll' and 'See You Later, Alligator', by which time the theatre floor was vibrating as thousands of feet beat out the rhythm in unison. The climax of the show, 'Rock Around the Clock', brought a truly memorable night to a very satisfactory conclusion. Hundreds of crazed teenagers congregated at the stage door until late in the evening hoping for another glimpse of their heroes.

Earlier in the proceedings, the support acts had been politely received despite being quite unsuitable for a rock'n'roll show. The Vic Lewis Orchestra, the comedy singing team of Kenneth Earle & Malcolm Vaughan, plus Desmond Lane warbling away merrily on his tin whistle, were not what

Aboard the Haley express. The blonde sitting in front of Bill is his wife, Cuppy.

the teenage audience had come to hear. It would be some time, however, before Britain got away from the variety show mentality which under different circumstances might well have seen Haley sharing the stage with a conjuror, a juggler and a troupe of performing dogs.

The tour was almost a complete sell-out. Serious riots by gangs of teddy boys had been predicted, but happily did not materialise, and the Comets continued to be welcomed everywhere they went. The strain on Haley was enormous and the pressure increased when they flew to Ireland at the end of February for two nights at the Royal Theatre, Dublin. In Glasgow, the regular support acts were augmented by the bizarre-sounding Johnny Wilson Rock'n'Roll Formation Dancers. Up in Manchester, two university students came to the hotel to acquire Bill's bathwater, which they wanted to sell for Rag Week. He gave them a shirt as well. Within a few years, one of the students — David Frost — would himself become a showbusiness personality.

On 4 March, Haley was presented with a gold disc at the Savoy Hotel by the head of Decca Records, Edward Lewis, in recognition of 'Rock Around The Clock' becoming the first disc to sell in excess of a million copies in the UK. The saturation press coverage was maintained and Bill eventually scored no fewer than eight front pages in the *Daily Mirror*. Indeed, such was the paper's support, that they underwrote an extra night at the Dominion Theatre so that fans could *'say "so long" to Bill Haley'*.

For this final show of the tour, six thousand fans sold out both performances to hear Haley and his Comets with a changed support that featured Alma Cogan, the Jack Hylton Orchestra, Dennis Lotis and the penny whistle man, Desmond Lane. This show, like its predecessors, was an unqualified success and, when Bill Haley packed his bags to return to the States, he did so at the glorious peak of his career. He was never again able to attain the same level of support and within a few weeks his records would disappear from the charts on both sides of the Atlantic. Sad though his fall from grace was to be, nobody can take away from Bill Haley the fact that this, his first tour of Britain, was the most successful ever. Many others would follow him onto a British stage, but none have come close to matching his achievements.

TV appearances
Sunday Night At The London Palladium   24 February 1957

MITCHELL TOROK

February 1957			7	York	Rialto
18-23	London	Prince of Wales	8-13	Finsbury Park	Empire
24	Streatham Hill	Theatre	15-20	Brighton	Hippodrome
25-28	London	Prince of Wales	22-27	Birmingham	Hippodrome
March 1957			29-30	Chiswick	Empire
1-2	London	Prince of Wales	**May 1957**		
4-9	Glasgow	Empire	1-4	Chiswick	Empire
11-16	Edinburgh	Empire	5	Leicester	De Montfort Hall
18-23	Manchester	Hippodrome	6-11	London	Metropolitan
25-30	Newcastle	Empire	13-18	Cardiff	New Theatre
April 1957			20-25	Bristol	Hippodrome
1-6	Liverpool	Empire			
Promoter — Bernard Delfont					

Mitchell Torok's tour got off to a very poor start when his first-night television appearance at the London Palladium was slaughtered by the critics. British audiences were tired of American performers who keep saying how wonderful it is to be here, make jokes about drinking tea and mimic the English accent. Torok managed to do all three, which did not help his cause and, although he sang pleasantly enough, he never managed to overcome his embarrassing patter.

Supported on the tour by Ken Macintosh and his full orchestra, for his own spot Torok played guitar and used only pianist Bob Bromley and the orchestra drummer to back him. However, he lacked a charismatic stage presence, and his mixture of country music and rock'n'roll failed to make any real impact with the teenagers.

When the tour opened at the Prince of Wales Theatre, his programme included 'Caribbean', 'Singing The Blues', a spoof version of 'Hound Dog', 'Blueberry Hill', a Hank Williams medley and — tellingly — 'When Mexico Gave Up The Rhumba To Do The Rock'n'Roll'. He was not especially well received and was criticised in the press for offering up a string of western ditties which were so slow that his audience settled into a pleasant state of semi-consciousness.

There was little demand for one-nighters on the free Sundays between each weekly engagement, although he did play Leicester on a relatively uninspired bill which included Mick Mulligan and his band, George Melly, the Saints and the Alan Radcliffe Quartet, while at York the audience witnessed the debut of a new British instrumental combo, the John Barry Seven.

TV appearances
Sunday Night At The London Palladium	17 February 1957
The Jack Jackson Show	21 April 1957

THE PLATTERS

March 1957					
12	York	Rialto	16	Taunton	Gaumont
13	Leicester	De Montfort Hall	17	Plymouth	Odeon
14	Sheffield	City Hall	18	Salisbury	Gaumont
15	Bristol	Colston Hall	19	Leeds	Odeon
16	Cardiff	Capitol	20	Nottingham	Odeon
17	Hanley	Gaumont	21	Blackpool	Opera House
18-23	Birmingham	Hippodrome	22-27	Manchester	Palace
24	Bradford	Gaumont	28	Worcester	Gaumont
25-30	Glasgow	Empire	29-30	London	Palladium
31	Preston	Gaumont	**May 1957**		
April 1957			1-3	London	Palladium
7	Wolverhampton	Gaumont	5	Southampton	Gaumont
8-13	Liverpool	Empire	6-11	London	Palladium
14	Coventry	Gaumont	12	Hull	Regal
15	Cheltenham	Gaumont	13-18	Newcastle	Empire
			19	Kilburn	Gaumont State
Promoter — Leslie Macdonnell					

Vocal groups have always been an integral part of rock'n'roll, regularly accepted in America alongside the more frenetic exponents of the music. The Platters became the first such act to visit Britain with their classic line-up of Tony Williams (lead tenor), Herb Reed (bass), David Lynch (second tenor), Paul Robi (baritone) and the glamorous Zola Taylor, known as 'The Dish'. They were accompanied by their musical director and pianist Rupert Branker. The Vic Lewis Orchestra, fresh from the Haley tour, provided the backing until mid-April, although Jack Parnell and his band were used for the Sunday concerts.

The opening night at York was a sensation. On an unexpectedly hot day, both atmospherically and musically, the Platters played to capacity houses taking six curtain calls at the first show and many more at the second. They were polished, visual and could all sing well.

They bounced on stage to a tumultuous welcome and launched straight into the gutsy rocker 'Dance With Me Henry' featuring Zola Taylor and the bass vocals of Herb Reed, who raised screams with a snappy dance routine. Their set included 'The Great Pretender', 'You'll Never Never Know', and the novelty jump number 'Gum Drop', which was a showcase for Zola and baritone, Paul Robi. Lead vocalist Tony Williams continued with 'The Magic

23

Those fabulous Platters. Pianist Rudy Branker is seated at the keyboard.

Touch' and 'Only You', while David Lynch stepped up to the mike for a tearaway performance of 'All Night Long'. Zola ripped through 'He's Mine' from their film, *Rock All Night*, before the act closed with classy renditions of 'My Prayer' and 'Goodnight, Sweetheart, Goodnight'.

Ronnie Aldrich & The Squadronaires replaced the Vic Lewis Orchestra when the show reached Cheltenham, and for the week at the London Palladium the group co-starred with the Lonnie Donegan Skiffle Group and Leo de Lyon, who was described as '*America's zaniest musician*'. Their Manager, Buck Ram, made his first UK visit, flying into London to attend the opening night at the Palladium.

TV appearances
Sunday Night At The London Palladium   19 May 1957

FRANKIE LYMON & THE TEENAGERS

March 1957					
18-23	Liverpool	Empire	13	Brixton	Astoria
25-30	Bimingham	Hippodrome	14	Wolverhampton	Civic Hall
April 1957			15	Bristol	Colston Hall
1-6	London	Palladium	16	Leicester	De Montfort Hall
8-13	London	Palladium	17	Sheffield	City Hall
15-20	Manchester	Palace	18	Edmonton	Regal
22-30	Glasgow	Empire	27-31	Newcastle	Empire
May 1957			**June 1957**		
1-4	Glasgow	Empire	1	Newcastle	Empire
6-11	Stockton	Globe	3-8	Coventry	Theatre
Promoter — Arthur Howes					

Another rock'n'roll vocal group, the Teenagers, arrived on 15 March for nearly three months of theatre dates, and the British press seemed fascinated by them. A reception was held on their arrival, which immediately identified friction within the group. Fourteen year old lead vocalist Frankie Lymon as well as being youngest was also the recipient of most of the media attention — a fact which was not being well-received by the rest of ensemble: Joe Negroni (baritone), Sherman Garnes (bass), Herman Santiago (first tenor) and Jimmy Merchant (second tenor). Such internal jealousies cannot have been helped by the billing which was used at many of the venues, where the billboards promised: *'The Teenagers with Wonder Boy Frankie Lymon'*.

Lymon's tender age meant that he was subject to strict controls to comply with UK labour laws, and it was a requirement that a tutor accompany him throughout the tour to ensure that his education did not suffer. The Teenagers were represented in the States by the shadowy figure of mobster

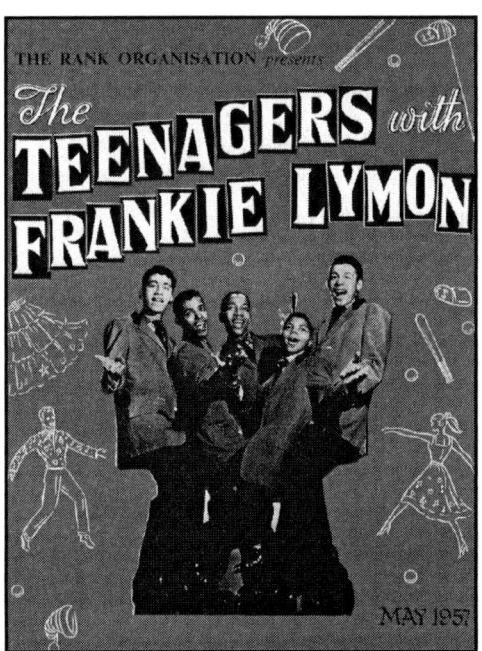

Morris Levy, and there appeared to be quite a contrast between his approach to the subject and that of the British education authorities, which was only resolved by a glamorous former nightclub cashier, Lulu Carter, being despatched from New York as Frankie's tutor, along with Jack Lewin from Levy's office in the role of tour manager.

The Teenagers were backed throughout their stay by the Larry Macklin Quintet, comprising Joe Ferris (drums), Bob Russell (bass), Jack Bickerton (tenor sax), George Burt (trumpet) and Macklin (piano). At the Liverpool Empire, they opened with 'I'm Not A Juvenile Delinquent' and inevitably the

spotlight focused largely on the diminutive Lymon and his raucous yet strangely attractive high treble voice. He had a microphone to himself while the other four Teenagers shared two others just a few feet to the side of him. The entire show was hot, wild, rock'n'roll and very visual.

They jumped around the stage doing a crazy itching-bug dance during 'I Promise To Remember', roared through 'The ABC's of Love' and waxed sentimental on 'I'm Not A Know It All'. Frankie had the girls and boys clapping in unison to 'Baby Baby' and then moved on through 'I Want You To Be My Girl' and 'Teenage Love'.   Only during one number did the warm-voiced quartet take over the spotlight from him, with Sherman Garnes, the six-foot-four bass singer doing some fine work on 'April Castles'. The act climaxed with the hugely popular 'Why Do Fools Fall In Love'.

After six weeks of variety, sharing billing with a mixed bag of jugglers, acrobats and comedians, the Teenagers had a week of one-nighters supported by Terry Lightfoot's Jazzmen, Chas McDevitt's Skiffle Group, Nancy Whiskey and Billie Anthony, and, after a short diversion to Ireland, the tour was wrapped up with further weeks at Newcastle and Coventry. One of the highlights of their visit was their memorable television appearance on the *London Palladium* show, dressed in fetching white sweaters with a giant letter 'T' emblazoned on the front.

Sadly, the divisions between Lymon and the Teenagers were exacerbated when he recorded an album consisting mainly of standards in London with the Norrie Paramor Orchestra, but pointedly without the rest of the group. It was therefore no surprise when he quit to go solo in July 1957, remarking that 'the headlines I received in Britain caused other members of the group to be jealous. Since our return to America, we have hardly spoken.'

The British tour was the beginning of the end for the Teenagers. Lymon's solo career was not a success and he eventually died of a heroin overdose on 28 February 1968. Without their high profile front-man, the group also quickly faded away and both Sherman Garnes and Joe Negroni died prematurely, the former on 26 February 1977 following imprisonment and open heart surgery, the latter on 5 September 1978 as a result of a brain tumour.

TV appearances
Sunday Night At The London Palladium   14 April 1957

FREDDIE BELL & THE BELLBOYS

May 1957			June 1957		
6-11	Liverpool	Empire	1	Glasgow	Empire
13-18	Cardiff	Gaumont	2	Bristol	Colston Hall
20-25	London	Dominion	3	Dudley	Hippodrome
27-31	Glasgow	Empire	4	Newcastle	City Hall
			5	Sheffield	City Hall
			6	Manchester	Free Trade Hall
Promoter — Harold Davison					

Freddie Bell from South Philadelphia and his band, the Bellboys, had made their name performing rock'n'roll in Las Vegas. They toured Britain jointly headlining with Britain's own favourites, Tommy Steele & The Steelemen, then at the peak of their popularity. Bell had never heard of Tommy until he arrived in the UK, but the two men hit it off immediately and it proved to be a very happy and immensely successful sellout tour. Press coverage was largely positive and noted the professionalism and musical ability of the Bellboys — Jack Kane (sax), Frankie Brent (bass), Jerry Mayo (trumpet), Russ Conti (piano) and Chick Keeney (drums). They closed the first half of each show, allowing Steele the final spot, but more than held their own.

Their debut at the Liverpool Empire was so successful that the music press speculated as to which of the two acts had won the popularity battle. Freddie and the boys ran on stage in striking flame-coloured jackets and kept up a tremendous pace, leaping and pivoting around in a series of well-drilled movements. The material included 'I Said It And I'm Glad', 'Shake A Hand', 'The Hucklebuck' and the all-action 'Go! Go! Go!'. Pianist Russ Conti was a natural comedian. Bell himself excelled with some magnificent trombone work in addition to his singing, and bass-player Frankie Brent performed his share of the vocals on 'Long Tall Sally' and 'Ling Ting Tong'. The set closed with renditions of 'Rock Around The Clock' and 'Giddy Up A Ding Dong' that shook the house.

Bell and Steele were mobbed at each venue, although Freddie was amused to find that Tommy's popularity did not extend as far as Glasgow, where the locals openly expressed their hatred for Cockneys. The level of attention they attracted was so high, in fact, that they were rarely able to leave the hotel and spent much of their spare time playing poker. Steele was a truly awful card player and Bellboys' drummer Chick Keeney practically lived off his winnings. Back in London, police escorts had to be arranged before they could hang out at Benny Green's club on a night off.

For the first four weeks of the tour, Steele and Bell were working with the usual gaggle of variety acts including French harmonica stars Trio Raisner and British comic duo Mike & Bernie Winters. The tour closed with five one-nighters on which the Bellboys starred with Chas McDevitt's Skiffle Group, Nancy Whiskey, Terry Lightfoot's Jazzmen and Yolanda, before moving on to play further shows in the Netherlands and France.

Bass player Frankie Brent did not go back to the States, returning to the UK after they played Paris. He left the Bellboys to try for a solo career and had two singles, 'Rockin' Shoes' and 'Be My Girl', released by Nixa during the second half of 1957.

TV appearances
Tonight   3 May 1957

CHARLIE GRACIE

August 1957			September 1957		
4	Southampton	Gaumont	2-7	Glasgow	Empire
5-10	London	Hippodrome	9-14	Manchester	Palace
12-17	London	Hippodrome	15	Bristol	Colston Hall
18	Blackpool	Opera House	16-21	Liverpool	Empire
19-24	Coventry	Theatre	22	Leicester	De Montfort Hall
25	Morecambe	Winter Gardens	23-28	Birmingham	Hippodrome
26-31	Stockton	Globe	29	Walthamstow	Granada
Promoter — Harold Davison					

Charlie Gracie's first UK tour proved to be highly successful, hitting the headlines even before the SS *Mauritania*, carrying the diminutive rock'n'roller, docked at Southampton on 3 August. Blonde balladeer Dorothy Squires quit the Hippodrome booking in a flurry of indignation rather than share top billing with the comparatively unknown Gracie. Her tantrum did no harm, merely providing welcome pre-tour publicity and an opportunity for Fredye Marshall, a black American jazz singer who replaced her, and who was featured on most of the shows along with the usual hotch-potch of variety acts.

Gracie travelled with his musical director, Dennis Ringrowe, drummer Joe Watson and his manager Bernie Rothbard. When the latter returned to the States, Charlie's father took his place for the duration of the trip.

The media had gathered like vultures when Gracie commenced his

GRANADA WALTHAMSTOW
CHARLIE GRACIE
Sunday Sept 29 1957 · *program sixpence*

season at the prestigious Hippodrome Theatre, and anything less than a highly-entertaining display would have seen him hung out to dry, for, although the music press were giving adequate column inches to rock'n'roll, there was little love for the music and any degree of failure would have been gleefully reported. In fact, he scored an emphatic hit with a fast-moving show which did not waste a second from the booming 'Talk To Me Baby' through 'Long Tall Sally', 'Ko Ko Mo' and 'Tutti Frutti'. After slowing the tempo for 'Trying', Charlie showed himself to be a master guitarist, scoring strongly with the instrumental 'Guitar Boogie Shuffle'. A cunningly fake opening of 'Whatever Will Be Will Be' led into a driving 'Hound Dog', and the act climaxed with his hits, 'Butterfly', 'Ninety-Nine Ways', and 'Fabulous'.

Only Charlie and his drummer appeared on stage during his shows, with the other accompaniment coming from the pit orchestra.

The early momentum was maintained throughout the tour, and at Walthamstow a frenzied mob of screaming teenagers made a determined effort to batter down the stage door, while at Bristol windows were broken as fans without tickets tried to smash their way into the theatre. After one show in Coventry, Charlie had his jacket completely shredded by excited fans.

Few recordings exist that illustrate the intensity of the early rock'n'roll shows in Britain, but happily a tape of Charlie's performance on 26 August did survive and in 1983 was released as an album by Rollercoaster Records, titled *Live At The Stockton Globe*. A proposed television appearance on *Star Time* could unfortunately not proceed on 3 October as Gracie came down with flu. His flight home also had to be deferred until he was well enough to travel.

TV appearances
Meet The Stars	11 August 1957
6.5 Special	17 August 1957

LITTLE RICHARD

In mid-September it was reported that the Gale Agency in the UK, in conjunction with the Jolly Joyce Agency in the USA, had lined up an Alan Freed rock'n'roll package to tour Britain for four weeks commencing 20 October. The artists participating would be Little Richard, the Moonglows, Teddy Randazzo and Jo-Ann Campbell. A week later this was amended to Little Richard and the Diamonds only. Then the tour dates were put back to February 1958, and finally the whole project fell apart in November with the news that Little Richard was quitting show business to enter the church.

PAUL ANKA

December 1957					
7	Elephant & Castle	Trocadero	17	Glasgow	Odeon
8	Kilburn	Gaumont State	18	Manchester	Odeon
9-14	Liverpool	Empire	19	Birmingham	Odeon
15	Bradford	Gaumont	20	Cardiff	Gaumont
16	Newcastle	Odeon	21	Nottingham	Odeon
			22	Edmonton	Regal
Promoters — Lew and Leslie Grade					

Sixteen year old Paul Anka arrived on 5 December for a whirlwind eighteen-day tour of the UK in the company of Canadian deejay Bill McCadden, who acted as tour manager. Backed by the John Barry Seven, Anka was supported by the Bob Cort Skiffle Group, Billie Anthony, the Four Gitson Sisters and compere Dickie Dawson, and proved enormously popular — especially with the female fans.

At Kilburn, he received one of the most rousing receptions ever given to a visiting singer and went straight into 'Tell Me That You Love Me' followed by 'Don't Gamble With Love'. The audience clapped their way through 'Gum Drop' and sat fully attentive during a belting version of 'I Believe'. He then moved to the front of the stage and appeared to fix his attention on a girl in the front stalls while singing his current hit, 'I Love You Baby'. He followed with a rocking version of 'Down By The Riverside' and the standard, 'White Christmas'. Finally, after whipping up the hand-claps for another rock'n'roll number, 'Shake Baby, Shake', he launched into 'Diana', the song that everybody wanted to hear.

With a very tight schedule, Anka somehow also managed to squeeze in a television appearance at the Palladium on the same night that he played Kilburn. A proposed spot on the *Jack Jackson Show*, however, proved impossible to finalise. On 22 December at Edmonton, he was presented with a gold disc by Joseph Lockwood, Managing Director of EMI, to commemorate a million UK sales of 'Diana'. The following day, he rushed back to the States to rehearse for his spot on a Patti Page Christmas Day TV special.

TV appearances
Sunday Night At The London Palladium   8 December 1957

CHAPTER THREE

1958

Boppin' At The High School Hop

In strictly commercial terms, rock'n'roll was at its peak at the beginning of 1958. The top American acts were all selling increasing volumes of the 45 rpm records which were now displacing the 78 format, while Elvis Presley, Little Richard, Buddy Holly, Jerry Lee Lewis, Paul Anka and the Everly Brothers were all riding high in the UK charts at the start of the year. There was, however, still no support or encouragement at all from the media, who never missed an opportunity to predict its imminent demise.

During April, it was widely reported that both skiffle and rock'n'roll would soon be blasted from the popularity stakes by a new South African music called kwela which was being introduced to the UK by Durban dancing teacher Mrs. Noele Andrews. She even demonstrated kwela on BBC-TV's *6.5 Special*, but without any noticeable sign of it catching on. Skiffle did begin to run out of steam the following month though, and many of the professional groups started to disband. By November it was the cha cha craze which was being championed as the probable replacement for rock'n'roll, and opportunist rockers Rory Blackwell & His Blackjacks even billed themselves as a 'rock a cha cha' band for a time.

British rock'n'roll really came alive. Tommy Steele no longer led the pack, but still performed the likes of 'Long Tall Sally' and 'Rebel Rock' in and among his novelty songs. Terry Dene should have been his natural successor but lacked the temperament for stardom. He was forever in the newspapers as his life gradually unravelled under the intense heat of public scrutiny, with both his marriage to ballad singer Edna Savage, and later his brief but disastrous period of military service providing further ammunition for the press to hammer rock'n'roll. Marty Wilde took over from Dene as Britain's premier rock'n'roller, but even his period of dominance would be brief, because Cliff Richard burst into the limelight during the autumn with 'Move It' — arguably the best British rock'n'roll record of all time.

At the start of 1958, *6.5 Special* was the only significant television show aimed specifically at the rock'n'roll generation. Two separate and competing '*6.5 Special*' roadshows set out to work the theatres, one starring Don Lang and Jimmy Jackson and the other Wee Willie Harris and Tony Crombie. Harris was one of the best British rockers and has always been vastly underrated. Perhaps this is because it was his stage gimmicks rather than his singing that tended to attract all the attention, as demonstrated by *Melody Maker*'s usual vitriolic write-up of his performance on the *6.5 Special*

At The 2i's tour: '*I can't even find the right adjectives to describe the colour of his hair. The nearest in my experience was the sun setting over the Egyptian desert after a sandstorm... It gives him the look of a rather grotesque chrysanthemum.*' The two *6.5 Special* packages eventually met at Brighton in a head-to-head over Easter, but in the end neither triumphed and there were empty seats at both theatres.

One of the most important developments during 1958 was the success in June of an ATV networked show, *Oh Boy!* It was produced by Jack Good and featured seventeen songs in thirty-five minutes, thereby claiming to be the fastest show on television — and a welcome improvement over *6.5 Special*, the format of which was becoming rather played-out. *Oh Boy!* was so well received that it was developed into a weekly series commencing in September. In time, this would lead to more American rock'n'rollers guesting on British television, but initially it was merely a vehicle to project home-grown talent. Although the vocalists came from the younger generation, Humphrey Lyttleton was speaking for many when he commented on all the jazz musicians hiding behind dark glasses on *Oh Boy!* and *6.5 Special*: 'It is an oversight that the Wolfenden Report on Prostitution has not investigated them,' he pronounced.

Surprisingly, there was no glut of visiting rock'n'rollers in 1958. The Americans were still fully occupied back home making money and, in truth, the extraordinary revelations that accompanied Jerry Lee Lewis' tour probably had a negative influence on other similar projects that may have been under consideration. Outside the rock'n'roll field, black gospel singers Marie Knight and Sister Rosetta Tharpe both toured Britain, as did bluesmen Muddy Waters, Sonny Terry and Brownie McGhee. Pop singer Georgia Gibbs, who had bolstered her career with wimpish recordings of rock'n'roll classics, came over for a television appearance, and the fabulous Billie Holiday performed for a single night at the Royal Festival Hall in London. Even jazz and vaudeville veteran Timmie Rogers spent six weeks in variety and opened for Liberace at the Palladium during April. Rogers had dabbled in rock'n'roll and scored an American hit with 'Back To School Again', which was covered in Britain by Wee Willie Harris. On balance however, 1958 was not a classic year for live music. The great package shows were still a couple of years away.

TOMMY SANDS

In January, it was reported that Tommy Sands, the US teenage sensation would be flying to Britain in time for the premiere of his movie, *Sing, Boy, Sing*, which was taking place at the Rialto in London on Thursday, 27 February. The trip was to be funded by 20th Century Fox, but while in London Sands would undertake concert appearances as well. It was even strongly hinted that he would star on ATV's prestigious *Sunday Night At The London Palladium*. In the event, however, Sands didn't make it and his movie was launched without him. A couple of months later, he admitted in an interview that he had been too scared to fly.

BUDDY HOLLY & THE CRICKETS

March 1958					
1	Elephant & Castle	Trocadero	13	East Ham	Granada
2	Kilburn	Gaumont State	14	Woolwich	Granada
3	Southampton	Gaumont	15	Ipswich	Gaumont
4	Sheffield	City Hall	16	Leicester	De Montfort Hall
5	Stockton	Globe	17	Doncaster	Gaumont
6	Newcastle	City Hall	18	Wigan	Ritz
7	Wolverhampton	Gaumont	19	Hull	Regal
8	Nottingham	Odeon	20	Liverpool	Philharmonic Hall
9	Bradford	Gaumont	21	Walthamstow	Granada
10	Birmingham	Town Hall	22	Salisbury	Gaumont
11	Worcester	Paramount	23	Bristol	Colston Hall
12	Croydon	Davis	24	Cardiff	Capitol
			25	Hammersmith	Gaumont
Promoters — Lew and Leslie Grade					

There was always something special about the British tour by Buddy Holly & The Crickets. Holly's premature death at the age of twenty-two has frozen him forever young in the consciousness of that generation of teenagers who were so influenced by him and his music, yet, even without such retrospective sentiments, his tour was special even at the time. In one respect, this was because he visited Britain at the absolute peak of his popularity, whereas so many American rock'n'rollers either toured on the back of a single hit record or delayed working overseas until their popularity in the States had started to fade.

Buddy and the Crickets had four records — 'Oh Boy!', 'Peggy Sue', 'Listen To Me' and 'Maybe Baby' — in the British charts during March 1958 and were just about the hottest act around. In addition, it can also be argued that this was the first proper British rock'n'roll package tour, as opposed to a rock'n'roller being accommodated on a variety bill designed not for teenagers, but for all-round family entertainment. There were no week-long bookings; it was all one-night stands, and the supporting acts, Gary Miller, the Tanner Sisters, Ronnie Keene's Orchestra with vocalist Lynne Adams and compere Des O'Connor, while not rock'n'rollers, were at least thought to have more appeal to the teenagers than the customary array of comedians, jugglers and performing dogs.

There was something else that was different about Buddy Holly & The Crickets: Bill Haley's Comets and Freddie Bell's Bellboys consisted of experienced and trained musicians and featured saxes, trombones and even pedal steel guitar in their line-ups. Solo performers like Paul Anka and Charlie Gracie had been backed in Britain by the house orchestras. Holly, in contrast, sang and played guitar supported by Joe B. Mauldin on double bass and Jerry Allison on drums. Both Joe and Jerry also sang back-up vocals. They were a complete unit and the basic rockabilly format of guitar, bass and drums first popularised in the States by Elvis Presley and Carl Perkins was now being demonstrated for the first time in Britain by genuine American rock'n'rollers.

It was also the sheer ordinariness of Buddy Holly that provided much of his appeal. Lacking Presley's smouldering good looks, he was bespectacled and rather gangly-looking. Yet he proved while in Britain that

The Crickets guest on BBC-TV's *Off The Record.*

he could rock'n'roll with the best. All across the land, spotty teenagers started to strum imaginary guitars and dream of stardom. The Crickets' British tour unarguably inspired a whole generation of British teenagers to try and sing or play guitar. They all wanted to be Buddy Holly.

They flew into London on 28 February in the company of their manager, Norman Petty, and his wife, Vi. The record company had set up a reception during which many of the classic photographs of the Crickets were taken by top photographer Harry Hammond. These included publicity shots with England cricketers Denis Compton and Godfrey Evans and others of them dancing with a couple of pretty girls from *Valentine* magazine.

There was also a need for rehearsals, which took place in the Trocadero at London's Elephant & Castle on the afternoon of the first show. In the USA, the Crickets were used to playing on big package tours where each act was only allocated one or at the most two numbers, whereas in Britain they were now contracted to perform for up to thirty minutes. With this extended format they had a real opportunity to show the British public what they could do.

However, there was criticism of the opening night at the Elephant & Castle. *Melody Maker* reported disappointment that they were not on stage for a longer spot and that they performed all their hit records at the beginning of the set, leaving the audience with a feeling of anti-climax at the end.

Even their appearance on *Sunday Night At The London Palladium* was less than satisfactory. Technical faults with the sound balance gave rise to erroneous speculation that they did not sound the same as on their records. Viewers were surprised to find that the Crickets were not closing the show, but with a stage appearance scheduled that same evening at the Kilburn Gaumont State, their live TV slot had to be fitted in early enough for them to reach the venue in time.

Any doubts about Buddy and the Crickets were swept away within the first few days of the tour. By the time they reached Bradford on the 9th, the set had been revised so that 'Peggy Sue' and 'Oh Boy!' were performed later in the show, giving the proceedings a more balanced feel. Audience reaction was incredible throughout and Holly proved himself to be a real rocker.

Immediately prior to their arrival on stage, Des O'Connor sang a couple of songs and tried to control the excitement of the fans who had their eyes fixed on the near empty stage where Joe's double bass was lying in wait for them. A short introduction produced a wave of applause and the three men ran on stage, picked up their instruments, and within seconds the familiar sound of Holly's Fender guitar heralded the start of a non-stop, all-action rock'n'roll show of the highest quality.

Little footage of Holly on stage has survived and nothing that can now be viewed on celluloid adequately conveys just how animated he was as a live performer. As they worked their way through 'Maybe Baby', 'Money Honey' and a faster-than-expected version of 'Everyday', he fell to his knees during one guitar break, danced back and forth across the stage, first encouraging Joe B. to ride his double bass, then exhorting Jerry to beat harder on the drums. Other songs performed that night included 'Ready Teddy', 'Great Balls Of Fire', a supercharged 'Be-Bop-A-Lula' and inevitably 'That'll Be The Day'. Holly's vocals were magnificent, and the audience wouldn't let them go. Eventually the national anthem had to be played before the management could clear the theatre.

Souvenir Programme

Despite the warm reception they received, not all their concerts were well attended. At the first house in Newcastle, there were so many empty rows that Des O'Connor felt moved to make a quip about the place being a multi-storey car park during the day.

Two further television performances were squeezed into the near-impossible schedule, but without a single free night there was little chance for more than a hurried sightseeing expedition in London and a trip round the Austin Motor Works while in the

Midlands. Otherwise, it was strictly rock'n'roll as they were whisked from town to town, and each fresh night meant packed theatres and a string of encores.

Only the final show at Hammersmith was a slight disappointment. They had to rush from the theatre to the airport to catch their plane home, and so closed the first half of the show. Shortly before they were due on stage, Buddy and Joe B. were clowning around backstage and Holly had his two front teeth accidentally knocked out, leaving him far from enthusiastic about performing at all. Norman Petty did persuade him to go out and face the audience but not surprisingly Buddy's final show in Britain was far from his best, as he struggled to contort his face and avoid showing off the gap in his teeth.

A year later, one of popular music's most infamous tragedies took place when on 3 February 1959, the plane carrying Holly, Ritchie Valens, and the Big Bopper crashed into a cornfield outside Mason City, Iowa, killing all three men. The death of Buddy Holly has with some justification been described as 'the day the music died'.

TV appearances

Cool For Cats	28 February 1958
Sunday Night At The London Palladium	2 March 1958
See You, Soho	13 March 1958
Off The Record	25 March 1958 (screened 27 March 1958)

PAUL ANKA

March 1958				
1	Aberdeen	Music Hall	13 Rochester	Gaumont
2	Dundee	Caird Hall	14 Dudley	Hippodrome
3	Edinburgh	Usher Hall	15 York	Rialto
4	Newcastle	City Hall	16 Hull	City Hall
5	Sheffield	City Hall	17 Stockton	Globe
6	Leicester	De Montfort Hall	18 Manchester	King's Hall
7	Brighton	Dome	19 Liverpool	Philharmonic
8	Slough	Adelphi	20 Lincoln	Savoy
9	Harrow	Dominion	21 Hanley	Victoria Hall
10	Bristol	Colston Hall	22 Croydon	Davis
11	Plymouth	Theatre Royal	23 St. Albans	Odeon *(matinée)*
12	Bournemouth	Winter Gardens	Romford	Odeon
Promoter — Harold Fielding				

Running concurrently with the Buddy Holly tour was the second Paul Anka package. The sixteen year old Canadian may have been shaping up as more of a teen idol than a committed rock'n'roller, but his many female fans could not have cared less about that. Reviews of his opening night at Aberdeen commented on his remarkable sense of showmanship, his assured stage presence, and in particular the infectious grin which was apparent throughout his twenty-five minute appearance. Wasting no time on lengthy introductions, Anka tore through his act building it to a terrific climax with 'Diana', 'You Are My Destiny' and 'I Love You Baby', while Vic Hammett & His

Orchestra laid down a strong, lively beat behind him. Also featured were Lorrae Desmond, the musical comedy of the Kentones, pianist Roy Stevens, and compere Reg Thompson.

The show at the Brighton Dome was the subject of a frenzied demonstration by female fans. After drowning Anka's first house performance with screams and squeals, a crowd of struggling girls besieged the stage door chanting: 'We want Paul!' Panels of glass were smashed and fans charged the barricades. A uniformed attendant had to retire for treatment as a splinter of glass sliced his leg. The coach conveying the artists was plastered with kisses and lipstick messages when a howling mob of teenage girls tried to swarm into it and had to be restrained by the police.

TV appearances
Cool For Cats   26 March 1958

PAT BOONE

April 1958
5   Elephant & Castle   Trocadero
Promoter unknown

By this time, press speculation over the relative merits of Pat or Elvis as the 'King Of Rock'n'Roll' had thankfully subsided, but nevertheless the news that Boone and his wife were to fly into London from Hollywood on Good Friday still created a good deal of interest. *New Musical Express*'s Maurice Kinn had only recently returned from a trip to the States during which he had presented Pat with a pair of engraved candlesticks commemorating his twin successes in the paper's readers' poll, which had voted him both the *'World's Outstanding Singer'* and *'Favourite American Singer'* of 1957.

The acceptable face of bad old rock'n'roll ensured that the Trocadero's box office was inundated with calls, and the demand for tickets was such that local magistrates were persuaded to allow the sale of additional standing tickets for the two concerts, thereby increasing the capacity to 3,600 for each house. Did Boone receive special treatment because of his clean-cut image or would the magistrates have been equally generous to the fans of Elvis Presley? We shall never know, but can probably hazard a reasonably accurate guess.

In a forty-five minute set, Boone strolled around the stage clicking his fingers enthusiastically to 'Love Letters In The Sand', followed by his current hit, 'Wonderful Time Up There', then two film numbers, 'April Love' and — in answer to calls from the audience — 'Bernadine'. He closed with 'Rock Around The Clock', performed in his own inimitable style. Backing was provided by the Ken Mackintosh Orchestra, who had earlier performed their own set. After the show, Shirley Boone, who was standing at the side of the cinema, had to be rescued from a mob of admiring girls seeking autographs.

The following day, Pat headlined *Sunday Night At The London Palladium* before travelling on to Europe for a short vacation. Prior to his departure, he was asked to comment on speculation that his fans had a higher IQ than those of Presley. After pondering the question, he hinted that they probably did, as they now tended to request songs like 'Begin The Beguine' rather than 'Tutti Frutti'.

TV appearances
Sunday Night At The London Palladium   6 April 1958

CHARLIE GRACIE

April 1958			27	East Ham	Granada
6	Bristol	Colston Hall	28-30	Glasgow	Empire
7-12	Liverpool	Empire	**May 1958**		
13	Hull	Regal	1-3	Glasgow	Empire
14-19	Birmingham	Hippodrome	4	York	Rialto
20	Bradford	St. George's Hall	5-10	Newcastle	Empire
21-26	Finsbury Park	Empire	11	Woolwich	Granada
Promoters — Lew and Leslie Grade, Harold Davison					

Charlie's brief spell as a major chart act had already passed by the time he returned for his second British tour. Such had been the impact of his first visit, however, that he had created genuine demand. 'He's the first of the rock'n'rollers to give a real performance,' commented promoter Harold Davison. 'We've had hundreds of letters begging us to bring him back.'

Charlie had married only two weeks before the tour and his bride, Joan, a nineteen year old former telephonist, accompanied him to Britain. Coincidentally, they crossed the Atlantic on the same flight as Pat and Shirley Boone.

There were some empty seats at Colston Hall, Bristol when the tour kicked off, but Gracie's fans made themselves heard and, as on his first trip, the instrumental, 'Guitar Boogie Shuffle' could not fail. Some of the audience were heard comparing Charlie's voice to that of Tommy Steele as he rocked through newer material like 'Crazy Girl' as well as his hits, 'Fabulous', 'Butterfly', and 'Ninety-Nine Ways'. Ronnie Aldrich & The Squadronaires provided the backing on the one-nighters. Otherwise, Gracie worked with the pit orchestra as before.

Prior to flying home to the States on 12 May, Charlie pronounced himself happy with the visit: 'My audience compared very favourably with those that attended the shows on my last trip,' he said. He promised to return, but could never have guessed that it would be twenty-one long years before he would again set foot on a British stage.

TV appearances
Saturday Spectacular   5 April 1958
The Big Show   8 April 1958

THE JOHNNY OTIS SHOW

An ambitious project was proposed for April 1958. The Johnny Otis Show would tour Britain for four weeks commencing 6 April, and Otis would bring his full rock'n'roll entourage with him including Marie Adams, the Three Tons Of Joy, Mel Williams, Don & Dewey and Jimmy Nolen. His partner and personal manager, Hal Ziegler eventually confirmed that contracts had been signed and exchanged with the Grades, but the first hint of a problem arose when the commencement date of the tour was put back a week owing to a delay in obtaining details for the work permits. Sadly, the whole venture disintegrated shortly afterwards when it was revealed that the Musicians' Union had refused to grant permits, and without them the Ministry of Labour would not approve the tour.

MARVIN RAINWATER

April 1958			May 1958		
20	London	Coliseum	1-3	Liverpool	Empire
21-26	Manchester	Hippodrome	5-10	Glasgow	Empire
27	Leicester	De Montfort Hall	12-17	Newcastle	Empire
28-29	Liverpool	Empire			
30	Heswall	Cleaver Hospital			
	Liverpool	Empire			
Promoter unknown					

Marvin Rainwater was an established name in United States. His ballad, 'Gonna Find Me A Bluebird', had been a major record in both the pop and country charts a year earlier. What he wanted now was a rock'n'roll hit: 'I came up with this idea for a new song on the piano one day up in New York. I played it to my brother Ray, who was my manager, but he said that it was rubbish. I persuaded them to put it out anyway, but they banned it. They said it was dirty, 'cos I sang that I'd been 'had', and she's a whole lotta woman and has gotta have a whole lotta man. They said it was sexually explicit. People were going wild about it, but when they said it was dirty the order came down that they couldn't play it on the networks in the US, so they killed my record. Then all of a sudden news came trickling back from England that it was doing something.'

Whatever were the BBC thinking about? Usually so eager to preserve the moral sensibilities of their listeners — Gene Vincent's 'Woman Love' had been banned nearly two years earlier for the simple reason that they couldn't understand the lyrics but feared they might be suggestive — they allowed 'Whole Lotta Woman' to be freely heard by impressionable teenagers who flocked to the record stores to buy copies. It shot to No. 1 on the charts during the first week of April, and Marvin, who was completely unknown in Britain only a week earlier, flew in from New York on 10 April for a major tour preceded by two important television appearances.

In view of Rainwater's country background, it was not surprising that his act included a tribute to Hank Williams, but reviews of his Palladium appearance noted that 'Whole Lotta Woman' was very close to that rock'n'roll style which was being written off, perhaps prematurely.

On 15 April, Marvin and his brother Ray travelled to Bristol to meet up with Johnny Duncan & The Blue Grass Boys who were to back him on his personal appearances. The following day he spent at the EMI studios in London recording two new songs, 'I Dig You Baby' and the hastily retitled 'Dance Me Daddy'. No-one was prepared to risk the BBC's wrath a second time: 'I recorded that wimp song 'Dance Me Daddy'. They wouldn't let me do it properly, 'cos this one was supposed to be dirty as well. Now I'm back doing it as 'Rock Me Daddy' — the way it was supposed to be,' Rainwater recalled many years later.

He headlined a package which, in addition to Johnny Duncan & The Blue Grass Boys also featured the Basil Kirchin Band, Phil Fernando and compere Dickie Dawson. 'I was the most thrilled person who ever lived. It was my first time out of the USA. We went over well because of 'Whole Lotta Woman', but they didn't really understand me.'

The music press didn't really want to understand. They still hated rock'n'roll. *Melody Maker* in particular were really only interested in Marvin's blue cowboy boots: 'They called me *'The man in the blue boots'*. What kind of compliment is that? In other words, everything I sang or said meant nothing — but I have blue boots on. It is hard to overcome that sort of prejudice. I hadn't got their attention, had I?'

In fact, *Melody Maker* ignored the applause of the audience and chose instead to speculate how ludicrous it was for a man of thirty-four to be singing rock'n'roll. After completing an hour-long rock'n'roll show at the Americana in Newark during July 2001, Marvin roared with laughter as he recalled the events of 1958. He seemed to derive particular pleasure from the news that *Melody Maker* had gone bust a year or so earlier. At the time, probably very few people in Britain expected that either Marvin Rainwater or rock'n'roll would outlive the sanctimonious *Melody Maker*, but as they say, he who laughs last...

TV appearances

Sunday Night At The London Palladium	13 April 1958
Saturday Spectacular	19 April 1958
Cool For Cats	19 May 1958
The Jack Jackson Show	24 May 1958

THE TRENIERS

May 1958		
5-10	London	Palladium
12-17	London	Palladium
Promoters — Lew and Leslie Grade		

Las Vegas rock'n'rollers, the Treniers, arrived on 1 May for a lengthy stay in the UK, the first segment of which comprised a fortnight at the London Palladium, supporting balladier Johnnie Ray. British fans had only a limited knowledge of the Treniers, who were better known in the UK for their appearances in the rock'n'roll movies, *The Girl Can't Help It* and *Don't Knock*

The Rock, than for their record sales.

Claude and Cliff Trenier had started performing together as the Trenier Twins during the Forties, and the act had soon expanded to include two other brothers, Milton and Buddy. Their show was a dynamic mixture of singing, dancing and comedy, the rocking sounds being produced by the combined talents of Don Hill (tenor sax), Gene Gilbeaux (piano), James Johnson (bass) and Henry Green (drums). The eight man line-up was described in *NME* as *'The most exuberant and colourful big beat combo ever to visit these shores'*. Songs like 'Rockin' Is Our Bizness', 'Go! Go! Go!', 'Out Of The Bushes' and 'Rock Me All Night Long' were all performed in their quite unique style which obliges the listener to pay full attention at all times to obtain the benefit of their complete range of visual antics. Most of the audience were at the Palladium specifically to see Johnnie Ray, but in the Treniers they had the opportunity to enjoy a highly professional and exciting supporting act.

TV appearances
Sunday Night At The Prince Of Wales   18 May 1958

JERRY LEE LEWIS
THE TRENIERS

May 1958		
24 Edmonton	Regal	
25 Kilburn	Gaumont State	
26 Tooting	Granada	
Promoters — Lew and Leslie Grade		

Britain was not ready for the arrival of Jerry Lee Lewis. The wild man from Ferriday, Louisiana had burst on to the British charts in September 1957 with 'Whole Lotta Shakin' Goin On' and had become one of the hottest teenage acts and a genuine contender for Presley's crown as the King Of Rock'n'Roll. His tour promised to be a monster. The proposed schedule comprised nearly forty theatre dates with two shows a night and a stage act that was so exciting and different from anything else that British audiences had ever experienced that his visit was always destined to attract the headlines. Unfortunately, nobody could have predicted quite how things would go so terribly wrong for all concerned as the media's hatred of rock'n'roll resurfaced with a vengeance.

Perhaps there was a sign of things to come when the plane carrying Lewis and his entourage had to make an emergency landing in Ireland after one of its engines burst into flames. Was this some sort of divine warning that the whole project was ill-fated? If so, nobody was listening, because a replacement aircraft soon enabled them to complete their journey to London where a horde of press men and photographers was waiting. Jerry was accompanied on his great adventure by his manager, Oscar Davis, drummer Russ Smith and bass-player J.W. Brown. Also travelling were Jerry's sister, Frankie Jean, J.W. Brown's wife Lois, and their two children Myra and Rusty.

What the world did not know but were about to find out was that Jerry

Before the fall: Jerry Lee tears it up at the Tooting Granada.

and Myra Brown had married on 12 December 1957 at the wedding chapel in Hernando, Mississippi. It was a stray newspaper reporter, left behind when the main scrum pursued Lewis through the airport terminal, who got lucky with the big story. Myra was happy to be travelling with her husband and proud to reveal the news of their marriage, which was not even general knowledge back in the States. What she failed to appreciate was just how interesting the whole affair was about to become to the British people, with seemingly everybody having an opinion on the subject.

The basic problem was that twenty-two year old Lewis had been married twice before. He had still not been divorced from his second wife, Jane Mitcham, at the time of his wedding to Myra, so in an attempt at damage

limitation he conceded the additional fact that she was his first cousin. Sensing that this entire news item was being badly received by the British press, he exaggerated her age to fifteen, a number which would surely be acceptable. It wasn't, and the news broke like an explosion, especially when Myra's true age was found to be only thirteen. Ironically Jerry's sister, Frankie Jean, escaped unnoticed. Had anybody bothered to enquire, she would have told them that she was already pregnant at fifteen, having been married at twelve. They do things a little different in Louisiana.

The scandal was front page news, and when the tour opened two days later at Edmonton it was difficult for anybody to concentrate on the music against a background of seething indignation. Britain in the Fifties still retained many Victorian values and was collectively recoiling in horror at the prospect of this rock'n'roll monster. Police called at the Westbury Hotel in Mayfair and inspected Myra's passport in the presence of her parents. Myra confided that she was still awaiting news from Mississippi as to the legality of the marriage. Her mother, Lois, said: 'The first my husband and I knew about this marriage was when we found the certificate in a drawer at home. If I find it is not valid, they will get married again quickly. I will insist on that.'

In the midst of all this insanity, the tour commenced, with the Treniers and the Hedley Ward Trio supporting. There was far greater press interest than would normally have been expected, and Jerry Lee made no concessions to try and win them over. He was reported to have leapt on stage at Edmonton and attacked the Steinway *'like an enraged buffalo'.* For the second house at Kilburn, he opened with 'Lawdy Miss Clawdy' and 'Good Golly Miss Molly', before peeling off his jacket and sitting at the piano calmly combing his long blond hair back into position. The audience applauded and he tore into 'It'll Be Me', during which he stood up, danced around, knelt at the piano and then sat down again, digging at the treble notes with the heel of his boot. The pace slowed for 'You Win Again' before he erupted into 'Down The Line', kicking the piano stool across the stage. Both sides of his new American record followed next, the bluesy piano on 'Fools Like Me' contrasting with the out-and-out rock'n'roll of 'High School Confidential'. Lewis then put everything into 'Whole Lotta Shakin' Goin' On', even coming to the front of the stage and lying down to describe the intimate details of the song.

With the audience at fever pitch, he closed with a roaring 'Great Balls Of Fire'. It was a masterly performance, but one which was too wild, too extreme and way too threatening for Britain to stomach in the light of everything else.

The true effects of the bad publicity were felt the following night at Tooting when Jerry was booed and jeered by a section of the audience. He taunted them: 'I'm alive. I sure hope you ain't half as dead as you sound.'

Teenagers responded with: 'Go home, baby snatcher!' and gave him a torrid time throughout his twenty-seven minute act. Lewis was wearing a custard-yellow suit with black sequined braiding, as if to underline his determination to stand out from the men in grey suits. The barracking continued after the show when a group gathered at the stage door still shouting insults.

Meanwhile back in Room 127 at Westbury Hotel, Jerry lunched on steak, strawberries and cream and watched television. 'I was a bigamist at sixteen,' he conceded. 'I have not told the full truth about my marriages before, but last night I had an abusive telephone call from my second wife, Jane. She said: "You're giving me lots of good publicity back here, but you won't see your son when you get back home." My marriage to Jane was invalid under US law. I married Dorothy Barton when I was fourteen. I was just a brat and I didn't know what I was doing. She was a good girl, but I decided to leave her after a year 'cos I realised I was too young for marriage. Then I met Jane. She was as wild as the wind. I met her one week before my divorce from Dorothy, so I married her bigamously. There it is. That is the truth. I hadn't meant to tell it, but now it's all come out. I was a young fool. My father should have put his foot on my neck and beaten a worm out of me.

I'm a good boy and I want everybody to know that. Myra and I are very happy. I am buying her a wedding ring soon.'

The package was due to move to Birmingham, but the Tooting show proved the final straw. The Granada cinema chain and the Grade organisation called a halt and Jerry Lee Lewis and his party were bundled unceremoniously onto a flight back to the States that very day, his career in ruins. He left behind an estimated £35,000 of unfulfilled bookings and a scandal that reverberated on for weeks. Sir Frank Medlicotte, Member of Parliament for Norfolk Central even raised the matter in the House of Commons, by observing: 'We have more than enough rock'n'roll entertainers of our own without importing them from overseas.' Iain MacLeod, Minister of Labour, agreed with him that it was 'a thoroughly unpleasant case'.

THE TRENIERS

May 1958					
27	Birmingham	Odeon	13	Ipswich	Gaumont
28	Preston	Public Hall	14	Woolwich	Granada
29	Glasgow	Odeon	15	East Ham	Granada
30	Edinburgh	New Victoria	16	Leicester	De Montfort Hall
31	Newcastle	Odeon	17	Doncaster	Gaumont
June 1958			18	Hanley	Gaumont
1	Liverpool	Odeon	19	Chester	Gaumont
2	Manchester	Odeon	20	Slough	Adelphi
3	Coventry	Gaumont	21	Salisbury	Gaumont
4	Worcester	Gaumont	22	Plymouth	Odeon
5	Cardiff	Capitol	23	Taunton	Gaumont
6	Cheltenham	Gaumont	24	Southampton	Gaumont
7	Wolverhampton	Gaumont	25	Bournemouth	Gaumont
8	Bradford	Gaumont	26	Rochester	Gaumont
9	Nottingham	Odeon	27	Southend	Gaumont
10	Leeds	Odeon	28	Elephant & Castle	Trocadero
11	Sheffield	City Hall	29	Guildford	Gaumont
12	Norwich	Carlton	30	Bovington	USAF
Promoters — Lew and Leslie Grade					

The banishment of Jerry Lee Lewis resulted in a major predicament for the tour organisers. Sixty-eight shows had still to be completed at thirty-four venues and the Treniers were left to carry the can. At the Birmingham Odeon, Jerry Lee was replaced by the eminently forgettable Terry Burton and Jerry Allen & His Trio. Predictably, there was a stampede to the box office as the public demanded their money back.

By the next night at Preston the tour had been re-shaped. The Treniers and the Hedley Ward Trio were joined by the Chas McDevitt Group — the word 'Skiffle' had recently been dropped from their title — and by an unknown South London teenage rock'n'roller, Terry Wayne. Attendances were generally patchy, but the tour did at least limp through to a conclusion largely thanks to the dynamic and exciting stage antics of The Treniers.

By the time the package reached Manchester, it was being reported that those who had stayed away were missing a treat. Claude and Cliff Trenier were now being referred to as the *'daddies of rock'n'roll'*, and every report remarked upon their astonishing vitality. Favourable comments also referred to the technique and control of drummer Henry Green, the exhibitionism of bassist James Johnson, and the fine alto sax playing of Don Hill. When the long tour finally came to an end, the Treniers crossed the English Channel to play shows in Germany and Belgium, including an appearance at the *World Fair* in Brussels.

TV appearances

Saturday Spectacular   21 June 1958

JACKIE WILSON

An unsuccessful attempt was made for Jackie Wilson to tour Britain for four weeks starting in July. It was an exciting prospect, as reports of his dynamic stage act had already crossed the Atlantic. Sadly, it would still be many years before this great entertainer appeared live for his British fans.

CONNIE FRANCIS

August 1958		
17	Blackpool	Opera House
18-23	Glasgow	Empire
24	Blackpool	Opera House
Promoters — Lew and Leslie Grade		

Connie flew into London on 13 August accompanied by her mother and her manager, George Scheck. A party aboard the SS *Queen Elizabeth* was staged by EMI Records and she spent her first evening in England cruising the Thames between Westminster and Greenwich in the company of both press and disc-jockeys. She made two separate appearances on ATV's *Saturday Spectacular*, the second along with Lonnie Donegan.

According to promoter Leslie Grade, Connie did terrific business during her week in Glasgow. 'I want her back for a longer stay,' he said.

The majority of her audience were male and they showed great enthusiasm especially when she sang 'Who's Sorry Now'. While she didn't exactly tear the house down, she did carry her fans with her all the time, and they clapped and whistled their way through a set which comprised fifteen songs.

Plans had also been made for Connie to do some recording in London following her live shows, but these were delayed for a couple of days as she had picked up a painful throat ailment. She was eventually well enough to record two songs for the new Jayne Mansfield film, *The Sheriff Of Fractured Jaw*.

TV appearances

Saturday Spectacular   16 August 1958
Saturday Spectacular   27 August 1958 (screened 13 September 1958)

THE KALIN TWINS

September 1958			10	Manchester	Free Trade Hall
22-27	London	Prince of Wales	12	Liverpool	Empire
29-30	London	Prince of Wales	14	Leicester	De Montfort Hall
October 1958			15	Sheffield	City Hall
1-4	London	Prince of Wales	16	Newcastle	City Hall
5	Hanley	Victoria Hall	17	Birmingham	Town Hall
6	Blackpool	Odeon	18	York	Rialto
7	Wigan	Ritz	19	Bristol	Colston Hall
8	Glasgow	St. Andrew's Hall			
Promoters — Lew and Leslie Grade					

Hal and Herbie Kalin were riding the crest of a wave in September 1958. They arrived in Britain on Sunday 21st with their recording of 'When' occupying the No. 1 slot in the British singles chart, but sadly proved unable to live up to the star billing which this conferred.

The tour opened with two weeks in variety at the Prince of Wales theatre. There, they headlined a bill which comprised Michael Holliday, the Mudlarks, violinist Florian Zabach and comedian Jimmy Gay. However Holliday missed the first week due to illness and was replaced by veteran comedians Jimmy Jewel and Ben Warriss. The Kalins struggled to make an impact right from the start and early reviews compared them unfavourably with the Mudlarks, who were described as being more than a match for the Americans.

On their provincial dates, the twins were joined by trumpeter Eddie Calvert, the Most Brothers, the Londonaires, compere Tony Martin and a young teenage rock'n'roller named Cliff Richard. It was sheer bad luck that Cliff Richard's 'Move It' was racing up the charts just when the Kalin Twins should have been cashing in on their own hit. As Cliff's popularity increased, so each night proved more difficult for them until the package reached Newcastle where Cliff was given his wildest reception to date. Screaming girls blocked both exits from the stage and Tony Martin was unable to announce the Kalins over chants of 'We Want Cliff!' Eventually, Cliff had to come out on stage and calm things down before they could perform.

TV appearances
Sunday Night At The London Palladium	28 September 1958
Saturday Spectacular	4 October 1958
6.5 Special	11 October 1958

ALAN FREED

It was announced in July that London agent David Rabin had just returned from a US visit with a signed contract for Alan Freed to embark upon a twenty-one day tour commencing 11 October. Freed would bring to Britain a touring rock'n'roll package which featured Chuck Berry, the Champs, Danny & The Juniors, Screamin' Jay Hawkins and Jo-Ann Campell. This mouthwatering prospect was tempered only by an option clause in the contract which allowed Rabin a limited time period to make his final decision regarding acceptance. In the end, the guarantees were never paid and the bad publicity arising from the Lewis debacle was cited as the reason for the cancellation.

PAT BOONE

November 1958
3   London   Coliseum
Promoter unknown

Pat Boone's links with rock'n'roll were becoming increasingly tenuous by the time he joined an all-star cast for the 1958 *Royal Variety Performance*. Appearing with him were Eartha Kitt, Max Bygraves, Frankie Vaughan, the Beverley Sisters and Roy Castle, along with the orchestras of Cyril Stapleton, Mantovani and Victor Sylvester. The comedy was provided by Tony Hancock, Bernard Bresslaw, Bruce Forsyth and Charlie Drake. Boone performed three numbers, opening with 'Lazy River', followed by a romantic rendition of 'April Love' and a routine 'St. Louis Blues'. Royal guest Princess Margaret was known to be a rock'n'roll fan, but Pat missed his opportunity to woo her with 'Tutti Frutti'.

CHAPTER FOUR

1959

Early To Bed

1959 was the year when everything ground to a halt. Rock'n'roll records still figured in the British charts, but with noticeably less regularity than in the past. Tours to the UK almost stopped completely and it really did seem as if the rock'n'roll era was drawing to a close. Two people must be given credit for breathing life into the corpse. Jack Good for one had not given up on rock'n'roll. He continued to produce exciting and innovative television programmes and was astute enough to realise that the real talent was to be found in the States. He fought long and hard to secure American rock'n'rollers to guest on his shows, *Oh Boy!* and *Boy Meets Girls*, and never wavered in his enthusiasm for the music. Likewise, Larry Parnes kept rock'n'roll on the road. He managed a large number of British acts and, in the absence of any American visitors, did at least keep rock'n'roll in the dance halls and theatres. Elsewhere, there was little support to be found, and the BBC even managed to ban 'Charlie Brown' by the Coasters because it included the word 'spitball', which they feared would encourage delinquency. Bernard Bresslaw's version of the same song was, however, considered fit for broadcast.

Cliff Richard was now the undisputed leader of British rock'n'roll. He had overtaken Marty Wilde after the latter became engaged in a public spat with his record company over their insistence that he record with session musicians rather than his own band, the Wildcats. Wilde claimed: 'In the past, my records have been corny and square, and the kids can spot that a mile off', while session drummer Phil Seaman countered: 'I'm afraid Marty doesn't know a crotchet from a hatchet.' Wilde was right though, and until the producers and the musicians could develop both a love and a feel for the music, British attempts at rock'n'roll were destined to remain distinctly sub-standard. The hapless Terry Dene spent much of the year attempting comebacks, while newer names from the Parnes stable — Billy Fury, Vince Eager and Dickie Pride — were busy supplanting themselves in the public's affections.

It was not just rock'n'roll tours which were in short supply. Very few American singers came to the UK during 1959, although former Ink Spot Bill Kenny undertook a long tour and even made an appearance on *Oh Boy!* Other visitors that year included Josh White, Dinah Washington, Billy Eckstine and bluesmen Champion Jack Dupree, Sonny Terry and Brownie McGhee. Jim Ed, Maxine and Bonnie Brown made a brief appearance on *Boy Meets Girls* in November when their record 'The Three Bells' was flying high in the charts, but overall the optimistic thought was that things could only get better... and happily they did.

THE EVERLY BROTHERS

Britain got its first glimpse of Don and Phil Everly during a whistle-stop promotional tour of Europe which found them visiting eight countries in ten days in the company of the Chordettes and crooner Andy Williams. All three acts recorded in the States for Cadence Records and label boss Archie Bleyer had arranged for the Everlys to appear as non-performing guests on ITV's late-night *Cool For Cats* show on 16 January.

"NEW MUSICAL EXPRESS"

1959 ANNUAL 100 PAGES 3/6d.

PRESENTING THE WORLD'S TOP DISC STARS ON PARADE

Thanks —
and Holiday
Greetings to
our friends
in Britain.

We look forward
to seeing you
all soon.

DON & PHIL
THE
EVERLY BROTHERS

The schedule was a tight one, and was thrown into disarray when their flight touched down almost an hour late. They were bundled into a car and whisked through London to the studios in Wembley where they barely had time to remove their overcoats before being thrust in front of the cameras for a brief interview with host Kent Walton, who also presented them with the *NME* award for *'Best Vocal Group of 1958'*. The following morning, they guested on the BBC Light Programme's *Saturday Club*, and later joined Andy Williams and the Chordettes at a reception thrown by Decca Records at the Savoy Hotel. Less than twenty-four hours after arriving in Britain, they were gone again, on a flight bound for Brussels.

TV appearances
Cool For Cats   16 January 1959

PAUL ANKA

Paul Anka concluded a highly successful season at the Olympia, Paris on 19 January and flew into London the following afternoon to commence rehearsals for the second broadcast in Associated Rediffusion's ambitious new TV series, *The 1959 Show*. The programme, on which he appeared with Indian singer Amru Sani, Petula Clark, Johnny Duncan & The Blue Grass Boys and Mike Preston was shown on Thursday, 22 January. The following day he departed for a twelve-day tour of Italy. An interesting project whereby Anka would return in March and co-star with Cliff Richard for two weeks at London's Palace Theatre sadly never got off the drawing board.

TV appearances
The 1959 Show   22 January 1959

CONNIE FRANCIS

February 1959			9-14	Glasgow	Empire
25-28	London	Palace	15	Newcastle	City Hall
March 1959			16-21	Liverpool	Empire
1	Bristol	Colston Hall	22	Leicester	De Montfort Hall
2-7	London	Palace			
Promoters — Lew and Leslie Grade					

Connie Francis returned for a second tour, again accompanied by her mother and manager George Scheck. She confirmed her love of rock'n'roll in several interviews, and on two separate occasions visited that Mecca of British rock'n'roll, the 2i's Coffee Bar in Soho — a sharp contrast to the luxury of her suite at the Savoy Hotel. While in London, she made two high-profile television appearances including *Saturday Spectacular* (on which she co-starred with Johnnie Ray) and also found the time to record an album of ballads at EMI's Abbey Road Studios, titled *My Thanks To You*.

Connie's live shows were well received. For her weekly engagements, she was accompanied by the theatre orchestras and supported by the Hedley Ward Trio and Italian crooner Toni Dalli. On the three Sunday night concerts, she worked with Frank Weir & His Orchestra.

Her act was a well-balanced mix of rock'n'roll, ballads and spirituals including 'You Always Hurt The One You Love', 'Rock-A-Bye Baby', 'Hallelujah, I Love Him So' and the Laurie London smash, 'He's Got The Whole World In His Hands'. But it was during her own songs, 'Carolina Moon', 'Who's Sorry Now', the infectious 'Stupid Cupid' and her latest, 'My Happiness', that the thirty-minute set really came alive.

When asked to explain the drought of live rock'n'roll acts from the States, she explained: 'The reason many American stars don't come to Britain is that they are frightened. Britain is so different. Sometimes a star can arrive with disc hits and then not make any impression at all. What they don't realise is that, if they are a success in Britain, they can keep coming for ten years and still be welcome — which is more than they can do in America.'

TV appearances
*Sunday Night At The London Palladiu*m   8 March 1959
Saturday Spectacular   23 March 1959 (screened 28 March 1959)

BRENDA LEE

By this time, Jack Good's fast-moving *Oh Boy!* Saturday evening TV show had become compulsory viewing for British rock'n'roll fans, regularly featuring up to a dozen different acts. Cliff Richard and Marty Wilde took it in turns to head a cast of home-grown rockers, and the positive effect of such intense exposure on the careers of these performers cannot be overstated. Jack Good had already expressed a wish to expand his show to include American guests and on 4 April Brenda Lee become the first Yank to appear on *Oh Boy!*

Brenda's early success in the States with songs like 'Rock The Bop'

A very young-looking Brenda Lee makes her first UK TV appearance on *Oh Boy!*

and 'Dynamite' had not been repeated in the UK, and her brief trip was therefore an important promotional visit. She had just completed a successful five-week season at the Paris Olympia when Tommy Steele dropped out of *Oh Boy!* at short notice. She flew into London on 2 April as a last-minute replacement, and two days later was introduced to British audiences as 'Little Brenda Lee'. She performed both sides of her current US single, opening with 'Hummin' The Blues' and concluding with a rocking version of 'Bill Bailey Won't You Please Come Home', which featured a fine sax solo from show stalwart Red Price. Also appearing were Dickie Pride, Tony Sheridan, Don Lang, Neville Taylor and Mike Preston as well as regulars Cherry Wainer, the Vernons Girls and Lord Rockingham's XI. Brenda made a strong impression on her British TV debut and flew on to Milan the following day.

TV appearances
Oh Boy!   4 April 1959

DALE HAWKINS

A major rock'n'roll package tour was announced to play twenty-one consecutive nights of concerts commencing 22 April 1959. The scheme was a joint venture involving Leslie Grade and Paul Anka's manager, Irving Feld, and was to feature Conway Twitty, the Poni-Tails, Bobby Darin, the Diamonds, Duane Eddy and Dale Hawkins. There was barely time to get excited by this fascinating prospect when it was killed off by the Musicians Union, who would not sanction the tour without equivalent British musicians going to America in exchange.

CONWAY TWITTY

With the total absence of any live tours, Britain was being starved of authentic American rock'n'roll. Only Jack Good seemed to be in touch with what the fans wanted, and in April he announced his intention to include more American guests among the cast of *Oh Boy!* Attempts to secure the services of Jackie Wilson proved unsuccessful, but on 5 May Conway Twitty flew into London with his manager, Don Seat. He appeared twice on the show, backed on both occasions by Tony Sheridan & The Wreckers. On Sunday, 10 May, Twitty made a flying visit to Germany with the intention of renewing his friendship with Elvis Presley, who was stationed there with the US Army. He missed him by two hours when Presley was summoned for a duty patrol, and instead spent the day in the company of Elvis's father and grandmother. After his second appearance on *Oh Boy!*, he flew back to the States for a tour of one-night stands.

TV appearances
Oh Boy!   9 May 1959
Oh Boy!   16 May 1959

JERRY LEE LEWIS

Another target for Jack Good was Jerry Lee Lewis, who was struggling to rebuild his career after the previous year's child-bride scandal. A letter from Jerry Lee's manager, Jud Phillips, had appeared in the music press during February making clear that he bore no ill-feelings and was anxious to return to England. However, even Jack Good's persuasive powers were unsuccessful on this occasion. The British authorities had not forgotten Lewis and all attempts to secure him a work permit were firmly refused.

PAUL ANKA

May 1959			June 1959		
11-16	Birmingham	Hippodrome	1-6	Manchester	Hippodrome
18-22	Liverpool	Empire	8-13	Newcastle	Empire
25-30	Glasgow	Empire			
Promoter — Tito Burns					

Paul Anka's commitment to his British fans could not be faulted. This was his third UK tour, and he opened at Birmingham with a rousing version of 'Gum Drop', delivered as always with an abundance of confidence and showmanship. After 'Your Cheating Heart', he varied the tempo with the beat ballad 'Don't Gamble With Love', before taking on the spiritual 'Down By The Riverside' at a rocking pace. He continued with 'You Are My Destiny' and, after a brief interlude kissing girls in front of the stage, followed on with 'Diana', 'Midnight' and 'It Doesn't Matter Anymore'. After performing his latest release, 'I Miss You', he closed strongly with 'I Love You Baby' and '(All Of A Sudden) My Heart Sings'.

It was a good, solid performance, but in truth audience reaction was noticeably less frenzied than on his previous trips. Through no fault of his own, Anka seemed to have lost ground — an impression that was confirmed by Leslie MacDonnell, joint Managing Director of Moss Empires. He cited Anka's five-week tour as having been 'disappointing'. Still, there was some consolation for Paul when he flew back to the States to start work on a new movie, *The Private Lives Of Adam And Eve*, along with the voluptuous Mamie Van Doren.

TV appearances

Drumbeat	17 May 1959 (screened 20 June 1959)
Sunday Break	7 June 1959

THE PLATTERS

With 'Smoke Gets In Your Eyes' high in the British charts, a second Platters tour of two months' duration was announced. It was due to commence on 18 May. Sadly, Zola Taylor, the lady Platter, fell ill and was too sick to travel. At first it was hoped that by rescheduling the early dates the tour could still continue, but when Zola failed to recover in time, the whole project was scrapped with only vague talk of a new tour later in the year to sustain the disappointed fans.

THE PONI-TAILS

August 1959		
3	Coventry	Theatre
Promoter unknown		

Oh Boy! came to an end on 30 May 1959, and producer Jack Good transferred his considerable energies to a new ABC-TV programme, *Boy Meets Girls*. Although this show lacked much of the frantic excitement of its predecessor, it would at least deliver some highly memorable American guests. Not to be outdone, BBC-TV's *Drumbeat* become embroiled in a Saturday evening ratings battle which directly resulted in the only stage appearance by LaVerne Novak, Patti McCabe and Toni Cistone — collectively known as the Poni-Tails.

The three girls from Cleveland flew into London on 8 July and were met at the airport by the entire cast of *Drumbeat* including Bob Miller & The Millermen, the John Barry Seven and the programme's producer, Stewart Morris, who underlined his credibility by informing the assembled press of plans to also secure the services of Lloyd Price and Brook Benton. The Poni-Tails were literally played into the country and three days later made their first appearance on *Drumbeat*, guesting live and performing their two hits, 'Born Too Late' and 'Early To Bed'. They were backed throughout their visit by Bob Miller & The Millermen.

A live show at the Coventry Theatre was arranged at relatively short notice for Bank Holiday Monday. The girls dressed for their twenty-minute spot in pastel green blouses and flowered skirts, and held the audience in the palms of their hands with a varied set that included their latest release, 'Moody', a rocking version of 'Yes Sir, That's My Baby' and a storming 'Yakety Yak' to close. They remained in Britain long enough to appear four times on *Drumbeat* and to tele-record three further spots.

Primarily on a promotional visit, the girls also visited Ireland, while back in the UK they even looked in on hospitals, performing for the patients. They finally departed to Wiesbaden in Germany for a series of concerts at US military bases.

TV appearances

Drumbeat	11 July 1959
Drumbeat	15 July 1959 (screened 18 July 1959)
Trinder Box	18 July 1959
Drumbeat	21 July 1959 (screened 15 August 1959)
Drumbeat	21 July 1959 (screened 22 August 1959)
Drumbeat	21 July 1959 (screened 29 August 1959)
Drumbeat	25 July 1959
Drumbeat	1 August 1959

CONNIE FRANCIS

Connie flew into London on 19 August while 'Lipstick On Your Collar' was high in the UK charts. She was entertained that evening at a lavish reception at the Dorchester Hotel but, although there was vague talk of squeezing a television spot into her schedule, the purpose of her visit was an ambitious recording session which it was hoped would provide enough material for three further albums. Sadly, rock'n'roll did not feature anywhere on the agenda. Connie was already moving into other fields and would apportion significantly less of her time to rock'n'roll in the future.

Freddy Cannon on *Boy Meets Girls*. Behind him is the unmistakable figure of Joe Brown.

JOHNNY CASH

It would be many years before Johnny Cash became a major player with British audiences, but in September 1959 he became the first US act to appear on ABC-TV's *Boy Meets Girls*. He was featured singing 'Katy Too' — one of his less memorable numbers — and, although there was talk of a second spot being filmed for later transmission, it appears that only the one song was ever aired. The only real memory of Cash's brief appearance was his rather exotic cowboy boots. British rock'n'roller Joe Brown was especially taken with them and persuaded Cash to send him a similar pair from the States, which he regularly wore on *Boy Meets Girls* thereafter.

TV appearances
Boy Meets Girls   19 September 1959

FREDDY CANNON

Jack Good's promise of US guest stars for *Boy Meets Girls* led to appearances by Sammy Turner singing 'Lavender Blue' and Jerry Keller with 'Here Comes Summer'. Abortive attempts were also made to secure the services of LaVern Baker, Fabian, Frankie Avalon and Jackie Wilson, but as things turned out, the next rock'n'roller to be featured on the show was Freddy Cannon, who performed 'Tallahassee Lassie' and tele-recorded 'Way Down Yonder In New Orleans' for transmission the following week.

TV appearances

Boy Meets Girls	13 November 1959 (screened 21 November 1959)
Boy Meets Girls	14 November 1959

DOC POMUS & MORT SHUMAN

New York songwriters Pomus & Shuman, best known as composers of the smash hit, 'A Teenager In Love', flew into Britain to take part in *Boy Meets Girls*. Shuman performed 'I'm A Man', a recent US hit for Fabian, and Jack Good even persuaded him to record the song while in London for a single release on Decca.

TV appearances

Boy Meets Girls	21 November 1959

GENE VINCENT

December 1959		
6	Tooting	Granada
Promoter — Larry Parnes		

1959 was unquestionably the bleakest year ever for live rock'n'roll in the UK. Never before nor since have there been less Americans performing in Britain, and at the time it really did seem that the prophets of doom were being proved correct. Ironically, one single stage appearance during the final month of the year can be identified as the start of the second phase of rock'n'roll tours in Britain. On a cold Sunday evening in South-West London, Gene Vincent limped on stage, and from the moment he grabbed the microphone and rolled his eyes to the heavens, nothing was quite the same again.

Gene was brought to the UK by Jack Good specifically to appear on *Boy Meets Girls*. He flew into London on Saturday, 5 December and performed live on BBC radio's *Saturday Club* only three hours after his plane had landed. Later that day, he attended a reception thrown for him by EMI Records at the new Bagatelle Club in Mayfair. Among the guests were Marty Wilde and his wife. Marty had wed Joyce Baker, one of the Vernons Girls, in Greenwich only three days earlier, but had no immediate prospect of a honeymoon owing to a string of personal appearances that had been lined up for him in addition to his TV commitments. The following night, Marty was to headline a show at the Tooting Granada which featured the cream of impresario Larry Parnes' stable of rock'n'roll acts: Dickie Pride, Billy Fury, Vince Eager, Duffy Power, Johnny Gentle, Julian X, Sally Kelly, Terry Dene, the Viscounts and compere Billy Raymond. Parnes augmented this already formidable cast by including Gene Vincent as special guest.

Not surprisingly, there was a capacity audience at Tooting. Vincent closed the first half and produced a stunning performance that showed him to be way above the rest of the acts in terms of stagecraft and showmanship.

Wearing a red and black sweater with jet black trousers and backed by Joe Brown and his group, he demonstrated the full range of his unique talent, hoisting the mike stand above his head before swinging his leg over the top of it, prowling the stage in that peculiar half-crouching stance of his, while all the time singing in that unexpectedly melodic voice. It was noticeable that there had been little rehearsal time, but this did not detract from the power and impact of Gene's debut performance. The audience were ecstatic, and many fans gathered behind the theatre yelling for Gene and hammering in vain on the stage door.

The next few days were spent rehearsing for *Boy Meets Girls*, and on Thursday, 10 December Gene travelled up to the Didsbury Studios in Manchester from where the show was transmitted. The following day, two sequences were recorded. Gene singing, 'Wild Cat', 'Frankie And Johnny', 'Bluejean Bop' and 'Say Mama' was aired on 19 December, while 'Rocky Road Blues', 'Five Days, Five Days', 'I Got A Baby' and 'Right Here On Earth' were held back for transmission on Christmas Eve (moved from the usual Saturday spot to accommodate the Christmas TV schedules). Previous American guests on *Boy Meets Girls* had been restricted to one song only, but Vincent had made such an immense impression on Jack Good that he was prepared to build the whole show around him three weeks running.

On Saturday, 12 December, the vast majority of British fans — at least those not fortunate enough to have been at the Tooting Granada — got their first look at Gene Vincent. He performed live on *Boy Meets Girls* and sang 'Baby Blue', 'Be-Bop-A-Lula' and 'Summertime'. At last one of the heavyweight rock'n'rollers was back in Britain! There was tremendous interest, and Gene was rapidly signed up by Parnes for a theatre tour in January. In the meantime, he flew off to Paris for a string of appearances in France and Germany, having whetted the appetites of British audiences starved for so long of the real thing.

TV appearances

Boy Meets Girls	11 December 1959 (screened 19 December 1959)
Boy Meets Girls	11 December 1959 (screened 24 December 1959)
Boy Meets Girls	12 December 1959

CHAPTER FIVE

1960

C'mon Everybody

If rock'n'roll was the music of the Fifties, then our story should already be drawing to a close. Happily, the opposite was the case, as the Gene Vincent–Eddie Cochran tour heralded the start of the great package shows which in time would bring the music to cinemas and theatres up and down the land and give British audiences the opportunity to enjoy live performances by most of the great rock'n'rollers. The days of variety bills were fortunately at an end, and even though much of the homegrown talent lagged a long way behind the Americans, at least now promoters were catering for teenage audiences rather than trying to force feed them with totally inappropriate supporting bills.

When rock'n'roll first materialised, there was nobody in Britain willing or able to play the music except for a handful of mercenary jazz musicians. This situation had gradually improved and in every district there were now singers and musicians rocking away in local halls and youth clubs striving to be the next Elvis or the next Duane Eddy.

The scene in Wales — always a hotbed of rock'n'roll — is a prime example of this underground activity. As early as 1956, a group called the Alley Cats were performing rock'n'roll, and they were soon followed by the Solid Six, the Heartbeats and the Raiders — the latter being a trio containing a very young Dave Edmunds. By the late Fifties, the Backbeats were a fixture on the local scene and were joined by Tommy Scott & The Senates, who did not threaten to break through to national prominence until Scott toned down his image and changed his name to Tom Jones. Another key person in Welsh rock'n'roll was Cal Ford, a country singer who was among the first to perform rockabilly and present the Sun sound to UK audiences. Most of these names never achieved more than local fame, but they all contributed to the spread of the Devil's Music — and what was happening in Wales was being repeated right across the land.

In 1960, Cliff Richard remained at the pinnacle of British rock'n'roll, although he had already started moving away from the hip-swivelling excesses of 'Move It' and 'High Class Baby'. Liverpudlian Billy Fury was almost as popular as Cliff in the North of England, while others like Joe Brown, Johnny Kidd & The Pirates, Danny Rivers and Dave Sampson were out on the road delivering rock'n'roll to the masses. Elsewhere, Tommy Steele was at the Old Vic playing Squire Lumpkin in *She Stoops To Conquer*, and Marty Wilde would soon be preparing for his appearance on ABC-TV's

Christmas Day panto. A new song had been specially commissioned for him titled 'The Lobster Quadrille Rock', which had a rock'n'roll backing and lyrics from *Alice In Wonderland*. Oh, the joys of being a family entertainer!

Outside of rock'n'roll, 1960 was the year of the girls: Judy Garland, Sarah Vaughan, Ella Fitzgerald and Eartha Kitt all appeared in concert, while Kay Starr and Jane Morgan came over for television work and the Andrews Sisters undertook a season of cabaret at the Talk Of The Town. Annette Funicello (in Britain to film the movie, *The Horsemasters*, for Disney) interrupted her schedule to appear on *Juke Box Jury*, while hot-gospeller Sister Rosetta Tharpe made her third British tour during April, working with the Chris Barber Band. Otherwise, Eddie Fisher, Sammy Davis Jnr. and Paul Robeson made personal appearances amidst a blaze of publicity, while blues pianists Memphis Slim and Little Brother Montgomery performed to specialist audiences following no publicity at all. The Kingston Trio were scheduled to play the Royal Festival Hall, but pulled out when they couldn't agree an acceptable fee. Future country superstar Johnny Cash even came over for a vacation, although on this occasion he left his guitar at home.

GENE VINCENT

January 1960			12	Aylesbury	Granada
6	Maidstone	Granada	13	Bedford	Granada
7	Harrow	Granada	14	Kettering	Granada
8	Dartford	Granada	15	Grantham	Granada
9	Rugby	Granada	16	Mansfield	Granada
10	Walthamstow	Granada	17	Slough	Adelphi
11	Kingston	Granada			
Promoter — Larry Parnes					

Gene Vincent's television exposure via *Boy Meets Girls* and his guest spot at the Granada, Tooting in December 1959 had created a massive demand for further appearances from the 'Screaming End' (as he had been described earlier in his career). He had rounded off the year with gigs in France and Germany, which included a mob scene in Paris during which his new black suede jacket — purchased specially for his British TV appearances — was torn from his back and shredded by over-excited French fans.

Larry Parnes had wasted no time in setting up theatre dates for Vincent and by the time he returned to the UK on 5 January there were a dozen gigs waiting for him which the promoter was busily marketing as the '*Be-Bop-A-Lula Tour*'. Gene was the headliner on a package which also featured Wee Willie Harris, Lance Fortune, Al Saxon, Keith Kelly, the Bachelors and compere Don Arden. His backing was provided by Tony Crombie & The Rockets.

The tour opened at the Granada, Maidstone on a cold wintry evening. One by one the supporting acts came and went. Harris gave his usual far-out performance, while Al Saxon managed to badly cut himself on his banjo and ended his spot with blood running down the side of his face. The tension and excitement of the occasion grew steadily, until finally it was time for Gene to

Rare shot of Gene in pre-leather days, wearing a green suit. Unknown venue.

appear.

He limped on stage, dragging his crippled leg, a gaunt and frail figure dressed in a short-sleeved shirt with leopard-skin markings and dark trousers. His act that evening was sensational and — just as at Tooting — the teenagers were stunned by the excitement and animal-like ferocity of it. Of all the rock'n'rollers who had visited Britain up to this point, probably only Jerry Lee Lewis could be compared to this dangerous, uncontrolled, yet incredibly exhilarating performer who had the ability to affect an audience in this way. Jerry, of course, had been driven away by the Establishment. Gene Vincent was here to stay and would return many, many times to keep the rock'n'roll flame burning brightly.

Every night of this short tour helped to build his reputation. Larry Parnes quickly began putting together an itinerary for future shows and everybody connected with the package could see that Gene was making his mark with the British public. One man who was in close enough proximity to see precisely the impact that he was making was the compere Don Arden, himself a man who had harboured ambitions as a singer. Arden and Vincent would soon become inextricably linked and would enjoy very much a

love-hate relationship. Gene was a difficult, abrasive and at times near-impossible person to work with. Arden would become both his manager and the promoter of his many tours of the UK. He was fortunate to witness the Gene Vincent phenomenon at this early stage and astute enough to see that in Gene he had found a real rock'n'roll hero.

THE PLATTERS

January 1960						
13	Sheffield	City Hall		19	Portsmouth	Guildhall
14	Newcastle	City Hall		20	Cardiff	Odeon
15	Glasgow	Odeon		22	Bristol	Colston Hall
16	Manchester	Free Trade Hall		23	Hammersmith	Gaumont
18	Birmingham	Odeon		24	Leicester	De Montfort Hall
Promoters — Harold Davison and Arthur Howes						

The second Platters tour had been originally scheduled for a nine-week marathon commencing in May 1959, but had been first delayed and then cancelled after Zola Taylor became ill. However, there were problems in rescheduling the dates and the revised itinerary was considerably shorter than originally envisaged. They were supported by Cuddly Dudley and were to be backed by Leslie 'Jiver' Hutchinson's Band, but tragically the Jamaican-born bandleader was killed in a car crash near Bury St. Edmunds on 22 November. He was replaced by Carl Barriteau & His Band.

The five original Platters, comprising Tony Williams, Zola Taylor,

David Lynch, Herb Reed and Paul Robi flew into the UK after a short tour of military bases in Germany. Without a doubt the high point of their visit was the television appearance of 17 January on *Sunday Night At The London Palladium*. The show was watched by an incredible 19·5 million viewers — still one of the highest-ever audience figures for a light entertainment show on British television. The reason for the massive interest was that they were co-starring with Cliff Richard, who at that time was at the peak of his early popularity. The group took the opportunity to showcase their new single, 'Harbour Lights'. Four days later they also appeared on the ATV show, *Startime*.

TV appearances

Sunday Night At The London Palladium	17 January 1960
Val Parnell's Startime	21 January 1960

EDDIE COCHRAN
GENE VINCENT

January 1960			24	Stockton	Globe
24	Ipswich	Gaumont	26	Cardiff	Gaumont
28	Coventry	Gaumont	29	Leeds	Empire
29	Worcester	Gaumont	**March 1960**		
30	Bradford	Gaumont	1-5	Leeds	Empire
31	Southampton	Guildhall	7-12	Birmingham	Hippodrome
February 1960			14-19	Liverpool	Empire
1-6	Glasgow	Empire	21-26	Newcastle	Empire
7	Sheffield	Gaumont	28-31	Manchester	Hippodrome
13	Woolwich	Granada	**April 1960**		
14	Taunton	Gaumont	1-2	Manchester	Hippodrome
18	Leicester	De Montfort Hall	4-9	Finsbury Park	Empire
20	Dundee	Caird Hall	11-14	Bristol	Hippodrome
21	Wembley	Empire Pool	16	Bristol	Hippodrome
Promoter — Larry Parnes					

Gene Vincent's impact on British audiences cannot be understated. His ferocious stage act and his exposure through the *Boy Meets Girls* television show had stirred up tremendous interest just at the time when rock'n'roll was supposed to be fading away. While he was still busily working through his short tour of the Granada circuit, fellow rock'n'roller Eddie Cochran flew into Britain, arriving on 10 January for what was originally intended to be no more than a five-week tour. Cochran was well-known in the UK and his rock'n'roll classic, 'Somethin' Else', had only recently slipped out of the British charts. In fact, Gene and Eddie were old friends who had first met in 1956 during the filming of *The Girl Can't Help It*, and pairing them together as headliners on a touring rock'n'roll package was an inspired choice. Box offices were besieged for tickets and 'House Full' notices were posted almost everywhere they went.

Eddie was entertained at a record company reception before being whisked up to Manchester on 12 January to commence rehearsals for two appearances on *Boy Meets Girls*, one of which went out live on 16 January,

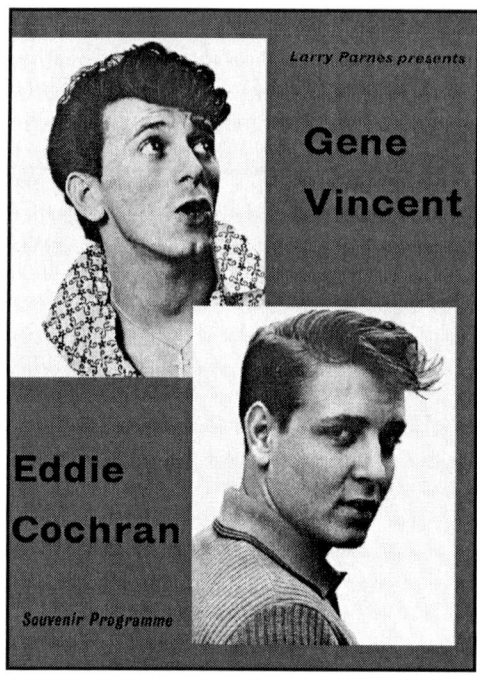

Larry Parnes presents

Gene

Vincent

Eddie

Cochran

Souvenir Programme

the other being recorded for later broadcast.

The tour got underway at Ipswich eight days later with support from Vince Eager & The Quiet Three, the Viscounts, Tony Sheridan and compere Billy Raymond. Eddie, who usually closed the first half of the show, was backed by Marty Wilde's group, the Wildcats, comprising Big Jim Sullivan (guitar), Tony Belcher (guitar), plus two future members of the Shadows, Brian Locking (bass) and Brian Bennett (drums). Gene worked with the Beat Boys, namely Colin Green (guitar), Vince Cooze (bass), Red Reece (drums), Georgie Fame (piano) and Billy McVay (saxophone). As the tour threaded its way around Britain, more and more dates were added, while the support acts varied and at different times included Billy Fury, Joe Brown, Peter Wynne, Dean Webb, Sally Kelly, Georgie Fame (in some instances performing as 'Lance Fortune') and Johnny Gentle.

At Sheffield, Cochran hit the stage dressed in a red shirt, silver waistcoat and leather trousers, plugged in his Gretsch and began playing with his back to the audience before swinging round and tearing into the vocal of 'Somethin' Else'. British audiences had no idea that he was such an accomplished guitarist, and as he worked his way through 'Twenty Flight Rock', 'C'mon Everybody', a brooding 'Milk Cow Blues' and a highly original treatment of 'What'd I Say', his instrumental prowess added another dimension to the proceedings. 'Summertime Blues' was the climax of his exciting and aggressive set. Girls were screaming and the atmosphere was electric throughout.

Gene Vincent had now adopted his 'black leather' image, on the recommendation of Jack Good, who saw him as a tragic Shakespearian figure and encouraged him, if anything, to accentuate his limp and to make a feature of his crippled leg. Dressed all in black, complete with leather gloves, his set was wilder and more extreme than ever. The British press found it hard to summon up much praise for the show, which by and large was panned almost everywhere it went. The critics may not have understood rock'n'roll but the teenage audiences did, and both Gene and Eddie were swept along on a solid wave of enthusiasm.

At Coventry, girls were screaming throughout and Gene scored with a moving version of 'Summertime', while at Worcester, Eddie drove the audience wild with a steamy 'Hallelujah, I Love Her So'. On a very cold night in Bradford, Gene stormed off stage after hecklers interrupted 'Over The

Rainbow'. It had been snowing and the ground was covered in slush, but Eddie managed to turn 'cold' into 'cool' with a masterful display and a quite sizzling 'Twenty Flight Rock'. By the time the show reached Southampton, Cochran was suffering with laryngitis, but struggled through, while at Glasgow the audience made so much noise that the vocals could hardly be heard, although 'C'mon Everybody' proved to be the showstopper.

Things got completely out of hand in Dundee, where bedlam led to fighting, girls fainting and several youths being ejected from the auditorium. The police were called and three people were arrested and charged with assault and breaches of the peace. Near the end of Gene's set a girl climbed on stage and kissed him, whereupon dozens more joined her and the singer became lost in the crowd. Attendants eventually cleared the stage and Vincent tried to continue with the show, but when Cochran and Vince Eager joined him for a final song, an avalanche of screaming fans — twice as many as before — rushed the stage and the whole proceedings deteriorated into chaos. One attendant had the sleeve torn from his jacket, a door was smashed, several seats destroyed, toilet fittings and towel rails were wrenched off the wall, and, to add insult to injury, a metal bust of Sir James Caird — donor of the Caird Hall — was removed from its base, thrown around the foyer and badly dented. This was not behaviour that was likely to gather positive reviews from the media, but it was shaking up a storm and rock'n'roll fans were enjoying every minute of it.

On 21 February, both men performed at the prestigious *New Musical Express Poll Winners' Concert* at Wembley on a bill that also featured Cliff Richard, Lonnie Donegan, Billy Fury, Marty Wilde, Emile Ford, the Mudlarks, Craig Douglas, the John Barry Seven, Dave Sampson, Bert Weedon and compere Pete Murray. Adam Faith appeared as a late replacement for Alma Cogan who was sick. Gene's manager, Norm Riley, and his wife, Darlene, were both present to see him perform 'Say Mama' and a raunchy 'Be-Bop-A-Lula', during which at one point he lay on his back holding the microphone stand vertically above him. Eddie was also in a very lively mood and literally pranced across the stage as he sang 'Somethin' Else', 'Hallelujah, I Love Her So', 'Sweet Little Sixteen' and

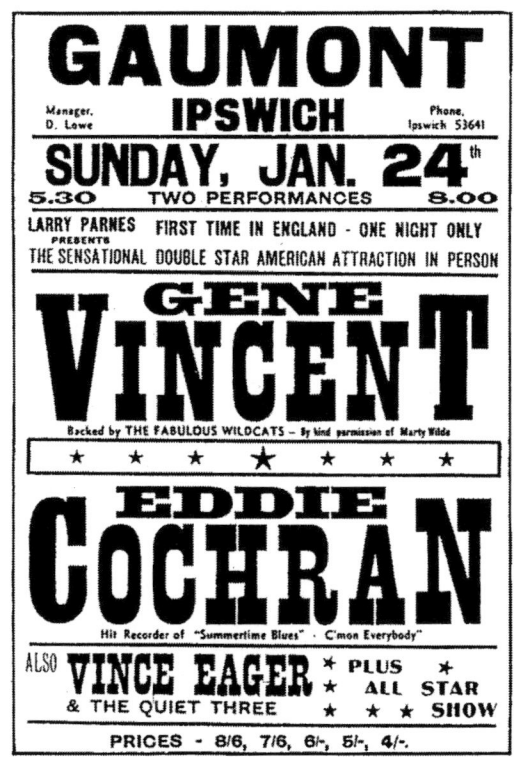

GAUMONT

Manager, D. Lowe **IPSWICH** Phone, Ipswich 53641

SUNDAY, JAN. 24th

5.30   TWO PERFORMANCES   8.00

LARRY PARNES   FIRST TIME IN ENGLAND - ONE NIGHT ONLY
PRESENTS
THE SENSATIONAL DOUBLE STAR AMERICAN ATTRACTION IN PERSON

GENE
VINCENT

Backed by THE FABULOUS WILDCATS - By kind permission of Marty Wilde

★ ★ ★ ★ ★ ★ ★

EDDIE
COCHRAN

Hit Recorder of "Summertime Blues" · C'mon Everybody"

ALSO VINCE EAGER ★ PLUS ★
& THE QUIET THREE ★ ALL STAR ★ ★ SHOW

PRICES - 8/6, 7/6, 6/-, 5/-, 4/-.

Eddie on *Boy Meets Girls.*

'C'mon Everybody'.

So great was the success of the Vincent–Cochran tour, that Larry Parnes was inundated with requests for further bookings and the original five-week itinerary was soon open-ended as more dates were confirmed, and both men rapidly rebooked on *Boy Meets Girls*.

There was more crowd trouble at Cardiff, where Tony Sheridan was barracked and met with a hail of lit cigarettes from impatient Gene Vincent fans. There was much screaming and shouting, and again it was Cochran's 'C'mon Everybody', which stole the show. The local press described Vincent as *'a leather-clad spaceman from another planet'*.

In Leeds, after another exhilarating evening, both Gene and Eddie crossed the street to a dance hall where they were entertained by disc jockey Jimmy Savile, and where they signed literally hundreds of autographs. Earlier, the St. John's Ambulance Service had been kept busy when several girls near the front fainted and had to be rescued from the baying mob.

Gene Vincent's crippled leg was a constant source of pain and discomfort, and even though he utilised this disability almost as a stage prop it was nevertheless a very real problem for him, and on several occasions during this tour — and indeed throughout his career — he performed in considerable pain. Even so, he would never cancel a show if he could possibly help it and invariably struggled on when common sense dictated otherwise. On 30 March, he collapsed in Manchester suffering from pleurisy and was replaced briefly by Peter Wynne before rejoining the tour again.

Eddie sang a memorable 'Sittin' In The Balcony' at Liverpool and not for the first time stunned his audience with his virtuosic guitar-picking.

During the week-long residency at Newcastle, Vincent rocked his way through 'Bluejean Bop', 'Wild Cat', 'Dance To The Bop' and a wonderful interpretation of Jack Scott's 'What In The World's Come Over You' before closing his show with a slow and menacing 'Be-Bop-A-Lula'. The whole cast including Billy Fury and Georgie Fame came together for a grand finale of 'Shake, Rattle And Roll'.

It seemed as if the tour would roll on for much of the year — a sure sign that Gene and Eddie were confounding all the critics who continued to treat rock'n'roll as if it was the direct cause of an unpleasant smell. Both men were putting so much into their acts that fatigue was starting to set in and Eddie in particular was reportedly homesick.

Larry Parnes decided that they would take a ten-day break after concluding the residency at Bristol. This would allow Eddie the opportunity to return home and even do some recording, while Gene, who never seemed to rest, could play shows in Paris. The whole troupe would reassemble at the end of April, when further gigs were scheduled for Hanley, Lewisham, Cheltenham, Salisbury, Guildford, Halifax, Chester, Wolverhampton and Romford. Even this was far from the end, as Parnes still had numerous other venues under consideration and was even looking into the possibility of summer seasons at Blackpool, Bournemouth and other resorts. Rock'n'roll was flying, and interest among British fans had never been greater.

The final show at the Bristol Hippodrome took place on 16 April — Easter Saturday. The supporting acts were the Tony Sheridan Trio, Georgie Fame, Peter Wynne, Johnny Gentle and compere Billy Raymond. The Wildcats were not available to back Gene as they were working with Mary Wilde at the Palladium, so the Beat Boys doubled up and backed both Americans. Once again, it was Eddie's superb guitar-playing that was the defining memory for many of the fans fortunate enough to witness what proved to be his last show.

For Cochran himself, weary and homesick, the final curtain could not come soon enough. A taxi had been organised to get him back to London in readiness for his flight home the following afternoon, and he was insistent that he wanted to make the journey immediately rather than wait until the morning.

The taxi was a Ford Consul and it set off from the Royal Hotel, Bristol at around 11.00 pm with Gene, Eddie and Sharon Sheeley, Eddie's American songwriter-girlfriend in the back, and tour manager Pat Thompkins sitting up front with the driver, George Martin. With no modern motorway yet in place, the journey involved driving through Bath and across to Chippenham to pick up the old A4 road.

Somewhere around Chippenham the driver lost his way and doubled back to regain his bearings, in the course of which he lost control of the vehicle while driving downhill. The car spun backwards into a concrete lamppost and landed up partly on the road and partly up a grass verge. The rear left-hand side of the taxi took the worst of the impact. Sharon Sheeley was sitting in the most vulnerable seat and received injuries to her back and pelvis. Eddie leaned across immediately before the point of impact and shielded her with his body, thereby almost certainly saving her life. He was thrown out of the vehicle when the door flew open. Gene suffered head injuries and broke his collarbone. Both the driver and Pat Thompkins in the front were unhurt.

The accident occurred shortly after midnight on 17 April. An ambulance dispatched them first to Chippenham Cottage Hospital and then on to the casualty unit at St. Martin's Hospital in Bath where Eddie was found to have serious head and chest injuries. He remained unconscious, and during the day his condition gradually deteriorated until he finally died at 4.10 pm. A subsequent post mortem showed that although his skull was not fractured, there had been severe haemorrhaging and an accumulation of fluid and bruising within the brain tissue.

News of the crash broke on Easter Monday, 18 April and not surprisingly it remained a major story for several days. Sharon and Gene were visited in hospital by Don and Phil Everly and the Crickets, who were themselves engaged on a British tour. Friends and fans alike were stunned by the news of Eddie's death.

Gene Vincent discharged himself from St. Martin's and flew back to the States on 20 April. Eddie's body made the same journey the following day. He was buried at Forest Lawn Cemetery in Cypress, Los Angeles at 10.00 am on Monday, 25 April.

The taxi driver, George Martin, appeared in court at Bristol Assizes on 24 June charged with causing death by dangerous driving. He was found guilty of driving the Ford Consul at excessive speed and received a fine of £50. He was disqualified from driving for a period of fifteen years.

Cochran's tragic demise at the age of only twenty-one is one of the great tragedies of rock'n'roll ranking alongside the plane crash only a year earlier which claimed the lives of Buddy Holly, the Big Bopper and Ritchie Valens. Somehow, for British fans, the fact that Eddie died in the UK while bringing so much pleasure to so many people made it even worse. Like Buddy Holly, Eddie Cochran will always be remembered and remains forever young in the memories of those who recall that fateful night.

TV appearances (Eddie Cochran)

Boy Meets Girls	15 January 1960 (screened 23 January 1960)
Boy Meets Girls	16 January 1960
Lunch Box	12 March 1960

TV appearances (Eddie Cochran and Gene Vincent)

Boy Meets Girls	19 February 1960 (screened 20 February 1960)
Boy Meets Girls	19 February 1960 (screened 27 February 1960)

Rockin' Ronnie on *Boy Meets Girls*. The sax-player nearest to the camera is Red Price.

RONNIE HAWKINS

The latest American rock'n'roller to appear on *Boy Meets Girls* was Arkansas-born Ronnie Hawkins, who had scored hits back home with 'Mary Lou' and 'Forty Days' but was practically unknown in Britain. He arrived along with his drummer, Levon Helm, and was featured on the show for two consecutive weeks performing first 'Forty Days' and then 'Southern Love'.

Hawkins was pleasantly surprised by the quality of the British musicians on *Boy Meets Girls*: 'They had one of the greatest horn-players I've ever heard in my life; Red Price was his name and he was as close to King

71

Curtis as anybody has been. Then there was this little girl, Cherry Wainer, who played organ and was fuckin' unbelievable, and a young kid called Joe Brown playing guitar in a pair of boots that Johnny Cash had given him. If I could have taken him back with me, he could have become the greatest picker of them all.'

TV appearances
Boy Meets Girls	29 January 1960 (screened 6 February 1960)
Boy Meets Girls	30 January 1960

OTIS BLACKWELL

The man who wrote such rock'n'roll classics as 'All Shook Up', 'Great Balls Of Fire' and 'Don't Be Cruel' was lined up to be the latest guest for *Boy Meets Girls* on 6 February. This seemed an odd choice, as Otis Blackwell was virtually unknown in the UK even as a songwriter, while almost nobody had any idea that he also harboured ambitions as a singer and piano-player. In the end, his abilities as a performer remained a mystery when he cried off citing illness as his excuse. He never did get another opportunity to appear in Britain and died in Nashville on 6 May 2002 after a long illness.

PAT BOONE

Pat's new movie, *Journey To The Centre Of The Earth*, had opened in the UK during January and was his first opportunity to tackle a serious acting role. He accepted a booking on *Sunday Night At The London Palladium*, arriving with his wife, Shirley, on 12 February. His stay was very brief, as it had to be squeezed in between recordings for his weekly US television show, but he did find time for a visit to an East London football match to watch Leyton Orient play Aston Villa.

TV appearances
Sunday Night At The London Palladium	14 February 1960

ELVIS PRESLEY

One name that figures very rarely in this book is that of Elvis Presley. His importance in the world of rock'n'roll is without question, but as he hardly ever set foot outside the USA, he can be no more than a peripheral figure in any study of live music in Britain. He did, however, visit the UK on one occasion at the end of his spell of service in the US Army. On 3 March 1960, Sgt. Elvis Presley stopped off for a couple of hours at Prestwick Airport in Scotland before completing his journey from Germany back to the States.

News of his arrival leaked out and a gaggle of local fans were there to greet him. It would be exhilarating to report that somebody handed Elvis a guitar and that he serenaded his fans with impromptu versions of 'Hound Dog' and 'That's All Right', but sadly this was not the case. He did sign some autographs, but otherwise remained under the close supervision of Colonel Russell Fisher and Major Ed Miller of 1631 USAF Unit, until his plane was ready to continue its journey across the Atlantic.

Togetherness: Duane Eddy, Clyde McPhatter and Bobby Darin.

DUANE EDDY
BOBBY DARIN
CLYDE McPHATTER

March 1960			April 1960		
18	Lewisham	Gaumont	1-2	Liverpool	Empire
19	Edmonton	Regal	3	Birmingham	Hippodrome
20	Leicester	De Montfort Hall	4	Bristol	Colston Hall
21-26	Glasgow	Empire	6	Leeds	Odeon
27	Newcastle	City Hall	7	Sheffield	Gaumont
28-31	Liverpool	Empire	8	Manchester	Odeon
			9	Elephant & Castle	Trocadero
			10	Guildford	Odeon
Promoters — Leslie Grade and Arthur Howes					

For the first time in Britain, here was a package show containing three American rock'n'roll acts, each quite different from the other and with their own distinctive styles. Travelling with his manager/producer Lee Hazlewood, Duane Eddy was backed by his own group, the Rebels, comprising Jim Horn (saxophone), Dave Campbell (bass), Larry Knechtel (piano) and Jimmy Troxel (drums), while McPhatter and Darin were backed throughout the tour by Bob Miller & The Millermen. Also on the package were Emile Ford & The Checkmates and compere Alan Field.

The show proved to be a controversial event because of the

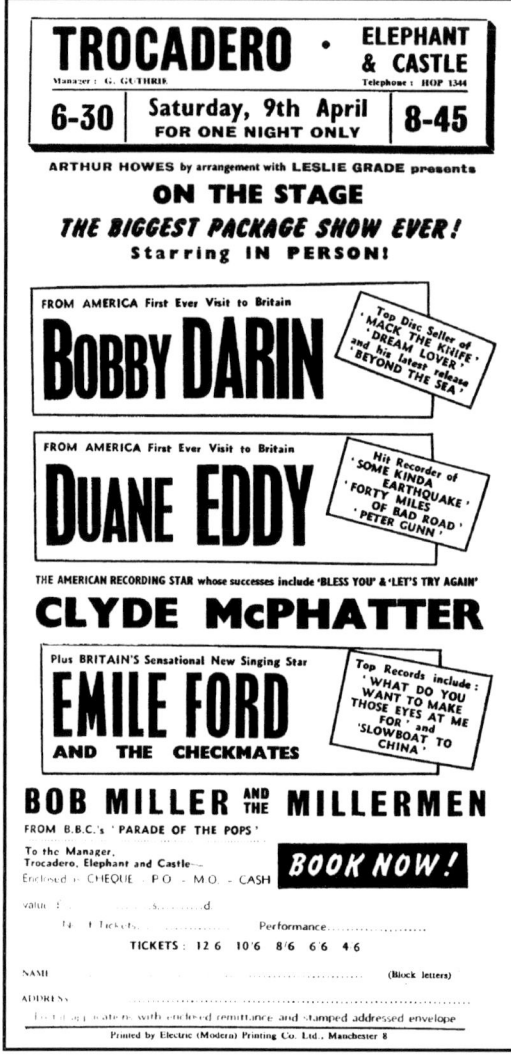

interaction between Bobby Darin and his audiences. Darin had started out as a rock'n'roller and it was songs like 'Plain Jane', 'Queen Of The Hop' and even the novelty rocker 'Splish Splash' that had made his name. Latterly however, he had expressed the desire to drop rock'n'roll in favour of a new style that was a good deal closer to Frank Sinatra than Elvis Presley. He had scored British hits with both 'La Mer (Beyond The Sea)' and 'Mack The Knife' complete with orchestral backings and it was the new mature, crooning Darin rather than Darin the rocker who arrived in the UK, unaware that not all his fans were of similar mind.

On opening night at Lewisham, it was Clyde McPhatter who was the first American on stage. He impressed with a short act that got off to a strong start via a powerful 'Money Honey'. The ex-Drifter then continued with 'Just To Hold My Hand', 'Without Love (There Is Nothing)' and a knockout 'Think Me A Kiss'. The Millermen played too loud, but Clyde's wonderful high-pitched voice still rose above them and he closed with a moving 'Have Mercy Baby'.

Duane Eddy & The Rebels could not have been a greater contrast. They commenced with a raw, pulsating and very loud 'Peter Gunn'. The audience were then swept along with 'Cannonball', 'Rebel Rouser' and 'Some Kinda Earthquake'. Duane never spoke and hardly moved, leaving saxman Jim Horn to jump and shake around, but the excitement that the five men created was extraordinary. His twangy guitar only relaxed for a colourful interpretation of '3.30 Blues' before thundering on through 'Yep!' and his latest single, 'Bonnie Came Back'. He and the Rebels were undoubtedly the hit of the night, and so great was the applause that he was obliged to make a brief speech of thanks to the fans who were still demanding more.

Bobby Darin was in trouble right from the start as he launched into a finger-snapping 'Swing Low, Sweet Chariot' and an unrocking 'Lonesome

Bobby guests on ATV's *Saturday Spectacular.*

Road'. The audience seemed restless as he crooned his way through 'Dream Lover' and 'Clementine' and finally lost patience with 'My Funny Valentine'. Darin seemed visibly shaken when the barracking started but did at least have the personality to put the hecklers in their place. Sensibly, he moved on to a lively 'Splish Splash' before sitting down at the piano and delivering a punchy 'I Got A Woman', finally closing with 'La Mer (Beyond The Sea)', 'All Night Long' and 'Mack The Knife'. The press were largely supportive, condemning the uncouth behaviour of the ill-mannered minority, but Darin was neither the first nor by any means the last to learn that rock'n'roll audiences want rock'n'roll and not a poor man's Sinatra.

As the tour progressed, Darin did fare better at some locations than at others, and he gradually adapted his act to include a higher proportion of rock'n'roll. Overall however, it was Duane Eddy who proved the star of the show and his twangy guitar style became a real hit with British audiences. On 5 April, all three men participated in ATV's *Saturday Spectacular*, with Duane playing guitar for Bobby on 'Country Boy'. Darin did not appear on the final night of the tour at Guildford.

TV appearances (Bobby Darin, Duane Eddy and Clyde McPhatter)
Saturday Spectacular   5 April 1960 (screened 23 April 1960)

TV appearances (Bobby Darin)
Sunday Night At The London Palladium   10 April 1960

THE EVERLY BROTHERS

April 1960				
3	London	New Victoria	16 Sheffield	City Hall
4	Ipswich	Gaumont	17 Leicester	De Montfort Hall
5	Portsmouth	Guildhall	18 Bristol	Colston Hall
7	Edinburgh	Usher Hall	19 Leeds	Odeon
8	Glasgow	Odeon	20 York	Rialto
9	Doncaster	Gaumont	21 Wolverhampton	Gaumont
10	Hull	ABC Regal	22 Manchester	Free Trade Hall
11	Stockton	Globe	23 Newcastle	City Hall
12	Derby	Gaumont	24 Liverpool	Empire
13	Edmonton	Regal	25 Cardiff	Gaumont
15	London	New Victoria	26 Birmingham	Odeon

Promoter — Arthur Howes

'Cathy's Clown', the first Everly Brothers single to be issued by Warner Brothers, soared to No. 1 in the UK charts during April, which confirmed the excellent timing of their British tour.

Don and Phil flew into London on 1 April along with their manager, Wesley Rose, and their backing musicians, who turned out to be none other than the Crickets: Jerry Allison (drums) and Joe B. Maudlin (double bass) — both of whom had toured the UK with Buddy Holly in March 1958 — plus Holly's replacement, singer/guitarist Sonny Curtis. Although the presence of the Crickets became public knowledge, they extraordinarily never performed under their own name at any stage of the tour, merely playing largely unseen in the background, although their involvement did provide the Everly Brothers with quality accompaniment of the highest order. The remainder of the package comprised the Dallas Boys, Cherry Wainer and Don Storer, Lance Fortune, Danny Hunter, the Flee-Rekkers, the Freddy Lloyd Five and compere Tony Marsh.

The opening night at London's New Victoria drew a near-capacity audience. The brothers were smartly attired in black suits and white shirts and the familiar harmonies of 'Wake Up Little Susie' gave immediate notice that their fans were in for a night to remember. Their crisp vocals tore through 'Bye Bye Love' before they dropped the pace for 'All I Have To Do Is Dream'. Happily, they experienced none of the hostility that had been directed at Bobby Darin when he had attempted ballads only days earlier, and this thought seemed to have registered with Don, who thanked the audience for applauding so enthusiastically. Then it was back to rock'n'roll with 'Bird Dog', 'Be-Bop-A-Lula' and a frantic '('Til) I Kissed You'. The set closed rather abruptly after a lively rendition of 'Cathy's Clown'. The crowd were cheering for more, but instead of an encore the safety curtain was dropped and the National Anthem played to signify that the show was over. Press reports all agreed that the Everlys were a great success and worthy of the big reputations that had preceded their arrival.

By an unkind quirk of fate, the package was scheduled to appear in Bristol on the night following the death of Eddie Cochran in nearby Chippenham. The show on 18 April did go ahead, but proved to be an enormously emotional occasion for both audience and entertainers alike. The

Startime with Don and Phil. Behind them is Crickets drummer Jerry Allison.

Crickets had played on Eddie's last recording session in January, and he was also well known to both Don and Phil.

During their visit the Everlys also appeared twice on ATV's *Startime* with Alma Cogan, but they turned down a spot on *Sunday Night At The London Palladium* scheduled for 1 May, plus a gig at the Paris Olympia on 30 April as they wanted to fly home to Nashville for a short break before commencing a gruelling tour of Australia. The Everly Brothers were immensely popular in Britain at this time and this, their first British tour, both cemented their popularity and created the demand for a quick return.

TV appearances

Val Parnell's Startime	6 April 1960 (screened 7 April 1960)
Val Parnell's Startime	14 April 1960
Saturday Spectacular	? April 1960 (screened 6 August 1960)

JOHNNY PRESTON

April 1960			May 1960		
10	Southend	Odeon	1	Chelmsford	Odeon
11-14	Liverpool	Empire	2	Brighton	Essoldo
15	Slough	Adelphi	3	Tunbridge Wells	Essoldo
16	Liverpool	Empire	4	Sutton	Granada
18-23	Leeds	Empire	5	Scunthorpe	Pavilion
25-30	Finsbury Park	Empire	6	Barrow	Coliseum
			7	Burnley	Palace
Promoter — Don Arden					

Texan Johnny Preston had recently scored a massive UK hit with the novelty rocker 'Running Bear', but was hitherto unknown on this side of the Atlantic. He became the first American act to have a tour promoted by Don Arden — a promoter who would win few friends with his somewhat extreme business methods, but who over the next few years would promote some of the greatest rock'n'roll tours ever to be seen in Britain. His venture with Johnny Preston was not among his greatest successes however. The package did no more than average business around the theatres despite a line-up that included Wee Willie Harris, Tony Crombie, Chris Wayne, the Echoes (who also backed Preston), the Four Jays and Arden himself as compere. On one or two shows the acts varied to include Jerry Lordan, Billy Fury and the Lindy Sisters.

Preston turned out to be an unspectacular performer who appeared to be suffering with nerves. The opening show of the tour took place at Southend, and he kicked off with a bright version of Neil Sedaka's 'Oh Carol', followed by 'You Got What It Takes' on which he switched to falsetto on occasions. 'Harbour Lights' was not a good idea, his voice going flat once or twice as he struggled through the song, though he did have a decent stab at 'Mack The Knife'. Then he tried out his newest record, 'Cradle Of Love' and the Shirley & Lee-inspired novelty, 'Feel So Fine', before closing his twenty-minute spot with a surprisingly lukewarm 'Running Bear'. Although the fans shouted for more, no encores were forthcoming.

Johnny Preston was accompanied in Britain by his wife Jeanell and their four month old daughter, Tracie, as well as his manager, Bill Hall, and his wife. He also made one television appearance, becoming the first American panellist to take part in the new BBC show, *Juke Box Jury*.

TV appearances

Juke Box Jury	14 April 1960 (screened 30 April 1960)

DUANE EDDY

April 1960		
11-16	Finsbury Park	Empire
17	Cheltenham	Gaumont
18-23	Liverpool	Empire
24	East Ham	Granada
Promoters — Leslie Grade and Arthur Howes		

Duane Eddy had done so well on the package tour with Bobby Darin and Clyde McPhatter that he remained in Britain for a further fortnight heading up a show which also featured Frank Ifield, Kathy Kirby, the Four Playboys, Alan Randall and compere Des O'Connor. It was a sure indication of the popularity of Duane and the Rebels that they were re-booked in Liverpool only sixteen days after their first appearance at the Empire. When his tour finally came to an end, Eddy flew to Paris on 25 April.

JACK SCOTT

Having got Johnny Preston's tour underway, Don Arden next turned his attention to a proposed eight-week visit by Canadian Jack Scott, which was originally scheduled to commence on 18 April. However, Jack proved a less straightforward proposition and negotiations became so protracted that the date of his British debut was initially put back to 23 May and eventually shelved indefinitely.

GENE VINCENT

April 1960					
30	Hanley	Gaumont	12	Halifax	Odeon
May 1960			13	Chester	Gaumont
1	Lewisham	Gaumont	14	Wolverhampton	Gaumont
5	Cheltenham	Gaumont	15	Romford	Odeon
6	Salisbury	Gaumont	16-21	Brighton	Hippodrome
7	Guildford	Odeon	**June 1960**		
8	Hull	ABC Regal	6-11	Glasgow	Empire
			13-18	Nottingham	Theatre Royal
Promoter — Larry Parnes					

The Cochran–Vincent tour had ground to a halt after the tragic accident of 17 April, but reassembled only a fortnight later with pop singer Jerry Keller now headlining alongside Gene. Eddie Cochran was irreplaceable, but Keller warbling 'Here Comes Summer' with a smug grin on his face was no sort of substitute. Nero & The Gladiators backed Keller while Vincent worked with the Beat Boys. The support acts were Lance Fortune, the Viscounts, Peter Wynne, Vince Taylor, Davy Jones and Georgie Fame. Inevitably, Larry Parnes mixed and matched as other commitments arose and consequently Sally Kelly, Billy Fury, Joe Brown, Michael Cox, Duffy Power and Dickie Pride also participated at different times as the tour threaded its way around the country.

Gene looked far from well, his usual gaunt appearance failing to disguise the pressures — both physical and mental — under which he was operating. During his performance at Lewisham, he continually rubbed his left shoulder, a clear indication that the collarbone, damaged in the car wreck, had not fully recovered. He made a short speech in tribute to his friend before announcing: 'I want to sing for you now, Eddie's favourite song.' Girls in the audience sobbed uncontrollably as he performed a sad but gentle rendition of 'Over The Rainbow', before launching into a powerful 'Be-Bop-A-Lula'.

At this time, it seemed as if working in front of an audience was the only thing that could get Gene through the day, and throughout this period he put everything into his act. On 11 June, he collapsed in Glasgow and was taken to hospital, only to discharge himself against doctor's orders in time to play both houses at the Empire that same evening. In fact, his week in Glasgow was memorable for at least two separate riots while he was on stage, and the theatre shut down for a ten-week refurbishment immediately the singer and his fans had departed.

During the later stages of the tour, Gene publicly announced on more than one occasion that his eighteen month old daughter, Melody, had died of pneumonia. Not surprisingly, he cut short his commitments in the UK and flew home to the States on 19 June leaving Joe Brown to replace him at residencies in Liverpool, Birmingham and Cardiff. This incident has always been shrouded with mystery, especially when it turned out that Melody was alive and well. Gene later claimed that he had been the victim of a cruel and sick hoax, whereas his wife, Darlene, was convinced that he had made up the whole story as a means of terminating his contract with Larry Parnes.

DAVY JONES

Black American singer Davy Jones, who had been featured as an opening act on the most recent Gene Vincent tour, is worthy of additional comment. He had arrived in Britain with a minimum of publicity but an interesting pedigree. He had been a member of the Rays, and in 1959 sang second tenor on their US hit 'Silhouettes', and additionally had co-written the song 'Soldier Boy', a fine version of which appeared on Presley's latest album, *Elvis Is Back*.

Jones was briefly added to Larry Parnes' roster of acts, but as press reports made reference to his clowning and acrobatics, it seems that he was more intent on developing a cabaret-style career, rather than pursuing his roots as a rock'n'roller. Jones is believed to have settled here for a time, probably in the North of England, and had at least five singles released on Pye and Piccadilly. He died in the States during 1995.

CONNIE FRANCIS

Connie flew into London on 4 May with her manager, George Scheck, primarily for an appearance on *Sunday Night At The London Palladium*. Her fan club organised a special party for her at Caxton Hall, while on 11 May she and Liberace were the guests of honour at the Variety Club of Great Britain's fourth annual *Golden Disc Luncheon* at the Dorchester Hotel, which was also attended by Cliff Richard, Adam Faith, Lonnie Donegan and Joan Regan. She returned to the USA on 19 May.

TV appearances
Sunday Night At The London Palladium	8 May 1960
Mantovani	? May 1960 (screened 29 May 1960)

JOHNNY PRESTON
CONWAY TWITTY

May 1960		
8	York	Rialto
9-14	Manchester	Palace
	Promoter — Don Arden	

Conway Twitty arrived for his British stage debut along with his drummer, Tommy 'Porkchop' Markham, and manager Don Seat. He was added to the Johnny Preston package with Wee Willie Harris, Chris Wayne & The Echoes, and Tony Crombie, but first made two television appearances, guesting on the BBC-TV's *Vera Lynn Presents* and Jack Good's new ABC-TV show, *Wham!*, on which he sang 'Lonely Blue Boy'.

TV appearances (Conway Twitty)
Wham!	30 April 1960
Vera Lynn Presents	7 May 1960

FREDDY CANNON

May 1960			11	Barking	Odeon
8	Tooting	Granada	12	Bournemouth	Gaumont
9	Worcester	Gaumont	13	Woolwich	Granada
10	Manchester	Free Trade Hall	14	Walthamstow	Granada
		Promoter — Don Arden			

Having failed to land Jack Scott, promoter Don Arden turned his attention to Freddy 'Boom Boom' Cannon, recently in the charts with 'Way Down Yonder In New Orleans', 'California Here I Come' and 'Indiana'. The American singer commenced his first British tour with seven one-nighters, backed by the Cannonballs and supported by Mike Preston, the Avons, the Four Jays and compere Bob Bain. Cherry Wainer had originally been booked, but was replaced at the last minute by the Avons.

FREDDY CANNON
JOHNNY PRESTON
CONWAY TWITTY

May 1960					
15	Newcastle	City Hall	23	Hull	Cecil
16	Birmingham	Odeon	24	Doncaster	Gaumont
17	Portsmouth	Guildhall	25	Leicester	De Montfort Hall
18	Derby	Gaumont	26	Swansea	Plaza
19	Stockton	Globe	27	Sheffield	City Hall
20	Bradford	Gaumont	28	Coventry	Gaumont
21	Edinburgh	Usher Hall	29	Bristol	Colston Hall
22	Liverpool	Empire	31	Cardiff	Gaumont
Promoter — Don Arden					

THE
LCKART BROS.
AND
DON ARDEN
PRESENT

CONWAY TWITTY

FREDDY CANNON

JOHNNY PRESTON

souvenir programme

Arden now brought together his three touring Americans for a triple-headed package that also contained Wee Willie Harris, Chris Wayne, Tony Crombie and Elaine Mansfield. Backing was again supplied by the Echoes and the Cannonballs.

The style of the package was both fast-moving and unusual. When it opened in Newcastle, it was reported to be *'the liveliest and most rocking show'* seen in those parts for quite some time.

Cannon displayed little in the way of subtlety, but put lots of enthusiasm into his hits, 'Tallahassee Lassie', 'California Here I Come' and 'Way Down Yonder In New Orleans' as well as trying out his new releases 'Jump Over' and 'The Urge'. Johnny Preston scored strongly on his uptempo numbers. 'Cradle Of Love' and 'Running Bear' had the girls screaming, but he still struggled with the slower material, neither 'Misty' nor 'Harbour Lights' really cutting it at all.

It was Conway Twitty who made the biggest impact. He smouldered his way through the beat ballads 'Mona Lisa', 'Heavenly' and 'What Am I Living For', received rapturous applause for 'It's Only Make Believe', and closed strongly with a rock'n'roll medley containing both 'Hound Dog' and 'Tutti Frutti'.

It was the intention that Johnny Preston and Freddy Cannon should work further dates together through to 16 June, but Preston unexpectedly split for home on 1 June. Conway Twitty flew to Italy for a television appearance in Rome two days later.

BOBBY RYDELL

It was announced that Bobby Rydell would come to Britain and co-star with Cliff Richard on ATV's *Saturday Spectacular* on 21 May. His British agent, Leslie Grade, worked with Cliff's manager, Tito Burns, to finalise the booking but their efforts were in vain. Rydell cancelled and flew to Hollywood for a screen test instead.

GENE VINCENT
FREDDY CANNON

June 1960		
1	Rochester	Gaumont
2	Norwich	Gaumont
3	Ipswich	Gaumont
4	York	Gaumont
Promoters — Larry Parnes and Don Arden		

Following Johnny Preston's premature departure, Freddy Cannon hooked up with the Gene Vincent–Jerry Keller package, which came back on the road following Gene's return from the States. Lance Fortune and Peter Wynne were the support acts.

Cannon's enthusiastic approach seemed to be paying off because 'The Urge' — one of his least-memorable singles — had climbed into the UK Top 20 during the last week of May. He would soon be joined there by Gene Vincent, who had cut 'Pistol Packin' Mama' at the Abbey Road Studios in London on 11 May. Both men were out-and-out rockers who bludgeoned their audience into submission — in sharp contrast to the rather wimpish efforts of Messrs. Keller, Wynne and Fortune. Interestingly, it was Vincent and Cannon who were selling the most records and receiving the loudest cheers at the end of each evening. Freddy Cannon missed the Rochester show because of a sore throat.

JOHNNY & THE HURRICANES

The Grade Organisation were behind an ambitious plan to bring the instrumental group, Johnny & The Hurricanes, to Britain for a tour scheduled to run from 5 June to 31 July. They were to headline a package containing the Crests, Dick Caruso and possibly Santo & Johnny. Three weeks after the initial announcement, the scheme collapsed as no suitable British acts could be found to work in the States to meet the Musicians' Union reciprocal exchange requirements.

FREDDY CANNON

June 1960		
10	Burnley	Palace
11	Liverpool	Silver Blades
12	Pontefract	Crescent
13-18	Glasgow	Empire
19	Doncaster	Astra
Promoters — Larry Parnes and Don Arden		

Freddy Cannon wrapped up his rather fragmented tour by playing a few more shows with Jerry Keller, the Viscounts and Don Fox. His backing was provided by the Tony Crombie Group. He was still suffering from a throat infection and missed some gigs between 5 and 9 June, but recovered sufficiently to finish the course. He then spent a week in Europe before flying home to the States on 28 June. Cliff Richard turned up at the airport to see him off.

JIMMY JONES

October 1960					
8	East Ham	Granada	23	Leeds	Odeon
9	Elephant & Castle	Trocadero	25	Glasgow	Odeon
10	Portsmouth	Guildhall	26	South Shields	Gaumont
12	Guildford	Odeon	28	Manchester	Odeon
13	Cardiff	Gaumont	29	Bradford	Gaumont
14	Bristol	Colston Hall	30	Worcester	Gaumont
15	Chester	Gaumont	31	Taunton	Gaumont
16	Liverpool	Empire	**November 1960**		
18	Finsbury Park	Astoria	1	Hanley	Victoria Hall
19	Sheffield	City Hall	2	Stockton	Hippodrome
20	Birmingham	Odeon	3	Dartford	Granada
22	Newcastle	City Hall	4	Kingston	Granada
Promoter — Arthur Howes					

A former member of Billy Ward's Dominoes, Jimmy headlined a large package billed as the *Jimmy Jones Spectacular*. Backed by Johnny Wiltshire & The Trebletones, and with a supporting cast comprising Mark Wynter, Michael Cox & The Hunters, the Brook Brothers, Dean Rogers & The Marauders, Janet Richmond, Kenny Lynch and compere Tony Marsh, it was far from being one of the strongest line-ups, and was further weakened when Cox missed the first few nights due to flu.

Jones was something of an unknown quantity. When interviewed, he went out of his way to stress that he favoured rock ballads over what he termed as the 'original, primitive rock'n'roll', yet when he hit the stage, he hardly paused for breath. He launched himself into 'The Twist', tap-danced, somersaulted, did the splits and finished up with a neck-roll. He was certainly a bundle of energy, if not quite a showstopper. The antics continued as he worked his way through 'Lonely Teardrops' and 'It's Now Or Never', finishing strongly with his three UK hits, 'Handy Man', 'Good Timin' ' and 'I Just Go For You'. During the early part of the tour, he was accompanied by his manager, Norm Riley.

CONNIE FRANCIS

October 1960		
29	Lewisham	Gaumont
30	Finsbury Park	Astoria
Promoter — Arthur Howes		

Connie Francis flew into London on 19 October primarily to play two television shows. For her stage appearances in London she worked with Cyril Stapleton's Showband, an intriguing line-up which included no less than five saxes, five trombones and four trumpets. Their version of 'In The Mood' nearly raised the roof.

The Lewisham Gaumont was reputed to attract the most difficult audience in South London, but on an exceptionally rainy night Connie triumphed over a large crowd with an act that concentrated mainly on uptempo material, although the ballad 'Mama' was especially well received. After performing her hits in a series of medleys, she surprised the audience with an Al Jolson tribute, and closed with a rousing gospel number, 'Yes Indeed'.

While in England, Connie had dinner with Cliff Richard and attended an Adam Faith concert in Northampton where she must have been rather conspicuous hiding behind a pair of dark glasses.

TV appearances

Sunday Night At The London Palladium	23 October 1960
Saturday Spectacular	5 November 1960

CHAPTER SIX

1961

Say Mama, Can I Go Out Tonight?

Rock'n'roll had not died, but it had become badly diluted. The showbusiness establishment and the media had fought long and hard in a combined effort against the wilder excesses of the music. Sure, they had tolerated Bill Haley when he was filling every theatre in Britain and the ringing of cash registers had drowned out the honking saxophones and the insistent beat of the drums, but few people in any position of power or authority ever actually admitted to *liking* it.

The watering-down process happened slowly and hardly anyone even noticed, but by 1961 Neil Sedaka, Bobby Rydell and Bobby Vee were suddenly the big name acts in the news. Their hits may still have been classed as 'rock'n'roll', but were veering ever further from the spirit of Little Richard and Jerry Lee Lewis, and closer to the safer, more acceptable pop music which Tin Pan Alley knew and understood. The Establishment had regained control.

What cannot be denied is that a significant proportion of the British public still wanted to see and hear real rock'n'roll, even if Marty Wilde was now following Tommy Steele through the exit door marked *'All-Round Entertainer'* by taking a starring role in the West End musical, *Bye Bye Birdie*, and Cliff Richard was attempting to broaden his appeal with a succession of sugary ballads. The much-maligned promoter Larry Parnes kept his options open with a touring package titled *Rock'n'Trad*, although trad jazz was never seriously thought of as much more than a passing novelty. However, when Parnes brought in producer Jack Good to choreograph a fast-moving, all-action show, *Rock'n'Trad* quickly evolved into a rock'n'roll extravaganza headed by Billy Fury and Joe Brown, and featuring as many as fifteen acts every night. It did tremendous business for more than four months and was later relaunched as *Rock'n'Trad 2*.

Few Americans visited Britain during this period, and one man must be credited with single-handedly keeping the flame alight. Gene Vincent was poised to commence his onslaught on what seemed like every theatre, dance hall, club, pub and assembly hall in the United Kingdom with an act which was a nightly reminder that a rock'n'roll show was supposed to be a visual, dynamic, exciting experience. Gene was hardly ever seen on British television, and rarely heard on the radio, but the fans flocked to see him and to witness one of the music's leading exponents at the peak of his powers.

JOHNNY BURNETTE
ROY ORBISON

In November 1960, it had been announced that Hollywood agent Norm Riley was in discussion with Leslie Grade regarding a four week tour for both Johnny Burnette and Roy Orbison commencing on 21 January. The following month, an interview with Burnette revealed that he was excitedly reading up on England and studying maps in anticipation of his arrival, but still no detailed itinerary was forthcoming. By Christmas, it was hinted that Brenda Lee may also be added to the bill, but early in the New Year the whole project was shelved with vague promises that it would be rescheduled later in the year. Needless to say, it wasn't.

GENE VINCENT

January 1961					
23	West Bromwich	Adelphi	12	East Ham	Granada
24	Ipswich	Savoy	13	Maidstone	Granada
25	Bristol	Top Twenty	14	Aylesbury	Granada
26	Reading	New Majestic	15	Bedford	Granada
27	Grimsby	Gaiety	16	Kettering	Granada
28	Nelson	Imperial	17	Grantham	Granada
29	Worksop	Monaco	18	Mansfield	Granada
30	Whitby	Spa	19	Slough	Adelphi
31	Doncaster	St. James St. Baths	20	Derby	*unknown venue*
February 1961			21	Oxford	Carfax
					Assembly Rooms
1	Leeds	Armley Baths	22	Mildenhall	USAF
2	Huddersfield	Empress	24	Winchester	Royal Lido
3	Galashiels	Volunteer Hall	25	Malvern	Winter Gardens
4	Hawick	Drill Hall	27	Kingston	Granada
5	Alconbury	USAF	28	Dartford	Granada
6	Rochester	Casino	**March 1961**		
7	Southport	Floral Hall	1	Greenford	Granada
8	Wigan	Empress	2	Woolwich	Granada
9	Barrow	Palais	3	Sutton	Granada
10	Northwich	Victory Memorial Hall	5	Rugby	Granada
11	Barnoldswick	Majestic	6	West Bromwich	Adelphi
Promoter — Don Arden					

Gene Vincent flew into the UK on 20 January and his schedule rapidly expanded as bookings came flooding in. The tour was divided into four segments commencing with ballroom dates up to 11 February, backed by Chris Wayne & The Echoes. For the next eight nights, he headlined a package billed as the *1961 All Star Parade*, backed by the Flee-Rekkers and supported by Jess Conrad, Mark Wynter, Michael Cox, Johnny Duncan & The Blue Grass Boys, the Four Jays, Screaming Lord Sutch, and comedians/comperes Mike and Bernie Winters. At Bedford, Vince Taylor replaced Mark Wynter. From 20 February, Vincent filled in with more ballrooms until the package regrouped for a further six nights. He continued to work with the Echoes until the end of the tour, while both the Flee-Rekkers and Jess Conrad departed to be replaced by Johnny Kidd & The Pirates. There was much chopping and changing during the later dates, and each of

GRANADA SUTTON MAR 3 1961
program sixpence

Terry Dene, Vince Taylor, Danny Rivers and Rory Blackwell participated in one or more shows. It sounds a confusing scenario, but then little involving the amazing Mr. Vincent was ever straight-forward.

Gene's return to Britain was just the tonic that rock'n'roll needed. His appearances drew large audiences — often to towns which had never previously hosted American rockers. At the East Ham Granada, the entire audience in the stalls left their seats and ran down to the front of the stage at the sight of his uninhibited display, and while Gene was kneeling on the floor and swirling the microphone stand around his head, the screams completely drowned the music. Wild, primitive rock'n'roll had returned to the UK.

A few days prior to his appearance in the Scottish border town of Hawick, a Gene Vincent imitator was shown on television miming to his records, and a rumour spread that it was not really Gene who would be appearing, but an impostor. His show drew an enormous crowd, and a deputation of Scottish teddy boys stormed the backstage area and eventually burst into Gene's dressing room. A startled Vincent pulled a gun and quickly persuaded them that he was the genuine article.

The tour seemed destined to go on forever, and more ballroom dates were being stacked up into April until it was announced that, for contractual reasons, its star had to return to the USA. Promoter Don Arden promised an early return. Gene had played forty nights with hardly a break.

BRENDA LEE

In mid-November it was announced that 'Little Miss Dynamite' would make her British stage debut on 11 February with four weeks of concerts and six days of television and radio appearances. The proposed tour was mentioned in the press on several occasions, but by 20 January it had been cancelled, apparently due to conflicts with her US commitments.

BRIAN HYLAND

The latest teenage sensation, Brian Hyland, was pencilled in to star on Larry Parnes' new package, *Don't Ban The Beat*, for a five-week run starting in February. Ultimately, however, it was an all-British cast that set out on the renamed *Rock'n'Trad 2* tour.

BOBBY RYDELL

March 1961	
3 Stockton	Globe
4 Walthamstow	Granada
5 Liverpool	Empire
Promoter — Arthur Howes	

As a contrast to Gene Vincent, British audiences had the chance to savour a brief visit by one of America's newer breed of teen idol. Bobby Rydell arrived in the UK on 17 February for a couple of TV appearances before travelling to Paris for a show with Emile Ford in front of five thousand people at the Palais des Sports, during which a near-riot took place. He then returned to England, where he jointly headlined with Jess Conrad on a mini-package which also featured the Brook Brothers, the Hunters and the Four Jays. Rydell was backed by the Red Price Combo.

TV appearances
Sunday Night At The London Palladium   19 February 1961
Val Parnell's Startime   22 February 1961 (screened 9 March 1961)

CONNIE FRANCIS

March 1961	
5 Wembley	Empire Pool
Promoter — *New Musical Express*	

During the Sixties, one of the big events of the year was the *NME Poll Winners' Concert* at Wembley. Connie Francis became the first winner from the *'World'* section to appear in person to receive her award, having been voted the *'World's Top Female Singer'* by a considerable margin.

She only flew in from Germany the day before the show and received a warm reception from the capacity crowd as she performed a medley of her hits including 'Robot Man', 'Lipstick On Your Collar' and 'Stupid Cupid', closing with a rocking version of 'When The Saints Go Marching In'. Connie also presented many of the awards at the end of the afternoon.

The 1961 *NME Poll Winners' Concert* featured no fewer than eighteen other acts. The undisputed favourites were the Shadows, who received rapturous applause, while the daily papers made much of the fact that Cliff Richard was booed by a section of the crowd when he tried to follow their spot. Others on the show included Billy Fury, Adam Faith, Bert Weedon,

Lonnie Donegan, Alma Cogan, the John Barry Seven and the Mudlarks. Extracts from the concert were televised by ABC-TV as *Big Night Out*. Connie remained in London until 14 March, recording yet another album at EMI's Abbey Road studios.

TV appearances
Big Night Out	5 March 1961 (screened 25 March 1961)
Sunday Night At The London Palladium	12 March 1961

GENE VINCENT

April 1961			7	Guildford	Plaza
30	Bradford	Gaumont	8-13	Belfast	Opera House
May 1961			15	Reading	New Majestic
1	Hull	Majestic	16	Kilburn	Gaumont State
2	Blyth	Roxy	17	Ilkeston	*unknown venue*
3	Loughborough	Essoldo	18	Chester	Majestic
4	Darlington	Majestic	19	Yeadon	Town Hall
5	Harrogate	Royal	20	Ebbw Vale	*unknown venue*
6	Stoke	King's Hall			
Promoter — Don Arden					

There had been speculation in the music press that Gene Vincent might return to the UK with his American band, the Blue Caps. In reality, the group had disbanded some two years earlier, but promoter Don Arden claimed it was Musicians' Union restrictions that had made this impossible. Instead, Gene worked — for the first of many times — with the British instrumental combo, Sounds Incorporated. The tour was another great success, and fresh bookings were already being set up long before 21 May when he departed for a short tour of South Africa.

TV appearances
Thank Your Lucky Stars	7 May 1961 (screened 13 May 1961)

GENE VINCENT

May 1961			9	Burslem	Queens Hall
30	Coventry	Majestic	10	Nottingham	Elizabethan
31	Buxton	Pavilion Gardens	12	Lincoln	Drill Hall
June 1961			13	Darlington	Majestic
2	Bedford	Corn Exchange	14	Newcastle	Majestic
6	Northwich	Victory Memorial Hall	23	Winchester	Royal Lido
7	Burgh Park	*unknown venue*	24	Basingstoke	Haymarket
8	Congleton	Drill Hall	25	Mansfield	Palais de Danse
Promoter — Don Arden					

Gene returned from South Africa on 29 May, and the following day was back in action at the Coventry Majestic. He continued to work with Sounds Incorporated, and despite little media interest, proved to be as popular as ever.

On 14 June, he fell down thirty steps after coming off stage in Newcastle and was knocked unconscious. His bad leg was further damaged in the accident, and dates scheduled for Motherwell, Carlisle, Nelson, Sheffield and Wolverhampton had to be cancelled. This also put paid to his participation in the *Rock Across The Channel* show on 18 June: an all-day cruise between Southend and Calais on the MV *Royal Daffodil* was to have been the venue for a floating rock'n'roll show co-starring Vincent, the Shadows and a host of support acts. He did, however, recover sufficiently to perform for the last three nights of the tour before flying back to the States on 26 June.

GENE VINCENT

July 1961			August 1961		
9	Blackpool	Queens	1	Slough	Carlton
10-15	Bristol	Hippodrome	2	Sunderland	Rink
16	Hull	Majestic	3	Inverness	*unknown venue*
17	West Bromwich	Adelphi	4	Wick	Boys' Brigade Hall
18	Penarth	Marina	5	Kirkaldy	Ice Rink
19	Cambridge	Rex	6	Cowdenbeath	Palais
20	Norwich	Grosvenor	7	Larbert	Dobbie Hall
21	Mildenhall	USAF	8	Airdrie	Town Hall
22	Morecambe	Floral Hall	9	Greenock	Palladium
25	Cirencester	Corn Hall	10	East Kilbride	*unknown venue*
26	Hitchin	Hermitage	11	Aberdeen	Beach
27	High Wycombe	Town Hall	13	Stirling	*unknown venue*
28	Shrewsbury	Granada	14	Glasgow	Barrowland
29	Morecambe	Floral Hall	16	Newcastle	Majestic
30	Torquay	Princess			
Promoter — Don Arden					

Interviewed at the start of his latest tour, Vincent displayed no illusions of becoming a family entertainer but merely expressed the wish to continue singing rock'n'roll and become a whole lot better at it. His legion of fans were well satisfied — as could be seen from his bulging date book.

Backed again by Sounds Incorporated, he kicked off in Blackpool supported by the Brook Brothers and Peter Elliott, followed by a week's residency in Bristol. During the last week of July he also managed to fit in a recording session for Capitol Records, at which he cut 'Spaceship To Mars' and 'I'm Going Home', a reworking of Bo Diddley's quirky 'Down Home Special'.

However, the physical strain of Vincent's act and his own frail health were always a cause for concern. During an arduous round of one-nighters in Scotland, he pushed himself beyond the limit, eventually collapsing after the show in Glasgow. He was kept in hospital for two days, only to discharge himself in time to perform at Newcastle. At this point, the tour ground to a halt. Gene was too mentally and physically exhausted to continue, and later bookings were cancelled. This included a spot on a big show at Wembley on 10 September, where he was to have lined up with Cliff Richard, Adam Faith and Billy Fury. He returned to the States on 19 August.

JOHNNY & THE HURRICANES

Rumours persisted throughout 1961 that the hit instrumental group, Johnny & The Hurricanes were about to undertake a British tour. Serious attempts were made to organise something for August and September, but nothing materialised. The complicated 'musician exchange' procedure appeared to be at least part of the problem.

PAUL ANKA

Paul Anka flew into the UK on 15 August to tele-record a one-hour spectacular for Granada TV. Taping took place on 24 August and also featured Canadian teenage star Linda Scott. Less than twenty-four hours later, he departed for Paris to film his part in the Daryl Zanuck movie, *The Longest Day.*

TV appearance
It's Paul Anka!   24 August 1961 (screened 3 January 1962)

CONNIE FRANCIS

Following a visit to Italy, Connie flew into London for a Palladium TV appearance on 24 September. Her stay was very brief, as she had to travel on to West Berlin to film a show with Ed Sullivan and Louis Armstrong before an audience of American servicemen.

TV appearances
Sunday Night At The London Palladium   24 September 1961

DION

With 'Runaround Sue' topping the US charts, it was perhaps surprising that Dion found the time to make a short promotional trip to Britain. Initial difficulties arose when the Ministry of Labour queried his application for a work permit, but everything was resolved and he and his manager, Sal Bonafede, arrived on 22 October. His hurried schedule included Scotland and Wales for regional TV appearances as well as a spot on ABC-TV's popular new music show, *Thank Your Lucky Stars.* Plans were formulated for a concert tour in 1962.

TV appearances
Discs A-Go-Go   26 October 1961
Spin Along   26 October 1961
Here And Now   28 October 1961
The One O'Clock Gang   ? October 1961
Thank Your Lucky Stars   4 November 1961

GENE VINCENT

November 1961					
6	Kilmarnock	Rex	20	Slough	Adelphi
7	Arbroath	Palais de Danse	21	Kilburn	Gaumont State
8	Ardrossan	Castlecraigs	22	Hull	Majestic
9	Elgin	Two Red Shoes	23	Darlington	Majestic
10	Perth	City Hall	24	Nelson	Imperial
11	Huntly	*unknown venue*	25	Grimsby	Gaiety
12	Rosewell	Miners' Institute	26	Southall	*unknown venue*
14	Sunderland	Rink	27	West Bromwich	Adelphi
15	Middlesbrough	Astoria	28	Epsom	Ebbisham Hall
16	Crewe	New	29	Bedford	Corn Exchange
17	Southampton	Park	**December 1961**		
18	Leytonstone	*unknown venue*	1	Croydon	Fairfield Halls
19	Southsea	Savoy	2	Prestatyn	Royal Lido
			3	Manchester	Oasis
Promoter — Don Arden					

Five years earlier, variety theatres had been the showcase for rock'n'roll. Increasingly, ballrooms were now taking over and Mr. L.B. Fancourt, head booker at Top Rank, had no doubt who had done the most business for them during 1961: 'Gene Vincent has visited most of our ballrooms this year,' he said. 'He has been to some of them several times, and wherever he goes, he is a tremendous draw. The Flee-Rekkers and Lord Sutch are two other successful acts, but nobody comes close to Vincent in box-office results.'

Gene was back in Britain on 5 November, and the following day returned to his Scottish expedition with Sounds Incorporated in tow, and support from Johnny Kidd & The Pirates, Johnny Duncan & The Blue Grass Boys and Jess Conrad. Even the music press were now speculating that he was overdoing things, but he ploughed on

regardless. As his tour travelled back and forth across the country, he even found time to film his spot in the movie *It's Trad Dad* — 'Spaceship To Mars' — at Abbey Road Studios on 30 November. The day after his appearance at the Manchester Oasis, he returned home to the States.

TV appearances
Thank Your Lucky Stars   5 November 1961 (screened 11 November 1961)

DUANE EDDY

Paul Anka and his manager, Irving Feld, were reported to be bringing Duane Eddy and possibly also Clarence 'Frogman' Henry to the UK for a lengthy visit. First reports indicated that it would be timed to coincide with the release of Eddy's movie, *A Thunder Of Drums*, in October. Later, a November start seemed more realistic, but eventually the whole project was deferred so that Duane could bring his own band, the Rebels, in April for a projected package tour which — in deference to the latest dance craze from the USA — would also include Chubby Checker.

CHUBBY CHECKER

Checker made a lightning visit to the UK for eight days as part of a whirlwind tour of Europe. No live shows were contemplated, but he undertook an exhaustive round of interviews and made three television appearances, including a starring role in Granada's *Trad With A Twist*, which was recorded in Manchester and also featured the Viscounts, Linda Scott and the jazz bands of Chris Barber and Terry Lightfoot.

TV appearances

Trad With A Twist	15 December 1961 (screened 17 January 1962)
Thank Your Lucky Stars	17 December 1961 (screened 30 December 1961)
Here And Now	19 December 1961 (screened 29 December 1961)

CHAPTER SEVEN

1962

Come On Everybody, Let's Twist!

'The first position is kinda like a boxer's stance. Then you move your hips like you're wiping yourself with a towel. Your body goes back and forth in one direction, your hands go in the other direction. From that point on, you ad-lib energetically.' Such was Chubby Checker's description of the twist. The new dance craze had been going strong in the States for some time, but started to spread like a rash in Britain early in 1962. For a short time at least, it did succeed in beefing up an increasingly limp music scene and many rock'n'rollers scrambled onto the bandwagon with twist recordings of their own.

In Britain, rock'n'roll continued to quietly slip out of the news, although there was still a minority of prominent performers such as Johnny Kidd and Joe Brown who were serving up the real thing. Many people would claim that rock'n'roll was finished by 1962, and in purely commercial terms it is difficult to dispute this statement. Rock'n'roll records rarely made any impact on the charts any more, but there was a very welcome increase in tours, many of which were incredibly successful.

NEIL SEDAKA

Neil Sedaka's first trip to the UK was a last-minute booking for *Sunday Night At The London Palladium*. He flew into London from Puerto Rico on 13 January and appeared the following evening along with Kenny Ball's Jazzmen. Although his stay was brief, plans got underway for a short concert tour later in the year.

TV appearances
Sunday Night At The London Palladium   14 January 1962

BOBBY VEE
CLARENCE 'FROGMAN' HENRY
TONY ORLANDO

February 1962			16	Bristol	Colston Hall
9	Doncaster	Gaumont	17	Leicester	De Montfort Hall
10	Tooting	Granada	18	Peterborough	Embassy
11	Liverpool	Empire	21	Blackburn	King George's Hall
12	Shrewsbury	Granada	22	Belfast	King's Hall
13	Portsmouth	Guildhall	23	Birmingham	Town Hall
14	Harrow	Granada	24	Walthamstow	Granada
15	Kingston	Granada	25	Bournemouth	Pavilion
Promoter — Arthur Howes					

Bobby Vee was the principal attraction on this very successful theatre tour. The Granadas were all sold out, and for the first time in fifteen years the 'House Full' notices were posted at Birmingham Town Hall. Vee arrived on 27 January accompanied by his manager, Arnie Mills, and producer Snuff Garrett. After a short promotional visit to Europe, the tour proceeded with only a two-day break during which Bobby was filmed singing 'At A Time Like This' for the movie, *Play It Cool*.

When the package opened at Doncaster, Tony Orlando almost stole the show. He opened with a rocker, 'You And Only You', but scored best with the big beat ballads 'Halfway To Paradise' and 'Stand By Me'. During the latter number, he left the stage and went down among the audience before returning to crown his act with 'Bless You'.

Earlier on, Clarence 'Frogman' Henry, with a toy frog mounted on top of his piano, had started with the song that gave him his nickname, 'Ain't Got No Home', following on with 'But I Do' and 'You Always Hurt The One You Love', before closing with his latest recording, 'A Little Too Much'.

The other acts featured on the tour were the Springfields, Suzy Cope, Jimmy Crawford and Billy Burden, plus the Ravens, who backed the three Americans. However, it was without question Bobby Vee that the greater proportion of the audience had come to see, his pop-rock material having always appealed more to the female fans who were clearly in the majority. Dressed in a smart grey suit, he launched straight into 'Rubber Ball' before continuing with Buddy Holly's 'Everyday', then 'Walking With My Angel', 'How Many Tears' and his latest hit, 'Run To Him'. His final number, 'Take Good Care Of My Baby', signalled several minutes of applause.

Vee was scheduled to travel on to Paris on 26 February, but a violent snowstorm caused him to change his arrangements, and he eventually flew out to Barcelona two days later.

TV appearances (Bobby Vee)

Thank Your Lucky Stars	28 January 1962 (screened 3 February 1962)
Young At Heart	31 January 1962
Sunday Night At The London Palladium	4 February 1962
Day By Day	13 February 1962
Wednesday Magazine	14 February 1962
Juke Box Jury	24 February 1962

TV appearances (Tony Orlando)

Tuesday Rendezvous	30 January 1962
Thank Your Lucky Stars	4 February 1962 (screened 10 February 1962)
Young At Heart	7 February 1962
Beat	20 February 1962 (screened 1 March 1962)
Juke Box Jury	24 February 1962

TV appearances (Clarence 'Frogman' Henry)

Thank Your Lucky Stars	8 February 1962 (screened 17 February 1962)
Beat	20 February 1962 (screened 8 March 1962)

BOBBY RYDELL

In February, Bobby Rydell became the latest American artist to visit Britain for promotional purposes, although there was briefly talk of personal appearances which never got beyond the negotiating stage. His visit was the first leg of a month in Europe and he flew in on 9 February for two TV slots, and returned at the end of his trek around Europe for a late booking on *Thank Your Lucky Stars*, on which he co-starred with Billy Fury.

TV appearances

Sunday Night At The London Palladium	11 February 1962
The Alma Cogan Show	13 February 1962 (screened 14 February 1962)
Thank Your Lucky Stars	3 March 1962

PAUL ANKA

As part of a gruelling tour of Europe involving eleven European cities in three weeks, Paul Anka stopped off in London on 23 February and stayed in the country just long enough to join Tony Orlando on the panel of BBC-TV's *Juke Box Jury* before continuing on to Paris.

TV appearances
Juke Box Jury   24 February 1962

TONY ORLANDO

February 1962			March 1962		
26	Leyton	Baths	1	Oxford	Town Hall
27	Wallington	Public Hall	2	Birmingham	Plaza
28	Manchester	Oasis	3	Aylesbury	Grosvenor
			4	Southsea	Savoy
Promoter — Malcolm Rose					

When the Bobby Vee tour ended, Tony Orlando remained in England for a further week of ballroom dates with Jimmy Crawford and the Ravens. Although best known for his dramatic ballads, Orlando confirmed in interviews that he enjoyed singing rock'n'roll, and revealed that Frankie Lymon & The Teenagers were among his influences.

TV appearances
Thank Your Lucky Stars   ? March 1962 (screened 10 March 1962)

BRENDA LEE
GENE VINCENT

March 1962			8	Tooting	Granada
31	Brighton	Essoldo	9	Sheffield	City Hall
April 1962			10	Birmingham	Town Hall
2	Newcastle	City Hall	11	Leicester	De Montfort Hall
3	Birkenhead	Essoldo	12	Worcester	Gaumont
4	Glasgow	St. Andrew's Hall	13	Bristol	Colston Hall
5	Blackburn	King George's Hall	14	Portsmouth	Guildhall
6	Woolwich	Granada	15	Slough	Adelphi
7	Walthamstow	Granada	16	Norwich	Theatre Royal
Promoter — Don Arden					

There was a high level of interest in Brenda Lee's first British tour, and pairing her with Gene Vincent under the banner of *'The King and Queen of Rock'* was an adept piece of marketing. The package also featured UK instrumental outfits Nero & The Gladiators and Sounds Incorporated (who backed the American acts), Rory Blackwell & His Blackjacks and compere Bob Bain.

The tour kicked off at Brighton with Vincent looking healthier and happier than for some time after a four-month rest back in California. Dressed in the all-white leather outfit he wore in the recently-released

Brenda appears on *Sunday Night At The London Palladium* with Sounds Incorporated.

It's Trad, Dad, he received a tremendous reception. Despite microphone problems during 'Lucille', he tore through his regular act with 'Say Mama', 'Bluejean Bop' and 'She She Little Sheila', leading into a tremendous climax via 'Be-Bop-A-Lula' and a romping, stomping 'Tutti Frutti'.

Brenda commenced her show with an explosive version of 'Dynamite'. She continued with a mixture of ballads and rockers. 'Eventually' was taken at a slow pace, but she accelerated into top gear for 'Dum Dum', and gave 'Kansas City' a real workout. The highlight of her act was 'Sweet Nothin's', where her delivery alternated between a rasping growl and a sensual whisper that had her listeners entranced.

On 15 April, Brenda made an unexpected appearance during the afternoon at Wembley, not to sing, but to present some of the awards at the *NME Poll Winners' Concert*. Gene did not appear on the Bristol show, being replaced by Jess Conrad.

TV appearances (Brenda Lee)
Sunday Night At The London Palladium	1 April 1962
Thank Your Lucky Stars	7 April 1962
Juke Box Jury	7 April 1962

TV appearances (Gene Vincent)
Thank Your Lucky Stars	14 April 1962

GENE VINCENT

April 1962			26	Wakefield	Playhouse
1	Stoke	Essoldo	27	Broadstairs	Grand
13	Cannock	Danilo	28	Aylesbury	Walton Hall
17	High Wycombe	Plaza	29	East Ham	Granada
18	Birmingham	Plaza	30	Southampton	Guildhall
	Birmingham	Ritz	**May 1962**		
19	Newmarket	Memorial Hall	1	Greenford	Granada
	Lynford	Country	2	Sutton	Granada
20	Bedford	County	4	Swindon	Locarno
21	Torquay	Town Hall	5	New Brighton	Tower
22	Westbury	Bista	6	Southall	Community Centre
23	Stockton	Hippodrome		Putney	*unknown venue*
24	Keighley	Essoldo	8	Bristol	Colston Hall
25	Stockport	Essoldo			

Promoters — Don Arden and George Cooper

On 1 April, while Brenda Lee was appearing on the nation's television screens from the Palladium, Gene Vincent played a one-nighter at Stoke backed by the Condors and supported by Ricky Valance, Tommy Bruce, Vince Eager, Peter Wynne and Danny Rivers. Such was his drawing power at the time that promoter Don Arden was inundated with offers for bookings from all over Britain, and immediately following the Brenda Lee tour Gene set out on another mixed bag of ballroom and theatre dates, working mainly with Sounds Incorporated, although the Echoes were used at both Cannock and Westbury. This culminated with a mini-package that played East Ham, Greenford and Sutton, where Gene and Sounds Incorporated headlined over Jimmy Justice, Jess Conrad, Emile Ford, Patti Brook and the Allisons. After squeezing in some more shows in early May (including one with Jerry Lee Lewis at Bristol on 8 May), he departed for a tour of France and Germany.

NEIL SEDAKA

April 1962		
20	London	Palladium
21	Manchester	Odeon
22	Liverpool	Odeon

Promoter — Vic Lewis

Neil Sedaka made a short visit to the UK over the Easter weekend co-starring with Adam Faith on a bill that included Emile Ford & The Checkmates, Ted Heath & His Phase Four Music, the Raindrops and compere Gary Marshall. Closing the first half, and backed by the Ted Heath band, he performed his hits including 'Oh Carol', 'The Diary', 'Stairway To Heaven' and 'Calendar Girl'. In a varied act he included his version of 'Lazy River' and even gave a deft piano solo, interpreting Chopin's 'Fantasie Impromptu' — quite a contrast to his closing number, 'Happy Birthday Sweet Sixteen'. He only stayed in Britain for five days before jetting off to Bermuda on 23 April.

TV appearances
Juke Box Jury   21 April 1962

GARY 'US' BONDS
JOHNNY BURNETTE

April 1962			May 1962		
21	Glasgow	St. Andrew's Hall	1	Aylesbury	Granada
22	Birmingham	Hippodrome	2	Kingston	Granada
23	Portsmouth	Guildhall	3	Harrow	Granada
24	Leicester	De Montfort Hall	4	Grantham	Granada
25	Doncaster	Gaumont	5	Mansfield	Granada
26	Worcester	Gaumont	6	Tooting	Granada
27	Bristol	Colston Hall	7	Plymouth	ABC
28	Bournemouth	Winter Gardens	8	Maidstone	Granada
29	Rugby	Granada	9	Bedford	Granada
30	Dartford	Granada	10	Kettering	Granada
			11	Woolwich	Granada
			12	Slough	Adelphi
			13	Walthamstow	Granada

Promoter — George Cooper

GRANADA
presents

ROCK 'N
TWIST
U.S.A.

program one shilling

This was a first British tour for both Johnny Burnette and Gary 'US' Bonds, who were accompanied by a third American, ballad singer Gene McDaniels, and a full cast of home-grown UK talent including Danny Rivers, Roly Daniels, the Flee-Rekkers and the Condors, as well as Mark Wynter, who both sang and compered.

Johnny Burnette appeared during the first half and concentrated on his hits, 'Little Boy Sad', 'Dreamin' and 'You're Sixteen', before accelerating into a storming 'Johnny B. Goode'. The Flee-Rekkers provided the backing, augmented by Burnette's own guitarist, Al Vescovo.

Bonds topped the bill and was likewise ably backed by the Flee-Rekkers. At the Birmingham Hippodrome, his high-energy act had the audience clapping along right from the opening number, 'New Orleans'. He worked through 'Pretty Girls Everywhere', 'School Is Out', and 'Quarter To Three' before finishing with an energetic 'Dear Lady Twist' and a marathon 'Twist Twist Señora'.

TV appearances (Gary 'US' Bonds)
Thank Your Lucky Stars　　　　21 April 1962
Juke Box Jury　　　　28 April 1962 *(unconfirmed)*

TV appearances (Johnny Burnette)
Thank Your Lucky Stars　　　　21 April 1962
Juke Box Jury　　　　28 April 1962

Johnny appears on *Thank Your Lucky Stars*.

PAT BOONE

Pat Boone spent the early part of 1962 in England shooting his latest movie, *The Main Attraction*. He rented a house in Richmond, Surrey, and there was continuing press speculation that some weekend concerts might be arranged to fit in with the filming schedule. As things turned out, however, nothing materialised and Pat's fans had to content themselves with a solitary TV appearance.

TV appearances
Sunday Night At The London Palladium   29 April 1962

JERRY LEE LEWIS

April 1962				9	Sheffield	City Hall
29	Newcastle	City Hall		10	Bradford	St. George's Hall
30	Leicester	De Montfort Hall		11	Birmingham	Ritz
May 1962					Birmingham	Plaza
1	Birmingham	Town Hall		12	Norwich	Theatre Royal
2	Cardiff	Sophia Gardens		13	Hull	Cecil
3	Blackburn	King George's Hall		14	Mitcham	Majestic
4	Grimsby	Gaiety		15	Tunbridge Wells	Essoldo
5	Portsmouth	Guildhall		16	Wigan	Empress
6	Cannock	Danilo		17	New Brighton	Tower
7	Brighton	Essoldo		18	Glasgow	St. Andrew's Hall
8	Bristol	Colston Hall		19	Nelson	Imperial
Promoter — Don Arden						

        The return of Jerry Lee Lewis to British shores was a major event for rock'n'roll. Since the disastrous episode of May 1958, his career had slumped badly. Record sales had dried up, friends had deserted him, and within the music business he had become something of a pariah. This immensely talented and charismatic performer was reduced to playing one-nighters in small clubs and bars the length and breadth of the United States for a fraction of the fee that he had commanded before the scandal of his child bride engulfed him. If the British media had been the instrument of his downfall, it was to be the loyalty and belief of the British fans that played a big part in the gradual rebuilding of his career.

        Rumours of a British tour had persisted for some months before it was finally confirmed in the music press that Lewis had signed for three

weeks of club and theatre dates for promoter Don Arden. This time, no objections were raised in official quarters. The British Establishment had made their point concerning Jerry's unconventional lifestyle four years earlier and, with his return being a much more low-key affair, such publicity as could be found was generally warm and welcoming — the return of the prodigal son.

        The life of Jerry Lee Lewis is a catalogue of triumphs and tragedies. A few days before he was due to fly to England, his three year old son, Steve Allen Lewis, drowned in the pool at their home. Jerry's arrival was delayed for two days while first an inquest and then the funeral took place, but on 28 April he landed back on British soil accompanied by his drummer, Ernie Bowman, and manager Jud Phillips. His mind must surely have been in turmoil. The death of his son coupled with inevitable apprehension as to what sort of reception he would receive placed him under almost intolerable pressure. British fans flocked to the box offices in droves, but had no way of knowing that they were about to witness perhaps the wildest rock'n'roll tour ever to ever play the British Isles.

At 26, Jerry Lee was young, fit and strong. He was physically at his peak and had something to prove. All his anger, hurt and frustration were channelled into an unbelievable display of rock'n'roll entertainment that even today remains a vivid memory for those who were fortunate enough to be present. Promoter Don Arden had no difficulty in filling his date book, even if many were less than top-line venues. There were no shows in central London, Manchester or Liverpool, and if Grimsby, Tunbridge Wells and Wigan were not the most prestigious locations to host *'The Greatest Live Show On Earth'*, Jerry Lee is unlikely to have even noticed.

The first batch of gigs was arranged as a package with support from Johnny Kidd & The Pirates, Vince Eager, the Bachelors, Mark Eden, the Viscounts, Danny Storm, Buddy Britten and Stewart Gaston. Lewis was ably backed throughout the tour by the Echoes.

Reports of the show at Leicester's De Montfort Hall which appeared in the music press suggested it was the most exciting so far seen on a British stage. Opening with a frantic 'Down The Line', Lewis received an incredible ovation for a performance that was the living epitome of rock'n'roll. After dropping the tempo for Hank Williams' 'You Win Again', he tore through 'Breathless' and 'High School Confidential' with his mane of wavy blonde hair flying in all directions. Both 'Great Balls Of Fire' and 'What'd I Say' received fantastic audience reaction which increased still further as he pounded his way into 'Whole Lotta Shakin' Goin' On'. Brought back for an encore, he launched into 'Good Golly Miss Molly', leaving the seething crowd physically drained but still clapping and yelling for more.

Two nights later at Cardiff, the safety curtain had to be dropped towards the end of the second house to prevent a riot. Jerry, exotically dressed in a scarlet and black suit, cranked up the excitement, throwing his head back in wild abandon as his stiff fingers pounded the piano keys. Then, swinging one leg up onto the keyboard, he began knocking out the rhythm with the heel of his elegant black boot. The atmosphere was positively electric, and a multitude of teenage girls and youths left their seats and surged towards the stage, grappling with officials who attempted to restrain them.

At Grimsby, Jerry Lee and the Echoes appeared without the support acts, while at Bristol the package was augmented by the welcome inclusion of Gene Vincent. After they played St. George's Hall, Bradford the package split up and Lewis continued with the Echoes and a variety of support acts which at different venues included the Allisons and Tommy Bruce. He headlined at New Brighton on a massive show titled *Rockerscope '62* for promoter Bob Wooler, with thirteen other acts that included Mersey Beat favourites Billy J. Kramer, the Big Three, the Undertakers and Kingsize Taylor — names that would soon become nationally known when the Liverpool sound came to dominate the music scene.

Lewis continued to confound the critics. Rock'n'roll was supposed to be fading away, yet the hysteria being created every night of this tour was solid evidence to the contrary. Most long-time fans agree that Lewis was at his wildest during 1962, but as it is highly unlikely that anybody witnessed all of his performances in Britain, comparisons between one show and another cannot be substantiated. Yet, over the years, the two performances at the Majestic, Mitcham on 14 May have acquired legendary status.

That night, Jerry seemed exceptionally calm and controlled. Wearing a gold lamé jacket, he played and sang magnificently, building his act to an orgasmic peak where he literally attacked his piano, tearing pieces off it and hurling the stool across the stage.

Rock'n'roll is very much a visual art, and those fortunate enough to have been present at Mitcham can at least lay claim to have seen Jerry Lee Lewis at his absolute best. Taking this hypothesis a stage further, if — as many would claim — Lewis at his best is as good as it gets, then surely a case can be made that his performance at Mitcham was the greatest rock'n'roll show ever seen in Britain.

THE PLATTERS

On 15 May, the Platters interrupted a tour of Spain to fly into London to tele-record a guest appearance on the ambitious ATV series *Broadway Goes Latin* with Edmundo Ros & His Orchestra. Since their last British tour in January 1960, lead singer Tony Williams had left the group to pursue a solo career, so Herb Reed, David Lynch, Paul Robi and Zola Taylor were joined on this brief three-day visit by his replacement, Sonny Turner, and their new musical director, Willie Jones.

TV appearances
Broadway Goes Latin   6 May 1962 (screened 6 October 1962)

BRUCE CHANNEL
DELBERT McCLINTON

June 1962					
4	Maidstone	Granada	18	Cheltenham	Town Hall
5	Aylesbury	Granada	19	Waltham Cross	Imperial
6	Bedford	Granada	20	Oxford	Town Hall
7	Mansfield	Granada	21	Liverpool	Cavern
8	Grantham	Granada		New Brighton	Tower
9	Tooting	Granada	22	Handsworth	Plaza
10	Walthamstow	Granada	23	Wisbech	Corn Exchange
11	Dartford	Granada	24	Bristol	Colston Hall
12	Kettering	Granada	25	Reading	New Majestic
13	Woolwich	Granada	26	Wallington	Public Hall
14	Kingston	Granada	28	Camberley	Agincourt
15	Harrow	Granada	29	Gravesend	Co-op
16	Slough	Adelphi	30	Bletchley	Wilton Hall
17	Rugby	Granada	**July 1962**		
			1	Manchester	Oasis
Promoter — George Cooper					

This lengthy tour provided the necessary proof that it is financially unwise to build a show around a new singer solely on the strength of one hit record. Texan Bruce Channel had scored massively on both sides of the Atlantic with 'Hey! Baby', featuring the distinctive harmonica of Delbert McClinton, but was otherwise completely unknown in Britain.

The first half of the tour comprised a package made up of Frank Ifield, Johnny Kidd & The Pirates, Cliff Bennett & The Rebel Rousers, Dick Charlesworth & His City Gents, Beryl Bryden, Jackie Lynn, Bobby Shafto, Jay & Tommy Scott, Bobby Brown and compere Diz Disley. Channel and McClinton were backed by the Barons, and although this represented a sizeable line-up, it was not one of the strongest assembled.

Channel flew in on 4 June with his manager, Marvin Montgomery, and eccentric record producer Major Bill Smith. He was driven straight from the airport to the Maidstone Granada. After several hours of rehearsal, and with no allowance for fatigue or jet lag, he opened the same evening. A thick-set figure in a light grey suit, he walked out on to the stage behind his harmonica player, Delbert McClinton, and went straight into 'What'd I Say'. This was followed by his latest release, 'Number One Man', 'It's Now Or Never' and a decent stab at

Clarence Henry's 'Ain't Got No Home'. The pace increased for 'Whole Lotta Shakin' Goin' On' and he finished off — inevitably — with 'Hey! Baby'. Channel was on stage for less than twenty minutes. McClinton's spot on the show stretched to no more than two numbers, during which he performed bluesy versions of 'Got My Mojo Working' and 'Dream Baby'.

Press reports were mixed to say the least, and the seemingly interminable procession of mainly uninspiring support acts did not help. The Aylesbury show was reported to be less than half full, the production was slow, and too many of the acts below standard. Channel came across as a likeable young man, but hardly a star after one hit record. Nevertheless, the package ran its course. Changes were made to the support with Mike Sarne, the John Barry Seven, Joe Brown, the Allisons and Nelson Keene each joining the troupe for one or more shows. Bruce and Delbert even got a glimpse of the future when they played a matinée at the Cavern in Liverpool, and on the same evening shared billing with the Beatles and the Big Three at the New Brighton Tower.

While in England, McClinton also cut two sessions for Decca Records under the supervision of Major Bill Smith and Dick Rowe, with ex-Shadow Tony Meehan playing drums.

CONNIE FRANCIS

Connie spent the last week of June 1962 at EMI Studios in London recording four songs for her new film, *Follow The Boys*. She returned on 31 July for one day to re-record one of the numbers.

GENE VINCENT

June 1962		11	Bradford	Majestic
17 *Twist Across The Channel*		12	Hull	Majestic
July 1962		13	Shrewsbury	Music Hall
1 Liverpool	Cavern	14	Spennymoor	Clarence
2 Leyton	Coronation Gardens	15	Blackpool	Queen's
3 Swindon	McKilroy's	16	Staines	Town Hall
4 Birmingham	Ritz	19	Wallington	Town Hall
Birmingham	Plaza	20	Whitehaven	Empress
5 Herne Bay	King's Hall	21	Northwich	Victory Memorial Hall
6 Gravesend	*unknown venue*	22	Blackpool	Queen's
7 Manchester	Oasis	24	Southport	Floral Hall
8 Torquay	Princess	25	Newcastle	Majestic
9 West Bromwich	Adelphi	26	Darlington	Majestic
10 Kilburn	Gaumont State			
Promoter — Don Arden				

Since early May, Gene Vincent had been undertaking tours of both France and Germany. He returned to the UK in time to headline the *Twist Across The Channel* jaunt between London and Calais.

On the domestic front, he and his future English wife, Margaret Russell, were negotiating the purchase of a house in Kent, and during June

Gene made an application to the Home Office for permission to settle permanently in the UK.

Don Arden had no difficulty in securing another block of ballroom dates and Vincent spent most of July on the road with Sounds Incorporated. His pulling power was as strong as ever with the public, but by now his efforts were gaining only limited publicity and no exposure at all on television. He did find time to re-record 'Be-Bop-A-Lula' with a twist tempo, backed by the Charles Blackwell Orchestra — 'Be-Bop-A-Lula '62' — but otherwise it was just the daily grind of one-nighters, followed at the end of July by a short tour of Italy.

CHUBBY CHECKER

September 1962					
2	Blackpool	Opera House	13	Hull	ABC
3	Bristol	Colston Hall	14	Norwich	Theatre Royal
4	Wolverhampton	Gaumont	15	Portsmouth	Guildhall
6	Manchester	Apollo	16	Leicester	De Montfort Hall
7	Stockton	Globe	19	Birmingham	Town Hall
8	Newcastle	City Hall	21	East Ham	Granada
9	Liverpool	Empire	22	Sheffield	City Hall
12	Leeds	Odeon	23	Birmingham	Granada
Promoter — Arthur Howes					

Billed as the 'Twist Extravaganza', the indefatigable Mr. Checker gyrated his way around Britain in the autumn of '62 at the helm of a sizeable package which also featured the Brook Brothers, the Kestrels, Susan Singer, Chas McDevitt and Shirley Douglas, the Gary Edwards Combo, the Semi-Tones and compere Bob Bain. He was backed by the Red Price Orchestra.

The initial fascination for the twist and its many spin-off dances was beginning to lessen, but Chubby's unswerving enthusiasm and dedication to the cause carried his audiences along with him. At Colston Hall, Bristol he had them twisting in the aisles and by the end of the evening many were up on stage dancing with him. His energetic act included 'The Fly' which — he assured everyone — was the newest American dance sensation. He did throw in a moving rendition of 'Georgia On My Mind', but the main body of his show was 'The Twist', 'Twistin' Party' and 'Let's Twist Again'. Called back time and again, he closed his dynamic set with 'I'd Love To Dance All Night' and his fans were left with little doubt that he meant it.

During his stay he recorded a thirty-minute special, *The Twist King*, for ABC-TV and, with a two-day break in his schedule after the Leicester show, fitted in a short trip to Paris in the company of his musical director, Frank Owens.

TV appearances

The Twist King	? September 1962 (screened 7 September 1962)
Thank Your Lucky Stars	? September 1962 (screened 13 October 1962)

DION
DEL SHANNON
BUZZ CLIFFORD

September 1962					
16	Brighton	Palladium	23	Walthamstow	Granada
17	Portsmouth	Guildhall	24	Kettering	Granada
18	Mansfield	Granada	25	Bristol	Colston Hall
19	Bedford	Granada	26	Bournemouth	Winter Gardens
20	Maidstone	Granada	27	Birmingham	Town Hall
21	Kingston	Granada	28	Harrow	Granada
22	Slough	Adelphi	29	Tooting	Granada
			30	Leicester	De Montfort Hall
Promoter — Tito Burns					

GRANADA SEPTEMBER 1962

program
one shilling

The opening night of this triple-header tour took place at the Brighton Palladium Ice Rink, where the acoustics were far from perfect. All three Americans were backed by the New York Twisters, and although their own set with front-man Peppi went over well enough, they seemed inadequately rehearsed as a backing group.

Buzz Clifford's performance, too, was disappointing. He only sang three numbers, 'No-One Loves Me But You', 'Ya Ya' and his 'Baby Sittin' Boogie' hit. He got only limited audience reaction and was clearly uncomfortable with his accompaniment.

Del Shannon proved to be the sensation of the show and received an enthusiastic response from more than 1,500 fans. His act commenced with 'So Long Baby', followed by 'Hey Little Girl' and then 'Cry Myself To Sleep', on which he played his own lead guitar. The show-stopper proved to be his version of Orbison's 'Crying', which had the girls screaming and going wild. Shannon closed with 'Hats Off To Larry' and 'Runaway'.

The final act of the night was Dion, who looked elegant in a shiny black suit. He danced around the stage and put plenty into his delivery, but was obviously having trouble with the backing band. 'Teenager In Love', 'Little Diane' and an energetic 'Stagger Lee' went over well, but it wasn't until his final number, 'Runaround Sue' that he really won over the crowd.

Also on the show were Joe Brown & The Bruvvers, the Allisons, Suzy Cope and comedians Wallace & Duval.

TV appearances (Dion)

Thank Your Lucky Stars	10 September 1962 (screened 29 September 1962)
Juke Box Jury	15 September 1962
Thank Your Lucky Stars	10 September 1962 (screened 13 October 1962)

TV appearances (Del Shannon)

Thank Your Lucky Stars	? September 1962 (screened 29 September 1962

TV appearances (Buzz Clifford)

Thank Your Lucky Stars	10 September 1962 (screened 27 October 1962)

FREDDY CANNON
DEL SHANNON
BUZZ CLIFFORD

October 1962			4	Manchester	Apollo
1	Huddersfield	ABC	5	Carlisle	Lonsdale
2	Cleethorpes	ABC	6	Newcastle	City Hall
3	Sheffield	City Hall	7	Liverpool	Empire
Promoter — Tito Burns					

Dion returned home at the end of September, while the package continued for a further week around the North of England with Freddy Cannon replacing him. Jet Harris & The Jetblacks joined the show instead of Joe Brown, although both Joe and the John Barry Seven appeared on one or more of the dates. Otherwise the line-up remained the same.

The backing provided by the New York Twisters was still attracting adverse comment when the show played at Huddersfield. It was reported that Cannon's voice was often inaudible as he worked through a string of his best-known numbers concluding with 'Palisades Park', which the audience had called for incessantly. Despite this, they still wanted more as he left the stage.

TV appearances (Freddy Cannon)

Thank Your Lucky Stars	30 September 1962 (screened 6 October 1962)

FREDDY CANNON

October 1962			12	Bimingham	Plaza
8	Reading	New Majestic		Old Hill	Plaza
9	Wallington	Public Hall	13	Nelson	Imperial
11	Kew	Boat House	14	Southsea	Savoy
Promoter — Tito Burns					

Freddy remained in Britain for a further week and played a series of low-key club and ballroom dates with Peppi & The New York Twisters before returning to the States on 16 October. He returned for a few days at the end of November to film his two songs in the movie, *Just For Fun*: 'I Gotta Get Up Early In The Morning' and 'The Ups And Downs Of Love'.

TV appearances

Thank Your Lucky Stars	? November 1962 (screened 8 December 1962)

LITTLE RICHARD
SAM COOKE
GENE VINCENT

October 1962					
8	Doncaster	Gaumont	18	Maidstone	Granada
9	Mansfield	Granada	19	Kingston	Granada
10	Birmingham	Town Hall	20	Slough	Adelphi
11	Grantham	Granada	21	Walthamstow	Granada
12	New Brighton	Tower	22	Newcastle	City Hall
13	Woolwich	Granada	23	Sheffield	City Hall
14	Brighton	Hippodrome	24	Kettering	Granada
15	Bristol	Colston Hall	25	Harrow	Granada
16	Southampton	Gaumont	26	Aylesbury	Granada
17	Bedford	Granada	27	Tooting	Granada
			28	Liverpool	Empire
Promoter — Don Arden					

     For the first-ever British tour by both Little Richard and Sam Cooke, Don Arden put together a strong package which also featured Jet Harris & The Jetblacks, the Breakaways, compere Bob Bain, and the instrumental combo Sounds Incorporated, who also backed both of the show's stars.

     Richard travelled to the UK by ship, docking at Southampton on 5 October, and was accompanied throughout the tour by sixteen year old keyboard wizard and future recording star, Billy Preston. There was much speculation as to whether Richard would perform rock'n'roll or gospel, and at the first performance in Doncaster he stormed on to the stage in a white baggy suit singing 'Joy, Joy, Joy'. He followed with 'He Got What He Wanted' and an emotional rendition of 'I Believe' before frustrating the audience with snatches of his rock'n'roll classics. Later that evening, however, the

second house found the erratic Mr. Penniman on top form. He tore the place apart with 'Long Tall Sally', 'Lucille', 'Good Golly Miss Molly' and 'Tutti Frutti', at one point running into the audience where several girls dissolved into helpless hysterics.

     Sam Cooke missed the opening show altogether because his plane was delayed by bad weather, and in his absence the fans were amazed to find none other than Gene Vincent stepping out of the audience to sing 'Be-Bop-A-Lula' from the auditorium. It transpired that his work permit had expired and he was not permitted to sing on a British stage again until March 1963. Never one to be overly concerned by

Sam Cooke and Little Richard backstage in London.

regulations, Vincent appeared at several venues during the tour, performing from the audience as well as introducing Little Richard's act.

Cooke arrived in time for the second house at Doncaster, accompanied by guitarist Cliff White and drummer Al Gardner, both former members of Ray Charles's band. Earlier on in his career, he had on several occasions publicly denounced rock'n'roll, but now appeared to have become caught up in the twist craze. He gave a very polished performance including 'Cupid', 'You Send Me', 'Chain Gang' and to round off, an exuberant 'Twistin' The Night Away'.

Such was the public's interest in the tour that an estimated two hundred fans congregated outside a restaurant in Doncaster where Richard, Cooke and Arden were enjoying a meal. Eventually, to keep the peace, they permitted the crowd to file through to the table and collect autographs. Meanwhile, a similar crowd had gathered at a nearby pub to watch Gene Vincent and Jet Harris playing darts.

The tour proved to be a great success and both headliners made television appearances on ABC-TV's *Thank Your Lucky Stars*, although Cooke initially turned the show down because the fee was too small, but later changed his mind.

On 12 and 26 October the package minus Little Richard played the Shrewsbury and Aylesbury Granadas, while he appeared at ballrooms in New Brighton and Trentham. Sam Cooke missed the final night of the tour, as he had been booked to co-star with the veteran entertainer, Sophie Tucker, at the Palace Theatre, Manchester. Ominously, his replacement at the Liverpool Empire were the Beatles, then newcomers to the charts with 'Love Me Do'. In the months ahead, the success of the British beat groups was to dramatically affect the careers of the American rock'n'rollers.

Little Richard sailed to Germany on 29 October for further dates. Sadly, Sam Cooke would never again return to Britain as he was shot dead on 11 December 1964 at a motel in Los Angeles following a drunken fracas with a young lady he had picked up at a party.

TV appearances (Little Richard)
Thank Your Lucky Stars   13 October 1962

TV appearances (Sam Cooke)
Thank Your Lucky Stars   14 October 1962 (screened 10 November 1962)

THE EVERLY BROTHERS

October 1962			26	Plymouth	ABC
14	East Ham	Granada	27	Bournemouth	Winter Gardens
15	Hull	ABC	28	Ipswich	Gaumont
16	Stockton	Globe	31	Portsmouth	Guildhall
17	Sheffield	City Hall	**November 1962**		
18	Lincoln	ABC	1	Bristol	Colston Hall
19	Leeds	Odeon	2	Cheltenham	Gaumont
20	Newcastle	City Hall	3	Cardiff	Sophia Gardens
22	Cambridge	Regal	4	Birmingham	Hippodrome
23	Croydon	ABC	7	Huddersfield	ABC
24	Kingston	ABC	8	Manchester	Apollo
25	Exeter	ABC	11	Liverpool	Empire
Promoter — Arthur Howes					

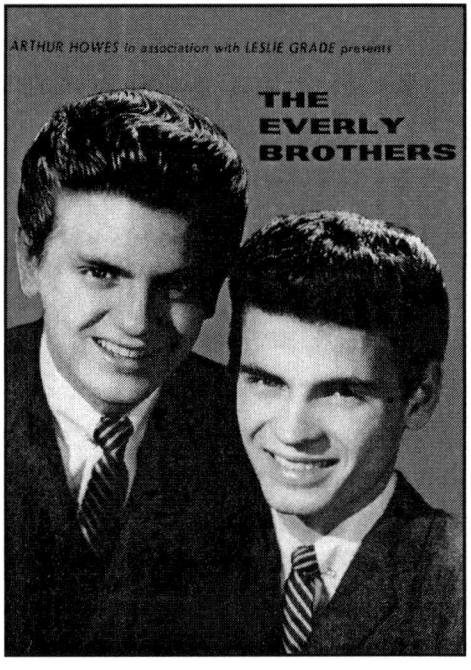

The second Everly Brothers tour promised almost a month of work with a supporting cast comprising Ketty Lester, Frank Ifield, Dean Rogers, the Vernons Girls, the Terry Young Five and comedian Norman Collier. However, it very nearly failed to materialise. Phil flew into London on 11 October, and the first hint of a problem came when Don reportedly missed two planes and didn't arrive until the following day.

What exactly happened after that is shrouded in mystery but, when the tour opened at the East Ham Granada, only one Everly Brother was in attendance. It was reported that Don collapsed during rehearsals with a severe stomach ailment due to overwork and nervous exhaustion, and immediately returned to the States. Later claims advanced the more sinister explanation that he had tried to take his life. It is now known that Don Everly was battling a severe addiction to the prescription drug, Ritalin, at the time, and it is highly probable that this was the cause of his erratic behaviour.

Phil made the first solo appearance of his life at East Ham, backed by the Everly Trio: Don Peake (guitar), Joey Paige (bass) and Chuck Blackwell (drums). He started rather nervously with 'Lucille', but, encouraged by a supportive audience, managed to negotiate his way through a succession of Everly hits, even expanding into a lively version of 'Let's Twist Again' before closing with 'Bye Bye Love'. 'I've never felt so scared,' he admitted afterwards. Proposed radio and television broadcasts including *Thank Your Lucky Stars* and *Sunday Night At The London Palladium* were cancelled, but Phil stuck to his task and steered the tour through to a not unsuccessful conclusion.

B. BUMBLE & THE STINGERS

October 1962			November 1962		
19-20	Liverpool	Cavern	2	Torquay	Town Hall
21	Manchester	Oasis	3	Bletchley	Wilton Hall
23	High Wycombe	Town Hall	4	Southsea	Savoy
25	Scunthorpe	Baths	5	East Ham	Granada
26	Old Hill	Plaza	6	Southport	Floral Hall
	Handsworth	Plaza	8	Greenford	Granada
27	Romford	Wykham Hall	9	Birmingham	Town Hall
28	Southall	Community Centre	10	Stoke	King's Hall
29	Reading	New Majestic	11	Newcastle	City Hall
30	Waltham Cross	Imperial	12	Stechford	Atlas
31	Bedford	Corn Exchange	13	Sheffield	City Hall
			14	Redruth	Flamingo
			15	Bristol	Colston Hall
			16	Croydon	Fairfield Halls
			17	Dunstable	California
Promoter — George Cooper					

The piano instrumental 'Nut Rocker' had topped the charts for the quaintly-named B. Bumble & The Stingers during May, but even at the time it was rightly perceived as being a novelty item rather than the start of a worthwhile career for Mr. Bumble. It was, therefore, something of a surprise when a touring band was put together for an entire month of personal appearances around the UK.

The band arrived on 17 October, their flight having been delayed for two and a half hours by fog. B. Bumble turned out to be a roly-poly piano player supported by Don Orr on drums, Terry Anderson on lead guitar and Jimmy King on rhythm guitar (the latter an alias for one-time rockabilly singer Lou Josie, who had recorded for Argo in 1958).

The tour itself was a mishmash of ballroom and theatre dates, ironically commencing at the Cavern in Liverpool the very week that the

Beatles gained their first British chart entry. For the theatre dates, they were billed with Joe Brown & The Bruvvers, Vince Eager, Johnny Kidd & The Pirates, Chris Wayne & The Echoes, the Tornados and Bobby Shafto, but there was much chopping and changing, and at different times they were also joined by Michael Cox, Bert Weedon, Tommy Bruce, the Flee-Rekkers and Ricky Valance. Media interest in Mr. Bumble was negligible, but reports of the Cavern show confirmed that his material was ideal for twisting or jiving to, although he had little to offer as a stage personality. In addition to the instrumentals, Bumble vocalised on 'What'd I Say' and 'Let The Four Winds Blow', while Jimmy King tried his hand at 'I Remember You'.

One small claim to fame is that, on 16 November 1962, B. Bumble & The Stingers became the first rock show to appear at Croydon's new Fairfield Halls.

PAT BOONE

October 1962		
25 London Plaza		
	Promoter unknown	

During the last week of October, it was announced that plans for a second Little Richard tour had been scrapped as he did not consider his voice to be in good enough shape. Somehow, a one-off appearance by Pat Boone was never going to be an acceptable substitute.

The occasion was the world premiere of Pat's new movie, *The Main Attraction*, and the audience, which included Princess Marina, were treated to thirty minutes of lush ballads like 'It All Depends On You' and 'April Love'. The highlight of the act was a comedy version of 'Speedy Gonzales', on which he was assisted by compere Pete Murray. The whole show was devoid of any other rock'n'roll content. Boone's rocking days were now well and truly behind him, and from this point he ceases to be in any way relevant to this book. Interestingly, his entire show was performed with a pre-recorded backing and no live musicians on the stage. The would-be King of Rock'n'Roll had evolved into the King of Karaoke!

TV appearances
Sunday Night At The London Palladium   21 October 1962
Thank Your Lucky Stars   17 November 1962

THE CRICKETS
BOBBY VEE

November 1962					
3	Sheffield	City Hall	14	Bedford	Granada
4	Leicester	De Montfort Hall	15	Maidstone	Granada
5	Birmingham	Town Hall	16	Kingston	Granada
6	Portsmouth	Guildhall	17	Slough	Adelphi
7	Bradford	Gaumont	18	Walthamstow	Granada
8	Doncaster	Gaumont	19	Mansfield	Granada
9	Worcester	Gaumont	20	Kettering	Granada
10	Bournemouth	Winter Gardens	21	Manchester	Odeon
11	Brighton	Essoldo	22	Birkenhead	Essoldo
12	Woolwich	Granada	23	Harrow	Granada
13	Aylesbury	Granada	24	Tooting	Granada
			25	Bristol	Colston Hall
Promoter — Tito Burns					

Touring England for the first time in their own name since the loss of Buddy Holly would in itself have been sufficient burden for the Crickets, but when Sonny Curtis, Jerry Naylor and Glen D. Hardin arrived on 26 October, their drummer and leader, Jerry Allison, was also absent. Special leave had been promised to him by the USAF, but this was abruptly postponed and later cancelled altogether as a result of the Cuban missile crisis. Don Groom, drummer with Mike Berry's Outlaws, substituted for Allison throughout the tour and did a fine job at such short notice. Bobby Vee flew in from Rome a day after the Crickets and was backed on the tour by the Nu-Notes, augmented by his own pianist, Ward Dunkirk. The rest of the acts comprised Ronnie Carroll, Mike Berry & The Outlaws, Russ Sainty, Frank Kelly & The Hunters, Johnny de Little and compere Frank Berry.

Not surprisingly, most of the press attention centred on the absence of Jerry Allison, but on the opening night at Sheffield the remaining Crickets demonstrated their adaptability with a strong set that commenced with 'Peggy Sue', 'That'll Be The Day, and 'Oh Boy!'. Naylor and Curtis then harmonised on 'Don't Ever Change', before Mike Berry came on stage and took over the vocal duties for 'Raining In My Heart' and 'I'm Gonna Love You Too'. Naylor performed a novelty song, 'Lou's Got The Flu', with the aid of a tambourine, while Hardin's piano playing was prominently featured on 'Summertime Blues'.

The ever-popular Bobby Vee gave a professional display, opening with 'Rubber Ball' and 'More Than I Can Say'. In addition to his many hit songs, he also included a medley of 'Baby Face', 'You Must Have Been A Beautiful Baby' and a smooth version of 'Personality'. The Crickets joined him on stage for 'Someday' and a raucous 'Bo Diddley'.

Happily, the tour survived Jerry Allison's absence and was well received around the country. Plans for the Crickets to remain in the UK for a further week of ballroom dates did not, however, materialise and they flew on to Amsterdam on 27 November.

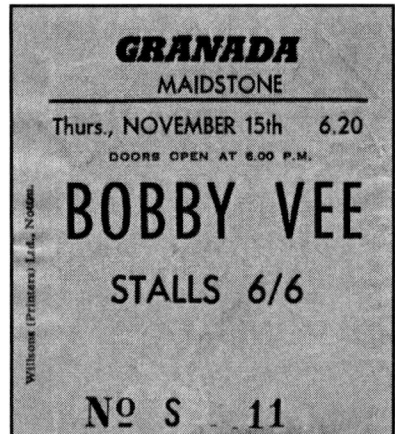

TV appearances (Crickets and Bobby Vee)

Thank Your Lucky Stars	? November 1962 (screened 3 November 1962)
Kingsley Amis Goes Pop	? November 1962 (screened 14 November 1962)
Thank Your Lucky Stars	6 November 1962 (screened 1 December 1962)

TV appearances (Bobby Vee)

Thank Your Lucky Stars	13 November 1962 (screened 5 January 1963)
People and Places	21 November 1962
Juke Box Jury	24 November 1962

TV appearances (Crickets)

Thank Your Lucky Stars	? November 1962 (screened 12 January 1963)

GENE VINCENT

November 1962			December 1962		
21	York	Rialto	1	Norwich	Theatre Royal
22	Portsmouth	Guildhall	2	Ipswich	Gaumont
23	Salisbury	Gaumont	3	Shrewsbury	Granada
24	Brighton	Essoldo	4	Wakefield	Regal
25	Worcester	Gaumont	5	Carlisle	Lonsdale
26	Edmonton	Granada	6	Chesterfield	ABC
27	Tunbridge Wells	Essoldo	7	Harrow	Granada
28	Bedford	Granada	8	Slough	Adelphi
29	Maidstone	Granada	9	Leicester	De Montfort Hall
30	Kingston	Granada			
Promoter — Don Arden					

Gene Vincent's fans were both surprised and delighted to learn that the Ministry of Labour had given special dispensation for him to re-commence touring despite his work permit having expired. Adam Faith topped the bill on a package which also featured the Roulettes, Chance Gordon, Johnny Wiltshire & The Trebletones, and compere Dave Reid. Vincent was once again backed by the Echoes, but this was not a happy tour for him. His leg was so painful that on some dates he was obliged to perform sitting on a stool. In fact, the inflammation became so severe that he was forced to enter Middlesex Hospital on 27 December for a bone graft operation.

CONNIE FRANCIS

Connie flew in and out of London on 15 December, crossing the Atlantic twice in one day, for a short session dubbing dialogue at Elstree Studios for her latest film, *Follow The Boys*. Her visit was made against doctor's orders as she was suffering from bronchitis at the time. She returned from the UK to Guantanamo Air Base in Cuba to appear on an *Ed Sullivan Show* special.

CHAPTER EIGHT

1963

Will You Still Love Me Tomorrow?

Don Arden, the self-styled 'godfather of rock'n'roll', has not enjoyed a very good public image. Over the years, various television and newspaper stories have given a frightening insight into his allegedly violent and uncompromising business methods, and few if any of the performers who worked for him have had anything positive to say on his behalf. For the fans, however, it is a different story. It was Arden who promoted many of the greatest package tours of the early Sixties, and thanks to him British audiences were able to enjoy concerts by the likes of Gene Vincent, Jerry Lee Lewis and Little Richard in their prime. This was a wonderful time for live rock'n'roll music as more and more American acts crossed the Atlantic and played high-profile theatre dates around the country. Almost every week the music press carried news and information about proposed tours, and even though many of the artists now struggled to shift sufficient quantities of their latest recordings, the live shows were generally well-supported.

As 1963 progressed, so the onslaught of Beatlemania swept the nation, gradually expanding to incorporate a host of other beat groups. Liverpool suddenly seemed like the centre of the universe, but much of the material performed by the early beat groups was derived directly from rock'n'roll, and this did have the effect of creating a demand for personal appearances by acts who were otherwise out of the public eye. Chuck Berry, Carl Perkins and Bo Diddley would all tour Britain for the very first time over the next year or so, and may well otherwise not have had the opportunity, but for the awakening of interest brought about by — often sadly inadequate — cover versions of their classic records. However, this short-term benefit would soon be outweighed by the public's almost total infatuation with the British beat groups. The Americans would be swept aside and within a couple of years the Beatles would lead the world down the cul-de-sac to drugs, hippies and electronic music. Not everybody was listening, however. A minority, albeit a significant one, was not ready to hang up their rock'n'roll shoes, and would cling loyally to the music that they loved. But, as far as 1963 was concerned, it was the high-point for the package tours, so thanks for the memories, Mr. Arden.

JOHNNY & THE HURRICANES

January 1963					
15	Kilburn	Gaumont State	23	Aylesbury	Granada
16	Alderley Edge	Regent Hall	24	Portsmouth	Guildhall
17	Harrow	Granada	25	Kingston	Granada
18	Birmingham	Ritz	26	Slough	Adelphi
	Birmingham	Plaza	27	Tooting	Granada
19	Leyton	Baths	28	Grantham	Granada
	Romford	Wykham Hall	29	Bradford	St. George's Hall
20	Newcastle	City Hall	31	Scunthorpe	Baths
21	Bedford	Granada	**February 1963**		
22	Maidstone	Granada	1	Stafford	Trentham Gardens
			2	Nelson	Imperial
Promoter — Don Arden					

The ill-fated *Juke Box Doubles* tour was one of Don Arden's less successful projects, although the current craze for tribute bands suggests that perhaps he was merely ahead of his time. Disc-jockey Jimmy Savile was signed up as compere, while a largely unknown bunch of hopefuls took turns at impersonating the stars. Brad Newman (as Elvis), Steve Francis (Billy Fury), Sally Green (Brenda Lee), Dev Douglas (Adam Faith), Dru Harvey (Gene Vincent) and the Jokers (the Shadows), represented a cheapskate production that completely failed to spark any real interest from the public.

Johnny & The Hurricanes had the difficult task of topping the bill and even they contained only leader and sax-player Johnny Paris from the original line-up. The other Hurricanes who accompanied Paris on his trip across the Atlantic were Eddie Fields (organ), Billy Marsh (guitar), Bobby Cantrell (bass) and Jay Drake (drums).

The tour opened at Kilburn to a lukewarm reception. The British acts were at best mediocre, and the Hurricanes unexciting. Their guitar was indistinct, the organ lacking bite, and only Paris' fluent tenor sax carried them through their mainly instrumental set.

By the time they reached Bradford, the show was falling apart at the seams. Ticket sales were so poor that the two houses were merged into one, but even that started late and was further disrupted by a power cut midway through the Jokers' act. Johnny Paris even conspired to forget the words to 'Speedy Gonzales', and would have been better served sticking to his instrumental hits. The small audience were filing out of the theatre long before the end.

Eventually, the tour collapsed and the last seven nights, including Stockport, Coventry and Bath, were cancelled. *Juke Box Doubles* was not an encouraging start to the year.

BRIAN HYLAND
LITTLE EVA

February 1963					
2	Cardiff	Sophia Gardens	17	Leicester	De Montfort Hall
3	Brighton	Hippodrome	18	Portsmouth	Guildhall
4	Bristol	Colston Hall	19	Dartford	Granada
5	Guildford	Odeon	20	Aylesbury	Granada
6	Sheffield	City Hall	21	Lincoln	ABC
7	Newcastle	City Hall	22	Kingston	Granada
8	Woolwich	Granada	23	Slough	Adelphi
9	Bournemouth	Winter Gardens	24	Tooting	Granada
10	Liverpool	Empire	25	Birmingham	Town Hall
11	Mansfield	Granada	26	Grantham	Granada
12	Cleethorpes	ABC	27	Bedford	Granada
13	York	Rialto	28	Dover	ABC
14	Maidstone	Granada	**March 1963**		
15	Harrow	Granada	1	Hanley	Victoria Hall
16	Walthamstow	Granada	2	Bradford	Gaumont
			3	Blackburn	King George's Hall
Promoter — Don Arden					

Nineteen year old Brian Hyland and Little Eva, two years his junior, represented the new generation of American acts. Backed by the Rhythm & Blues Quintet and supported by the Brook Brothers, the Chariots, Johnny Temple and compere Dave Reid, they set off on a lengthy tour of provincial theatres. Joey Dee had originally been scheduled to tour, but when he dropped out the vivacious Eva Boyd proved a popular replacement.

On the opening night at Cardiff, Hyland showed himself to be a pro despite his comparative youth, and his act contained a larger proportion of

uptempo rock'n'roll than might have been anticipated from his records. Shaking his mane of unruly hair from side to side, he burst onto the stage with a ferocious 'Early In The Morning', followed by 'The Wanderer', then worked through his hits, 'Warmed Over Kisses', 'Ginny Come Lately' and 'Sealed With A Kiss', though he tended to talk too much between songs. Also included was a punchy version of Charlie Rich's 'Lonely Weekends', while he played lead guitar on 'Oh, Lonesome Me'. His final number was a rocking 'What'd I Say'.

Little Eva's lack of experience had been evident when she closed the first half, showing little stagecraft or confidence. She quickly improved, however, and by the following night at Brighton her

123

warm smile, big eyes and flexible body entranced the audience who were soon singing along to 'Zip-A-Dee-Doo-Dah' and clapping through 'Hey! Baby'. She faltered at the opening to 'Keep Your Hands Off My Baby', but recovered and ended with a torrid version of 'Loco-motion'.

At Guildford, police with dogs had to be called to the Odeon after rioting teenage girls tried to smash their way into Brian Hyland's dressing room. He was hit by flying glass and had to be evacuated to another part of the building.

TV appearances (Brian Hyland)

Juke Box Jury	26 January 1963
Scene At 6.30	28 January 1963
Thank Your Lucky Stars	2 February 1963

TV appearances (Little Eva)

Tonight	? February 1963
Scene at 6.30	6 February 1963
Thank Your Lucky Stars	24 February 1963 (screened 2 March 1963)

BOBBY DARIN

Three years after his controversial British tour with Duane Eddy, Bobby Darin was lined up to return in February, and the opening dates at Portsmouth and Hammersmith had already been announced when he pulled out, citing his Hollywood commitments. Like Pat Boone, Darin had already left rock'n'roll behind some time ago and was carving out a career for himself as a latter-day Sinatra. He had long ceased to be of interest to rock'n'roll fans.

GENE VINCENT

February 1963			29	Nottingham	Albert Hall
17	London	Pigalle	30	Sunderland	Odeon
March 1963			31	Blackburn	King George's Hall
1	Stockport	Astoria	**April 1963**		
2	Macclesfield	El Rio	3	Torquay	400 Ballroom
3	Stoke	King's Hall	4	Plymouth	Majestic
5	Kilburn	Gaumont State	5	Redruth	Flamingo
16	East Grinstead	Whitehall	6	Penzance	Grand Casino
22	Llanelly	Ritz	**May 1963**		
24	Southport	Odeon	4	Prestatyn	Royal Lido
Promoter — Don Arden					

Still very much of interest was the indefatigable Mr. Vincent, who started the year with a clutch of dates in France before making an appearance at a private party at the exclusive Pigalle nightclub in London. This was followed by a short tour of Germany starting on 20 February, and a handful of dates in the UK during March.

The four shows between 24 and 31 March were as part of a mini-package which also featured Jet Harris & Tony Meehan, John Leyton,

Patti Brook, Johnny Temple, the Voltairs and compere Ray Peters, following which Gene penetrated the far South-West of England, taking rock'n'roll for a rare excursion into Devon and Cornwall.

CHRIS MONTEZ
TOMMY ROE

March 1963					
9	East Ham	Granada	20	Romford	Ritz
10	Birmingham	Hippodrome	21	Croydon	ABC
12	Bedford	Granada	22	Doncaster	Gaumont
13	York	Rialto	23	Newcastle	City Hall
14	Wolverhampton	Gaumont	24	Liverpool	Empire
15	Bristol	Colston Hall	26	Mansfield	Granada
16	Sheffield	City Hall	27	Northampton	ABC
17	Peterborough	Embassy	28	Exeter	ABC
18	Gloucester	ABC	29	Lewisham	Odeon
19	Cambridge	ABC	30	Portsmouth	Guildhall
			31	Leicester	De Montfort Hall
Promoter — Arthur Howes					

When Tommy Roe and Chris Montez arrived in the UK they could have had no inkling that they were walking into the eye of a storm of monumental proportions. Billed as the headliners on a routine package show, they would not have known that their support acts were to be compere Tony Marsh, the Terry Young Six (who also backed both Americans), Debbie Lee, the Viscounts and... the Beatles.

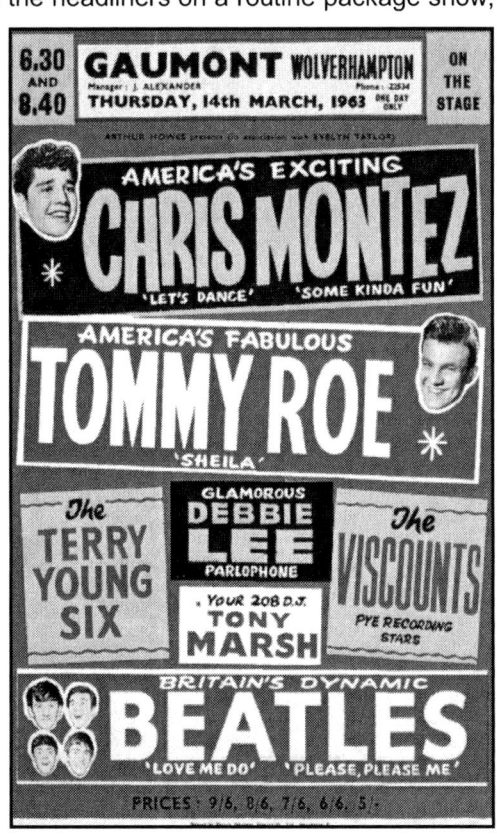

Those so-lovable mop-tops from Liverpool were still unknown in the USA, but were riding high in the British charts with their second hit, 'Please, Please Me', and the early signs of Beatlemania were soon apparent. Both Roe and Montez had a difficult time on the opening night at East Ham and, although both showed themselves to be competent performers, they would probably have required some divine intervention to overcome the hysteria that followed them from town to town.

Roe was the first to appear. Tall and slim, he came on smartly dressed in a grey jacket and black trousers. His act opened with 'Whole Lotta Shakin' Goin' On' and included 'The Folk Singer' (his latest single), 'Maybellene', 'Sheila' and a hand-clapping, gospel-styled 'There's A Great Day Coming'. He seemed a little shy with the audience, but did receive some enthusiastic screams after breaking into a rather sedate twist.

Chris Montez was a little bundle of energy. His set, which was built around his two hits, 'Let's Dance' and 'Some Kinda Fun', also included a rip-roaring 'Bony Moronie', an uptempo rocker sung entirely in Spanish, and a ballad, 'You're The One', which went down extremely well with the ladies in the audience. Throughout the proceedings, Montez danced around the stage like a whirling dervish, removing first his jacket, then his tie, finishing his act bathed in sweat and with his shirt unbuttoned.

Neither Roe nor Montez could be faulted for lack of effort, but the tidal wave of support for the Beatles was too much for them. As the tour progressed, the running order was changed so that the Beatles could close the show and the two headliners became bit-part players on the tour. From now on, the profile of the American rock'n'rollers would be reduced as the British beat groups began to gain a stranglehold on the music scene.

TV appearances (Tommy Roe)

On The Scene	4 March 1963
Thank Your Lucky Stars	9 March 1963 (screened 27 April 1963)

TV appearances (Chris Montez)

Juke Box Jury	9 March 1963
Thank Your Lucky Stars	9 March 1963

BRENDA LEE

March 1963					
11	Cardiff	Capitol	20	Birmingham	Town Hall
12	Worcester	Gaumont	21	Bristol	Colston Hall
13	Brighton	Hippodrome	22	Kingston	Granada
14	Harrow	Granada	23	Slough	Adelphi
15	Woolwich	Granada	24	Coventry	Theatre
16	Walthamstow	Granada	25	Portsmouth	Guildhall
17	Newcastle	City Hall	26	Belfast	Kings Hall
18	Sheffield	City Hall	29	Manchester	Odeon
19	Liverpool	Odeon	30	Bournemouth	Winter Gardens
			31	Tooting	Granada
Promoter — Don Arden					

The second Brenda Lee tour took place whilst she was at the peak of her popularity. Polls of the time clearly demonstrated that she had overtaken Connie Francis and was now unquestionably the most popular female singer with British audiences. The year had not started well for her, however: a serious house fire had forced Brenda and her family to evacuate their Nashville home during January.

She arrived in Britain after a short tour of Germany, and for her trek around the UK was joined by Mike Berry & The Outlaws, Tony Sheridan, the

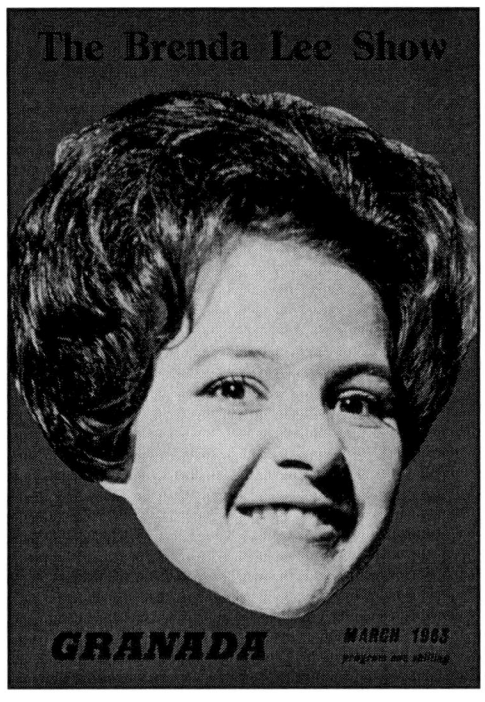

The Brenda Lee Show

GRANADA   MARCH 1963
program and spelling

Bachelors, Steve Perry and compere Bob Bain. As before, she was backed by Sounds Incorporated, who had themselves only recently returned from a three-week tour of the States.

British audiences were known to favour Brenda's uptempo material, so her thirty-minute act was tailored accordingly. A packed auditorium at Cardiff heard her open strongly with 'Lover Come Back To Me', 'Let's Jump The Broomstick' and 'Here Comes That Feeling'. Other bouncy rockers which had the fans in uproar included 'Speak To Me Pretty' and 'What'd I Say', but it was her latest hit — the slow ballad 'All Alone Am I' — which received the most prolonged cheers.

TV appearances

Thank Your Lucky Stars	10 March 1963 (screened 16 March 1963)
Here Come The Girls	16 March 1963 (screened 1 May 1963)
Thank Your Lucky Stars	22 March 1963 (screened 13 April 1963)
Scene at 6.30	29 March 1963

CHRIS MONTEZ

April 1963					
			8	West Bromwich	Adelphi
1	Southsea	Savoy		Birmingham	Atlas
2	East Grinstead	Whitehall	9	Hayes	Botwell House
3	Kings Lynn	Corn Exchange	10	Farnborough	Town Hall
4	Manchester	Northern Sporting	11	Birmingham	Plaza
5	Llanelly	Ritz		Old Hill	Plaza
6	Maidstone	Agricultural	12	Nelson	Imperial
7	Marylebone	Londoner	13	Chelmsford	Corn Exchange
	Harlesden	Westmore	15	Oxford	Town Hall
Promoter — Arthur Howes					

After the Tommy Roe–Chris Montez package had run its course, Chris Montez stayed in the UK for a further fortnight of club and dancehall dates backed by the Eagles. This must have come as a welcome relief after three weeks under siege from marauding Beatles' fans.

DEL SHANNON

April 1963			May 1963		
18	London	Royal Albert Hall	2	Wolverhampton	Civic Hall
19	Taunton	*unknown venue*	3	Kingston	Granada
20	Bournemouth	Winter Gardens	4	Tooting	Granada
21	Leicester	De Montfort Hall	5	Walthamstow	Granada
22	Norwich	Theatre Royal	7	Bedford	Granada
23	Birmingham	Town Hall	8	Woolwich	Granada
24	York	Rialto	9	Brighton	Essoldo
25	Manchester	Odeon	10	Portsmouth	Guildhall
26	Newcastle	Odeon	11	Cardiff	Sophia Gardens
27	Bradford	Gaumont	12	Bristol	Colston Hall
28	Liverpool	Empire	13	East Grinstead	Whitehall
29	Stoke	Essoldo	15	Kilburn	Gaumont State
30	Hammersmith	Odeon			
Promoter — Tito Burns					

On his second UK tour, Del Shannon co-starred with the diminutive pop-country singer, Johnny Tillotson, who had scored a UK No. 1 hit with 'Poetry In Motion' at the end of 1960. Shannon was backed throughout his stay by the Eagles. Other acts featured on the tour were Kenny Lynch, the Springfields, Peppi, Rey Anton and Jerry Stevens.

The main tour kicked off at Bournemouth, but Shannon had been in Britain since 13 April and played two earlier shows at the Royal Albert Hall and in Taunton. The Albert Hall gig was an elaborate affair organised by the BBC and also featured John Leyton, the Bachelors, Susan Maughan, Matt Monro, the Springfields, the Vernons Girls, Shane Fenton and the Beatles.

Del had so far clocked up seven Top Ten hits in Britain and was a major attraction, the tour proving a great success. An extra show at Kilburn was added at the end, on which he starred with the Four Seasons on a bill that also included the Brook Brothers, Freddie & The Dreamers and the Terry Young Six. Shannon left the UK on 17 May to do further shows in Sweden.

TV appearances

Thank Your Lucky Stars	20 April 1963
Scene at 6.30	25 April 1963
Juke Box Jury	4 May 1963 (screened 11 May 1963)

DEE DEE SHARP

May 1963		
4	Old Hill	Plaza
Promoter unknown		

Dee Dee Sharp, a seventeen year old Philadelphia schoolgirl, made just one public appearance during a three-day promotional visit to Britain. She gave a creditable performance showcasing her new record — yet another new dance craze — called 'Do The Bird'. She was backed by the Viscounts.

TV appearances
Thank Your Lucky Stars   ? May 1963 (screened 11 May 1963)

JERRY LEE LEWIS
GENE VINCENT

May 1963		
6	Birmingham	Town Hall
7	Sheffield	City Hall
8	York	Rialto
9	Croydon	Fairfield Halls
10	Bristol	Colston Hall
11	Bournemouth	Winter Gardens
12	Newcastle	City Hall
Promoter — Don Arden		

The overwhelming success of Jerry Lee's 1962 tour deemed it inevitable that he would make an early return to the UK, and there was a very positive response to the pairing with Gene Vincent for a week of provincial theatre dates. What did not receive such a positive reaction was Don Arden's decision to give equal billing to ex-Tornado Heinz Burt in the pre-tour publicity.

Tolerance and patience are not qualities to be found in abundance among rock'n'roll audiences and this tour set the pattern for many that followed. Inadequate or inappropriate support acts could expect a torrid time from fans waiting impatiently for their favourites, especially if their performance was substandard. In addition to the wretched Heinz, Gene and Jerry Lee lined up with such forgettables as Andy Cavell & The Saints, Dev Douglas, Mickie Most, Brad Newman and compere Chris Carlsen — some of them survivors from January's ill-fated *Juke Box Doubles* tour. Vincent was backed by Dru Harvey & The Jokers masquerading as the Blue Caps, while Jerry Lee was paired with the Outlaws, including guitarist Ritchie Blackmore and bass-player Chas Hodges.

When the package opened at Birmingham, fans paraded through the city centre carrying a giant *'Jerry Lee Lewis'* banner and, even before the show got underway, were shouting and clapping and calling for their hero. The early acts were treated with contempt, but not much open hostility, although Mickie Most's efforts gave new meaning to the word mediocre.

Vincent closed the first half with a short but highly effective set that included 'Chain Gang' and 'Be-Bop-A-Lula'. But why on earth was he restricted to only five songs?

Heinz must have felt akin to a human sacrifice as he opened his act. He had been designated the penultimate spot on the show and had neither the experience nor the ability to make any positive impact when faced with an over-excited audience who had sat through too much dross already. His cause was not aided by microphone problems and an overloud backing, but the boos from the fans would certainly have left him in no doubt that his efforts were far from being appreciated.

In stark contrast, headliner Jerry Lee Lewis was quite simply magnificent. He slammed his way through the old favourites including 'Hound Dog', 'You Win Again', 'Don't Be Cruel', 'Good Golly Miss Molly', 'Whole Lotta Shakin' ' and 'Great Balls Of Fire'. His fans were jiving in the aisles, stamping, shouting and begging for more. As far as they were concerned, he could do no wrong, and after he left the stage the cries of 'We want Jerry!' echoed around the hall for several minutes.

Despite his popularity, the Establishment was still apprehensive about Lewis, and — significantly — he again failed to secure a central London concert or any coverage on British television.

TV appearances (Gene Vincent)

Thank Your Lucky Stars	27 April 1963
Scene At 6.30	20 May 1963

ROY ORBISON

May 1963					
			29	Manchester	Odeon
18	Slough	Granada	31	Southend	Odeon
19	Hanley	Gaumont	**June 1963**		
20	Southampton	Gaumont	1	Tooting	Granada
22	Ipswich	Gaumont	2	Brighton	Hippodrome
23	Nottingham	Odeon	3	Woolwich	Granada
24	Walthamstow	Granada	4	Birmingham	Town Hall
25	Sheffield	City Hall	5	Leeds	Odeon
26	Liverpool	Empire	7	Glasgow	Odeon
27	Cardiff	Capitol	8	Manchester	City Hall
28	Worcester	Gaumont	9	Blackburn	King George's Hall
Promoter — Peter Walsh					

When negotiations to bring Duane Eddy to Britain fell though, and Texan Roy Orbison was announced as his replacement, it felt almost as if he were being handed a poisoned chalice. Tommy Roe and Chris Montez had been overwhelmed by the early effects of Beatlemania when they toured in March.

Two months later, the position had worsened considerably and the hysteria had now extended to embrace the so-called 'Liverpool Sound'. Every youth on Merseyside who could strum a guitar or vaguely carry a tune was having a record contract thrust at him, as the media and public alike climbed aboard the latest bandwagon. At the pinnacle stood the Beatles and Gerry &

The Pacemakers — each with a recent No. 1 hit — and, inevitably, the news that they would headline a package tour together caused enormous interest. Roy Orbison was announced as 'special guest star' and was placed third on the bill. The days were over when visiting American rock'n'rollers would automatically receive top billing in preference to the local acts.

The pattern of the tour became clear on the opening night at Slough. Compere Tony Marsh and the early support acts, Ian Crawford, Erkey Grant, the Terry Young Six (who also backed Roy) and David Macbeth struggled to make any impact in advance of Gerry & The Pacemakers, who scored well as their segment closed the first half.

After the intermission, Orbison had the apparently hopeless task of entertaining the largely female audience who were all impatiently waiting for the Beatles. Without a single movement, he calmed them with a haunting rendition of 'Only The Lonely', before his own harmonica introduction switched into 'Candy Man'. His third number, the hypnotic 'Running Scared', won the day and following tumultuous applause he was obliged to encore the final chorus. He continued with a rocking 'What'd I Say', 'Crying', 'Dream Baby', 'Falling' (his latest single), and rounded off a terrific act with 'In Dreams'. Sustained applause and cheers brought him back three times as the audience momentarily forgot about the Beatles — a quite incredible feat by the unassuming Orbison. Indeed, it is doubtful whether any other performer in the world could have held back the raging tide of Beatlemania at that time.

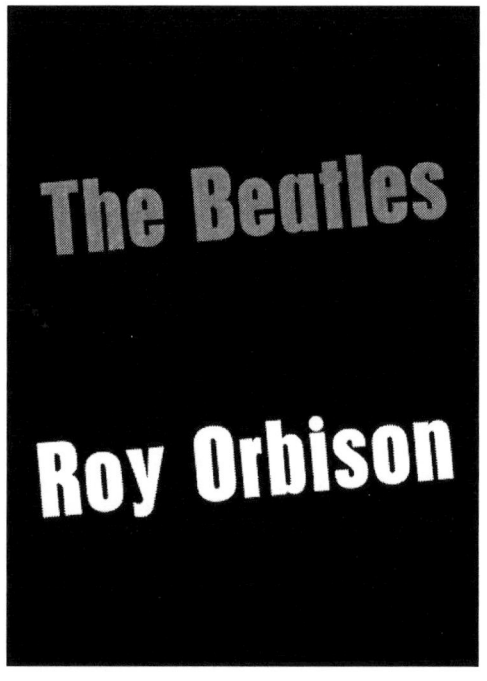

TV appearances
Scene At 6.30   30 May 1963

1963

ROCK TWIST JIVE

CHANNEL CROSSING

with

JERRY LEE LEWIS

and The Outlaws

on the

MV ROYAL DAFFODIL

Whit Saturday 1st June 1963

from Southend to Boulogne

Hello, Rockers, Twisters and Jivers:

Welcome aboard the MV Royal Daffodil. We intend to make this the most enjoyable and exciting trip yet. We have organised for you a day packed with many things to help you to enjoy yourself.

There will be plenty of opportunity to dance all your favourite dances to the non-stop music provided by all the top line artists aboard the ship, and when you arrive in Boulogne you will be greeted by the Mayor and other prominent members of the community.

When you disembark in Boulogne, you are free to go where you please, but there will be a terrific Teen-beat show in the Casino, with French, American, and English stars specially selected for your entertainment.

JERRY LEE LEWIS

May 1963			30	Coventry	Matrix Hall
27	Bath	Royal Hall	31	Stoke	King's Hall
28	Wallington	Public Hall	**June 1963**		
	East Grinstead	Whitehall	1	*Rock-Twist-Jive Across The Channel*	
29	Birmingham	Plaza	2	Liverpool	Empire
	Birmingham	Ritz			
Promoter — Don Arden					

After dates in Hamburg and a short tour of US military bases in Germany, Jerry Lee returned to the UK and teamed up with the Outlaws, again for a short sequence of ballroom dates.

On 1 June, he spearheaded what was billed as *Rock–Twist–Jive Across The Channel.* Some eight hundred teenagers packed on to the ferry at Southend for a day trip to Boulogne, with more than a dozen acts aboard to entertain them — the most prominent of which were Nero & The Gladiators,

Ricky Valance, Johnny Angel and the Flee-Rekkers.

Jerry Lee did not perform on the outward voyage but, after a visit to the local casino in Boulogne for what was advertised as *'a terrific Teen-beat show'*, gave a rousing display of rock'n'roll music with a performance that lasted nearly an hour during the return leg to Southend.

The whole episode attracted lurid headlines in the more hysterical Sunday papers with vivid accounts of teenagers crazed with drink fighting the French police on the streets. In reality, only some half a dozen youths got involved in a fight with French teenagers on the quayside, but the incident was blown up out of all proportion. Nevertheless the prospect of Jerry Lee Lewis and eight hundred fans on a boat does seem like a recipe for disaster, so perhaps the French authorities had a lucky escape.

DEL SHANNON

June 1963		
1	Nelson	Imperial
2	Scarborough	Futurist
3	Hayes	Botwell House
	East Grinstead	Whitehall
Promoter — Tito Burns		

After touring Europe and Israel, Del Shannon returned to the UK for four more dates, the highlight of which was a headlining appearance at a large open-air festival held on Whit Monday at Botwell Park, Hayes, Middlesex. More than 8,000 fans supported the event and twenty-one acts participated, including Gerry & The Pacemakers, Vince Taylor, Eden Kane, Billy J. Kramer, Jackie Lynton and Brian Poole & The Tremeloes — but it was Screaming Lord Sutch who grabbed the headlines, emerging from a blazing coffin at the start of his act and later swinging on a rope out into the audience.

BOBBY CURTOLA

Canadian singer Bobby Curtola arrived in Britain on 3 June for a promotional visit. Largely unknown in this country, his arrival made little impact, though the British public did get the chance to see him on *Thank Your Lucky Stars* along with John Leyton and Tommy Bruce.

TV appearances
Thank Your Lucky Stars   ? June 1963 (screened 15 June 1963)

JOHNNY CYMBAL

June 1963			16	Birmingham	Plaza
7	Birmingham	Ritz	17	St. Albans	Market Hall
8	Margate	Dreamland	18	East Grinstead	Whitehall
9	Southsea	Savoy	19	Frome	Grand
11	Muddiford	BURE	20	Aldershot	New Central
12	Redruth	Flamingo		Farnborough	Town Hall
13	Liverpool	Locarno	21	Hayes	Botwell House
14	Morecambe	Floral Hall	22	Northwich	Victory Memorial Hall
15	Lincoln	Drill Hall	23	Manchester	Belle Vue
Promoter unknown					

A ballroom tour by Johnny Cymbal did not prove to be a headline-grabber in June 1963 as the Liverpool beat groups took it in turns to leapfrog up the charts. A Scottish-born American who came originally from Ochiltree in Ayrshire but had emigrated with his family in 1952, Johnny did at least receive favourable reviews when his tour opened in Birmingham.

Backed by the Premiers, he included rock'n'roll favourites like 'Johnny B. Goode', 'Love Me' and 'Whole Lotta Shakin' Goin' On' in his act, as well as a smattering of comedy, dancing and even impressions: Presley, Holly and Paul & Paula came over best. Surprisingly, his latest record — a controversial 'death' ballad called 'Teenage Heaven' — was not included, but his only British hit, 'Mr. Bass Man', was adequate compensation and proved to be a popular closing number.

TV appearances
Lucky Stars Summer Spin   ? June 1963 (screened 13 July 1963)

GENE VINCENT

June 1963			August 1963		
15	Redhill	Market Hall	4	Bournemouth	Gaumont
16	Camberley	Agincourt	11	Folkestone	Odeon
27	Liverpool	Locarno	18	Blackpool	ABC
July 1963			25	Great Yarmouth	ABC
5	London	Alexandra Palace	31	Wimbledon	Palais
7	Weston-super-Mare	Odeon	**September 1963**		
14	Southend	Odeon	1	Llandudno	Odeon
19	Llanelly	Ritz	3	Waltham Cross	Imperial
21	Llandudno	Odeon	6	Banbury	Winter Gardens
26	East Grinstead	Whitehall	8	Bournemouth	Gaumont
27	Buxton	Pavilion Gardens	13	Pwllheli	Town Hall
	Birmingham	Bingley Hall	15	Manchester	Top Ten
28	Southport	Floral Hall			
Promoter — Don Arden					

Perhaps mercifully in view of his fragile health, Gene Vincent carried a lighter workload during the summer of 1963 compared to the never-ending tours of 1961–62. He had, however, been performing in Europe, and a show at the Alhambra in Paris proved particularly memorable with three thousand screaming fans rioting, after which the iron safety curtain had to be lowered at the end of his act.

The gig at Liverpool on 27 June was one of the first times that Gene was backed by the Outlaws, although on some other occasions he still had Sounds Incorporated in tow. At Alexandra Palace, he headed a lengthy bill for an all-nighter which also featured the John Barry Seven, Cyril Davies & His Rhythm & Blues All Stars and Screaming Lord Sutch, while at the *Birmingham Beat Festival* on 27 July he appeared with Billy J. Kramer, Freddie & The Dreamers and Freddie Starr.

TV appearances

Lucky Stars Summer Spin	20 July 1963
Lucky Stars Summer Spin	7 September 1963

CONNIE FRANCIS

July 1963
3   Glasgow   Alhambra
Promoter unknown

Connie was booked to appear on the *Scottish Royal Variety Show* along with a plethora of British talent including the Springfields, Max Bygraves, Yana, Acker Bilk and comedian Bob Monkhouse. Her record sales and popularity in Britain had slumped in recent months. As she explained: 'I've had too many slow numbers released here. I'm gonna rock for Britain!' All of which sounded like good news for the Queen and Prince Philip, who were attending the concert.

True to her word, she opened her act with 'Do You Love Me', but very swiftly altered the mood with a medley of Jolson, Caruso and Cohan material, and a dramatic rendition of the Anthony Newley hit, 'What Kind Of Fool Am I'. In fairness to Connie, she always spoke positively about rock'n'roll and seemed perfectly at ease with her early hits, but by the summer of 1963 her days as a rock'n'roller were over and she was moving effortlessly into the more sophisticated world of cabaret.

CHUBBY CHECKER

Chubby was busily twisting his way around Ireland during July when it was first suggested that he might be able to guest on one of the TV shows in the UK. Bookings were made and then cancelled when they proved impossible to accommodate into his schedule. Eventually, he managed to squeeze in a lightning visit from Paris for two screen appearances. He barely had time to swivel his hips before he was gone again, though he did return briefly in mid-September for a recording session with Tony Hatch.

TV appearances

A Swingin' Time	15 August 1963
Lucky Stars Summer Spin	? August 1963 (screened 17 August 1963)

TOMMY ROE

September 1963					
13	Cambridge	ABC	6	Liverpool	Empire
14	Bedford	Granada	7	Reading	Olympia
15	Colchester	Odeon	8	Trowbridge	Gaumont
16	Bristol	Colston Hall	9	Luton	Odeon
17	Cleethorpes	ABC	10	Romford	Odeon
18	Carlisle	ABC	11	Croydon	Fairfield Halls
19	Chesterfield	ABC	12	Cardiff	Sophia Gardens
20	Wolverhampton	Gaumont	13	Bournemouth	Winter Gardens
21	Worcester	Gaumont	14	Newport	Majestic
22	Leicester	De Montfort Hall	15	Kilburn	Gaumont State
24	Portsmouth	Guildhall	16	Farnborough	Town Hall
25	Gloucester	ABC	17	Salisbury	City Hall
26	Shrewsbury	Granada	18	East Grinstead	Whitehall
27	Wakefield	ABC	19	Handsworth	Plaza
28	Mansfield	Granada	20	Southsea	Savoy
29	Peterborough	Embassy	21	Bath	Pavilion
October 1963			22	Middlesbrough	Astoria
1	Dartford	Granada	23	Dunfermline	Kinema
2	York	Rialto	24	Aberdeen	Palace
4	Blackpool	Winter Gardens	25	Kircaldy	Raith
5	Taunton	Gaumont	26	Nelson	Imperial
			27	Haslemere	Ritz
Promoter – Arthur Howes					

Only six months or so after touring the UK with Chris Montez and the Beatles, Tommy Roe returned for a marathon of one-nighters during which he clocked up quite extraordinary mileage, travelling up and down the country on a schedule that must have been incredibly gruelling.

The tour was divided into three segments, commencing with a package headlined by the latest Liverpool rage, Billy J. Kramer & The Dakotas. Tommy was backed by the Remo Four, and the other featured acts were the Fourmost, Tommy Quickly, Heinz & The Saints, the Dennisons, Johnny Sandon and compere Chris Carlsen. His act had not changed greatly since his last visit, although, when the tour opened at Cambridge, he kicked off with a rousing 'Early In The Morning' and also threw in a slow number, 'You Might As Well Forget Him', as well as playing his hits.

The Kramer package terminated after Liverpool, and two days later Roe joined forces with the Searchers and Freddie & The Dreamers for a further week of theatre appearances. He then moved into the ballrooms, and negotiated a trek up to Scotland before finally departing for Ireland on 28 October.

TV appearances
Ready Steady Go	6 September 1963
Juke Box Jury	7 September 1963
A Swingin' Time	12 September 1963
Scene At 6.30	4 October 1963

ROY ORBISON
BOB LUMAN

September 1963			26	East Ham	Granada
14	Walthamstow	Granada	27	Kingston	Granada
15	Hanley	Gaumont	28	Slough	Adelphi
16	Southampton	Gaumont	29	Bristol	Colston Hall
17	Tooting	Granada	30	Birmingham	Odeon
18	York	Rialto	**October 1963**		
19	Nottingham	Odeon	1	Rochester	Gaumont
20	Glasgow	Odeon	2	Bedford	Granada
21	Sheffield	City Hall	3	Leeds	Odeon
22	Liverpool	Empire	4	Scarborough	Futurist
23	Manchester	Odeon	5	Newcastle	City Hall
25	Harrow	Granada	6	Blackburn	King George's Hall
Promoter — Peter Walsh					

The extraordinary success of Roy Orbison's first tour demanded an early return to the UK, and he was booked as headliner on a show that also featured three of the most popular current chart acts: Freddie & The Dreamers, the Searchers and Brian Poole & The Tremeloes. Surprisingly, Bob Luman — two years after his last British hit — was also included, but hidden away fifth on the bill. The remainder of the line-up comprised Cherry Roland, Gary & Lee, compere Tony Marsh plus Terry Young's Sons Of The Piltdown Men, who backed both Orbison and Luman.

Roy arrived fresh from shows in Hamburg, and stopped off at Decca's studios in London to record some material under the supervision of Monument label boss Fred Foster. A little over a year later, one of the songs from this session, 'Pretty Paper', would become a Top Ten hit for him in the UK. Roy's subdued and somewhat melancholy style was a welcome contrast to the thrashing beat groups, and his popularity was such that he consistently stole the honours as the show travelled around the country.

Bob Luman's contribution was relatively modest. When interviewed, he described himself as a 'rockabilly singer' — an expression rarely heard in the UK before the Seventies. There was little evidence of his rock'n'roll heritage though. His short act was more in the pop-country mould, including 'I Remember You' and his best-known hit, 'Let's Think About Living'.

TV appearances (Roy Orbison)
Ready Steady Go   13 September 1963
Thank Your Lucky Stars   ? October (screened 19 October 1963)

JOHNNY THUNDER

September 1963			29	Southsea	Savoy
20	Winchester	Royal Lido	30	Newport	*unknown venue*
21	Weymouth	Drill Hall	**October 1963**		
22	Chatham	*unknown venue*	1	Birmingham	*unknown venue*
23	Reading	Top Rank	2	Gorleston	*unknown venue*
24	Kilburn	Gaumont State	4	Whitehaven	Empress
25	Lowestoft	Royal Hotel	5	Prestatyn	Royal Lido
27	Handsworth	Plaza	6	Oldham	Astoria
Promoter — Roy Tempest					

Prior to the late Seventies, it was most unusual for an American rock'n'roller to tour Britain without first securing at least one UK hit to create the demand for personal appearances. Johnny Thunder was an exception, undertaking a short excursion around the ballroom circuit despite a singular lack of interest from British record buyers, who had comprehensively ignored his American success with 'Loop De Loop'.

Despite this in-built disadvantage, Thunder put on an energetic act and received a surprisingly good reception. At Kilburn, he made an immediate visual impact, emerging smartly dressed in a crisp white suit and open black shirt. The audience were roused by 'Twist And Shout', followed by a Sam Cooke-style rendition of 'Frankie And Johnny'. Other numbers included 'Shout', 'Stand By Me', 'What'd I Say' and a relaxed 'Jailer Bring Me Water'. An exciting and enjoyable act closed with 'Loop De Loop', before a well-deserved encore of 'Stagger Lee'. Thunder was backed by the Rikki Alan Trio, although much of the tour advertising billed them as either 'The Thunderers' or 'The Thundermen'. Presumably this was an attempt to mislead the public into believing that he had brought his own band with him from the USA.

FREDDY CANNON

September 1963		
18	Farnborough	Town Hall
20	Old Hill	Plaza
	Handsworth	Plaza
21	East Grinstead	Whitehall
Promoter unknown		

Freddy Cannon arrived in the UK on 14 September for a ten-day visit during which he guested on two TV shows and made a number of very low-key ballroom appearances. His visit was a last-minute booking and was barely reported at all by the music press. His backing on this occasion was provided by the Giants.

TV appearances
A Swingin' Time ? September 1963 (screened 19 September 1963)
Thank Your Lucky Stars ? September 1963 (screened 28 September 1963)

GENE VINCENT

September 1963			October 1963		
28	Hastings	Pier	1	Wallington	Public Hall
29	Manchester	*unknown venue*	2	Stourbridge	Town Hall
30	Bath	Pavilion	3	Kidderminster	*unknown venue*
			19-21	Belfast	Boom Boom
Promoter — Don Arden					

Gene had been scheduled to spend much of September in Germany, including several appearances at the infamous Star Club in Hamburg, but the booking collapsed, so several more British ballroom dates with the Outlaws were quickly added to the tail of his June–September UK tour. He spent most of October on a lengthy tour of France.

THE EVERLY BROTHERS
BO DIDDLEY
LITTLE RICHARD

September 1963					
29	London	New Victoria	19	Bradford	Gaumont
October 1963			20	Hanley	Gaumont
1	Streatham	Odeon	22	Sheffield	Gaumont
2	Edmonton	Regal	23	Nottingham	Odeon
3	Southend	Odeon	24	Birmingham	Odeon
4	Guildford	Odeon	25	Taunton	Gaumont
5	Watford	Gaumont	26	Bournemouth	Gaumont
6	Cardiff	Capitol	27	Salisbury	Gaumont
8	Cheltenham	Odeon	28	East Ham	Granada (*Little Richard*)
9	Worcester	Gaumont		Manchester	Oasis (*Bo Diddley*)
10	Wolverhampton	Gaumont	29	Southampton	Gaumont
11	Derby	Gaumont	30	St. Albans	Odeon
12	Doncaster	Gaumont	31	Lewisham	Odeon
13	Liverpool	Odeon	**November 1963**		
16	Manchester	Odeon	1	Rochester	Odeon
17	Glasgow	Odeon	2	Ipswich	Gaumont
18	Newcastle	Odeon	3	Hammersmith	Odeon
Promoter — Don Arden					

A long, chaotic, but ultimately successful tour commenced with the Everly Brothers topping the bill, Bo Diddley making his eagerly-awaited UK debut, and support being provided by Julie Grant, the Flintstones, Mickie Most and compere Bob Bain... plus an up-and-coming London group called the Rolling Stones. Germany's Rattles had also been in the frame at one point, but in the event didn't make the final selection.

The Everlys were backed as before by their own trio — Don Peake (guitar), Joey Paige (bass) and Jim Gordon (drums) — and the opening night

audience at the New Victoria gave them an enthusiastic welcome back to Britain, seemingly pleased to see Don Everly looking fit and well again.

They opened strongly with 'Lucille' and stomped through 'Walk Right Back' and 'Wake Up Little Susie' before slowing the pace for 'Cathy's Clown'. The temperature rose again for 'Rip It Up' and 'Bye Bye Love' before they rounded off the night by alternating the mood between fast and slow: 'All I Have To Do Is Dream, 'Keep A-Knockin' ', 'So Sad' and a raucous 'Be-Bop-A-Lula'. It was a superbly polished performance.

Due to Musicians' Union restrictions, Bo Diddley had only been able to bring his maraca-player, Jerome Green, and his glamorous guitarist, Norma-Jean Wofford, otherwise known as 'The Duchess', so his backing was augmented by the Flintstones. The media — and, indeed, many of his fans — were fascinated by the Duchess, whose stage attire comprised a skin-tight gold lamé catsuit, and it was erroneously reported that she was Bo's sister. Diddley himself was no slouch in the fashion stakes either, appearing on *Thank Your Lucky Stars* in a gold brocade suit, the impact of which was sadly lost when viewed on black-and-white television.

His set was well-received throughout the tour, especially the song to which he gave his name, and it is fair to say that his style and stage act were immensely influential to the new breed of British bands, particularly the Rolling Stones and the Pretty Things. What is less easy to explain is why he was only allotted enough time to sing three songs each night on the tour. Surely a longer spot would have been justified for such an innovative and dynamic performer?

Despite critical acclaim for the package, advance ticket sales were worryingly slow and so it was announced that Little Richard would be added as a joint headliner. He flew into the UK on 4 October in time to appear at Watford the following night.

As usual with the erratic Mr. Penniman, nobody knew exactly what to expect. After his last British tour, he had vowed never to sing rock'n'roll again, but the Watford audience were greeted with 'Long Tall Sally', 'Rip It Up', 'Tutti Frutti' and 'Lucille'. By the time he'd got half-way through his act, Richard had already shed his jacket, shirt, tie and shoes, and was driving the fans into a frenzy with his antics: one minute leaping off the stage with the microphone in his hand, the next climbing on top of his piano. There could have been no better antidote for poor ticket sales, and indeed, the tour went

Bo and Duchess mime to 'Pretty Thing' on *Thank Your Lucky Stars.*

on to play to packed houses almost everywhere.

Bo, Jerome and the Duchess made three visits to London's R&B club, the Scene (where Guy Stevens was the resident deejay) and Bo sat in with the house band, much to the delight of the audience. A similar thing happened in Newcastle, where Jerome Green played and sang with the Alan Price Combo (soon to become the Animals) at the Club A Go Go.

Little Richard meanwhile continued to confuse everybody including himself, telling *Record Mirror*: 'I want people to forget me as a rock'n'roller. I'm going to be an evangelist like Billy Graham!'

Surprisingly, the Everly Brothers made no television appearances, claiming that their schedule was too tight to accommodate them. They were also not included in the booking for 28 October, when Richard headed up the package at the East Ham Granada. Bo, Jerome and the Duchess were also absent at East Ham, playing a club date in Manchester instead.

The Everlys were accompanied by their wives, Venetia and Jackie, and when the tour finally ended Don flew home straight away as Venetia was suffering with flu, while Phil stayed on to assist their bass-player, Joey Paige, who was recording a session at Decca Studios. (Paige, who had previously toured in the States with Dicky Doo & The Don'ts, had ambitions of a solo career. He remained in Britain for several weeks and landed a week of cabaret work in Manchester during December.)

TV appearances (Bo Diddley)

Thank Your Lucky Stars	22 September 1963 (screened 28 September 1963)
Scene at 6.30	24 September 1963
Ready Steady Go	27 September 1963
Juke Box Jury	28 September 1963 *(unconfirmed)*

DEL SHANNON

October 1963						
4	Lewisham	Odeon		20	Birmingham	Hippodrome
5	Southampton	Gaumont		21	Slough	Adelphi
6	Leicester	De Montfort Hall		23	Harrow	Granada
7	Walthamstow	Granada		24	Kingston	Granada
8	Huddersfield	ABC		25	Woolwich	Granada
9	Manchester	Apollo		26	Colchester	Odeon
11	Belfast	Adelphi		27	Luton	ABC
12	Bristol	Colston Hall		29	Maidstone	Granada
13	Coventry	Theatre		30	Croydon	ABC
15	Portsmouth	Guildhall		31	Cambridge	ABC
16	York	Rialto		**November 1963**		
17	Bolton	Odeon		1	Lincoln	ABC
18	Leeds	Odeon		2	Sunderland	Empire
19	Sheffield	City Hall		3	Liverpool	Empire
Promoter — Arthur Howes						

Several major tours took place in the autumn of 1963, but few of them passed off without incident. Del Shannon was scheduled to star alongside Jet Harris & Tony Meehan and Gerry & The Pacemakers for a month of theatre dates. However, disaster struck three weeks beforehand, when a chauffeur-driven car carrying Harris and singer Billie Davis hit a bus in Evesham, Worcestershire, injuring them both and forcing him to withdraw from the tour while his partner carried on billed as the 'Tony Meehan Combo'. The other supporting acts on the package were Duffy Power, Cilla Black, the Bachelors, the Blue Diamonds (who also backed Del Shannon) and compere Bryan Burdon. To make matters worse, Meehan subsequently fell ill and missed the first five nights, but despite such an inauspicious start the tour generally did well.

Gerry & The Pacemakers topped the bill, while Del Shannon closed the first half, but at Lewisham the lack of rehearsal time was noticeable, and there was little rapport between Shannon and his backing band. Nevertheless, he received a sympathetic reception for a set which contained a selection of his hits and — perhaps more surprisingly — a strong version of Conway Twitty's 'It's Only Make Believe'.

Arrangements were in hand for Del to remain in the UK for a further week so that he could tour Scotland, but this did not materialise and he flew back across the Atlantic to undertake an extensive Canadian tour with the Crystals instead.

TV appearances

Thank Your Lucky Stars	? October 1963 (screened 5 October 1963)
Ready Steady Go	25 October 1963

BILL HALEY & HIS COMETS

Bill Haley had overdosed on publicity at the time of his first British tour in February 1957, but had since slipped out of the news. Promoter Peter Walsh was reported to have set up a return visit for Haley and the Comets with the opening night at Dunstable on 5 October. Although the tour fell through, it was heartening to learn that plans were afoot for Haley to return to the UK in the near future.

JOHNNY CASH

October 1963	
10 Manchester	Astoria Irish
11 Camden Town	Irish Social
Promoter unknown	

Although many of Johnny Cash's Sun recordings had been released in Britain and he had been seen once on national television when guesting on *Boy Meets Girls* in 1959, he was still little known at the time of his first tour, which centred on Ireland plus several US military bases in the UK. Publicity was negligible for his British debut at the Astoria Irish Club, where Johnny was accompanied by the Tennessee Three — guitarist Luther Perkins, bass-player Marshall Grant and drummer W.S. 'Fluke' Holland. This was a quiet and inauspicious debut on British soil for the 'Man In Black' who would become a firm favourite with UK audiences in the years to come.

Johnny at the Irish Social Club, Manchester.

DEE DEE SHARP

October 1963		
19	Grantham	Granada
20	Bournemouth	Winter Gardens
21	Mansfield	Granada
22	Kettering	Granada
23	Bedford	Granada
24	Aylesbury	Granada
25	Greenford	Granada
27	Dartford	Granada
28	Edmonton	Granada
29	Rugby	Granada
30	Haslemere	Rex
31	Scunthorpe	Baths
November 1963		
1	Leyton	Baths
2	Malvern	Winter Gardens
3	Manchester	Top Ten

Promoter — George Cooper

Johnny Kidd & The Pirates, Heinz and Dee Dee Sharp were the mainstays of yet another rock'n'roll package, which varied in personnel from day to day but included Joe Brown, Vince Eager, the Big Three, Gerry & The Pacemakers and the Caravelles. Prior to the first show, Dee Dee confirmed her credentials: 'I'll be singing rock'n'roll numbers, and maybe a few gospel-influenced songs.'

At Edmonton, she looked stunning in a ravishing red evening dress with a pink cummerbund and sequined top. Backed by the Sundowners, she opened with a highly original interpretation of 'Twist And Shout' and worked through 'Do The Bird', 'Wild!' (her latest US hit), 'Cradle of Love' and 'Da Doo Ron Ron' before closing

GRANADA OCTOBER 1963

program one shilling

with an emotional 'Stand By Me', kneeling for part of the song on a darkened stage. She well deserved the cheers at the end of her act.

Three weeks of ballroom dates had been lined up for Dee Dee to follow her theatre commitments, but on 4 November she unexpectedly flew home when her grandmother was taken ill. Duffy Power replaced her at Norwich, and Bert Weedon at Croydon, which were the final two theatre bookings. It was confidently predicted that she would return, but eventually the ballroom dates were all scrapped. Her place on *Juke Box Jury* was taken by actress Jane Asher.

TV appearances
Ready Steady Go   18 October 1963

DION

October 1963			24	Manchester	Odeon
19	Finsbury Park	Astoria	25	Leeds	Odeon
20	Hammersmith	Odeon	26	Lewisham	Odeon
21	Luton	Odeon	27	Nottingham	Odeon
22	Cardiff	Capitol	28	Birmingham	Odeon
23	Liverpool	Odeon			
Promoter — Vic Lewis					

Dion was the only rock'n'roller among the five American acts who undertook a short tour which was confidently billed as *'The Greatest Record Show of 1963'.* He was billed under his full name — Dion di Mucci — as part of an attempt to portray a more mature image. His co-stars were Brook Benton, Timi Yuro, Lesley Gore and Trini Lopez. All were backed by the Ken Thorne Orchestra and the shows compered by Jerry Stevens. The tour was restricted to ten days because of Lesley Gore's school commitments.

Dion closed the first half but, at least at Finsbury Park, did not seem comfortable with the Thorne Orchestra. His material showed that he was anxious to change his image, but his vocal interpretation of a modern jazz standard, 'Moanin' ', contrasted awkwardly with 'Runaround Sue'. He really did not fare terribly well and looked ill at ease in his well-pressed tuxedo, and it was Benton and Lopez who proved the main successes of the package.

Timi Yuro stayed on in Britain for additional cabaret bookings, but was obliged to return home following a car wreck in the Midlands, which left her slightly injured.

TV appearances
Ready Steady Go   18 October 1963
Thank Your Lucky Stars   ? November 1963 (screened 9 November 1963)

JOHNNY BURNETTE

November 1963			8	East Grinstead	Whitehall
1	Handsworth	Plaza	9	Nelson	Imperial
2	Prestatyn	Royal Lido	11	Bridgwater	Town Hall
3	Southsea	Savoy	12	Cardiff	*unknown venue*
4	Reading	New Majestic	13	Hitchin	Hermitage
5	Kilburn	Gaumont State	15	Dunstable	California
6	Farnborough	Town Hall	16	Boston	Gliderdrome
7	Lowestoft	Royal Hotel	17	Manchester	Princess
Promoter — Roy Tempest					

Johnny Burnette's second tour was a very low-key affair. So low-key in fact, that years later many of his fans were still unaware that he had ever returned to the UK at all. The music press gave his visit scant coverage, and the dates that were announced seemed to be changed or contradicted elsewhere. This chaotic state of affairs would soon become a regular feature of British rock'n'roll tours. Fans would have to pay attention to even find out who was visiting the UK. Second-rate tours with second-rate organisation would soon become the order of the day for many years to come.

Johnny arrived in Britain bearing a painful black eye, which he had acquired while making an Australian TV appearance on the *Mike Walsh Show*. His fellow guest had been Bongo, the boxing kangaroo. Burnette, having boxed seriously in his youth, had been cajoled into trying his luck, only to receive a real battering from his marsupial opponent.

However, it is showbiz tradition that the show must go on, and by the time he took the stage at Kilburn in front of a small audience, there was little sign remaining of his facial injuries.

Backed by the Rebounds throughout the tour, Johnny appeared smartly dressed in a black, braid-edged suit and an open-necked white shirt. He opened with a driving version of 'Johnny B. Goode' followed by his hits, 'Dreamin'' and 'Little Boy Sad'. He then rocked his way through 'Bony Moronie' and two more of his own recordings, 'Big Big World' and 'Cincinnatti Fireball'. His closing number was another hit, 'You're Sixteen'. For his well-deserved encore, Burnette reached back to his days as vocalist with the Rock'n'Roll Trio and roared his way through a wild version of 'Tear It Up'.

There was to be no third tour by Johnny Burnette. Tragically, he drowned in a fishing accident on 14 August 1964.

TV appearances

Scene At 6.30	30 October 1963
Thank Your Lucky Stars	? November 1963 (screened 16 November 1963)
Five O'Clock Club	19 November 1963

TOMMY ROE

Tommy Roe's tour, which had started as far back as 13 September, seemed to be never-ending. Having completed his UK dates on 27 October, he was now working his way around Ireland and planning to undertake further theatre gigs in England from 8 November along with Dave Berry, Brian Poole & The Tremeloes and the Searchers. At the last minute, he pulled out and returned home, being replaced by Dusty Springfield.

DUANE EDDY
THE SHIRELLES
LITTLE RICHARD

November 1963					
9	Edmonton	Regal	14	Kingston	Granada
10	Woolwich	Granada	15	Stockton	ABC
11	Harrow	Granada	16	Brixton	Astoria
13	Cardiff	Sophia Gardens	17	Southend	Odeon
Promoter — Don Arden					

There had been several abortive attempts to bring Duane Eddy back to Britain following his successful tour in March 1960, but invariably problems arose with the Musicians' Union over the inclusion of his band, the Rebels.

Recording at Granada.

The most recent attempt had been engineered by promoter Arthur Howes for a tour in October 1963, but this failed when an exchange agreement for the Rebels could not be secured.

It was, therefore, something of a surprise when rival promoter Don Arden announced that both Duane and the Rebels were to be included in his latest package, and that an exchange deal had been finalised whereby the virtually unknown Malcolm Mitchell & His Trio would work in New York for the duration of the period that the Rebels were in the UK. Subsequent events revealed that Arden's optimism had been somewhat premature, but Eddy and his Rebels — Al Casey (bass), Jim Horn (sax) and Bob Taylor (drums) — flew into Britain in early November, where they were joined by a second saxophone player, British sessionman Rex Morris (a former member of Lord Rockingham's XI).

Little Richard had remained in the UK following the conclusion of the Everlys–Diddley tour and was joined by the Shirelles, who were making their first appearance over here. Both Richard and the Shirelles were backed by the Flintstones, while Mickie Most, the Roof-Raisers and compere Ray Cameron completed the package.

Granada Television recorded a 45-minute special on 8 November starring Richard and also featuring the Shirelles. It proved immensely popular when it was screened a couple of months later, and remains an exciting reminder of just how good the exasperating Mr. Penniman could be when focusing all his attention on rock'n'roll.

The tour experienced more than its share of difficulties, commencing

The Shirelles with their guitarist, Joe Richardson.

on the opening night at Edmonton, where Duane Eddy could not appear for the first house because his group's instruments and equipment had been delayed arriving from Europe. Nevertheless, when he and the Rebels finally appeared for the late show, they were rewarded with a tremendous reception. The audience were supplied with a feast of twang as they worked through the familiar titles, 'Detour', 'Cannonball' and 'Peter Gunn'. Duane introduced 'Some Kinda Earthquake' as 'a tender love song' and continued the instrumental assault with 'Shazam!' and 'Forty Miles Of Bad Road'. The pace dropped for 'The Lonely One' and the jazz-flavoured '3.30 Blues', before a rocking finale with 'Hard Times' and 'Rebel-Rouser'. He accepted four curtain calls.

Earlier in the proceedings, the Shirelles had earned their own share of the applause. Shirley Alston, Doris Kenner, Beverly Lee and Micki Harris were wearing black dresses with Cinderella-style flared hems and opened their act with 'Everybody Loves A Lover'. Doris and Shirley alternated on lead vocals while the other girls chanted in harmony close by. Their big hit, 'Will You Love Me Tomorrow' went over well, as did 'Tonight's The Night'. They increased the tempo for 'Twist And Shout' and closed with 'When The Saints Go Marching In', during which their musical director and guitarist, Joe Richardson (who also sat in with the Flintstones during Little Richard's set) jumped around with some way-out movements. The four girls finished off with a high-stepping dance routine, which brought whistles and cheers as they left the stage.

Little Richard himself was likewise in fantastic form, performing a typical selection of his rock'n'roll classics. During a thirteen-minute workout on 'Whole Lotta Shakin' Goin' On', he stripped to the waist and at one point

149

leapt on top of the piano. He closed with 'Good Golly Miss Molly' to a tumultuous wave of stamping and cheering.

On the fourth night of the tour, it became clear that the problems with work permits were far from settled. The Rebels were forbidden to appear, and the audience at Cardiff were baffled by the sight of Duane Eddy coming on stage with only an acoustic guitar. He performed just three songs, 'Scarlet Ribbons', 'Streets of Laredo' and his own 'Along Came Linda', that night. On some subsequent shows, the Rebels were replaced by the British combo, the Hi-Fi's.

As if there were not enough problems already, Little Richard left the tour before the Kingston show and returned to the States. The temperamental Mr. Penniman had injured his ankle and went home for treatment. Quite what medical condition necessitated this action is unclear, but the demand for urgent attention seemed especially curious when he declined to fly and left by ship for New York on 15 November.

Gene Vincent stepped in to replace Richard at Kingston, while Jimmy Justice took over at Stockton and Southend. Joey Paige, ex-bass player for the Everlys, was also drafted in to shore up the ailing tour. At this point, Duane flew to Paris for a concert appearance on 19 November, providing Don Arden with a little breathing space to lick his wounds and regroup.

TV appearance (Little Richard and the Shirelles)
It's Little Richard!   8 November 1963 (screened 8 January 1964)

GENE VINCENT

November 1963			December 1963		
9	Putney	St. Mary's Hall	7	Eccles	New Majestic
14	Kingston	Granada	12	Birmingham	Town Hall
Promoter — Don Arden					

Gene finished the year as part of the Duane Eddy–Shirelles package, but did also slip in a few other dates. His appearance at Putney was his first with a new backing group, the Shouts. At Kingston, he was a late replacement for the ailing Little Richard. His booking at the New Majestic in Eccles was as part of the grand opening weekend for a new club, where he was again teamed with the Outlaws. At Birmingham Town Hall, he starred alongside Johnny Kidd & The Pirates on a sizeable bill that also included Heinz, Wayne Fontana & The Mindbenders and the Rockin' Berries.

TV appearances
Thank Your Lucky Stars   ? December 1963 (screened 14 December 1963)
Discs A-Go-Go   30 December 1963

BOBBY RYDELL

November 1963			December 1963		
10	Peterborough	Embassy	1	Liverpool	Empire
12	Cambridge	ABC	4	Exeter	ABC
13	York	Rialto	5	Plymouth	ABC
15	Croydon	ABC	6	Luton	ABC
16	Southampton	Gaumont	7	Bournemouth	Winter Gardens
19	Nottingham	Odeon	8	Birmingham	Hippodrome
20	Doncaster	Gaumont	9	Manchester	Plaza
21	Scarborough	Futurist	10	Bristol	Colston Hall
22	Sheffield	City Hall	11	Wolverhampton	Gaumont
23	Slough	Adelphi	12	Manchester	Apollo
24	Ipswich	Gaumont	13	Stockton	ABC
26	Romford	Ritz	14	Leeds	Odeon
27	Kingston	ABC	15	Hull	ABC
29	Belfast	ABC			
30	Blackpool	Opera House			

Promoter — Arthur Howes

Presented by Arthur Howes

HELEN SHAPIRO BOBBY RYDELL

Souvenir Programme

Bobby Rydell arrived in Britain for the Royal Premiere of his movie, *Bye Bye Birdie*, at the Odeon, Marble Arch on 7 November. Although he played the part of a rock'n'roll singer in the film, he seemed anxious to stress his all-round talents whilst in Britain, clearly looking towards a career in films and cabaret.

He was billed second to Helen Shapiro on a package that also included the Spotniks, the Chants, the Harlems, the Trebletones and compere Alan Field. Each night also featured a guest star (or stars), who varied from venue to venue. These included Brian Poole & The Tremeloes, Heinz, the Fourmost, the Searchers and the Hollies.

At Cambridge, Rydell closed the first half with a solid set which included 'Wild One', 'Sway', 'Forget Him' and 'Volare'. He surprised the audience by playing drums on 'C Jam Blues', and closed with 'When The Saints Go Marching In'.

TV appearances

Thank Your Lucky Stars	10 November 1963 (screened 23 November 1963)
Sunday Night At The London Palladium	17 November 1963
They've Sold A Million	? November 1963 (screened 5 February 1964)
Five O'Clock Club	26 November 1963

DUANE EDDY
THE SHIRELLES
GENE VINCENT
GARY 'US' BONDS

November 1963					
20	Sheffield	City Hall	25	Luton	Odeon
21	Croydon	Fairfield Halls	26	Liverpool	Odeon
22	Lewisham	Gaumont	27	Leeds	Odeon
23	Bournemouth	Winter Gardens	28	Manchester	Odeon
24	Leicester	De Montfort Hall	29	Birmingham	Odeon
			30	Glasgow	Odeon
Promoter — Don Arden					

Duane Eddy returned from Paris and the package rolled back onto the road with the addition of Carter–Lewis & The Southerners — another new band which included both Jimmy Page and Viv Prince in their line-up. Despite the attraction of three American acts, advance bookings were still causing concern, so Gary 'US' Bonds was drafted in to join the tour, arriving in time to appear at Leicester. There was now so much interest in the British beat groups that the Americans were really feeling the pinch. Even with four heavyweight acts paired together, it was a struggle to move the tickets in sufficient quantity.

FAIRFIELD HALLS - CROYDON
General Manager   T. J. PYPER, M.I.M.E.M.   Phone - CROydon 929
6.45 – THURSDAY, NOVEMBER 21st – 8.50
TWO PERFORMANCES ONLY

ON THE STAGE FOR ONE DAY ONLY
DON ARDEN ENTERPRISES LTD. presents

DUANE EDDY
THE SHIRELLES
CARTER LEWIS & THE SOUTHERNERS

| THE FLINTSTONES | MICKIE MOST ★ RAY CAMERON | THE ROOF-RAISERS |

SPECIAL GUEST ARTISTE
GENE VINCENT

TICKETS :   10/6   8/6   7/6   5/-
From Fairfield Halls Booking Office - Tel. CROydon 9291

GARY 'US' BONDS

December 1963		
1	Manchester	Princess
	Manchester	Domino
15	Manchester	Empress
Promoter — Don Arden		

Gary 'US' Bonds remained behind after the Duane Eddy package finally came to an end. His presence in Britain was totally ignored by the music media — no interviews, no publicity, no television — although he possibly filled in the days between his Manchester gigs with some promotional appearances in Europe.

CHAPTER NINE

1964

Need A Shot Of Rhythm & Blues

1964 was the year when Britain discovered the blues. Up to this point, the few bluesmen who did visit the UK — such as Muddy Waters and Jimmy Rushing — did so off the back of the jazz club circuit, touring with the likes of Chris Barber or Humphrey Lyttleton. The Beatles, and to an even greater extent the Rolling Stones, introduced to a wider British audience all manner of delightfully obscure black artists and aroused in at least some of the record-buying public a curiosity to look beyond the cover version and check out the real thing.

This commendable state of affairs presented fresh opportunities for several bluesmen who were otherwise merely marking time back home, and amongst the names who toured Britain during the year were Sonny Boy Williamson, John Lee Hooker, Jimmy Reed, Jimmy Witherspoon, Little Walter and Howlin' Wolf. (It is interesting to contrast this with the almost total lack of interest in country music. It was rarely written about, and no C&W artists of note visited Britain at all in 1964, with the exception of a brief promotional trip by Skeeter Davis and a short club tour by Hank Locklin.)

Where did all this leave rock'n'roll? The answer is: nowhere. The very name 'rock'n'roll' was now totally out of vogue, and any performer wishing to survive had to discard such an outdated label and get with it. The solution proved to be 'R&B' — rhythm and blues. This wonderful new music that was modern and vibrant and alive and very much the latest thing was *the* sound of 1964. Don't look so disinterested. Chuck Berry and Bo Diddley are 'R&B', so is Carl Perkins, and probably Bill Haley as well... it is only a label after all is said and done.

GENE VINCENT

January 1964			February 1964		
4	Cirencester	Bingham Hall	3	Kingsley	Victoria
7	Sheffield	Saints	6	Liverpool	Locarno
11	Lowestoft	South Pier	12	Bristol	Corn Exchange
17	Wimbledon	Palais	14	Hounslow	Baths
18	Burnley	Casino	16	Kingston	Cellar
23	Stockbridge	Club	22	Loughborough	Town Hall
24	Edmonton	Continental	28	Leicester	Granby Hall
25	Bristol	University	29	East Grinstead	Whitehall
			March 1964		
			7	Orpington	Civic Halls
Promoter — Don Arden					

The changing face of popular music had made little impression on Gene Vincent. Backed by the Shouts, he continued to perform a solid rock'n'roll show and to draw healthy crowds wherever he appeared. By the standards of later years, his sets were short — rarely exceeding ten songs.

His show at the Wimbledon Palais was typical. Dressed in his familiar black leather suit, Gene opened with 'Say Mama' and 'Good Golly Miss Molly', interspersed two of his more recent recordings, 'La-Den-Da-Den-Da-Da' and 'Where Have You Been', then accelerated into 'She She Little Sheila'. A slow, plaintive rendition of 'Lavender Blue' led into 'Be-Bop-A-Lula' and he closed out with 'You Are My Sunshine'.

Seven weeks later at Orpington, his act had changed to include 'Rocky Road Blues', 'Rip It Up', 'I'm Going Home' and 'Long Tall Sally', but was still unashamedly rock'n'roll, making no concessions to the latest trends. He may have been swimming against the tide, but his loyal fans loved him for it.

On 7 March, Gene made one of his rare television appearances (singing the woeful 'Humpity Dumpty'), and the following day flew on to Paris for more shows with the Shouts.

TV appearances
Thank Your Lucky Stars   ? March 1964 (screened 7 March 1964)

THE RONETTES

January 1964					
5	Haslemere	Rex	15	Bedford	Granada
6	Harrow	Granada	17	Nuneaton	Co-op
7	Slough	Adelphi	18	Malvern	Winter Gardens
8	Maidstone	Granada	19	Coventry	Theatre
9	Kettering	Granada	20	Woolwich	Granada
10	Walthamstow	Granada	21	Lowestoft	South Pier
11	Old Hill	Plaza	22	Shrewsbury	Granada
	Handsworth	Plaza	24	Dundee	Caird Hall
12	Tooting	Granada	25	Paisley	Town Hall
14	Mansfield	Granada	26	Leicester	De Montfort Hall
			27	Bristol	Colston Hall
Promoter — George Cooper					

British audiences had never experienced an act quite like the Ronettes, who co-starred with the Rolling Stones on the first package tour of

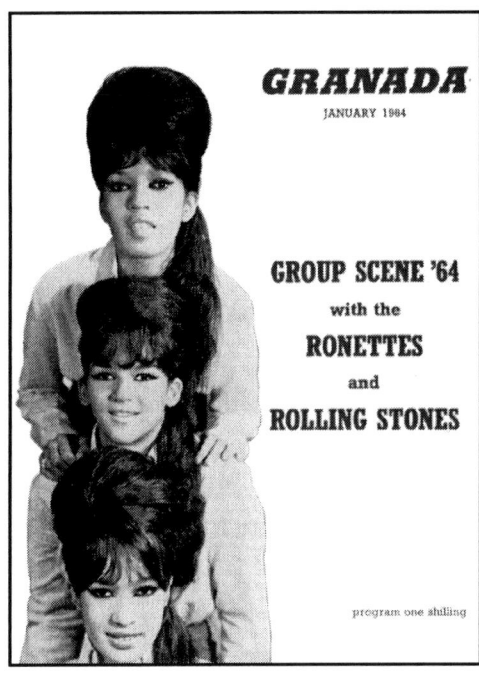

GRANADA

JANUARY 1964

GROUP SCENE '64

with the

RONETTES

and

ROLLING STONES

program one shilling

1964. Ronnie Bennett, her older sister Estelle and their cousin, Nedra Talley, were the first exponents of the Phil Spector Sound to visit the UK. It may not have been possible to faithfully re-create on stage Spector's incredible 'Wall Of Sound', but the girls served up a dynamic, exciting and sexy act that had every red-blooded male in the audience yelling for more, long before the end of the show.

At Harlow, the three girls ran on stage wearing diamante-encrusted pale orange sheath dresses, which were split high up the side so that their long legs were clearly visible as they sang and danced 'The Twist'. Ronnie moved around the stage with a hand-mike while the other two harmonised on 'Be My Baby'. This was followed by 'Everybody Loves A Lover' and 'Will You Love Me Tomorrow', Esther singing lead on the latter. The Cheynes provided steady backing throughout and with all three girls dancing provocatively around the stage during 'Baby I Love You' the audience were at fever pitch. They encored with the ever-popular 'What'd I Say', finishing up with an even sexier dance across the stage which nearly provoked a riot.

The package did brisk business around the theatres, and featured popular support from Marty Wilde & The Wildcats, the Swinging Blue Jeans, Dave Berry & The Cruisers and compere Al Paige. In addition, various guest artists were added to the bill, and each night different combinations of Johnny Kidd & The Pirates, Joe Brown & The Bruvvers, Freddie & The Dreamers and Bern Elliott & The Fenmen appeared alongside the regulars.

Ronnie and Estelle were accompanied on the tour by their mother, who acted as chaperone. Phil Spector himself flew into Britain on 23 January for interviews and television appearances.

TV appearances

Ready Steady Go	3 January 1964
Thank Your Lucky Stars	*?* January 1964 (screened 25 January 1964)
They've Sold A Million	29 January 1964
Crackerjack	*?* January 1964

BEN E. KING

February 1964			20	Glasgow	Odeon
8	Nottingham	Odeon	21	Stockton	Globe
9	Liverpool	Empire	22	Newcastle	City Hall
10	Walthamstow	Gaumont	23	Scarborough	Futurist
11	Gloucester	ABC	25	Bedford	Granada
12	Cardiff	Capitol	26	Cleethorpes	ABC
13	Exeter	ABC	27	Doncaster	Gaumont
14	Plymouth	ABC	28	Northampton	ABC
15	Bournemouth	Winter Gardens	29	East Ham	Granada
16	Brighton	Hippodrome	**March 1964**		
18	Chesterfield	ABC	1	Leicester	De Montfort Hall
19	Carlisle	ABC			

Promoter — Arthur Howes

The first British tour by Ben E. King came as support act for Gerry & The Pacemakers. The ex-Drifter subsequently became a regular in the UK dancehalls throughout the Sixties and Seventies with an act that moved away from rock'n'roll and into the soul field, although he has often returned to his roots as one of the most well-respected of the Drifters' lead vocalists.

For his initial look at British audiences, Ben was backed by the ever-reliable Sounds Incorporated, while the remainder of the package comprised the Fourmost, Tommy Quickly, the Dennisons and compere Jimmy Tarbuck, but it was Gerry & The Pacemakers that the majority of the fans had come to see. King had the difficult task of preceding the Pacemakers, and on the opening night at Nottingham, Gerry's supporters made it clear that they were becoming impatient to see their favourite. His arrival on stage was greeted with little enthusiasm, but his opening number, 'Amor', was at least politely received. However, the Drifters classic, 'Save The Last Dance For Me', won them over and screams could even be heard during 'I Could Have Danced All Night'. King finished his short set with a punchy gospel version of 'You Are My Sunshine'.

TV appearances

Ready Steady Go	7 February 1964
Thank Your Lucky Stars	? February 1964 (screened 22 February 1964)

THE CRYSTALS

February 1964					
16	Coventry	Theatre	8	Leicester	De Montfort Hall
17	Finsbury Park	Astoria	9	Stockton	Odeon
18	Luton	Odeon	10	Sunderland	Odeon
19	Bradford	Gaumont	11	York	Rialto
20	Bolton	Odeon	12	Scarborough	Futurist
21	Blackburn	Odeon	13	Woolwich	Granada
22	Blackpool	Opera House	14	Southampton	Gaumont
23	Liverpool	Empire	15	Birmingham	Hippodrome
24	Derby	Gaumont	16	Edinburgh	Usher Hall
25	Wolverhampton	Gaumont	17	Glasgow	Kelvin Hall
26	Worcester	Gaumont	18	Dundee	Caird Hall
27	Cheltenham	Odeon	19	Kettering	Granada
28	Bournemouth	Winter Gardens	20	Bristol	Colston Hall
March 1964			21	Slough	Adelphi
1	Portsmouth	Guildhall	22	Walthamstow	Granada
2	Kingston	Granada	23	Cardiff	Sophia Gardens
3	Chelmsford	Odeon	24	Stoke	Essoldo
4	Tunbridge Wells	Essoldo	25	Stockport	Essoldo
5	Guildford	Odeon	26	Mansfield	Granada
6	Harrow	Granada	27	Brighton	Essoldo
7	Norwich	Gaumont	28	Ipswich	Gaumont

Promoter — Larry Parnes

Hot on the heels of the Ronettes came the second Phil Spector-produced group to tour the UK. The Crystals — in the shape of Barbara Alston, Dee Dee Kennibrew, Lala Brooks and Frances Collins — were the main support to Joe Brown & The Bruvvers on a lengthy package titled *Your Lucky Stars*, which also featured Johnny Kidd & The Pirates, Heinz & The Saints, Mike Preston, Daryl Quist, the Sundowners, Kevin Kirk and compere Al Paige. Yet another new hit group, Manfred Mann, performed their own set as well as backing the Crystals.

The girls were greeted with wolf whistles when they ran on stage on the opening night at Coventry clad in tight black lace mini-skirts, and went straight into an energetic hip-shaking dance during 'Twistin' The Night Away'. The pace dropped for a faithful rendition of 'Then He Kissed Me', which drew enthusiastic applause, as did their latest single, 'I Wonder'. They then belted out a stirring 'He's A Rebel' before losing their way slightly with a limp version of the Beatles' 'From Me To You'. Although their performance had been somewhat marred by sound problems, with much of the vocal harmony being drowned out by the accompaniment, the girls finished strongly, bringing their short set to a close with a knockout 'Da Doo Ron Ron'.

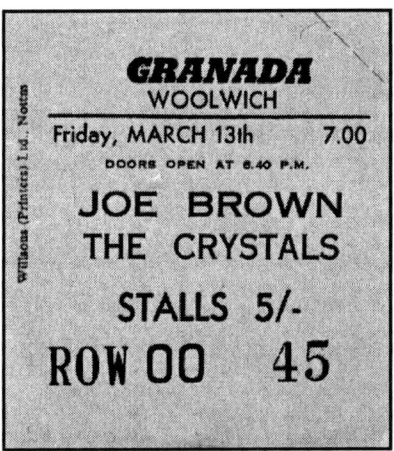

GRANADA
WOOLWICH
Friday, MARCH 13th   7.00
DOORS OPEN AT 6.40 P.M.
JOE BROWN
THE CRYSTALS
STALLS 5/-
ROW OO   45

TV appearances

They've Sold A Million	12 February 1964 (screened 8 April 1964)
Thank Your Lucky Stars	? February 1964 (screened 15 February 1964)
Ready Steady Go	14 February 1964

BOBBY VEE

February 1964			15	Bristol	Colston Hall
29	Slough	Adelphi	16	Cardiff	Capitol
March 1964			17	Worcester	Gaumont
1	Walthamstow	Granada	18	Birmingham	Odeon
2	Maidstone	Granada	19	Nottingham	Odeon
3	Kettering	Granada	20	East Ham	Granada
4	Ipswich	Odeon	21	Bournemouth	Winter Gardens
5	Manchester	Odeon	22	Leicester	De Montfort Hall
6	Mansfield	Granada	23	Kingston	Granada
7	Sheffield	City Hall	24	Doncaster	Gaumont
8	Hanley	Gaumont	25	Stockton	Odeon
9	Bolton	Odeon	26	Glasgow	Odeon
11	Leeds	Odeon	27	Aberdeen	Capitol
12	Bedford	Granada	28	Newcastle	City Hall
13	Southend	Odeon	29	Liverpool	Empire
14	Tooting	Granada			

Promoter — Peter Walsh

The third Bobby Vee tour found him no longer topping the bill, but providing the main support for the Searchers as part of a package that also included Dusty Springfield, the Echoes, Suzy Cope, Alan Davison, the Diamonds (who backed Vee), compere Tony Marsh, and another American, Big Dee Irwin. Agent Tito Burns had given Irwin a big build-up by describing him as 'a R&B artist in the style of Little Richard and Chuck Berry' — which was enough to grab the attention of the rock'n'roll enthusiasts. However, Big Dee turned out to be a big disappointment, having little connection with either rock'n'roll or R&B, serving up a pop-cabaret act that even included a bizarre take-off of Shirley Bassey.

Bobby Vee closed the first half throughout the tour with his usual polished act. Opening with a snappy version of 'Someday', he ran through a selection of his hits and also accompanied himself on acoustic guitar for 'Buddy's Song'. For the climax of his set, he performed two Holly numbers: the melancholy 'Raining In My Heart' and a belting version of 'Oh Boy!'.

Rock'n'roll fans remained fiercely divided over Vee. His pop-rock'n'roll was a long way from the excesses of Vincent or Lewis, and his rather soppy stage presence was far from everybody's taste.

TV appearances

Thank Your Lucky Stars	? February 1964 (screened 29 February 1964)
Scene At 6.30	? March 1964
Juke Box Jury	14 March 1964
Ready Steady Go	20 March 1964

GENE VINCENT

March 1964		
13	Kendal	*unknown venue*
14	Bletchley	Wilton Hall
21	Cardiff	Sophia Gardens
28	Southall	Community Centre

April 1964		
1	Bristol	Cresta
10	Birmingham	West End
11	Colwyn Bay	Pier
12	Rochdale	Pyramid
16	Birkenhead	Majestic
17	West Hartlepool	Town Hall
18	Catford	Savoy

Promoter — Don Arden

GRANADA TV MANCHESTER 3

invites you to a

WHOLE LOTTA' SHAKIN' GOIN' ON

with

JERRY LEE LEWIS

and

GENE VINCENT

THURSDAY, MAR. 19th. Doors 7-30 p.m.
No admittance after 8 o'clock

DRESS — Leathers, sweaters, shades, no ties.

GRANADA TV CENTRE Manchester 3 DEA 7211

Gene Vincent returned on 13 March from a short visit to France and went straight up to Kendal where he and the Shouts were back to business as usual. Although rarely included in his stage act, Gene was still flogging the hopeless 'Humpity Dumpity' when he made another of his infrequent television appearances on *Five O'Clock Club*.

The constant grind of travelling was not without its problems either. The Midlands-based Shouts got disastrously lost in East London on 29 March, and a gig at the 99 Club in Hackney had to be cancelled when they failed to show. Gene again flew out to Paris on 19 April.

TV appearances

Whole Lotta Shakin' Goin' On	19 March 1964 (screened 30 September 1964)
Five O'Clock Club	20 March 1964

JERRY LEE LEWIS

March 1964		
20	Birmingham	Town Hall
21	Newcastle	Club A Go Go
22	West Ham	Baths
23	Bloxwich	Baths
23	West Bromwich	Adelphi
24	Glasgow	Kelvin Hall
25	York	Rialto

26	Kingston	Cellar
27	Swadlincote	Rink
28	Coventry	Matrix Hall
29	Manchester	Belle Vue
April 1964		
2	Harrow	Beat City
3	Hereford	Hillside

Promoter — Don Arden

So much praise had been lavished on the Little Richard TV special after it was first shown in January, that it was inevitable that his great rival, Jerry Lee Lewis would be lined up for a similar project at the earliest opportunity.

When Lewis returned to Britain in March for a fortnight of mainly ballroom gigs, he'd hardly stepped off the plane before he was whisked off to the Granada studios in Manchester to tele-record a 45-minute spectacular, *Whole Lotta Shakin' Goin' On*, backed by the Nashville Teens. Gene Vincent

Shake it, baby, shake it!

and the Animals were also included in the production, which opened with the thunderous roar of five gleaming motor cycles accelerating on to the set, but it was Jerry Lee who stole the show with a frenzied performance that climaxed with him in full flight, his blond locks hanging in disarray as he belted out 'Whole Lotta Shakin' Goin' On' from on top of the piano as all around him the fans went crazy. Rock'n'roll may have become marginalised as far as mainstream pop music was concerned, but it still retained a substantial following — as was demonstrated when a reported fifteen million listeners tuned in to hear Lewis on *Saturday Club*.

Kicking off his tour at Birmingham Town Hall, Jerry Lee and the Nashville Teens topped the bill over seven contemporary groups including the Animals, the Rockin' Berries and the Flintstones. The show was completely Lewis', and two thousand screaming fans clamoured for more whenever he ended a song. As well as all his regular numbers, he included 'I'm On Fire' in his act, at one point placing his boot on the keyboard and crouching low over the piano before leaping to his feet with a wild scream. 'What'd I Say' was introduced with the promise: 'If you can't shake to this one, you can't shake it at all!' The 45-minute set finished once again with Lewis on top of the piano, his hair all over his face, shaking hands with the fans who were swarming onto the stage while at the same time belting out the lyrics to 'Hound Dog'. His performances on the other dates were reported to have been equally dynamic.

Shortly before departing for Hamburg on 4 April, he told *NME*'s Richard Green: 'Jerry ain't never gonna stop rockin'. They offered me a spot on a TV show in America if I would just go up there and do a number like Bobby Darin does. I told them to...'

TV appearances

Whole Lotta Shakin' Goin' On	19 March 1964 (screened 30 September 1964)
Scene At 6.30	19 March 1964 (screened 20 March 1964)

ROY ORBISON

April 1964			May 1964		
18	Slough	Adelphi	1	Southend	Odeon
19	Walthamstow	Granada	2	Tooting	Granada
20	Harrow	Granada	3	Coventry	Theatre
21	Southampton	Gaumont	4	Bedford	Granada
22	Kingston	Granada	5	Worcester	Gaumont
24	Bristol	Colston Hall	6	Birmingham	Odeon
25	East Ham	Granada	7	Doncaster	Gaumont
26	Leicester	De Montfort Hall	8	Sheffield	City Hall
27	Croydon	Fairfield Halls	9	Bolton	Odeon
28	Hanley	Gaumont	10	Liverpool	Empire
29	Ipswich	Gaumont	11	Manchester	Odeon
30	Nottingham	Gaumont	12	Leeds	Odeon
			14	Glasgow	Odeon
			15	Stockton	Odeon
			16	Newcastle	City Hall
			17	London	Prince of Wales
Promoters — Tito Burns and Peter Walsh					

The extent of Roy Orbison's popularity in Britain can be gauged by the fact that this was his third major tour within a year, and on this occasion he was deemed strong enough to headline an extensive package that also featured Freddie & The Dreamers, Tony Sheridan, Wayne Fontana & The Mindbenders, the Bobby Patrick Big Six, Chris Sandford & The Coronets, the Three Quarters, Ezz Reco & The Launchers and compere Glen Mason.

Roy was backed by the Federals augmented by session pianist Barry Booth, and by his American drummer, Paul Carrigan. Two drum kits on stage each night, along with girl trio the Three Quarters adding harmony vocals, plus even a trumpet and violins on some numbers, guaranteed a big sound as Roy worked through his hits including 'It's Over', which climbed to the No. 1 slot on the British charts during June. This was a very successful and happy period for Orbison, who had arrived early in Britain with his wife and one of his sons. They rented a flat in Westminster and spent several days sightseeing.

Almost without exception, the theatres were well attended, and audience reaction very positive. Freddie & The Dreamers were replaced by Brian Poole & The Tremeloes at Southend and Worcester, and Wayne Fontana by Dave Berry at Sheffield. On the afternoon of Sunday, 26 April, Roy appeared at the *NME Poll Winners' Concert* at Wembley, where he presented Joe Brown with an award for *'Top Vocal Personality'*. The package finally terminated at Newcastle, but Roy stayed on for an additional show at the Prince of Wales Theatre in London, where he appeared with Eden Kane, the Vernons Girls and Cliff Bennett at a special Sunday night concert promoted by Brian Epstein.

TV appearances

Ready Steady Go	17 April 1964
Thank Your Lucky Stars	2 May 1964
Scene At 6.30	11 May 1964

GENE VINCENT

April 1964				18	Liverpool	Warrel
22	Preston	Astoria		19	Wolverhampton	Civic Hall
23	Grays	*unknown venue*		21	Birmingham	Town Hall
24	Ashford	Corn Exchange		22	Weedon	New Hall
25	Abergavenny	Town Hall		23	Nantwich	Civic Hall
May 1964				25	Woolwich	Granada
1	Bath	Regency		29	Bridlington	Spa
6	Wolverhampton	Civic Hall		30	Loughborough	Town Hall
8	Welling	St. Michael's		31	Hammersmith	Odeon
10	Bristol	Colston Hall				
Promoter — Don Arden						

The spring of 1964 was a quiet time for Gene Vincent. Returning from France to the usual mixed bag of ballroom dates with the Shouts, he found his previously hectic schedule finally easing down, with much of his live work being restricted to weekends. Nevertheless, he remained busy, laying down tracks for his *Shakin' Up A Storm* album at the Olympic Sound Studios in London and playing high-profile gigs at Woolwich and Hammersmith (where he appeared alongside Chuck Berry and Carl Perkins) and at Birmingham (where he was teamed up with Little Richard).

TV appearances
Juke Box Jury   30 May 1964

LITTLE RICHARD
DON & DEWEY

May 1964				16	Lowestoft	Royal Hotel
9	Coventry	Matrix Hall		17	Nelson	Imperial
10	Manchester	Oasis		18	Belfast	Boom Boom
11	Bath	Pavilion		21	Birmingham	Town Hall
13	Crewe	Town Hall		23	Lincoln	Drill Hall
	Stoke	King's Hall			Scunthorpe	Drill Hall
14	Scarborough	Spa Hall		26	Wimbledon	Palais
15	Birkenhead	Plaza				
Promoter — Don Arden						

Little Richard's profile in the UK had been significantly raised by his sensational performance on the Granada TV special that was first screened on 8 January, and subsequently repeated on several other occasions. It had been publicised as his farewell performance before he retired for a second time to devote his life to religion, but few of his fans took this very seriously, especially as he had only recently been back in the studio cutting five brand new rock'n'roll numbers for Specialty Records in California.

He was scheduled to arrive on 8 May for his third British tour, opening on the same night at the Wimbledon Palais as well as making a TV appearance on ABC-TV's trendsetting *Ready Steady Go*. At the last minute, however, he discovered that his passport had expired and he had to travel to New York to obtain a new one, thereby delaying his arrival by twenty-four

Little Richard preaches the gospel at the Oasis Club, Manchester.

hours. When he did make his rescheduled appearance on *Ready Steady Go* later in the month, he caused a stir by refusing to mime — the usual format for the show — and insisting on performing live. It is certainly hard to imagine a dynamic and unpredictable entertainer like Little Richard ever feeling comfortable lip-synching to a record.

On his ballroom dates, Richard was backed by the Flintstones and guitarist Glenn Willings, along with Don 'Sugarcane' Harris and Dewey Terry, two of the musicians who had played on his recent record session. Don & Dewey were themselves Specialty recording artists, but in the UK were completely unknown and unbilled.

For his appearance at the new Oasis Club in Manchester, Richard included all five of his new songs, most notable of which was the explosive 'Bama Lama Bama Loo'. There were no gospel tunes. It was vintage Penniman rock'n'roll, the only difference being that he had dispensed with saxophones and replaced them with a much more guitar-based sound.

Half-way through the tour, Don & Dewey were awarded their own spot in addition to backing Richard. Music historian Bill Millar attended the rearranged Wimbledon gig and was amazed to see two wild-looking black men bound onto the stage dressed in salmon pink suits. They performed for only fifteen minutes, opening with their own 'Farmer John' and continuing with 'Shout' and 'What'd I Say'. Leaping around the stage in demented fashion throughout their supercharged act, they made an enormous impression on the audience, most of whom had never even heard of them before.

They were the perfect apéritif for what was to follow. Little Richard was on top form. Dressed in a turquoise suit with white ruffled shirt and silver shoes, he tore through his hits and also featured 'You Are My Sunshine',

'Baby What You Want Me To Do' and 'I Got A Woman' along with his expected itinerary.

Following his British tour, Richard travelled to Paris, where he appeared before a packed house at the Olympia. The show sparked a riot during which windows were smashed and more than fifty seats broken.

TV appearances
Ready Steady Go   22 May 1964

CHUCK BERRY
CARL PERKINS

May 1964					
9	Finsbury Park	Astoria	21	Croydon	ABC
10	Hammersmith	Odeon	22	Manchester	Odeon
11	Birmingham	Town Hall	23	Newcastle	City Hall
12	Nottingham	Odeon	24	Leicester	De Montfort Hall
13	Stockton	Globe	25	Woolwich	Granada
14	Sheffield	City Hall	26	Bolton	Odeon
15	Bradford	Gaumont	27	Glasgow	Odeon
16	Bournemouth	Winter Gardens	28	Bristol	Colston Hall
17	Liverpool	Odeon	29	Southend	Odeon
18	Southampton	Gaumont	30	Tottenham	Club Noreik
19	Plymouth	ABC		London	Beat City
20	Exeter	Savoy	31	Hammersmith	Odeon
Promoter — Don Arden					

Chuck Berry, one of the greatest rock'n'rollers, flew into London on 9 May to commence his first British tour. As the R&B craze had gathered momentum, Chuck's music had become increasingly fashionable and he arrived amid a blaze of publicity. He was still singing the same songs in the same way as he had a decade earlier at the beginning of his career, but now he was no longer spoken of as a 'rock'n'roller', but as the 'King of Rhythm & Blues'. A succession of British beat groups — not least the Beatles and the Rolling Stones — were performing and recording his songs, and now at last the man himself had crossed the Atlantic to accept the plaudits.

More surprisingly, Don

Arden also signed up Carl Perkins as one of the support acts. Perkins' career, which had promised so much when his 'Blue Suede Shoes' had briefly threatened to push Elvis out of the limelight, had disappeared from public view following a serious car wreck in 1956. Eight years on from his only British hit, he had been largely forgotten by all but a dedicated few, and was struggling both to reactivate his flagging career and also to come to terms with an increasing drink problem.

Carl at the Manchester Odeon.

The rehabilitation of Carl Perkins was to commence with this tour. The welcome he received from the British audiences and the renewed interest in his music helped him back on his feet and inspired him to put his life back on track.

Ever since the emergence of the Beatles there had been an increasing fragmentation in the musical tastes of the public, highlighted by the lifestyle differences of the mods and rockers, the former favouring the British beat groups while the latter remained loyal to the American rock'n'rollers. The intolerance between the two factions was hammered home — almost literally — in a series of Bank Holiday clashes at various seaside resorts, and was destined to resurface from time to time over the next decade whenever a promoter was foolish enough to misjudge the tastes of his audience.

The Berry–Perkins package also featured the Animals, the Swinging Blue Jeans, Kingsize Taylor & The Dominoes, the Other Two and compere Larry Burns. The act which was destined to suffer the most adverse audience reaction were the Swinging Blue Jeans, another Liverpool group, who performed in a bouncy pseudo-rock'n'roll style and who had recently charted with their own version of Little Richard's 'Good Golly Miss Molly'. They provoked strong reactions, being loved by their own legion of fans, while at the same time loathed by a significant number of the more fanatical rock'n'roll enthusiasts. Even before the tour got underway, it was obvious that they were in for a rocky ride.

Chuck at Sheffield City Hall.

Carl Perkins made a considerable impact at the Finsbury Park Astoria with a short, punchy set that included 'Mean Woman Blues', 'What'd I Say' and 'Blue Suede Shoes', but Chuck was unquestionably the star of the show.

Wearing a sober dark grey suit and ably backed by Kingsize Taylor & The Dominoes augmented by British rocker Roy Young on piano, he worked through 'School Day', 'Johnny B. Goode', 'Sweet Little Sixteen', 'Worried Life Blues', 'Nadine' and 'Maybelline', proving to be both a charismatic performer and a highly individual guitarist. The audience were mesmerised as he prowled around the stage and became ecstatic when he suddenly crouched low to perform his famous duckwalk. The following night at Hammersmith, crowd trouble stopped Berry's act after only fifteen minutes. Every time he did the duckwalk, the fans went crazy, and the management were panicked into lowering the safety curtain.

In stark contrast, the Swinging Blue Jeans ran into problems from the outset. On the opening night, they were booed continually through their act, and after the first house several youths went round to the stage door to threaten them. Ken Major of Edmonton vehemently voiced the feelings of the fans with a letter to *Record Mirror*: *'Have promoters any idea of billing a show? If they are bringing in great stars such as Jerry Lee Lewis, Little Richard or Chuck Berry, why do we have to sit through rubbish like the Swinging Blue Jeans? If the show is rock'n'roll, let's keep it that way.'*

His opinions were certainly shared by others, because the onslaught against the Swinging Blue Jeans persisted and they left the show halfway through the tour, understandably accepting an alternative and altogether more peaceful engagement elsewhere. The days when rock'n'roll fans would patiently sit through a string of variety acts were over. Notwithstanding the Blue Jeans debacle, however, the tour was a great success, with both Chuck and Carl being enthusiastically received wherever they appeared.

Gene Vincent was included in the package at Woolwich and, although Southend was scheduled to be the final night, an additional *'Farewell To Chuck'* show was added for 31 May at Hammersmith, again including Vincent. On the previous evening, Chuck played two London club dates with Kingsize Taylor & The Dominoes supported by Alexis Korner's Blues Incorporated. Sadly, a planned Granada TV special for Berry and Perkins did not materialise.

TV appearances (Chuck Berry)
Open House   30 May 1964

TV appearances (Carl Perkins)
Ready Steady Go   8 May 1964

TONY ORLANDO

May 1964			22	Salford	Whiskey A Go Go
15	Guildford	Civic Hall	23	Boston	Gliderdrome
16	Crewe	*unknown venue*	24	Southsea	Savoy
17	Manchester	Domino	30	Handsworth	Plaza
	Manchester	Princess	31	London	Beat City
Promoter — Roy Tempest					

This was a badly-publicised and absurdly chaotic tour. Such information as did appear in the music press was largely inaccurate. It was reported that Tony Orlando would be backed by the Pets, but appears to have worked with Brian Diamond & The Cutters instead. He had made a big impression on his first British tour in 1962, but this time made no impact at all despite three television appearances.

TV appearances
Thank Your Lucky Stars   10 May 1964 (screened 16 May 1964)
Scene At 6.30   19 May 1964
Open House   23 May 1964

LOUIS PRIMA

It was reported during May that Louis Prima and his band would be coming to Britain in February 1965 as part of a three-month European tour while Georgie Fame & The Blue Flames went over to America in exchange. Unfortunately, the project quickly ran into difficulties and was never mentioned again by the music press.

GENE VINCENT

June 1964			July 1964		
5	Plymouth	Majestic	3	Shoreditch	Town Hall
6	Runcorn	Scala	4	Tenbury Wells	Riverside
7	Bath	Forum	5	Blackpool	North Pier Pavilion
11	Swindon	Locarno	7	Wallington	Public Hall
12	Pontypridd	Municipal Hall	8	Stourbridge	Town Hall
13	Market Harborough	Continental	9	Birkenhead	Majestic
18	Newcastle	Mayfair	10	Dursley	Lister Hall
19	Southsea	Clarence Pier	11	Ulverston	Coronation Hall
20	Wisbech	Corn Exchange	12	Great Yarmouth	Britannia Pier
21	Burton	76 Club			
Promoter — Don Arden					

Sadly, Gene Vincent was ceasing to be quite the draw that he had been over the last four years. The cause was probably a combination of his own fragile health, allied to the fact that he was just too accessible. Don Arden had worked him into the ground, and even his most loyal fans were now loath to travel any great distance believing that there would always be another gig near their locality the following week.

His cause had also not been greatly helped by a succession of distinctly mediocre recordings, one of which — 'La-Den-Da-Den-Da-Da' — he performed on *Thank Your Lucky Stars* on 20 June. On 23 and 24 June, he finished recording the *Shakin' Up A Storm* album.

Most of his live appearances during June and July were routine ballroom or club gigs, although at Blackpool he headlined a gigantic bill with the Animals, while at Great Yarmouth he starred with Karl Denver, the Mojos and Mark Wynter. He then departed for another short trip to France.

TV appearances
Thank Your Lucky Stars   20 June 1964

CARL PERKINS

June 1964	
6 Manchester	Twisted Wheel
Promoter — Don Arden	

Following the Chuck Berry tour, Carl Perkins remained in England for the first week of June, making two further TV appearances and filming his segments for a movie called *Swinging UK*. The shoot took place in London on 4 June and featured Perkins singing 'Blue Suede Shoes' and 'Big Bad Blues'. He'd cut the latter tune (along with 'Lonely Heart') for Decca Records with the Nashville Teens on 22 May.

He was back in the studio again on 1 June, but this time as an invited guest of the Beatles. Carl attended their session at Abbey Road, during which it became clear to him that they were all enormous fans of his work. He remained in their company from early afternoon until late into the night, during which time they recorded their own version of 'Matchbox' and tried out several

other Perkins songs.

His first UK tour had proved an unexpected success. 'He was such an unknown quantity to us,' said Peter Grant from Don Arden's office. 'We just didn't realise how great he is.'

Carl's final gig of the tour was by far the wildest of the lot. He really let rip in the dark, sweaty Twisted Wheel club, including several different songs and some blistering guitar solos.

TV appearances

Scene At 6.30	4 June 1964
Ready Steady Go	5 June 1964

The Crickets on *Ready Steady Go*.

THE CRICKETS

June 1964			July 1964		
19	Wimbledon	Palais	1	Leicester	De Montfort Hall
23	Wisbech	Corn Exchange	2	Cleethorpes	Café d'Ansant
24	Cambridge	Corn Exchange	3	Hanley	The Place
25	Southsea	Savoy	4	London	Royal Albert Hall
26	Widnes	Plaza		Maidstone	Royal Star
27	Erdington	Carlton	11	Lowestoft	Royal Hotel
30	Manchester	Oasis			
Promoter — Vic Lewis					

The post-Holly Crickets seemed cursed by bad luck. In 1962, they had been obliged to tour Britain without drummer Jerry Allison, who had been unable to obtain leave from the US Air Force. On this occasion, the problem was rather more serious: vocalist Jerry Naylor had suffered a heart attack and was still recuperating when Jerry Allison, Sonny Curtis, Glen D. Hardin and replacement singer Buzz Cason flew into London on 19 June.

Fortunately, the fans seemed to accept the constantly changing line-up of the group, who were well received at the Royal Albert Hall along with Adam Faith, P.J. Proby, the Applejacks, Dante & The Infernos, the Cherokees and the Pickwicks, on a show billed as *'Big Beat Night'*. Generally, however, the tour was more low-key than previous visits. At Lowestoft, they were supported by Cliff Bennett & The Rebel Rousers, and at Erdington by the Moody Blues. On their first day in Britain, they appeared on *Ready Steady Go* along with bluesman John Lee Hooker.

TV appearances
Ready Steady Go	19 June 1964
Open House	20 June 1964

GENE VINCENT

July 1964			23	Great Yarmouth	Britannia Pier
17	Peterborough	Elweys Hall	24	Bath	Pavilion
18	Heacham	Public Hall	26	Hindley	Palace Casino
19	Great Yarmouth	Britannia Pier	28	Gravesend	Co-op
24	Leamington Spa	Assembly Hall	29	Grantham	Drill Hall
25	Aylesbury	Grosvenor	30	Ryde, IOW	*unknown venue*
August 1964			September 1964		
6	Harwich	Rivington Barn	6	Great Yarmouth	Britannia Pier
7	Morecambe	Floral Hall	13	Great Yarmouth	Britannia Pier
9	Great Yarmouth	Britannia Pier	20	Birmingham	Hippodrome
12	Bristol	Corn Exchange	22	Nelson	Imperial
15	Redhill	Market Hall	26	Manchester	Oasis
	Tottenham	Club Noreik	27	Bristol	Colston Hall
17	Tunbridge Wells	Assembly Rooms	October 1964		
20	Kidderminster	Town Hall	11	Manchester	Domino
22	Cardiff	Sophia Gardens		Manchester	Princess
Promoter — Don Arden					

Upon his return from his brief sojourn in France, Gene Vincent continued to tour with the Shouts. On his two Great Yarmouth appearances in September, he starred alongside both Marty Wilde and the Applejacks; at Birmingham, he appeared with the Animals and the Nashville Teens; at Nelson he was the support for Bill Haley & His Comets. Otherwise it was business as usual for Gene as he travelled the length and breadth of the country bringing rock'n'roll to the faithful.

BRENDA LEE

Brenda Lee arrived in Britain on 16 August for a promotional visit during which she recorded at Decca Studios with producer Mickie Most, cutting 'What'd I Say' and 'Is It True'. She expressed great pleasure at being back in England, and even spoke of possibly moving to live in the UK. The plan was that she would return to the States for a short break and then join Bill Haley & His Comets for a theatre tour. However, Brenda's daughter Julie had been born five weeks prematurely on 1 April, and she subsequently pulled out of the Haley tour, citing exhaustion as the reason. She was replaced by Manfred Mann.

TV appearances

Ready Steady Go	21 August 1964
The Beat Room	24 August 1964
Ready Steady Win	31 August 1964
Juke Box Jury	? August 1964

BILL HALEY & HIS COMETS

September 1964			October 1964		
18	Belfast	Boom Boom	1	Liverpool	Odeon
21	London	Flamingo	2	Portsmouth	Guildhall
22	Nelson	Imperial	3	Bournemouth	Winter Gardens
24	Cardiff	Sophia Gardens	4	Leicester	De Montfort Hall
25	Croydon	Fairfield Halls	5	Kilburn	Gaumont State
26	Finsbury Park	Astoria	6	Rochester	Odeon
27	Bristol	Colston Hall	7	Sheffield	City Hall
28	Birmingham	Town Hall	8	Stockton	Odeon
29	Manchester	Odeon	9	Manchester	Oasis
30	Newcastle	City Hall		Manchester	Astoria
			10	Nottingham	Odeon
			11	London	New Victoria
Promoter — Don Arden					

Prime Minister Harold Wilson once said that a week is a long time in politics. Well, seven and a half years is an eternity in rock'n'roll! Bill Haley had visited Britain in March 1957 at the peak of his popularity and been mobbed by adoring fans wherever he went. His tour had been an unqualified success and played to capacity crowds, yet his career nosedived as soon as he returned to the States and his name had rarely been mentioned in the music press since. Needless to say, his return to Britain in the post-Beatle era was a considerably less frenzied affair, but, although the media now treated him as something of an antique curiosity, there was still a solid body of fans who had remained loyal and who were delighted to welcome him back.

There had been a lot of hard times for Haley since the glory days of 1957 and the Comets had undergone almost a complete change of personnel. The new line-up comprised Johnny Kay (lead guitar), Rudy Pompilli (tenor sax), Dave Holly (drums), Nick Nastos (steel and rhythm guitars) and Al Rappa (double bass). Bill's long-time manager, Jolly Joyce, also made the trip.

The bulk of the tour consisted of theatre dates with Manfred Mann, the Nashville Teens, the Rockin' Berries, the Untamed Four, the Bobby Patrick Big Six and compere Bob Bain, but before the main package got underway, he also played gigs in Belfast, at London's Flamingo Club (with Zoot Money's Big Roll Band) and at Nelson's Imperial Ballroom, where Gene Vincent provided the support. The Flamingo gig was well-attended and Haley's spot sparked a minor riot, but at Nelson the crowd was disappointingly small and the usually packed ballroom floor seemed bare in comparison to a normal night.

Haley's act had not really altered at all. He still sang the old hits and, with Rudy honking the sax and Al Rappa climbing on the bass, the visual antics were unchanged as well. The 1957 tour had been so incredible that both media and public alike could not fail to notice the reduced impact, but Bill himself just seemed happy to be back in Britain. The press marvelled at how a man of 36 could still manage to sing rock'n'roll. When would it all end?

ASTORIA - Finsbury Park

DAVRON (THEATRICAL MANAGERS) LTD.
by arrangement with DON ARDEN presents
THE MANFRED MANN
and BILL HALEY SHOW
2nd Performance 9-0 p.m.
SATURDAY
SEPTEMBER **26**
STALLS 7/6

Q33

No ticket exchanged nor money refunded
THIS PORTION TO BE RETAINED

On 10 September Bill joined Brian Epstein among the judges for Rediffusion's *Ready Steady Win* TV talent show.

TV appearances

Ready Steady Go	8 September 1964 (screened 11 September 1964)
Ready Steady Win	10 September 1964 (screened 16 September 1964)
Juke Box Jury	12 September 1964
Lucky Stars Summer Spin	13 September 1964 (screened 19 September 1964)
Scene At 6.30	15 September 1964

THE RONETTES
BILL BLACK'S COMBO

September 1964					
25	Northampton	ABC	8	Bolton	Odeon
26	Mansfield	Granada	9	Grantham	Granada
27	Liverpool	Empire	10	Hull	ABC
29	Edinburgh	ABC	11	East Ham	Granada
30	Glasgow	Odeon	13	Bedford	Granada
October 1964			14	Brixton	Granada
2	Belfast	ABC	15	Guildford	Odeon
3	Sheffield	City Hall	16	Southampton	ABC
4	Stockton	ABC	17	Gloucester	ABC
7	Carlisle	ABC	18	Tooting	Granada
Promoter — Arthur Howes					

The days of the big package shows were coming to an end, and the second Ronettes tour of 1964 was far from a financial success. Co-starring with Billy J. Kramer & The Dakotas, the girls were — rather surprisingly — joined by Bill Black's Combo, fresh from a major US tour supporting the Beatles. Black himself had retired from the road two years earlier and did not make the trip, but in his place were to be found some of the top Memphis musicians, namely Reggie Young (guitar), Bob Tucker (bass), Ed Logan (saxophone), Clarice Vernon (organ) and Sammy Creason (drums). The surprise at their inclusion was not through doubts over their ability, rather that their work had so far proved singularly unappealing to British record-buyers, and it seems unlikely that the appearance of their name on the posters would have contributed greatly to ticket sales. The rest of the package comprised Cliff Bennett & The Rebel Rousers, the Yardbirds and compere Tim Connor. From 7 October, the Kinks were added to the line-up, presumably in an attempt to improve box office receipts.

Bill Black's Combo were only allocated a short spot of their own, in which they included 'Little Queenie' — the Chuck Berry tune that was their latest single. They also played behind the Ronettes but, despite their top-class backing, Ronnie, Nedra and Estelle were unable to repeat the level of excitement that they had created at the beginning of the year. The popularity of the British acts on the show was such that they had to fight every inch of the way as they performed 'Shout' and their new single, 'Do I Love You', along with their hits. With hindsight, perhaps they returned to the UK a little too soon after their first tour.

TV appearances (Ronettes)

Top Of The Pops	1 October 1964
Scene At 6.30	9 October 1964
Sunday Night At The London Palladium	11 October 1964
The Beat Room	12 October 1964
Thank Your Lucky Stars	24 October 1964

LITTLE EVA

September 1964			9	Milford Haven	Phil Centre
26	Hinckley	St. George's	10	Manchester	Discs A-Go-Go
October 1964			16	Wellington	Majestic
3	London	Beat City	18	Middleton	The Limit
4	Birkenhead	Majestic	24	Manchester	New Century Hall
6	Forest Gate	Lotus	26	Kingston	Cellar
8	Swindon	Locarno			
Promoter — Terry King					

Little Eva arrived in Britain with the intention of launching a new dance craze based on her latest record, 'Makin' With The Magilla'. 'The song is the signature tune of a kid's TV cartoon series,' she explained at her London press reception. 'It's a "monkey" beat with a difference.' Sadly for Eva, the world was not about to jump onto this particular bandwagon, and both her record and the tour sank without trace. Several shows were cancelled or rearranged at short notice. *Record Mirror* reported that she would be appearing with the Merseybeats, the Naturals and Screaming Lord Sutch, but after much chopping and changing it was mainly ballroom dates that survived, on which she was backed by Danny Storm & The Strollers. The almost total dominance of the British groups was now really hurting the visiting Americans, and sadly it would get a lot worse before it got better.

TV appearances

Ready Steady Go	25 September 1964
Lucky Stars Summer Spin	? September 1964
The Beat Room	3 October 1964
Discs A-Go-Go	12 October 1964

LITTLE RICHARD

Don Arden had announced a three-week tour of clubs and ballrooms commencing 2 October. A crowd of 1,500 turned up at the Queens Hall, Leeds for the opening night, only to be told that Richard would not be appearing. The Pretty Things were given the dubious honour of replacing him and were pelted with orange peel, sweets and coins for their trouble until eventually the audience were offered their money back when the situation started to get out of hand.

Apparently Richard had cabled Arden from New York on the day of the first show with the news that he was ill. A last-ditch attempt to bring in Jerry Lee Lewis proved equally unsuccessful.

ROY ORBISON

With 'Oh, Pretty Woman' perched proudly at the top of the British charts, the 'Big O' travelled to Britain on 16 October for a five-day flying visit. He headlined a *Palladium* TV show, appearing alongside jazz pianist Errol Garner and comedienne Beryl Reid, and tele-recorded a 40-minute spectacular for transmission the following evening.

TV appearances

Sunday Night At The London Palladium	18 October 1964
The Roy Orbison Show	20 October 1964 (screened 21 October 1964)

GENE VINCENT

October 1964			3	Manchester	Odeon
17	Finsbury Park	Astoria	4	Hanley	Gaumont
18	Coventry	Theatre	5	Wolverhampton	Gaumont
19	Harrow	Granada	6	Cheltenham	Odeon
20	Doncaster	Gaumont	7	Bournemouth	Winter Gardens
21	Newcastle	Odeon	8	Bristol	Colston Hall
22	Sheffield	Gaumont	10	Kettering	Granada
23	Bradford	Gaumont	11	Romford	Odeon
24	Blackpool	Opera House	12	Southend	Odeon
25	Liverpool	Empire	13	Ipswich	Gaumont
26	Kingston	Granada	14	Portsmouth	Guildhall
27	Southampton	Gaumont	15	Leicester	De Montfort Hall
28	Cardiff	Capitol	17	Woolwich	Granada
29	Birmingham	Odeon	18	Greenford	Granada
30	Nottingham	Odeon	19	Slough	Adelphi
31	Rochester	Odeon	20	Worcester	Gaumont
November 1964			21	Tooting	Granada
1	Lewisham	Odeon	22	Walthamstow	Granada
2	Bedford	Granada			
Promoters — George Cooper and Larry Parnes					

Billed as *'Big Beat Scene'*, this was Gene Vincent's biggest tour for some time, but one on which he must have felt increasingly out of place supporting yet another new generation of chart acts, few of whom would have been heard of at the start of the year. It is even doubtful that many of his own fans would have bothered to sit through the show, which featured the likes of the Applejacks, Millie, Lulu & The Luvvers, the Honeycombs, Daryl Quist, the Beat Merchants and the Puppets.

The Shouts were preparing to split from Gene and launch their own ultimately unsuccessful bid for stardom, so during this period he was backed by them on some shows, and by the Londoners on others. His act stayed true to rock'n'roll, however, opening at the Finsbury Park show with 'Say Mama', continuing with 'You Are My Sunshine', 'Corrine, Corinna' and 'Be-Bop-A-Lula', before closing his short spot with 'Baby Blue'.

THE ISLEY BROTHERS

October 1964			5	Kingston	ABC
17	Sheffield	City Hall	6	Chester	ABC
18	Liverpool	Empire	7	Doncaster	Gaumont
19	Huddersfield	ABC	8	Stockton	Odeon
21	Colchester	ABC	9	Glasgow	Odeon
22	Luton	Odeon	10	Chesterfield	ABC
23	Slough	Adelphi	11	Cleethorpes	ABC
24	Stoke	Essoldo	12	Birmingham	Odeon
25	Woolwich	Granada	13	East Ham	Granada
26	Taunton	Gaumont	14	Norwich	Theatre Royal
27	Exeter	Odeon	15	Coventry	Theatre
28	Gloucester	ABC	16	Nottingham	Odeon
29	Worcester	Gaumont	17	Bristol	Colston Hall
30	Maidstone	Granada	18	Croydon	ABC
31	Bournemouth	Winter Gardens	19	Tunbridge Wells	Essoldo
November 1964			20	Cannock	Essoldo
1	Portsmouth	Guildhall	21	Newcastle	City Hall
3	Cambridge	Regal	22	Manchester	Odeon
4	Leeds	Odeon			
Promoter — Tito Burns					

The Isley Brothers would go on to become one of the top soul music acts of the Seventies, but at the time of their first British tour they were still performing an energetic and highly visual rock'n'roll show with a strong Little Richard feel as well as the gospel influence of their formative years spent singing in the Baptist churches of Cincinnatti. Ronald, Rudolph and O'Kelly Isley, along with Dionne Warwick — another singer with a gospel background — were the principal support for the Searchers on an extensive theatre tour, which also featured Alan Elsdon & The Voodoos, the Zombies and Tony Sheveton. The comperes, comedy duo Syd & Eddie, also later went on to fame after they renamed themselves Little & Large. The Isleys also brought with them their American drummer, Charlie Duff.

Their physically exhausting act was well received, and most definitely rock'n'roll. They performed 'I'm Gonna Knock On Your Door', 'Twistin' With Linda', 'Nobody But Me', 'Twist And Shout' and their original 1959 arrangement of 'Shout' — a song that had been high in the British charts only a few months earlier thanks to a recent waxing by Lulu. Their live appearance on *Ready Steady Go* was so successful that they were rebooked for a second show, and although the tour generally went well, it did not pass without incident.   Dionne Warwick was injured in a road accident in mid-November and missed the final dates. Her replacement, Eden Kane, was not a universally popular choice and the venerable music historian Bill Millar was physically ejected from the East Ham Granada for overstating his protest.

TV appearances

Ready Steady Go	16 October 1964
The Beat Room	? November 1964 (screened 30 November 1964)
Ready Steady Go	27 November 1964
Thank Your Lucky Stars	28 November 1964

CARL PERKINS

October 1964			November 1964		
19	Liverpool	Odeon	1	Brighton	Hippodrome
20	Edmonton	Regal	2	Kilburn	Gaumont State
21	Romford	Odeon	3	Guildford	Odeon
22	Huddersfield	Essoldo	4	Croydon	Fairfield Halls
23	Ipswich	Gaumont	5	Sheffield	City Hall
24	Leicester	Odeon	6	Stoke	Essoldo
25	Newcastle	City Hall	7	Derby	Gaumont
26	Birmingham	Town Hall	8	Portsmouth	Guildhall
27	Stockton	Hippodrome	9	Rochester	Odeon
28	Edinburgh	Usher Hall	10	Lewisham	Odeon
29	Dumfries	Lyceum	11	Cardiff	Sophia Gardens
30	Stockport	Essoldo	12	Bristol	Colston Hall
31	Bradford	Gaumont	13	Watford	Odeon
			14	Manchester	Odeon
			15	Bournemouth	Winter Gardens
			20	Kingston	Cellar
			22	Handsworth	Plaza
Promoter — Don Arden					

Carl Perkins returned to the UK for a second visit only five months after the Chuck Berry tour on which he had played a relatively minor role. Don Arden was perceptive enough to appreciate that the rock'n'roll audiences were anxious to see more of Carl, and he was now promoted to second billing on a package headed by the Animals. Gene Vincent had also been included on the earliest tour announcements but he was replaced by American R&B singer Tommy Tucker. Both Americans were backed by the Quotations, and the remainder of the show comprised Elkie Brooks, the Plebs, the Nashville Teens, compere Ray Cameron and, on selected dates, a young lady called Barry St. John.

As it happens, Perkins very nearly missed the trip altogether, due to a freak accident the previous August. Taking a bow at the end of a gig near Memphis, he'd raised his left hand to wave and caught the exposed blades of a large cooling fan. By the time he reached hospital, he was already unconscious, having lost half the blood in his body. Indeed, the damage to his fingers was so serious that at first his doctors feared that he would never play guitar again. Although this initial diagnosis thankfully proved inaccurate, his wounds had still not properly healed and he was in considerable pain throughout his time in Britain.

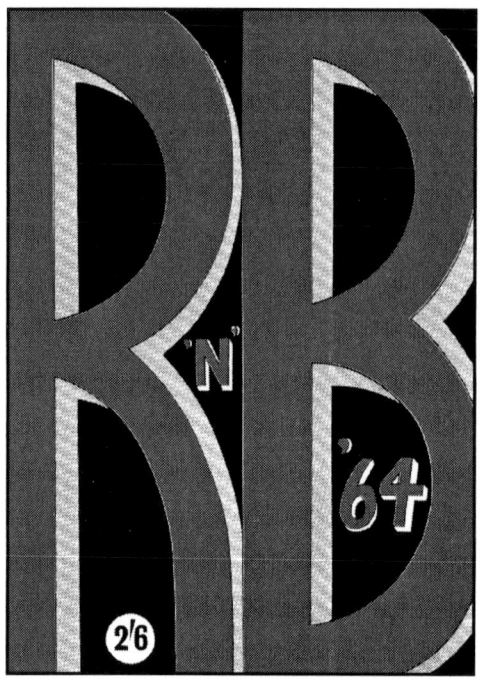

The tour was supposed to have opened at the Manchester Odeon on 18 October, but the Animals' commitments in the States forced a twenty-four hour postponement, with Liverpool becoming the first night instead. It was the Animals who got the lion's share of both publicity and audience response, but Carl went over well, with 'Blue Suede Shoes' inevitably being the song that everybody wanted to hear. Tommy Tucker also scored heavily with some rocking R&B including 'Long Tall Shorty', a jazz-flavoured 'Trouble in Mind' and his recent hit, 'Hi-Heel Sneakers'. However, there was criticism that the tour did not provide value for money, the acts were too short, the programme overpriced and crammed with adverts, and the theatre — at Edmonton at least — less than half full. The package finished at Bournemouth on 15 November, but Carl remained in England for a further week playing club dates at Handsworth and Kingston, and spending a day in the company of Jerry Lee Lewis on the film set of *Be My Guest*.

TV appearances

Ready Steady Go	9 October 1964
Beat Extra	19 October 1964

THE DIXIE CUPS

October 1964			November 1964		
23	Tunbridge Wells	Essoldo	1	Leicester	De Montfort Hall
24	Norwich	Theatre Royal	2	Dartford	Granada
25	Boston	Regal	3	Aylesbury	Granada
26	Haslemere	Rex	4	Grantham	Granada
27	Watford	Gaumont	6	Huddersfield	Essoldo
28	Ipswich	ABC	7	Handsworth	Plaza
29	Cannock	Danilo	8	Coventry	Theatre
30	Dunstable	California			
31	Scunthorpe	Baths			
Promoters — George Cooper and Larry Parnes					

With so many all-male beat groups dominating British popular music, the American vogue for all-girl singing groups provided a welcome contrast. The Dixie Cups from New Orleans, comprising sisters Rosa Lee and Barbara Ann Hawkins and their cousin, Joan Johnson, made their first overseas trip to participate on the Hollies' *Your Lucky Stars* tour along with Heinz & The Wild Boys, Jess Conrad, Wayne Gibson & The Dynamic Sounds, the Hi-Fi's and compere Larry Burns. The Tornados backed the girls as well as playing their own spot. In addition to the theatre tour, the Dixie Cups also worked ballrooms at Dunstable, Scunthorpe and Handsworth before moving on to Switzerland for a week of concerts.

The opening night at Tunbridge Wells was marred by over-amplification which almost completely drowned out Jess Conrad. However, the Dixie Cups fared somewhat better and certainly looked stunning in white blouses and tight black pants. Their act was relaxed and their husky singing style well received, with 'Chapel of Love' gaining the greatest applause.

TV appearances

Thank Your Lucky Stars	24 October 1964
The Beat Room	26 October 1964
Scene At 6.30	29 October 1964
Ready Steady Go	30 October 1964
Open House	31 October 1964

BRENDA LEE

November 1964			December 1964		
2	London	Palladium	1	Sheffield	City Hall
14	Finsbury Park	Astoria	4	Bristol	Colston Hall
16	Chelmsford	Odeon	5	Norwich	Theatre Royal
17	Guildford	Odeon	6	Wakefield	ABC
20	Handsworth	Plaza	7	London	Royal Albert Hall
	Old Hill	Plaza	8	Bedford	Granada
21	Wolverton	Palace	9	Kettering	Granada
	Dunstable	California	10	Walthamstow	Granada
22	Tooting	Granada	11	Slough	Adelphi
23	Maidstone	Granada	12	Blackpool	Opera House
25	Belfast	ABC			
28	Boston	Gliderdrome			
30	Birmingham	Town Hall			
Promoter — George Cooper					

Despite having dropped out of the Bill Haley tour in September through exhaustion, Brenda Lee returned to Britain only two months later, appearing on a star-studded bill at the Palladium that included Cilla Black, the Shadows, and comedians Tommy Cooper and Bob Newhart. The occasion was the *Royal Command Performance*, and the Queen was in the audience when Brenda performed her only number of the evening, the ballad 'All The Way'. Brenda wore a plain white dress, and one rather unkind report described her as looking *'somewhat tubby'*. Her Majesty spoke to her after the show and declared: 'I enjoyed your singing very much.' An unconfirmed report close to Buckingham Palace, however, indicated that she would have preferred to hear 'Let's Jump The Broomstick'. Brenda was backed by the John Barry Seven, and she was able to share her Royal triumph with her husband, Ronnie Shacklett, who was enjoying his first trip to the UK. Baby

Julie remained back at home in the USA.

After a short visit to perform two concerts in Germany, Brenda kicked off her main tour at Finsbury Park on 14 November. For most of the shows, she was backed by the John Barry Seven, but on this occasion appeared with the Bobby Patrick Big Six. She was feeling unwell and had been attended by a doctor only two hours before going on stage, but still gave a dynamic and professional performance that had the audience on their feet clapping and cheering enthusiastically. Opening with 'Dynamite' and 'Sweet Nothin's' followed by 'Let's Jump The Broomstick', she then alternated ballads like 'As Usual' and 'I Wish It Were Me' with rockers 'Tutti Frutti' and 'What'd I Say', before winding up with a vibrant rendition of 'When The Saints Go Marching In'.

The GEORGE COOPER ORGANISATION LTD. presents

Souvenir Programme
Two Shillings

The tour was a mixture of theatres and ballrooms, and Brenda's support acts varied from night to night, but for the theatres usually comprised a combination of Manfred Mann, Johnny Kidd & The Pirates, Heinz, Marty Wilde, Bern Elliott, the Flee-Rekkers and Wayne Fontana & The Mindbenders, while at the ballroom date in Wolverton, her opening act was Freddie 'Fingers' Lee & The Shriekers.

Although her days as an automatic chart draw in Britain were coming to an end, Brenda Lee remained in demand during 1964. Among several television appearances, a live performance on *Ready Steady Go* did not materialise, but she did participate in BBC2's *Top Beat*, a recorded concert from the Royal Albert Hall also featuring Dave Berry, the Yardbirds, Brian Poole & The Tremeloes, Sounds Incorporated and the American Motown group, the Miracles.

TV appearances

Royal Command Performance	2 November 1964 (screened 8 November 1964)
Open House	14 November 1964
It's Tarbuck!	27 November 1964 (screened 27 January 1965)
Thank Your Lucky Stars	28 November 1964
Top Beat	7 December 1964 (screened 9 December 1964)

CHUCK BERRY

A full-blown package tour starring Texan P.J. Proby, the Pretty Things and Motown singer Kim Weston had been arranged by promoter Robert Stigwood to run for twenty-four nights in November. Proby, who had earlier recorded some obscure rock'n'roll under the name of Jet Powers, was now permanently resident in Britain and struggling to handle his brief period of stardom. His difficult and erratic behaviour got him into a great deal of trouble, and immediately prior to this tour he fell out with Stigwood, and it was announced in the music press that his late replacement would be Chuck Berry. In the end, however, it proved too late to rescue the tour and the whole project had to be scrapped. Chuck did fly into Britain in November for a short business trip during which he set up a tour for Stigwood for the following January.

JERRY LEE LEWIS

November 1964			December 1964		
21	New Cross	Lawrie Grove Baths	1	Golders Green	Hippodrome
	Tottenham	Club Noreik	4	Wimbledon	Palais
22	Brighton	Hippodrome	5	Manchester	New Century Hall
23	Eltham	Baths	6	Handsworth	Plaza
	Chatham	Invicta		Kings Heath	*unknown venue*
26	Windsor	Ricky Tick	7	Birmingham	Town Hall
28	Peterborough	Palais			
	Wisbech	Corn Exchange			
Promoter — Don Arden					

Jerry Lee flew into Britain on 20 November for his second tour of 1964 and was backed throughout by the Plebs. The quality of the venues was disappointing. What on earth was he doing playing at Eltham Baths? The sad truth was that mainline interest in the master showman was declining as rock'n'roll became increasingly marginalised, the media concentrating almost entirely on the Beatles and the seemingly endless parade of new groups that now jockeyed for positions in the charts.

The itinerary was a rag-bag of ballrooms and second-rate theatres, but Lewis delivered the goods in his own inimitable style, with Gene Vincent joining him for

John Smith presents

THE
JERRY LEE LEWIS
SHOW

at the Brighton Hippodrome
on Sunday 22nd November

the shows at Birmingham Town Hall and Golders Green.   The latter event was sold out and generated sufficient audience activity for the management to panic and bring the police in to stop the show, citing unruly behaviour as the reason for their actions. Jerry Lee had not lost the ability to stir up his devoted fans, and as usual remained supremely confident and apparently oblivious to the changing world of popular music in which he was obliged to operate.

His appearance at Wisbech Corn Exchange was typical. Despite the entrance charge being hiked up by a staggering four shillings, the local rockers turned out in force and ensured an enthusiastic welcome for their hero. For his part, Lewis gave them their money's worth with forty-five minutes of non-stop

Jerry Lee rocks Wimbledon.

rock'n'roll, his songs ranging from 'Great Balls Of Fire' to his latest release, 'Hi-Heel Sneakers'. One minute, he was hammering the piano with both his hands and feet, while the next he was singing 'You Win Again' in a quiet, relaxed country style. He turned in steamy versions of both 'Mean Woman Blues' and 'Good Golly Miss Molly', and at the end of the evening was avidly pursued by an army of fans and autograph hunters.

Proposed gigs in the North East were cancelled to enable Jerry Lee to film a spot in the movie *Be My Guest*, for which he was reunited with the Nashville Teens. At Brighton, his support included the Yardbirds and Twinkle, while the Spencer Davis Group were on the bill at Birmingham.

TV appearances
Ready Steady Go   20 November 1964
Scene At 6.30   27 November 1964

GENE VINCENT

November 1964			December 1964		
23	West Bromwich	Adelphi	1	Golders Green	Hippodrome
24	Birmingham	In Town	7	Birmingham	Town Hall
25	Birmingham	Morgue	12	Wimbledon	Palais
26	Erdington	Carlton	17	Kings Norton	Bourneville Youth Club
29	Hassocks	The Downs			
Promoter — Don Arden					

Gene Vincent came straight off the October/November *Big Beat Scene* tour and continued with a clutch of dates in the Birmingham area. He was now working exclusively with the Londoners. Other than his two shows with Jerry Lee Lewis, December was a much quieter month.

His performance at Wimbledon Palais was typical Vincent: short but dynamic. Dressed as always in his trademark black leathers, he opened with 'Say Mama' and 'Baby Blue' — numbers most familiar to his audience and guaranteed to stir the emotions. He continued with 'Ac-Cent-Tchu-Ate The Positive' and an emotional rendition of 'What Am I Living For', perhaps less obvious material, but nevertheless well received by the fans. Then he pushed the pedal to the floor, crashed into top gear and was away, storming through 'Good Golly Miss Molly' and 'Long Tall Sally'. All the old movements were in evidence – the staring eyes, the mike stand swung around like a rag doll, and his injured leg dragging stiffly behind him as he jerkily prowled the stage. The pace slackened a little for 'Corinne, Corrina' before the inevitable 'Be-Bop-A-Lula' closed yet another night of rock'n'roll by the great man. True, his energy levels and the brilliance of his performances had declined somewhat over the past year, but a Gene Vincent show was still a magnificent occasion.

Gene flew home to the States for Christmas, where he spent time visiting his parents in New Mexico.

CHAPTER TEN

1965

Save The Last Dance For Me

The era of the package tour was finally coming to an end. During 1965, Don Arden withdrew from promoting American acts and by the end of the year it would be a rarity to find rock'n'roll in British theatres any more. What we were left with were chaotically-promoted ballroom tours that were inadequately advertised and subject to constantly changing dates. To make matters worse, the music press (with the exception of *Record Mirror*), had given up on rock'n'roll, so it was becoming even harder to glean information about forthcoming events.

A partial remedy for this state of affairs came about via the fan clubs, and in 1965 no self-respecting rock'n'roll singer would have been without one. Fan-based journalism was spearheaded by Breathless Dan Coffey's *Boppin' News*, probably the first specialist rock'n'roll magazine. Gradually, a whole host of journals evolved, the leading fan clubs being those representing Bill Haley, Little Richard and Gene Vincent, although even less prominent artists like Larry Williams and Ronnie Hawkins had enthusiastic fans looking after their interests and trying eagerly to outdo their competitors with the latest facts, news and information.

R&B was still very much in fashion, and blues artists continued to flock to Britain and play the clubs and ballroom circuit. During the course of the year, Buddy Guy, T-Bone Walker, Memphis Slim and Champion Jack Dupree all toured, and were joined by soul singers Marvin Gaye, the Miracles, Donnie Elbert and Sugar Pie DeSanto.

Country music on the other hand was still an unknown quantity to most people on this side of the Atlantic. Roger Miller toured off the back of his UK chart-topper, 'King Of The Road', but that was about all. Mervyn Conn — later to become the UK's top country music promoter — already had too much on his plate trying to promote Bo Diddley.

CHUCK BERRY

January 1965					
8	Lewisham	Odeon	20	Edinburgh	Usher Hall
9	Finsbury Park	Astoria	21	Glasgow	Odeon
10	Manchester	Odeon	22	Carlisle	ABC
11	Sheffield	Gaumont	23	Stockton	Odeon
12	Hanley	Gaumont	24	Liverpool	Empire
13	Leicester	Odeon	25	Chester	ABC
14	Cardiff	Capitol	26	Leeds	Odeon
15	Bristol	Colston Hall	27	Lincoln	ABC
16	Southampton	Gaumont	28	Wolverhampton	Gaumont
17	Birmingham	Hippodrome	29	Croydon	Fairfield Halls
18	Hull	ABC	30	Southend	Odeon
19	Newcastle	Odeon	31	Edmonton	Regal
Promoter — Robert Stigwood					

The second Chuck Berry tour found him heading up a package that included the Moody Blues, the Graham Bond Organization, Long John Baldry & The Hoochie Coochie Men, Winston G and compere Don Spencer, along with the Five Dimensions who backed Berry in addition to playing their own set. The Graham Bond Organization featured in their line-up both Jack Bruce and Ginger Baker, who would later find fame as members of Cream.

Unfortunately, Baldry fell ill and was replaced by Simon Scott just prior to the opening night. Scott was solidly booed for his trouble, and never came close to equalling the hype that accompanied the launch of his short-lived career. Without Baldry the bill did seem to lack suitable depth — a fact that was reflected at the box office, where promoter Robert Stigwood took a real caning. He explained: 'Audiences want to participate more. They are tired of sitting down and just watching.'

Chuck's popularity was not in question — indeed, his latest release, 'Promised Land', charted during the tour. Before leaving America he had assured Stigwood: 'I'm going to make that audience jump like they've never seen a rock'n'roll show before!'

Even so, the opening night at Lewisham was not without its difficulties. One heckler was told to shut his mouth, and when another youth began shouting during Chuck's comedy routine he snapped back: 'If everything you had was as big as your mouth, you wouldn't have to work!' There were no real surprises. Introduced as Chuck 'Crazy Legs' Berry, he opened with 'No Particular Place To Go', and worked through the

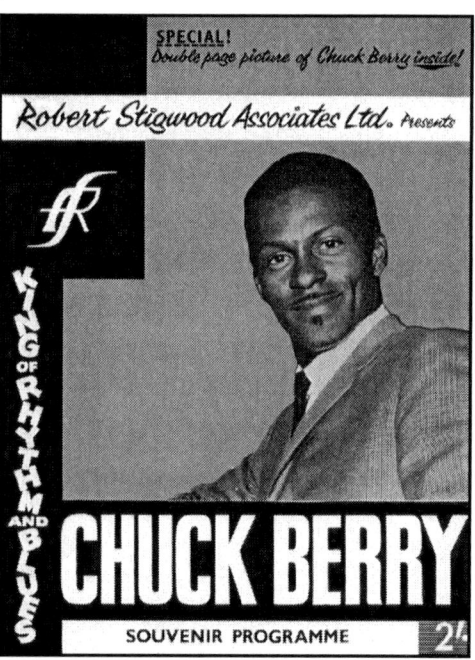

SPECIAL!
Double page picture of Chuck Berry inside!

Robert Stigwood Associates Ltd. Presents

KING OF RHYTHM AND BLUES

CHUCK BERRY

SOUVENIR PROGRAMME   2/-

likes of 'Nadine', 'Memphis Tennessee' and 'Sweet Little Sixteen' — all of which received thunderous applause — though, surprisingly, he did not bother to include his new hit.

Chuck and the Five Dimensions made two trips to the Pye Studios at Cumberland Place in London on 9 and 31 January, where they cut tracks for his next album, *Chuck Berry In London*. His sister, Lucy Ann, was employed by Chuck as his assistant for the duration of the tour, and it was proposed to record her while they were in London, but this plan had to be aborted when Chuck's own session overran. Amazingly, Berry did not appear on television at any time during his stay in Britain.

DEL SHANNON

Del flew into Britain on 13 January to promote his new disc, 'Keep Searchin' (We'll Follow The Sun)', and his efforts proved worthwhile when he scored his first British hit for over a year. Memorable among his TV appearances was *Ready Steady Go*, on which he appeared with the Righteous Brothers. On the BBC radio show *Pop Inn*, he guested with former rock'n'roller Paul Anka, who was himself engaged in a promotional visit to the UK. Interestingly, this was the first occasion on which the two men had met.

TV appearances

Scene At 6.30	14 January 1965
Top Of The Pops	14 January 1965
Ready Steady Go	15 January 1965
Five O'Clock Club	19 January 1965
Juke Box Jury	23 January 1965
Thank Your Lucky Stars	23 January 1965

JOHNNY THUNDER

January 1965					
15	Southsea	Savoy	23	Hinckley	St. George's
16	March	Marcham Hall	24	Cromer	Olympia
17	Manchester	Domino	28	Luton	Majestic
	Manchester	Princess	29	Nelson	Imperial
18	Reading	New Majestic	30	Crewe	Majestic
20	Newcastle	Majestic	31	Manchester	Oasis
21	Oldham	Astoria	**February 1965**		
22	Wellington	Majestic	1	Newport	Majestic
Promoter — Roy Tempest					

The adverts for Johnny Thunder's second British tour announced him as being *'Sonny Liston's ex-sparring partner'* and *'fresh from the Elvis Presley Show'*. He was backed by a mysterious group of British musicians billed as 'The Thunderbirds', or in some cases 'The Thunderbeats'. The tour did not pick up any great interest from the music press despite four television appearances, although at Nelson he did share billing with Herman's Hermits.

TV appearances

Ready Steady Go	? January 1965
Juke Box Jury	16 January 1965
Thank Your Lucky Stars	16 January 1965
The Beat Room	18 January 1965

GENE VINCENT

January 1965		
15	Stafford	Trentham Gardens
16	Liverpool	*unknown venue*
22	Bristol	*unknown venue*
24	East Grinstead	Whitehall

Promoter — Don Arden

The year opened quietly for Gene Vincent, with just a handful of gigs in January on which he was backed by the Londoners. Other dates were provisionally scheduled and then cancelled again. After so long in the limelight, the erratic and problem-laden Vincent was now squabbling badly with Don Arden and proving increasingly difficult to manage. On 6 February, he travelled to Germany for a short tour.

TOMMY ROE

January 1965					
29	Croydon	ABC	9	Manchester	ABC
30	Wolverhampton	Granada	10	Wigan	ABC
31	Luton	Ritz	11	Newcastle	City Hall
February 1965			12	Edinburgh	ABC
1	Northampton	ABC	13	Stockton	ABC
2	Gloucester	ABC	14	Hull	ABC
3	Exeter	ABC	16	Harrow	ABC
4	Plymouth	ABC	17	Cambridge	ABC
5	Bristol	Colston Hall	18	Chester	ABC
6	Cardiff	Capitol	19	Sheffield	City Hall
7	Southampton	ABC	20	Lincoln	ABC
			21	Liverpool	Empire

Promoters — Arthur Howes and Brian Epstein

Tommy Roe's career had been marking time since his two long British tours of 1963. The reason was that he had been called up by Uncle Sam and had only been released from his spell in the US Army in September 1964. He returned to the UK as a support act on a package jointly headlined by Cilla Black and P.J. Proby, which also featured the Fourmost, Sounds Incorporated, the Mike Cotton Sound, Tommy Quickly, the Remo Four and compere Bob Bain. Accompanying Roe on the tour were his American band, the Roemans.

His slot on the show was relatively modest — no more than three or four numbers. He seemed out of place in his shiny powder blue suit and slicked-back hair in the midst of the mod styles and regulation Beatle haircuts, but went over well enough, his haunting rendition of 'The Folk Singer' contrasting with the more raucous 'Susie-Q'.

Ultimately however, this package is not remembered for anything other than the virtual self-destruction of P.J. Proby. During the first night at Croydon, toilet rolls were thrown at him when he split his pants during a highly-provocative act. He continued in similar fashion the following night, until at Luton they brought down the safety curtain after only his first number, and he was forcibly removed from the stage and the 1,700-strong audience offered their money back. Proby was instantly banned from all the ABC venues on the tour and replaced by a new chart name — Tom Jones & The Squires. The hypocritical *NME* seethed with indignation at Proby's outrageous behaviour and demanded that he be deported.

TV appearances

Ready Steady Go	? February 1965
Thank Your Lucky Stars	? February 1965 (screened 13 March 1965)
Crackerjack	19 February 1965 *(unconfirmed)*
Five O'Clock Club	28 February 1965

SCREAMIN' JAY HAWKINS

February 1965					
2	Wallington	Public Hall	15	Kingston	Cellar
3	London	Flamingo	16	Bristol	Corn Exchange
4	Reading	Olympia	17	Woolwich	Black Cat
5	Wimbledon	Palais	18	Edmonton	Cook's Ferry Inn
6	East Grinstead	Whitehall	19	Nottingham	Dungeon
7	Bromley	Bromel		Manchester	Twisted Wheel
8	Woking	*unknown venue*	21	Camberley	Agincourt
9	Wallington	Public Hall	26	Newcastle	Club A Go Go
10	Windsor	Ricky Tick	27	Nelson	Imperial
12	Manchester	Domino	28	Birmingham	Marquee
	Manchester	Princess	**March 1965**		
13	London	Flamingo	13	London	Flamingo
14	Redcar	Coatham Hotel	**April 1965**		
			4	Stockport	Manor Lounge
Promoter — Don Arden					

If something was needed to revitalise rock'n'roll in Britain at a time when the great package shows were coming to an end, what better tonic could there have been than the arrival on 26 January of the unbelievable Screamin' Jay Hawkins for a month of club and ballroom dates. Jay was not widely known in the UK, and attendances at his shows tended to be patchy, but for the privileged few this was the first chance to witness this extraordinary showman in action. Jay had never — nor would ever — have a hit record in Britain, and his reputation was built entirely on his completely unpredictable and flamboyant stage act. His show was a heady mix of rocking rhythm and blues, augmented by every conceivable stage prop. Britain's own Screaming Lord Sutch had already built his own career along similar lines, but Screamin' Jay was the original — and a far superior singer, his powerful baritone voice alternating between straight ballads, wild R&B and the sort of incomprehensible insanity that would keep the men in white coats forever on standby.

Jay stuns the Saturday teatime audience of *Thank Your Lucky Stars*.

The tour opened at Wallington Town Hall, where the local dancers stared in disbelief as Hawkins ran on and off the stage, pounded the piano, screamed, performed the splits, and for an hour stormed his way through a non-stop glut of rock'n'roll classics, ably backed — as he was throughout the tour — by the Blues Set. The teenagers brought up on the likes of Freddie & The Dreamers went into collective shock. Screamin' Jay is an acquired taste and should probably have carried a Government Health Warning!

The following night at the Flamingo Club in London's Soho, there was

Is this man sane? Hamming it up on Granada-TV's *Late Scene*.

host of showbiz faces in the audience as Jay came on stage wearing a brightly-coloured cloak and clutching his cigarette-smoking skull, Henry. Alternately playing piano and saxophone, he yelled his way through an action-packed set, the highlights of which included 'The Whammy', 'Alligator Wine', 'Strange', 'Little Bitty Pretty One' and his best-known song, the mildly insane 'I Put A Spell On You'.

At Bromley the following Sunday, Jay got so carried away that he knocked over an amplifier while running round the ballroom. After returning to the stage, he made flames shoot from his fingertips while playing the sax. On this occasion, it was 'Feast Of The Mau Mau' and 'What'd I Say', that got the greatest cheers.

Jay and his wife Ginny remained in Britain longer than the original month and on 3 May he cut an album, *The Night And Day Of Screamin' Jay Hawkins*, at the Decca studios in London. More dates were being set up for the summer when suddenly on 4 June he had a furious argument with Don Arden and was observed oiling a revolver in anticipation of a confrontation with the promoter. Fortunately this never materialised, but Jay flew home the next day leaving much of his luggage in the care of friends — including Henry the skull, a pair of zebra-striped shoes, and a suitcase full of flash-powder and fuse boxes.

TV appearances

Gadzooks! It's All Happening	15 February 1965
Scene At 6.30	? February 1965
Late Scene	? February 1965
Thank Your Lucky Stars	6 March 1965

ROY ORBISON

February 1965					
16	Slough	Adelphi	4	Glasgow	Odeon
17	Belfast	ABC	5	Edinburgh	ABC
19	East Ham	Granada	6	Stockton	Globe
20	Finsbury Park	Astoria	9	Tooting	Granada
21	Birmingham	Hippodrome	10	Bedford	Granada
23	Plymouth	ABC	11	Southampton	Gaumont
24	Exeter	ABC	12	Cardiff	Capitol
25	Gloucester	ABC	13	Bristol	Colston Hall
26	Manchester	ABC	14	Coventry	Theatre
27	Wigan	ABC	16	Wolverhampton	Gaumont
28	Leicester	De Montfort Hall	17	Sheffield	Gaumont
March 1965			18	Newcastle	City Hall
1	Hull	ABC	19	Bradford	Gaumont
2	Leeds	Odeon	20	Blackpool	ABC
3	Carlisle	ABC	21	Liverpool	Empire

Promoter — Arthur Howes

Arthur Howes presents

2/-

Roy flew in from Australia on 15 February for what was now becoming his annual tour of Britain. Accompanied by his own group, the Candy Men, he headlined a package that included the Rockin' Berries, Marianne Faithfull, Cliff Bennett & The Rebel Rousers, the Untamed, the Three Quarters (who also sang backing vocals for Roy on the tour), Jon Mark and compere Frank Berry. His father, Orbie Lee, came with him in the role of tour manager, but it was reported that wife, Claudette, had remained at home with the children.

When the tour got underway at Slough, both houses were sold out. Roy opened with 'Only The Lonely' and 'Dream Baby' and worked though his standard routine, injecting some fire and pace with 'Mean Woman Blues', although a morbid version of 'Crying' was marred by the singing of the Three Quarters, who occasionally drowned him out. The set closed with a stomping version of 'Oh, Pretty Woman'.

One amusing aside demonstrated just how badly P.J. Proby had burned his bridges during the recent tour with Tommy Roe. The ABC venues would not even permit the Rockin' Berries to include a take-off of Proby in their act!

Most of the tour reviews commented on the fact that Orbison had lost weight and seemed haggard and drawn. Just as the tour was drawing to a close, it was revealed that his eight-year marriage to Claudette had ended in

November, but that so far only close friends and family knew. He did, however, add that he and Claudette were missing each other and that he had hopes of a reconciliation. He left England for ten days of concerts in Europe, commencing with a big show on 23 March at the Paris Olympia with Wanda Jackson.

TV appearances

Top Of The Pops	18 February 1965
Ready Steady Go	19 February 1965
Juke Box Jury	20 February 1965
Thank Your Lucky Stars	21 February 1965 (screened 27 February 1965)
Sunday Night At The London Palladium	7 March 1965

JOHNNY RIVERS

February 1965
20   London   Ad-Lib
Promoter unknown

Rare appearance on *Thank Your Lucky Stars.*

Johnny Rivers was a big US star who never quite succeeded in establishing himself in Britain. He arrived in London on 17 February for a promotional visit along with his musicians, Joe Osborne (bass) and Mickey Jones (drums), plus his recording manager Lou Adler. Rivers himself could see that there was work to be done and explained: 'There is no point in trying to set up any concerts at this stage until I'm better known here.'

So, the plan was for radio and television work plus one club date at London's fashionable Ad-Lib club, which could be used as a platform from which to launch him in Britain. The snag came when the Home Office refused to grant a work permit for Osborne and Jones, as Rivers would not play without them. He mimed his way through two television shows, appearing both times on the same night as Roy Orbison, but dropped out of *Gadzooks!* because they would not permit him to mime.

Mickey Jones in particular

was disappointed by the red tape, as he had previously toured in the UK with Trini Lopez without a work permit. After much discussion, the date at the Ad-Lib went ahead as a free gig with P.J. Proby and Beatles Paul McCartney and Ringo Starr among the famous faces who turned up to watch. The Johnny Rivers trio proved to be what *Record Mirror* described as 'a hard-swinging outfit'. They had a very tight sound and were especially impressive on his recent US hits, 'Memphis Tennessee' and 'Maybellene'. Also prominently featured was Rivers' latest recording, 'Midnight Special'.

Immediately prior to his arrival in Britain it had been reported that Rivers had frequently been seen escorting actress Mamie Van Doren. Perhaps the biggest disappointment of his brief visit to Britain was that the voluptuous Miss Van Doren did not make the trip with him. Rivers departed for further promotional work in Germany, where he was preparing to go into the studio and get his tongue around a German language version of 'Midnight Special'.

TV appearances

Ready Steady Go	19 February 1965
Thank Your Lucky Stars	21 February 1965 (screened 27 February 1965)

DEL SHANNON

February 1965			11	Dover	ABC
27	Sheffield	City Hall	12	Lewisham	Odeon
28	Liverpool	Empire	13	Colchester	Odeon
March 1965			14	Hammersmith	Commodore
1	Birmingham	Town Hall	16	Aldershot	ABC
2	Wolverhampton	Gaumont	17	Taunton	Gaumont
3	Manchester	Odeon	18	Worcester	Gaumont
5	Aberdeen	Capitol	19	Leeds	Odeon
6	Dundee	Caird Hall	20	Bolton	Odeon
7	Newcastle	City Hall	21	Hanley	Gaumont
9	Northampton	ABC	22	Glasgow	Odeon
10	Salisbury	Odeon			
Promoter — Peter Walsh					

With 'Keep Searchin'' flying high in the British charts, Del Shannon returned for his first British concert tour since October 1963. The intention had been for him to co-star with New York girl group the Shangri-Las, but they pulled out at the last minute owing to illness of Mary Weiss, the blonde Shangri-La. Shannon (backed by the Soul Savages) was left to tread the boards in the company of Wayne Fontana & The Mindbenders, Herman's Hermits, Just Four Men, Paul Dean and compere Jerry Stevens, while a new UK girl group called the Dollies was drafted in to replace the Shangri-Las. Dodie West joined the tour at Dundee, while both Twinkle and the Ivy League were added for selected dates as necessary. Wayne Fontana keeled over with exhaustion when the tour reached Salisbury, after which he was replaced by the Zephyrs.

On the opening night at Sheffield, Del showed himself to be in better vocal form than ever. He played his own lead guitar — a Gretsch 'Chet Atkins' — throughout the tour, and started strongly with 'Hey Little Girl' and 'Hats Off To Larry'. His falsetto trademark and hit songs like 'Swiss Maid',

'Little Town Flirt' and 'Runaway' were well in evidence, yet the surprise highlight of the act was a dramatic rendition of Gene Pitney's 'I'm Gonna Be Strong', during which he was picked out by a single spotlight as he built the emotion of the song to a gripping climax. He closed enjoyable act with 'Keep Searchin' ' and his new single, 'Stranger in Town'.

TV appearances

Thank Your Lucky Stars	20 March 1965
Five O'Clock Club	30 March 1965

GENE VINCENT

March 1965			7	Balloch	*unknown venue*
3	Dunfermline	Kinema	8	Newport	Majestic
5	Kirkaldy	Raith	14	Manchester	Princess
6	Glasgow	Centre		Manchester	Domino
Promoter — Don Arden					

By March 1965, Gene Vincent's health was giving increasing cause for concern. It was not just his long-standing leg injury that was the problem, either. It seemed as if his whole body was worn out after more than five years of live shows in the UK. Anybody who has undertaken a tour of one-night stands will realise how physically exhausting such a lifestyle can be, and Gene had kept up an impossible schedule for longer than anybody else. He had literally worked himself into the ground.

Several dates were cancelled, although he did appear at Dunfermline alongside Brian Poole & The Tremeloes. His backing group, the Londoners, had also now been replaced by the Puppets.

On 17 March, Gene was rushed to the Royal National Ear, Nose & Throat Hospital in London for an emergency operation, forcing Don Arden to cancel his remaining dates up to the end of March.

THE DRIFTERS

March 1965			April 1965		
24	London	Lyceum	1	Woking	Atlanta
26	London	Palladium		London	Cromwellian
29	Warrington	Parr Hall	2	Nelson	Imperial
	Stockport	*unknown venue*	3	Leyton	Baths
30	Hanley	The Place		Tottenham	Club Noreik
	Altrincham	Stafford Hall	4-9	Manchester	Buckingham
31	Rochdale	Cubiklub	10	Manchester	Oasis
	Bolton	Beachcomber	11	London	Pigalle
				Greenford	Starlite
Promoter — Don Arden					

One of the greatest rock'n'roll vocal groups, the Drifters, made their UK debut at the Lyceum in London's Strand on the same evening that the Queen was visiting the nearby Aldwych Theatre, and Princess Margaret and the Queen Mother were to be found at Covent Garden Opera House. Despite these alternative attractions, a huge crowd waited patiently until 11.00 pm when the familiar sound of 'Up On The Roof' set the scene for a memorable night's entertainment.

The personnel of the Drifters had been in a state of constant change since the group was formed in 1953 as a vehicle for the exquisite tenor voice of Clyde McPhatter, and the 1965 line-up comprised Johnny Moore, Charlie Thomas, Eugene Pearson, Johnny Terry and guitarist Billy Davis — the same faces who had recorded the classics 'Saturday Night At The Movies' and 'Under The Boardwalk' the previous year. Both numbers were of course included in a set stuffed full of great songs like 'Save The Last Dance For Me', 'At The Club', 'When My Little Girl Is Smiling' and 'This Magic Moment'. Johnny B. Great & The Quotations provided top-line backing while the Drifters themselves used the large stage to leap about, dance, wave their arms, sway, jerk and crouch. They closed their set with 'On Broadway' and 'There Goes My Baby', the latter earning such sustained cheers that they were obliged to return to the stage and sing it a second time.

The bulk of the tour was to comprise ballrooms, sometimes doubling to include early and late shows at different venues. Before they got underway however, the Drifters attended a press reception thrown in their honour, and were prominently photographed alongside Rolling Stone Brian Jones. They also played a midnight charity show at the London Palladium along with Roy Castle and Al Saxon.

The ballroom dates proved very successful and drew consistently good attendances, although a fire broke out in the basement of the Cromwellian Club only a few hours after their performance, resulting in thousands of pounds of damage.

TV appearances

Scene At 6.30	25 March 1965
Ready Steady Go	26 March 1965
Thank Your Lucky Stars	3 April 1965

BOBBY VEE

March 1965			April 1965		
25	Stockton	Odeon	1	Worcester	Gaumont
26	Newcastle	City Hall	2	Birmingham	Town Hall
27	Doncaster	Gaumont	3	Bradford	Gaumont
28	Liverpool	Empire	4	Bristol	Colston Hall
			7	Colchester	Odeon
			8	Salisbury	Odeon
			9	Taunton	Odeon
			10	Cardiff	Sophia Gardens
Promoter — Tito Burns					

The irrepressible Bobby Vee came bouncing back to Britain on 11 March and headed straight for the EMI studios in London for a session with Beatles' producer George Martin. This yielded 'Keep On Trying', which failed to dent the UK singles chart but gave him a minor hit in the States. His wife, Karen Bergen, accompanied him on the trip.

After a few days of promotional activity, Vee joined the *Big Beat Show Of 1965* package, where he was billed as a 'special guest'. The joint headliners were Dusty Springfield and the Searchers, supported by the Zombies, Tony Jackson & The Vibrations, George Meaton, Heinz & The Wild Ones and the Echoes. Bobby himself was no more than a bit-part player on this tour — in stark contract to his earlier visits when he had been a major attraction. Times had changed, and even an articulate and shrewd operator like Vee was feeling the pinch.

TV appearances

Ready Steady Go	19 March 1965
Thank Your Lucky Stars	27 March 1965

LARRY WILLIAMS
JOHNNY 'GUITAR' WATSON

March 1965			**April 1965**		
26	Leyton	Baths	1	Luton	Majestic
	London	Flamingo	2	Guildford	Ricky Tick
27	London	Flamingo		Richmond	Crawdaddy
28	Manchester	Domino	3	Manchester	Twisted Wheel
	Manchester	Princess	4	London	Flamingo
29	Newport	Majestic	5	Hanley	The Place
30	Swansea	R'N'B	6	London	Marquee
Promoter — Roy Tempest					

Almost without anybody noticing, the spring of 1965 had turned into a golden period for rock'n'roll in Britain. First Screamin' Jay, then the Drifters, and finally Larry Williams all made their UK stage debuts within a matter of two months. Quite why Williams had never visited Britain before is open to debate, as he would surely have been a massive success on one of the touring packages two or three years earlier. He arrived with his wife, Helen, and Texan guitar ace Johnny 'Guitar' Watson, for a short stay of less than two weeks during which he created a most favourable impression and even found time to record not one but two new albums.

Larry had no sooner arrived than he became caught up in the continuing debate over what precisely was rock'n'roll. He answered: 'We call it "rhythm and blues", but the white folks wanted a new name for it, so they invented "rock'n'roll"... but it doesn't matter, it's still the same thing.'

Big crowds turned out at most of the venues although some of the more puritan rock'n'roll fans were dismayed to find Larry had combed his hair forward in a sort-of Beatle style. In contrast, Johnny 'Guitar' Watson, with his greased-back bouffant looked the image of the perfect rocker and, although largely unknown in the UK prior to his arrival, went down extremely well performing his own numbers like 'Gangster Of Love' and (at Manchester's Twisted Wheel in particular) a show-stopping 'Looking Back'. Williams himself seemed to take a little time to win over the crowd, but at the Flamingo in London was soon pounding at the piano, and, with a repertoire that included 'Dizzy Miss Lizzy', 'Slow Down', 'Bony Moronie' and 'Short Fat Fannie' — all rock'n'roll standards — couldn't really fail. Backing throughout

The dynamic duo in action at Manchester.

the tour was supplied by the Stormsville Shakers.

Williams also proved himself to be a slick businessman, arranging two separate recording deals while in England. On 5 April, Mike Vernon produced a studio album in London for Decca entitled *The Larry Williams Show*, while the following night another album was recorded at the Marquee Club before a very enthusiastic audience that included none other than Screamin' Jay Hawkins. Larry even made passing reference to Jay in the lyrics to 'Long Tall Sally'. This live album was released by Sue under the title *Larry Williams On Stage* and came complete with introductions by Screaming Lord Sutch.

Sadly the dynamic Williams–Watson combination never returned to Britain again. Johnny 'Guitar' Watson did make a highly forgettable appearance back in London in November 1976, by which time he was peddling disco soul and bore no resemblance to the greasy rocker of 1965. He collapsed and died on stage in Yokohama, Japan on 17 May 1996.

The later life of Larry Williams is shrouded in mystery. It has been strongly rumoured that he became involved in various illegal activities including prostitution and drugs. What is not in doubt is that on 2 January 1980 he was found dead at his luxury home in Los Angeles, a .38 calibre bullet having entered his right temple. The police declared his death to be suicide, but continuing claims that it was a mobster killing have persisted. Certainly, casual enquiries on the subject have been discouraged rather forcibly, so perhaps we should leave this subject alone and move swiftly on.

GENE VINCENT

March 1965		May 1965	
31 Liverpool	Cavern	8 Stockport	Manor Lounge
April 1965			
8 Newport	*unknown venue*		
Promoter — Don Arden			

Gene Vincent's gigs were now becoming few and far between. His appearance at the Liverpool Cavern backed by the Dyaks was a one-off that was also filmed for French television. By mid-May he was back in hospital again, and Tommy Quickly & The Remo Four were hastily drafted in as replacements for a show in Manchester on 19 May.

CHUBBY CHECKER

Promoter Mervyn Conn set up five TV appearances for Chubby, who by this time had moved on from the twist and was now exhorting people to 'Do The Freddie', and there was talk of a concert to take place on 1 May. This did not materialise, though Conn did organise a tour for him in August instead.

TV appearances

Scene At 6.30	28 April 1965
Top Of The Pops	29 April 1965
Ready Steady Goes Live	30 April 1965
The Eamonn Andrews Show	2 May 1965
Thank Your Lucky Stars	? May 1965 (screened 8 May 1965)

THE EVERLY BROTHERS

Don and Phil returned to the UK in May 1965 for a promotional visit to plug their latest single and did the full routine of TV and radio shows. Just as a similar trip had paid off for Del Shannon earlier in the year, so 'The Price Of Love' entered the charts on 22 May, making all the hard graft worthwhile. Interestingly, they were backed on this occasion by Jim Gordon on drums, Sonny Curtis on guitar, and former Teddy Bear Marshall Leib on bass.

TV appearances

The Eamonn Andrews Show	2 May 1965
Scene At 6.30	5 May 1965
Top Of The Pops	6 May 1965
Five O'Clock Club	6 May 1965
Ready Steady Goes Live	7 May 1965
Thank Your Lucky Stars	9 May 1965 (screened 15 May 1965)
Gadzooks! It's All Happening	10 May 1965

BIG JOE TURNER

May 1965			14	Bath	Regency
7	Southall	Osterley Jazz Club	15	West Bridgford	Dancing Slipper
8	London	Royal Festival Hall	19	Aylesbury	Assembly Hall
9	Redcar	Coatham Hotel	21	Southall	Osterley Jazz Club
10	Birmingham	Digbeth Civic Hall	22-23	Manchester	Sports Guild
12	London	100 Club	26	Southampton	Concorde
Promoter unknown					

Joe Turner, the 'Boss Of The Blues', certainly did not regard himself as a rock'n'roll singer, nor for that matter was his British tour supported by any rock'n'roll fans, as his live appearances were held exclusively on the jazz circuit. Nevertheless, in hindsight, the man who recorded such wonderful tracks as 'Boogie Woogie Country Girl', 'Honey Hush', 'Chicken And The Hawk' and, of course, 'Shake, Rattle And Roll' deserves inclusion in any book about rock'n'roll music.

Joe toured Britain with US trumpeter Buck Clayton, trombonist Vic Dickerson and the Humphrey Lyttleton Band. At Southall, a large crowd packed out the rugby club pavilion where the Osterley Jazz Club held their meetings and the whole building swayed under the influence of ninety minutes of the blues. Turner belted out one number after another, while the accompaniment by Buck and Humph was little short of prodigious.

The main gig of the tour was at the Royal Festival Hall in London, where the concert was billed as *'Jazz From Kansas City'* and included Ben Webster, Ruby Braff and the Stan Tracey Trio. The first house ran late and Joe was only permitted three numbers, but even that was enough to demonstrate the power of his giant voice. For the second house, he got a longer spot and went down a storm.

TV appearances
Jazz 625 [Part 1]   8 May 1965 (screened 16 June 1965)
Jazz 625 [Part 2]   8 May 1965 (screened 3 November 1965)

FATS DOMINO

Hopes of a first British tour by Fats Domino and his band gathered momentum with an announcement by Don Arden that he was concluding arrangements for six or seven dates in May including London, Manchester, Liverpool, Glasgow and Birmingham. Notwithstanding the question of work permits, the sheer expense of bringing in a ten-piece orchestra was considerable and must surely have been the prime reason why the Fat Man had yet to visit the UK. Arden's ambitious scheme soon fell through and rival promoter Roy Tempest took over negotiations, promising a two-week tour in November. Once again, the whole scheme fizzled out into nothing.

JIMMY GILMER

Texan singer Jimmy Gilmer, who had scaled the heights of fame in 1963 when his 'Sugar Shack' topped the US charts, made an unexpected two-day visit to London during June in the company of Buddy Holly's former producer, Norman Petty. They were only making a brief stopover on the way home from Europe, but even so he received little support from his British record label, Stateside. With no television or radio appearances arranged, he was restricted to a couple of brief interviews with the music press.

GENE VINCENT

June-September 1965		
25 June-19 September Blackpool South Pier		
	Promoters — George Cooper and Larry Parnes	

The writing had been on the wall for some time, and the end of Gene Vincent's glorious era in Britain finally came with an ignominious summer season at the Rainbow Theatre on Blackpool's South Pier. Vincent had provided some of the wildest rock'n'roll ever seen on a British stage and had more than once stated publicly that rock'n'roll was all he wanted to do. He did not want to be an 'all-round entertainer', and a summer season at the seaside in competition with Tommy Trinder, Bob Monkhouse and Tommy Cooper was the last place he should have been, but a combination of insensitive management, changing trends and his own continuing health problems had all conspired against him. In addition, of course, Gene was not the easiest of people to deal with, and his own intractable behaviour had much to do with his downfall.

A summer season may have meant no travelling, but it meant no time off either. For six nights a week Gene and the Puppets were the main support for Gerry & The Pacemakers on a variety show that also featured the Karl Denver Trio, the Marionettes, Paul Andrews, Mick & Kirk and the Fox Miller Lovelies. On Sundays, he remained at the same venue performing as support to Manfred Mann.

Summer seasons can be like a graveyard for entertainers, and Gene must have realised that he had reached the end of the road. Depressed and downhearted, he flew back home to the States with no immediate plans to return.

As a postscript, in December 1965 the *NME* reported that the courts had ordered Gene to pay manager Don Arden £675 damages in respect of a contract breach. There was never going to be a happy ending.

ROY ORBISON

July 1965		
29	Belfast	Ulster Hall

Promoter — Phil Solomon

Roy Orbison stopped off in England for a few hours on his way to Ireland, where he had a string of dates in the South and just one appearance in Ulster. He brought with him the welcome news that he and his wife, Claudette, had settled their differences and were now reconciled.

CHUBBY CHECKER

August 1965			2	Bristol	Arnos
28	Portsmouth	Guildhall	17	Manchester	Asprey's
30	Weymouth	Pavilion	19-24	Newcastle	La Dolce Vita
31	Nelson	Imperial		Stockton	Fiesta
September 1965			26	Harlesden	Club 32
1	Manchester	New Luxor			
	Manchester	Empress			

Promoters — Joe Collins and Mervyn Conn

Poor old Chubby Checker was suffering from an identity crisis. After being so closely associated with the twist craze, it was extremely difficult for him to move on to fresh pastures now that the twist was decidedly passé.

At Weymouth, he walked off the stage after only ten minutes as a result of continual barracking from a section of the audience. There had been about three hundred people in the ballroom when he began his act, and dancing couples moved between Checker and the audience. It was when he appealed to them to sit down that several youths made it impossible for him to continue. He waited for the shouting to stop and then walked off. Later, he and his nine-piece band completed the act for the benefit of the seventy-odd fans who remained.

During the early part of September, Checker travelled on to do shows in Italy, France, Germany and Ireland before returning for a week in cabaret, doubling each night at Newcastle Upon Tyne and Stockton.

TV appearances

Top Of The Pops	26 August 1965
Scene At 6.30	? August 1965
Lucky Stars Summer Spin	4 September 1965

BO DIDDLEY

September 1965					
25	Nelson	Imperial	7	Rochdale	Cubiklub
26	Birmingham	*unknown venue*	8	Wimbledon	Palais
27	London	Flamingo		London	University
28	London	100 Club	9	Southampton	University
29	Bromley	Bromel		East Grinstead	Whitehall
October 1965			11	Edmonton	Cook's Ferry Inn
1	Manchester	Cavern	13	Loughborough	College
	Stockport	Manor Lounge		Sheffield	University
2	London	Flamingo	14	Oldham	Astoria
3	Manchester	Oasis	15	Exeter	University
5	Hanley	The Place	16	Chelsea	College
6	Bristol	Corn Exchange	17	Lewisham	El Partido

Promoters — Joe Collins and Mervyn Conn

Two years had elapsed since Bo Diddley first toured Britain so successfully in the company of Little Richard and the Everly Brothers. His return proved to be a disappointment for all concerned. Publicity for the tour was completely chaotic with conflicting dates being announced and then changed more than once, so that it was never clear precisely where and when he was appearing. Bo arrived on 25 September along with the Duchess and his drummer, Clifton James. It was hoped that Jerome Green would be coming as well, but he did not make the trip. It transpired that he had recently married and, put under severe pressure from his new bride to give up touring, had now left the group.

Generally, fans voiced their disapproval of Bo's new toned-down style, while the gigs were plagued by equipment problems, car breakdowns and disappointing attendances. At the Birdcage in Portsmouth, fans did attend in significant numbers but the star of the show never turned up, leaving two thousand people having their entrance money refunded. Promoter Mervyn Conn subsequently announced to the press that Diddley's car had broken down on the way to Portsmouth.

The trouble-strewn tour finally disintegrated when Bo cut and ran back to Chicago on 18 October, claiming that money was owed to him — an accusation that was hotly disputed by co-promoter Joe Collins: 'Bo Diddley says he wasn't paid, but he was,' he insisted.

The villain of the piece appears to have been Bo's manager, Frank Kocian, who conned him into undertaking an expenses-only 'promotional tour' while pocketing all the appearance fees himself.

Bo had been due to make a second appearance at London's 100 Club that evening, but it was ten minutes after he was due on stage that they got a call from his road manager to say that he would not be appearing, so yet again refunds had to be made to disappointed fans. The whole tour had degenerated into a complete fiasco.

TV appearances

The Eamonn Andrews Show	26 September 1965
Gadzooks! It's All Happening	27 September 1965
Thank Your Lucky Stars	2 October 1965
Discs A-Go-Go	6 October 1965
Ready Steady Go	8 October 1965

THE EVERLY BROTHERS

October 1965					
8	Bedford	Granada	19	Bristol	Colston Hall
9	Finsbury Park	Astoria	20	Portsmouth	ABC
10	Leicester	De Montfort Hall	21	Exeter	ABC
12	Edinburgh	ABC	22	Cardiff	Odeon
13	Glasgow	Odeon	23	Bournemouth	Winter Gardens
14	Newcastle	City Hall	24	East Ham	Granada
15	Leeds	Odeon	26	Lincoln	ABC
16	Blackpool	ABC	27	Chesterfield	ABC
17	Liverpool	Empire	28	Wigan	ABC
Promoter — Brian Epstein					

At one time, it looked as though Phil Everly would be repeating his solo tour of 1962 because his brother Don was only discharged from the US Marines immediately before they flew to the UK on 4 October. Promoter Brian Epstein set the tour up in association with the pirate station, Radio London, who plugged it ceaselessly as well as arranging a welcome for the Everlys at the airport.

They brought with them the Everly Trio, which now comprised Sonny Curtis (guitar), Dale Halcombe (bass) and Jim Gordon (drums), and joined a package titled *Star Scene '65*, along with Cilla Black, Billy J. Kramer & The Dakotas, Paddy, Klaus & Gibson, the Marionettes, the Alan Elsdon Band, Lionel Blair & His Kick Dancers and Radio London deejay Pete Brady, who acted as compere. *Melody Maker* reported that the Everlys were being paid

£7,000 a week by Epstein — a huge amount of money in 1965.

At Finsbury Park, Don and Phil come out on stage smartly attired in black suits, Phil's hair longer than on previous trips, in stark contrast to Don's short crop — a reminder of his spell in the Marines. They opened with 'Lucille', 'All I Have To Do Is Dream' and a raucous 'Price Of Love'. The mournful 'Cathy's Clown' raised an expected ovation, as did 'Bye Bye Love'. They also included newer pieces like 'Love Is Strange' (their latest release) and a folk tune called 'People Get Ready', which would have been more effective without the screamers. They closed their polished and highly-professional act with a show-stopping rendition of 'I Got A Woman'.

The tour did exceptionally good business at all eighteen venues, while on 18 October they were reported to have recorded their own half-hour TV special for Tyne-Tees, although it apparently was never screened.

TV appearances

Ready Steady Go	8 October 1965
Thank Your Lucky Stars	16 October 1965

DOCTOR ROSS

October 1965			18	Belfast	Ulster Hall
11	Croydon	Fairfield Halls	21	Bradford	St. George's Hall
15	Manchester	Free Trade Hall	22	Birmingham	Town Hall
16	Newcastle	City Hall	23	Bristol	Colston Hall
17	Glasgow	Concert Hall			
Promoter — National Jazz Federation					

Some eyebrows may be raised at the inclusion of Dr. Ross, who like Big Joe Turner was much more a bluesman than a rock'n'roller. However, he did become something of a cult hero to the rockabillies during the Eighties because of his Sun recordings and for that reason alone is considered worthy of our attention.

Dr. Isiah Ross was a one-man band exponent, a left-handed guitarist who sang and also played harmonica and drums. He came originally from Tunica, Mississippi but at the time of his first visit to Britain was residing in Detroit. He toured as part of an intriguing show that was billed as *'The 4th American Folk Blues Festival'* and also included Big Mama Thornton, Lonesome Jimmy Lee, Eddie Boyd, Buddy Guy, Fred Below, J.B. Lenoir, Walter 'Shakey' Horton, Roosevelt Sykes and Mississippi Fred McDowell.

For his slot, the Doctor set up in the centre of the stage with bass drum, cymbals, guitar and harmonica and performed 'Illinois Blues' and '32-20' before raising the temperature with an unexpected 'Good Rockin' Tonight'. Whilst receiving adequate applause, his act was clearly one that would have been more effective in a small club rather than a theatre environment.

CHUCK BERRY

By now, it had become clear that Chuck Berry was a very shrewd businessman. Eschewing the services of managers, he preferred to make his own deals, being just as tough a negotiator as the agents and promoters with whom he came into contact. A trio of promoters, Paddy Malynn, Joe Collins and Mervyn Conn, jointly announced a series of ballroom dates for Chuck, commencing in Portsmouth and including appearances in Boston, Nelson and at London's Flamingo Club. Shortly after the initial announcement, a further statement revealed that there were 'a lot of difficulties', until eventually the whole tour was shelved. Joe Collins confirmed: 'He won't be coming for me. I didn't agree to certain contractual obligations that were put up at the last minute.'

BEN E. KING

October 1965					
15	Hounslow	Zambesi	23	Nottingham	Birdcage
	London	Scotch of St. James		Sheffield	King Mojo
16	Birmingham	*unknown venue*	24	Hayes	Blue Moon
17	Kirklevington	Country	27	Cheltenham	*unknown venue*
18	London	Flamingo	28	Portsmouth	Birdcage
20	Liverpool	Cavern	29	Manchester	Twisted Wheel
21	Reading	Olympia	30	Cowley	*unknown venue*
22	Greenford	Starlite		Stepney	New All Star
	London	Flamingo	31	Bromley	Bromel
				London	Flamingo
Promoter — Roy Tempest					

When Ben E. King first toured Britain in February 1964, he had been part of a big package and his time allocation had been no more than fifteen minutes per show. He was therefore pleased to be able to perform his full repertoire on this highly-successful ballroom tour, on which he was backed by the Jimmy Brown Sound.

Audience response exceeded his wildest dreams. At the Cavern in Liverpool, chairs were smashed and girls fainted and had to be pulled out over the heads of the crowd. A smiling King told *Record Mirror*: 'Now I know how the Beatles feel. In all my years of singing I've only been afraid of fainting twice, and that was one of them.'

The previous night at the Flamingo Club, the normally cool London kids went crazy over Ben: 'There was one fellow that had me worried. He was six foot seven and kept shouting all through the act. Then at the end he rushed over and picked me up, and I thought my time had come, but all he did was shout: "Yeah, man!" '

The Drifters' hits like 'There Goes My Baby' and 'Save The Last Dance For Me' on which Ben had been the original vocalist, proved enormously popular — so much so that he was allocated four songs instead of the usual two on his *Ready Steady Go* appearance on 15 October.

TV appearances

Ready Steady Go	15 October 1965
Scene At 6.30	20 October 1965
Discs A-Go-Go	27 October 1965

The ever-popular Ben E. King mobbed at Manchester's Twisted Wheel.

BRENDA LEE

There had been continuing rumours that Brenda Lee would be touring the UK again before the end of 1965. Dates had originally been proposed for September and October, and finally promoter George Cooper came forward with firm proposals for sixteen concerts commencing 16 November. Before anybody had time to get excited, the whole scheme was scrapped to enable Brenda to entertain US troops in Vietnam.

JOHNNY CASH

The final non-event of the year was a short visit for two December concerts in London and Liverpool by Johnny Cash. The most interesting aspect of this project was the promoter. Although he was unsuccessful on this occasion, within a few years Mervyn Conn would not only be responsible for breaking Cash in the UK, but was also to play a major role in popularising country music in Europe. His day would come.

CHAPTER ELEVEN

1966

It's Saturday Night
And I Just Got Paid

As the Sixties wore on, so popular music continued to evolve. Every month the charts were crammed with new names, new sounds and absolutely no rock'n'roll. The R&B craze of 1964 had evaporated, and Don Arden was now fully occupied controlling the career of the Small Faces. Live rock'n'roll in Britain still had a following but little or no real organisation, and it was largely the efforts of promoter Roy Tempest that kept the scene alive at all. Moreover, the violence which had attached itself to the music in the Fifties was never far from the surface in 1966, and few people would have bet on it lasting for very much longer.

The British performers were gone as well. Stalwarts like Marty Wilde and Wee Willie Harris survived in the business by rebranding themselves as cabaret performers, albeit with acts that included healthy doses of rock'n'roll. Those like Terry Dene or Dickie Pride, who either couldn't or wouldn't change, had long since been swept aside. Even Screaming Lord Sutch had been obliged to alter his image and in 1966 was billing himself as 'Lord Caesar Sutch'.

Country music had still to make any real impact in Britain. Eddy Arnold got himself a UK Top Ten hit with 'Make The World Go Away' and came over for a brief visit, although more interestingly, Bill Monroe took his bluegrass music around the British clubs, but unsurprisingly received virtually no media interest at all.

Soul music of course continued to be in vogue and major acts seen in Britain during the year included Stevie Wonder, James Brown, Wilson Pickett, Don Covay, Solomon Burke and Otis Redding.

However, if you wanted to hear and see live rock'n'roll, you really had to pay attention. It was still out there, but sometimes you had to look very hard to find it.

At the Gainsborough in Pendleton on the last night of the tour.
Left to right: Gerhart Thrasher, Bobby Hendricks, Bobby Lee Hollis and Bill Pinkney.

THE ORIGINAL DRIFTERS

January 1966			23	Stepney	New All Star
14	Harlesden	32 Club	24	Wolverhampton	*unknown venue*
	Paddington	Cue	25	Harlow	*unknown venue*
15	Manchester	Oasis	26	Southampton	*unknown venue*
	Manchester	Twisted Wheel	27	Portsmouth	Birdcage
16	Birmingham	Brum Kavern	29	Northwich	Victory Memorial Hall
19	Nottingham	Dungeon		Manchester	Jigsaw
21	Golders Green	Refectory		Liverpool	Cavern *(all nighter)*
22	Dalston	Macador	30	Pendleton	Gainsborough
	Greenford	Starlite		Salford	Riverboat
Promoter — Roy Tempest					

The year started with a riddle: When is a Drifter not a Drifter? The answer is somewhat complicated, and this was the first of numerous occasions when the origins and identity of a group needed careful examination.

The Original Drifters comprised Gerhart Thrasher, Bobby Hendricks, Bobby Lee Hollis and Bill Pinkney — a completely different line-up to those who had toured Britain the previous spring. Thrasher and Pinkney had both been Drifters way back in 1953 when the Clyde McPhatter-led outfit recorded such rock'n'roll classics as 'Money Honey' and 'Such a Night'. Hendricks joined the group for a brief period in 1958, and his is the lead tenor voice on 'Drip Drop'.

When their manager, George Treadwell sacked the entire group later that year and replaced them with the Ben E. King ensemble, the 'Original Drifters' became the vehicle for the Gerhart Thrasher outfit to keep working.

So, it can be seen that the Original Drifters had much to offer, even though they did not have the credibility of being current Atlantic recording artists.

At the Brum Kavern in Birmingham they went on stage ridiculously late for a Sunday evening, but received an enthusiastic ovation from the fans who had been waiting impatiently for the show to begin. Their act was a fascinating mixture of material from their hit-producing namesakes — such as 'Up On The Roof' and 'On Broadway' — interspersed with 'Stand By Me' and other songs of similar vintage including 'Only You' and 'Night Time Is The Right Time'. By the end of the evening they had the place rocking, and persuaded members of the audience to join them on stage for 'If I Had A Hammer', before launching into 'Shout' for a fitting climax to a most exciting and visual act.

TV appearances

Stramash	? January 1966
Five O'Clock Club	28 January 1966

GARY 'US' BONDS
BEN E. KING
CLYDE McPHATTER
THE SHANGRI-LAS

Promoter Roy Tempest was now adopting the scatter-gun approach to his press statements. He would simultaneously list perhaps eight forthcoming tours by various rock'n'roll, pop or soul acts. Many were speculative at best and were never mentioned again after the initial announcement. Rock'n'roll acts that were promised for the early months of 1966 but failed to materialise were Gary 'US' Bonds, Clyde McPhatter, Ben E. King and the Shangri-Las.

CLARENCE 'FROGMAN' HENRY

March 1966					
4	Islington	Golden Star	12	Halifax	Marlborough Hall
5	Stepney	New All Star	14	Edmonton	Cook's Ferry Inn
	Dunstable	California	18	Camberley	Agincourt
6	Woolwich	Shakespeare		Windsor	Ricky Tick
7	London	Tiles	19	Manchester	Twisted Wheel
11	Lewisham	El Partido	20	Birmingham	Ritz
12	Accrington	Cavern		Birmingham	Plaza
Promoter — Mervyn Conn					

Four years after his first British tour, the Frogman returned to work the UK's clubs and ballrooms. There was little publicity for his visit and those who did manage to track him down were surprised to find that he had dispensed completely with the piano. This did seem a rather desperate move as his whole style had been based around the New Orleans rolling piano sound, but he explained that he was trying to get away from the keyboard because it 'hides a performer'.

At Tiles in London he sang for almost an hour but did not seem to be enjoying the experience any more than his tiny audience, a good number of whom might best have been described as apathetic teenagers. His set consisted of a mixture of ballads and rock'n'roll standards, but even proven winners like 'Kansas City', 'Hi-Heel Sneakers' and even his own 'Ain't Got No Home', failed to generate much enthusiasm. An all-purpose rock'n'roll medley incorporating 'Long Tall Sally', 'Whole Lotta Shakin', 'Jenny, Jenny' and 'Ko Ko Mo' likewise achieved little. In fact, it was the slower numbers like 'But I Do', 'Cherry Pie' and 'You Always Hurt The One You Love' that worked best, while on 'Blueberry Hill' Clarence sounded exactly like Fats Domino — but without the piano of course. All in all, a distinctly unmemorable tour. Even his proposed spot on *Ready Steady Go* was cancelled.

TV appearances
Scene At 6.30   9 March 1966

ROY ORBISON

March 1966			10	Leicester	De Montfort Hall
25	Finsbury Park	Astoria	11	Blackpool	Odeon
26	Birmingham	Odeon	14	Bristol	Colston Hall
27	Derby	Gaumont	15	Cardiff	Capitol
28	Walthamstow	Granada	16	Sheffield	City Hall
29	Chester	ABC	17	Liverpool	Empire
30	Wigan	ABC	19-20	Oxford	New
31	Glasgow	Odeon	22	Belfast	ABC
April 1966			23	Hammersmith	Odeon
1	Edinburgh	ABC	24	Ipswich	Gaumont
2	Newcastle	City Hall	27	Tooting	Granada
3	Leeds	Odeon	28	Luton	ABC
5	Wolverhampton	Gaumont	29	Portsmouth	Guildhall
6	Manchester	Odeon	30	Bournemouth	Winter Gardens
7	Stockton	ABC	May 1966		
8	Bradford	Gaumont	1	Wembley	Empire Pool
9	East Ham	Granada		Coventry	Theatre
Promoter — Arthur Howes					

Roy returned to Britain for another long theatre tour, this time co-starring with the Walker Brothers on a package that also promised Lulu & The Luvvers, the Marionettes, Kim D, the Quotations and compere Ray Cameron. In the event, Lulu split from her Luvvers a week before the tour commenced and performed as a solo act. She also missed three nights early on through laryngitis, her place being taken by the Irish girl, Perpetual Langley and the Untamed. Lulu also missed the Coventry show, where she was replaced by Dee Dee Warwick.

The tour kicked off at Finsbury Park with a typical Orbison performance notable for the inclusion of his new disc, the uptempo 'Twinkle Toes'. He was backed throughout his stay by the Barry Booth Orchestra. The music press speculated about whether Roy or the Walker Brothers were the more popular, but everybody seemed satisfied that the package contained something for everybody.

On 27 March, Roy went to watch the motorcycle scrambling at Hawkstone Park and was invited to ride the lap of honour with the race winners. He came off his machine and fell into a sandpit, but remounted to finish the lap. Later that evening, he performed two shows at Derby in considerable discomfort and afterwards it was confirmed that he had broken a bone in his foot. From then on he was obliged to perform his act seated on a stool. When she heard about his accident, Claudette Orbison flew to England to be with her husband.

On the afternoon of Sunday, 1 May, Roy appeared on a star-studded bill at Wembley at the *NME Poll Winners Concert*, and performed 'Twinkle Toes', 'Breaking Up Is Breaking My Heart' and 'Oh, Pretty Woman' before ten thousand fans. Also appearing were the Beatles, the Rolling Stones, Cliff Richard, the Shadows and a host of others.

A tragic postscript to Orbison's accident occurred in June, shortly after the tour was completed. Roy and Claudette were returning home from a motorcycling holiday, travelling on separate bikes. As they neared their Nashville home, a truck came out of a side road and collided with Claudette, who died in hospital a few hours later.

TV appearances

The London Palladium Show	20 March 1966
Top Of The Pops	24 March 1966
Crackerjack	25 March 1966
Five O'Clock Club	15 April 1966
Juke Box Jury	23 April 1966
A Whole Scene Going	27 April 1966
NME Poll Winners' Concert	1 May 1966 (screened 8 May 1966)

SCREAMIN' JAY HAWKINS

April 1966					
1	Brixton	Ram Jam	15	Nottingham	Dungeon
	Stepney	New All Star	16	Farnborough	Carousel
2	Manchester	Oasis	17	Bayswater	Douglas House (USAF)
3	Salford	Riverboat	18	Woking	Atlanta
5	Birmingham	Penthouse	19	Uxbridge	*unknown venue*
8	Paddington	Cue	20	Pendleton	Gainsborough
9	Manchester	Jigsaw		Salford	Riverboat
10	Handsworth	Plaza	21	Penarth	Paget Rooms
	Kings Heath	Ritz	22	London	Flamingo
12	London	Whiskey A Go Go	23	Boston	Gliderdrome
14	London	New Scene	24	Coventry	Leofric Hotel
Promoter — Roy Tempest					

Screamin' Jay returned to the UK on 1 April for what was originally scheduled as twelve nights of ballroom dates, but was soon extended to almost a month. Backed throughout by Herbie Goins & The Night-Timers, Jay was generally a little more restrained — at least by his standards — than on his first visit.

He opened at the Ram Jam in Brixton, highlights of which included 'Little Bitty Pretty One', 'Just Don't Care', 'Alligator Wine' and a manic version

Great moments in history: Screamin' Jay meets Screaming Lord Sutch.

'Shout'. He was given a rousing reception as he prowled around the stage, resplendent in his cape and clutching his skull, Henry, while simultaneously assaulting the audience with his deep baritone voice.

The tour was a mixed bag of venues. On Good Friday at Paddington, Hawkins co-starred with Don Covay on what was billed as a 'soul' show. The following night, he headlined in Manchester on a gig that also featured the

Impromptu session at the Twisted Wheel.

Graham Bond Organization. At the New Scene club in London, Lee Dorsey turned up to watch Jay perform in front of only a handful of people. Nevertheless, he still gave his best and added knockout versions of 'You Made Me Love You' and 'Ebb Tide' to his usual set. 'The Whammy', 'Yellow Coat' and 'I Put A Spell On You' were also high points of the evening.

For the show at the Flamingo, Jay appeared in a new stage outfit comprising a huge broad jacket and trousers of heavy silk brocade in a fetching white-and-gold pattern. He drew a sizeable audience on this occasion and included a great rocker, 'Mumblin' Blues', in his set. Needless to say, he went down famously and finished the night with three encores.

214

ARTHUR ALEXANDER

April 1966					
			9	Stevenage	Bowes Lyon House
1	Windsor	Ricky Tick		Stonebridge Park	West Indies
2	Brixton	Ram Jam	10	Nottingham	Beachcomber
	London	Flamingo	11	Bognor	Caribbean
3	Hanley	The Place	15	Stepney	New All Star
4	London	Scotch of St. James	16	Windsor	Ricky Tick
5	London	Marquee	17	Portsmouth	Birdcage
8	Farnborough	Carousel		Hassocks	The Downs
Promoter — Malcolm Rose					

Arthur at the Flamingo Club, London.

Arthur Alexander's only British tour ran concurrently with Screamin' Jay's visit, making April 1966 an exciting time for those fans whose musical knowledge and interests extended beyond the charts. Like Jay, Alexander never enjoyed the luxury of a British hit. His name had only come to the attention of the public through the many cover versions of his records (notably 'You Better Move On', 'Anna' and 'A Shot Of Rhythm & Blues), one or more of which seemed to feature in the repertoire of every self-respecting British group. His tour rarely ventured far from London and, with negligible press interest, the whole project seemed financially unwise.

He was backed throughout his stay by the seven-piece Jimmy Brown Sound. Arthur himself turned out to be a tall, lean man with a full head of lank, black, greasy hair. On stage he appeared reserved and undemonstrative, and showed little personality, simply standing and singing each song in turn with a voice and style faintly reminiscent of Sam Cooke.

At the Flamingo, he wore a black suit and frilly white shirt and opened with 'Pretty Girls Everywhere'. Audience response was positive and he progressed effortlessly through 'You Better Move On' and 'Stand By Me'. It was all very pleasant and well put-over. 'Anna' was followed by a rather limp version of 'If I Had A Hammer', but he recovered with 'Where Have You Been'. Halfway through the song, however, he glanced at his watch to confirm that he had completed his thirty minutes and walked off the stage, leaving the band to finish the song as best they could.

Arthur Alexander was a talented and massively-underrated artist, although not by any means an outstanding live performer. He died on 9 June 1993 in Cleveland, Ohio following a heart attack.

TV appearances

Scene At 6.30	31 March 1966
Five O'Clock Club	5 April 1966
Ready Steady Go	8 April 1966

The bubbly Dixie Cups at the Jigsaw, Manchester.

THE DIXIE CUPS

April 1966			May 1966		
23	Stepney	New All Star	4	Bromley	Bromel
24	Huntingdon	USAF	5	London	Whiskey A Go Go
26	Hounslow	Zambesi	6	London	Flamingo
28	Brixton	Ram Jam	7	Manchester	Jigsaw
30	Eastbourne	Catacombs			
	Paddington	Cue			
Promoter — Mervyn Conn					

The spring of 1966 saw the Dixie Cups make a welcome return to the UK. Joan Johnson, Barbara Hawkins and her sister Rosa Lee were teamed with soul singer Alvin Robinson for a low-key tour of the clubs and ballrooms.

It was originally planned for the girls to kick-start their tour with two theatre gigs at Leicester and Walthamstow, appearing with the Small Faces and Crispian St. Peters, but these were both cancelled at a late stage, possibly due to indifferent ticket sales. However, the dates that did survive went over well enough, with their hit records, 'Chapel Of Love' and 'Iko Iko' proving the most popular numbers. At the Flamingo, they shared billing with Geno Washington & His Ram Jam Band.

The girls were accompanied by their manager, Joe Jones (of 'You Talk Too Much' fame), although sadly he did not perform whilst in Britain. Barbara Hawkins appeared on *Juke Box Jury* on 23 April along with Roy Orbison.

TV appearances

Juke Box Jury [Barbara Hawkins only]	23 April 1966
A Whole Scene Going	27 April 1966
Ready Steady Go	29 April 1966

THE ORIGINAL DRIFTERS

May 1966			21	Manchester	Twisted Wheel
6	London	Tiles	22	Orpington	*unknown venue*
	Stepney	New All Star	24	West Hampstead	Klook's Kleek
7	Bayswater	Douglas House (USAF)	25	Salford	Riverboat
	Bishops Stortford	*unknown venue*		Pendleton	Gainsborough
8	Handsworth	Plaza	26	Erdington	Carlton
	Old Hill	Plaza		Birmingham	Penthouse
12	Brixton	Ram Jam	27	London	Flamingo
14	Manchester	Jigsaw	28	Manchester	University
	Manchester	Iron Door		Sheffield	King Mojo
15	Manchester	Oasis	29	Leigh	Garrick
16	Warrington	Parr Hall		Warrington	Towers
17	Nottingham	Dungeon	**June 1966**		
18	Purley	Orchid	5	Nottingham	Dungeon
19	London	Whiskey A Go Go	8	Handsworth	Plaza
20	Manchester	Domino		Kings Heath	Ritz
	Manchester	Princess			
Promoter — Roy Tempest					

Bill Pinkney, Bobby Hendricks, Bobby Lee Hollis and Gerhart Thrasher returned to the UK on 6 May for a second tour, which again did good business around the clubs. Backing this time around was provided by Trendsetters Ltd, and — unsurprisingly — their act had not significantly changed since January.

Their performance on the opening night at Tiles was probably typical. Smartly attired in check suits, white shirts and patent leather shoes, they started strongly with a rocking 'Ruby Baby', and then worked their way through a selection of Drifters' favourites including 'Under The Boardwalk', 'There Goes My Baby' and 'Up On The Roof'. Hendricks mainly sang lead in a high, almost falsetto voice, contrasting with Pinkney's bass and the strict harmonies from Hollis and Thrasher. The latter was clearly inebriated, which added a wholly uninhibited air to his performance, his strong voice revealing the gospel influences in his past. The highlight of the evening was Bobby

Hendricks' moving rendition of 'Only You', which momentarily calmed the otherwise rowdy audience. The set closed with the tactical error of inviting some of the fans to dance on the stage during 'If I Had A Hammer', and the predictable shambles ensued as too many exhibitionists grabbed the opportunity to take over the proceedings.

When the Original Drifters played a gig at Douglas House the following afternoon, the audience included Bobby Lewis, who was touring US military bases in Britain at the time. There were variations of the basic show from night to night, and worthy of mention are Pinkney's rousing version of 'Night Time Is The Right Time' and 'Try Me', Bobby Lee Hollis soloing on 'Stand By Me', and Hendricks' gentle 'I Love You For Sentimental Reasons', which was transformed into something quite different as Gerhart Thrasher strutted up and down the stage, yelling at the audience and firing a stream of hip phrases and jive talk across him.

The Original Drifters had so much to offer, yet were forced to operate in a twilight existence, despite the fact that a high proportion of their audiences neither knew nor cared that they were not the current line-up of the group who recorded for Atlantic. During the tour, Bobby Lee Hollis fell ill and dropped out, being replaced by a British soul singer called Ollie. However, the Drifters' story would soon become even more complex as totally bogus groups were brought to England to cash in on the name.

JOHNNY CASH

May 1966					
7	Liverpool	Empire	14	Manchester	Palace
8	Birmingham	Hippodrome	15	Hammersmith	Odeon
12	Newcastle	City Hall	17	Bayswater	Douglas House (USAF)
13	Glasgow	Odeon	20	Belfast	ABC
			22	Walthamstow	Granada
Promoters — Joe Collins and Mervyn Conn					

British audiences were just starting to latch on to the music of Johnny Cash in the spring of 1966. His early Sun recordings were eagerly sought by rock'n'roll fans and at least one far-sighted promoter had, through Cash, spotted the enormous and yet untapped potential for country music in the UK.

Mervyn Conn would soon become Europe's leading country promoter, but for now he and Joe Collins were taking a considerable risk. As well as Johnny and his wife June Carter, the tour also featured his backing group, the Tennessee Three (guitarist Luther Perkins, bassist Marshall Grant and drummer W.S. Holland), plus the Statler Brothers. Attendances were generally good and audiences most enthusiastic.

At Liverpool, Cash sang for over an hour — an extraordinary length of time given that sets in those days were generally no more than twenty or thirty minutes long. His rendition of two Dylan songs, 'Don't Think Twice' and 'It Ain't Me Babe', was particularly well received and — significantly — his recording of the latter gave him his first British hit the following month. Other numbers that went over well included 'Streets of Laredo', The Troubadour' and 'The One On The Right'.

Up in Glasgow, a swinging version of 'Orange Blossom Special' went down a storm and he was inundated with requests including 'Forty Shades Of Green' and, inevitably, 'I Walk The Line'.

THE EVERLY BROTHERS

Don and Phil spent some time in London during the first half of May, recording the album *Two Yanks In England*. During this period they also made an appearance on *Ready Steady Go*, as well as attending a lavish party thrown by Brian Epstein at the Savoy along with Cilla Black, Joe Brown and Patsy Ann Noble. They returned to the UK again in July for further work on the same album.

TV appearances
Ready Steady Go   ? May 1966 (screened 13 May 1966)

BEN E. KING

May 1966					
20	London	Flamingo	28	Paddington	Cue
	London	Scotch of St. James		Manor House	Kinky
21	Nottingham	Dungeon	29	Liverpool	Empire
	Manchester	Jigsaw	30	Farnborough	Carousel
22	Windsor	Ricky Tick	31	London	Marquee
	Harlesden	West Indies	**June 1966**		
23	London	Tiles	2	Birmingham	Penthouse
25	Purley	Orchid		Erdington	Carlton
26	Brixton	Ram Jam	3	Greenford	Starlite
	London	Whiskey A Go Go		Stepney	New All Star
27	Manchester	Domino	4	Manchester	Twisted Wheel
	Manchester	Princess	5	Brixton	Ram Jam
Promoter — Roy Tempest					

Ben E. King returned on 18 May for his third UK visit and further enhanced his reputation with some solid performances on Roy Tempest's club circuit. On this tour he worked with the Statesiders and pulled good crowds, appealing perhaps more to the soul fans than the rockers, but nevertheless always including some Drifters material in his repertoire.

At Tiles in London, he opened with a bouncy version of 'Just A Little Bit' and proceeded to deliver 'Save The Last Dance For Me', 'Don't Play That Song', 'Stand By Me' and 'Spanish Harlem' as part of a thirty-five minute set. Smartly dressed in a dark brownish-green suit, King smiled throughout as he shuffled from one foot to the other, occasionally clapping his hands. After a medley of soul tunes, he closed with a repeat of 'Stand By Me' and then some four or five encores of 'Yes'.

At the Ram Jam in Brixton, his show went over so well that he was rapidly re-booked for a second time on the final night of the tour.

TV appearances
Ready Steady Go   20 May 1966

GARY 'US' BONDS
FATS DOMINO
CLARENCE 'FROGMAN' HENRY

Promoter Roy Tempest's list of forthcoming tours for July included Gary 'US' Bonds, Clarence 'Frogman' Henry and Fats Domino, and one by one they all fizzled out. Domino was the biggest disappointment, as British audiences had yet to see him perform live. Tempest promised that he would play a series of large seaside venues including Blackpool, Bournemouth and Great Yarmouth, and claimed that Freddie & The Dreamers and then Gerry & The Pacemakers were to be contracted to tour the USA to comply with the Musicians' Union exchange agreement. Nothing materialised.

BIG JOE TURNER

September 1966		
28	London	Royal Albert Hall
29	Manchester	Free Trade Hall
Promoter — Harold Davison		

Big Joe Turner returned to the UK as part of the 1966 *American Blues Festival* along with Sleepy John Estes, Roosevelt Sykes, Little Brother Montgomery, Otis Rush, Junior Wells and Sippie Wallace. They arrived on 27 September and had a day of rehearsals before playing two major concert dates in London and Manchester. Turner's backing was supplied by Otis Rush (guitar), Freddie Below (drums), Jack Myers (bass) and Little Brother Montgomery (piano).

At the Royal Albert Hall, Joe seemed tired and sang without any noticeable enthusiasm, but thanks to his formidable stature and his rich resonant voice, was still able to make a positive impression as he worked through a selection of his hits. Highlights of his act included a slow rendition of 'Chains Of Love', a more rocking 'Hide And Seek' and his closing number, 'TV Mama'. For an encore that also marked the end of the concert, he was joined on stage by the rest of the cast for a chaotic 'Bye Bye Baby', during which Junior Wells grabbed the limelight by falling to the floor and screaming with complete abandon. Unfortunately, the show was running late and had to be brought to a sudden and rather unsatisfactory close halfway through the song.

On 30 September, the *AFBF* troupe recorded a TV special in Manchester for Granada on which Joe performed 'My Baby's A Jockey'.

TV appearances
Nothing But The Blues   30 September 1966 (screened 27 December 1966)

BILL HALEY & HIS COMETS

Bill Haley & His Comets were contracted to play shows in France during September, and promoter Barry Clayman tried unsuccessfully to follow this with a five-week UK tour commencing 9 October. A week in cabaret at the Fiesta in Stockton was provisionally lined up but by late September the project had been scrapped. However, the French dates did go ahead and Haley played a very successful show in Paris along with the Spencer Davis Group.

JERRY LEE LEWIS

October 1966			November 1966		
16-22	Bradford	Lyceum Rainbow	1-5	Stockton	Tito's
	Guiseley	Paradise		Middlesbrough	Marimba
23-29	South Shields	Latino	6	Birmingham	Hippodrome
	Newcastle	La Dolce Vita	7	Wimbledon	Theatre
30-31	Stockton	Tito's	9	London	Blaises
	Middlesbrough	Marimba	10-11	Leigh	Garrick
				Warrington	Towers
			12	Coventry	Matrix Hall
				London	Flamingo

Promoters — Barry Clayman, Maurice King and Colin Berlin

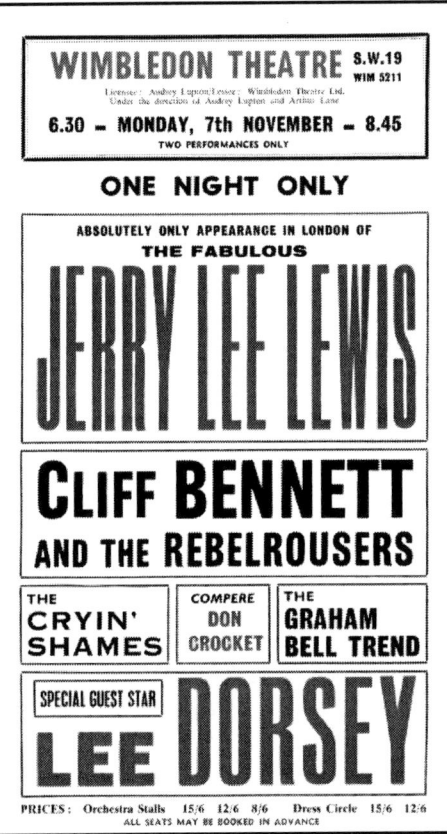

WIMBLEDON THEATRE S.W.19 WIM 5211

Licensee: Audrey Lupton/Lessee: Wimbledon Theatre Ltd.
Under the direction of Audrey Lupton and Arthur Lane

6.30 — MONDAY, 7th NOVEMBER — 8.45
TWO PERFORMANCES ONLY

ONE NIGHT ONLY

ABSOLUTELY ONLY APPEARANCE IN LONDON OF
THE FABULOUS

JERRY LEE LEWIS

CLIFF BENNETT
AND THE REBELROUSERS

THE **CRYIN' SHAMES**	COMPERE **DON CROCKET**	THE **GRAHAM BELL TREND**

SPECIAL GUEST STAR
LEE DORSEY

PRICES: Orchestra Stalls 15/6 12/6 8/6   Dress Circle 15/6 12/6
ALL SEATS MAY BE BOOKED IN ADVANCE

Almost two years had passed since Jerry Lee Lewis last visited Britain and his tour did not get off to a good start when bad weather prevented his plane leaving America on time, forcing the cancellation of the opening show at the Imperial Ballroom, Nelson. When he eventually arrived, he was met at the airport by Tom Jones, a long-time fan who had every reason to be extending his hospitality to Jerry. He had just plundered 'Green Green Grass Of Home' off Lewis' *Country Songs For City Folks* album, and the record would soar to the top of the British charts in early December, though many considered Jerry Lee's rendition to be infinitely superior.

Plans for a major TV special, provisionally titled *Tom And Jerry* did not come to fruition, and instead Jerry was packed off to the North of England for his first excursion into the scampi-and-

Jerry Lee in action at Wimbledon Theatre.

chips cabaret circuit. If anybody expected him to modify his behaviour in such circumstances, they were in for a disappointment. He opened at Bradford with a storming 'Down The Line' and played all his usual material including frantic versions of 'Mean Woman Blues', High School Confidential' and 'Hi-Heel Sneakers' before cooling down with a moving encore of 'Goodnight Irene'.

Jerry's appearance had changed since the 1964 tour. He had lost his lean, hungry look and had his hair cropped in a much shorter style. He wore a conservative dark suit and could easily have passed for a lawyer or an accountant until he opened his mouth to sing.

There were only two theatre dates — on consecutive nights at Birmingham and Wimbledon — with support from Lee Dorsey, Cliff Bennett & The Rebel Rousers (featuring former British rock'n'roller Roy Young on piano), the Cryin' Shames and the Graham Bell Trend. Lewis' backing was provided by his regular US crew, Morris Tarrant (drums) and Herman Hawkins (bass), although Johnny Kidd's Pirates were actually contracted to provide the backing to comply with Musicians' Union requirements. They were paid but did not play. Kidd himself had been tragically killed in a car crash only a week before Lewis arrived in the UK.

At Birmingham the sound system was first-rate, and he included standout versions of 'Let's Talk About Us' and 'Little Queenie', along with a magnificent 'Green, Green Grass Of Home'.

The following night at Wimbledon, the theatre was packed with a very rowdy audience containing a high percentage of teddy boys. Possibly the aggression that stemmed from the audience — where at least one fight broke out — affected him, but there was not a single slow number included in his set. He steamed through 'Lewis Boogie', 'Great Balls Of Fire', 'Good Golly Miss Molly' and the rest. It was another vintage night of rock'n'roll that ended with Jerry Lee on top of his piano and the audience invading the stage from all sides.

The tour concluded with appearances at Leigh and Warrington, with support from Dave Berry at both, and Marty Wilde at the latter. Finally, after an all-nighter at the Flamingo, Jerry flew on to Geneva, Switzerland on 13 November for more shows.

JOHNNY CASH

Only six months after his first Johnny Cash tour, Mervyn Conn tried to set up a further seven British dates in November as part of a longer European excursion. On this occasion he was unsuccessful, but if the time was still not quite right for Johnny Cash in the UK, at least Conn was proceeding along the right lines.

THE DIXIE CUPS

November 1966			12	Nottingham	Dungeon
4	Greenford	Starlite	15	Leicester	Palais de Danse
	Stepney	New All Star	16	Southampton	Mecca
5	Manchester	Twisted Wheel	18	Manchester	Domino
8	London	Whiskey A Go Go		Manchester	Princess
9	Purley	Orchid			
10	Birmingham	Cedar			
	Erdington	Carlton			
Promoter — Roy Tempest					

Barbara Ann and Rosa Lee Hawkins and Joan Johnson returned for their second tour of 1966 accompanied as before by their manager, Joe Jones. Backing was provided by the Thoughts. The girls were largely ignored by the music press but received a positive response in the ballrooms. At Southampton, an enthusiastic audience heard a thirty-minute set featuring 'Iko Iko', 'People Say', 'Chapel Of Love' and their newest single 'Daddy Said No', which they sang twice. The evening closed with a raucous version of 'Land Of A Thousand Dances'.

Nat Wilson, Cornel Gunter and Bobby Stegar in action at the Twisted Wheel, Manchester.

THE ORIGINAL COASTERS

November 1966				
5	Sheffield	Rawmarsh Baths	15 London	Whiskey A Go Go
	Sheffield	King Mojo	17 Crawley	Starlight
6	Nottingham	Beachcomber	19 Manchester	Twisted Wheel
	Nottingham	Britannia	Liverpool	Cavern
9	Southampton	Mecca	20 Manchester	Princess
11	Greenford	Starlite	Manchester	Domino
12	Manchester	Oasis	24 London	Whiskey A Go Go
13	London	Tiles	26 Boston	Gliderdrome
			Leicester	Burlesque
Promoter — Roy Tempest				

In November 1966 it was believed — wrongly as it turned out — that Roy Tempest was bringing into Britain the current line-up of Coasters for their first UK tour. Only later was it fully appreciated that stalwarts like Billy Guy and Carl Gardner were still active in the States, and that the trio which came to do battle around the ballrooms of Great Britain was in reality considerably less authentic than the Original Drifters had been. The group comprised Cornel Gunter, Nathaniel Wilson and Bobby Stegar. Wilson was formerly a member of the Shields, but only Gunter had any real connections with the Coasters, having been the second tenor to Carl Gardner's lead on several of their hit records.

Their tour proved to be reasonably successful, although the act was almost entirely constructed around the showmanship of Cornel Gunter. Their second appearance at London's Whiskey A Go Go was typical. They came on stage around 11.00 pm, Bobby and Nat smartly attired in grey suits, vividly contrasting with Cornel who was wearing what looked like a silver-green pyjama suit, complete with matching nail polish and eye make-up. His overt effeminacy led to the inevitable catcalls and barracking from the more homophobic among the audience, as he stormed into 'Poison Ivy' and an unusually fast 'Yakety Yak'.

There was much clowning around both between and during the numbers, during which Gunter pronounced himself 'prettier than both Mohammed Ali and Little Richard'. 'Young Blood' was one of the highlights of the evening, being an ideal vehicle for his rich and powerful voice. Bobby Stegar took the lead for 'Searchin' ', while Nat serenaded Gunter on 'My Girl'. Their hilarious antics during 'Little Egypt' easily held the attention of the audience, who were soon hand-clapping along to the gospel-flavoured 'Amen' and an unbelievably furious 'I Can't Help Myself'. 'Knock On Wood' led into an uptempo 'Charlie Brown' before they closed as they had begun with 'Poison Ivy'.

It would still be some time before authentic Coasters came to Britain, and although Gunter continued to front different versions of the group for many years to come, for him at least the clowning came to an abrupt halt on 26 January 1990 when he was shot dead in his car in Las Vegas by an unknown assailant.

BEN E. KING

November 1966			19	Sheffield	King Mojo
11	Stepney	New All Star		Nottingham	Dungeon
	London	Tiles	20	Greenford	Starlite
12	Manchester	Twisted Wheel	25	Paddington	Cue
14	Birmingham	Cedar		London	Scotch of St. James
15	West Hampstead	Klook's Kleek	26	Liverpool	Cavern
	Windsor	Ricky Tick	27	Coventry	Leofric Hotel
18	Manchester	Princess		Birmingham	Cedar
	Manchester	Domino			
Promoter — Roy Tempest					

Back for his second tour of 1966, Ben E. King's popularity with other musicians was highlighted when a packed Scotch of St. James included Eric Burdon, Georgie Fame, the Four Tops, John and Cynthia Lennon and Bobby Darin among those anxious to catch his act. Darin was in the UK for the first time since his 1960 tour, and managed some TV work and promotion, but was now far removed from his days as a rock'n'roller. He did enter into the spirit of things sufficiently to play drums on a couple of numbers at the Scotch, but it was Ben E. King that everybody had come to see, and he was well up to the mark, despite the temporary embarrassment of forgetting the lyrics to 'There Goes My Baby'. At Nottingham, Ben shared the billing with Lee Dorsey, while at Liverpool's Cavern a rather extraordinary promotion had him appearing with the Salvation Army group, the Joystrings.

Backed on the tour by the Senate, King was sufficiently impressed by the Scottish group's work to produce a session for them in London on 20 November, which included his own composition 'Can't Stop'. He was also popular enough to justify another spot on *Ready Steady Go*. He appeared on the same night as Little Richard, and after his own act was clearly visible to viewers, standing and clapping while Richard gave his usual excessive performance.

TV appearances
Ready Steady Go   25 November 1966

LITTLE RICHARD

November 1966			December 1966		
23	Chester	Top Rank	1-3	Edinburgh	Pentland
	Sheffield	University	4	Newcastle	City Hall
25	Portsmouth	Birdcage	5-10	Edinburgh	Pentland
26	Liverpool	Peppermint Lounge	11	London	Saville
	Nelson	Imperial	14	Stevenage	Locarno
27	Manchester	Princess		London	Blaises
	Manchester	Domino	16	West Houghton	Casino
28	Wigan	Casino		Burnley	Casino
30	Bolton	Casino	17	Folkestone	Toft's
				London	Flamingo
			18	Manchester	Princess
				Manchester	Domino

Promoters — Barry Clayman, Maurice King and Colin Berlin

Little Richard flew into Britain on 19 November, and — in welcome contrast to most recent rock'n'roll tours — was met with an abundance of coverage in the music press. This was probably not unconnected with the fact that the main gig was scheduled for the Saville Theatre in London's Shaftesbury Avenue. The Beatles' manager, Brian Epstein, had recently begun promoting Sunday evening concerts at the Saville, and his involvement provided the necessary press interest. Richard was accompanied by his mother, Leva Mae Penniman, his aunt Roberta and his cousin, Roy Chester. The latter had hopes of his own singing career and on at least one occasion (at the Princess in Manchester) performed a short guest spot.

Little Richard in typically energetic form at Manchester.

A press reception was arranged by EMI for Richard on 21 November, and it came as something of a relief when he contradicted earlier pronouncements on the subject by informing the world: 'I'm a rock'n'roll singer,' while claiming to no longer be a minister of the church.

Backed throughout by the Quotations, he packed in the crowds wherever he played. At Folkestone, his show was unusually short, but the insistent cheering of the audience finally coaxed him back on stage for an unscheduled encore. He had already left the building but came back and sang his final number wearing a heavy sheepskin coat.

The show at Wigan was an interesting contrast of styles, with Richard headlining and lounge bar crooner Vince Hill providing support.

On his way to the Princess Club at Manchester, Richard's car was involved in an accident and he performed with a badly cut lip and several painful bruises. The Princess was a semi-cabaret venue, but quickly loosened up. 'The piano isn't loud enough!' Richard screamed at the conclusion of 'Send Me Some Lovin' '. He then proceeded to tear the place apart with 'Rip It Up' and an extended version of 'Keep A-Knockin' ' which had the audience dancing and pushing their way to the front of the stage. He then told them: 'Even if I was dead and in a casket, I would still sing from there if the fans wanted me to' — an interesting proposition, and one which sent the crowd berserk, with cheering and yelling, before he closed out with a riotous 'Whole Lotta Shakin' Goin' On'.

For his appearance on *Ready Steady Go*, Richard wore a striking gold lamé jacket, and featured a lot of his distinctive piano playing on 'I Need Love' and 'Good Golly Miss Molly'.

Inevitably however, it was the Saville Theatre gig that secured the greatest interest. Showbiz celebrities including Mick Jagger, Dave Clark, Lionel Bart, Georgie Fame and Cilla Black were packed in with a seething mass of rockers and teddy boys. The concert was a sellout and the atmosphere electric right from the word go.

Opening the show were Bluesology, who sensibly performed an inoffensive set of rock'n'roll standards, but were given a pretty hard time by the audience. Their pianist, Reg Dwight, would later change his name to Elton John and become a flamboyant star in his own right, but at the Saville he remained in the shadow of Little Richard, one of rock'n'roll's greatest showmen.

The Alan Price Set closed the first half, and they too ran into immediate trouble from a hostile audience who were not prepared to sit through anything but rock'n'roll. Their efforts were met by catcalls, slow handclaps and constant barracking. Several items were thrown at the stage and the whole affair was teetering on the brink of disaster, especially when compere Eric Burdon came out and faced the audience, holding in his hand a spark plug which had earlier been thrown at Bluesology. He shouted above the din: 'These people are here to entertain you. If you don't like it, I suggest you leave the theatre and return when Little Richard appears.' More abuse followed and Burdon retreated with the audience now at fever pitch.

After a short interval which fortunately managed to calm the atmosphere somewhat, Burdon came back out to introduce the star of the show. In a creditable attempt to lighten the proceedings, he wore a metal ice bucket on his head and was clutching a steel dustbin lid in front of himself like a shield. 'All right you bastards,' he shouted — in perhaps the most unusual introduction ever heard from a compere's lips at a West End theatre — 'you want Little Richard — here he is!'

The patrons in the stalls rose as one and moved *en masse* to occupy the aisles closest to the stage as Little Richard started to hammer the piano keys and tear his way into 'Lucille'. He had been suffering with flu and needed to use an inhaler between numbers, but still had enough energy to teach the future Elton John a thing or two. Richard's hair was much longer on this tour and at the start of his act it was piled on his head in a gravity defying style which was soon shaken into oblivion. With long strands of dark hair hanging down his back and over his face, he screeched through 'The Girl Can't Help It' and a high-powered 'Send Me Some Lovin' '.

By the end of 'Good Golly Miss Molly', a girl fan had got on stage and embraced him before being ejected by the heavy-handed and overworked security. The piano took a further pasting during 'Rip It Up', 'Tutti Frutti' and 'Jenny, Jenny', by the end of which several drape-jacketed youths finally managed to clamber up onto the stage, some dancing, others writhing on the floor, before being unceremoniously hurled back into the audience. 'Ready Teddy' was cut short when the drummer screwed things up, and mid-way through 'Long Tall Sally' it became clear that Richard's voice was giving out completely. Nobody seemed to care. The whole theatre was being shaken to its foundations and he struggled through 'Whole Lotta Shakin' ' before finally leaving the stage bathed in perspiration.

Little Richard can sometimes frustrate his audiences by promising more than he actually delivers. At the Saville, he cut the crap and just played piano and sang without the gimmicks and the striptease. Real rock'n'roll doesn't come much better than that.

TV appearances

The Scene	23 November 1966
Top Of The Pops	24 November 1966
Ready Steady Go	25 November 1966
The Eamonn Andrews Show	11 December 1966
The Frost Programme	16 December 1966

THE ORIGINAL DRIFTERS

December 1966			10	Manchester	University
5	Birmingham	Cedar		Manchester	Twisted Wheel
8	Birmingham	Cedar		Sheffield	King Mojo *(all nighter)*
9	Manchester	Domino	11	Greenford	Starlite
	Manchester	Princess	13	Nottingham	Dungeon
Promoter — Roy Tempest					

The Original Drifters returned for their third British tour of 1966. Three visits within the year was a sure indication of their popularity on the club circuit. Media interest was zilch. This time, Bill Pinkney, Gerhart Thrasher and Bobby Hendricks were augmented by a fourth, anonymous Drifter, but the high standard of the shows was maintained and the public were quite unconcerned by the change in personnel.

CHAPTER TWELVE

1967

Just Want To Hear Some Of That Rock'n'Roll Music

1967 was the year when popular music overdosed on peace and love. Flower children predominated. Hippies rattled their beads and exhorted us all to meditate, while festivals of love sprang up all over the place. The Beatles hatched the monstrosity that they called *Sergeant Pepper* and a bland voice on the radio exhorted everyone to go to San Francisco and to 'be sure to wear some flowers in your hair'. The rockers had already put up with enough from the posturing mods, and found the hippies and their whole sleazy drug culture a completely alien experience. San Francisco was just not far enough away, and as for their damn flowers, they should be forced up into a wholly more appropriate part of the body, and as painfully as possible. The music press rarely gave rock'n'roll even a passing mention, concentrating instead on the likes of Moby Grape and the Electric Prunes. Many thought the world had suddenly gone mad.

As well as the rock'n'roll tours which continued to feed the hunger of the faithful, blues and soul remained in favour around the clubs and UK visitors during the year included Carla Thomas, Arthur Conley, John Lee Hooker, Mary Wells and Lee Dorsey.

British audiences were finally starting to become interested in country music, in no small part due to the enduring popularity of the late Jim Reeves. Hank Locklin and Carl Belew both worked the club circuit that year, while Bobby Bare, George Hamilton IV and Bobbie Gentry all made promotional visits. Jim Ed Brown even managed a TV appearance with David Frost, while former Sun artist David Houston interrupted a European tour to appear at the opening of a new club in Liverpool, only to run into work permit difficulties which prevented him from performing. Country music had an important connection with rock'n'roll and only now was it starting to build more than a tiny minority audience in Britain.

ROY ORBISON

Roy commenced the New Year with a lightning visit to the UK to appear on the *London Palladium Show*. He flew into London with his father, but only stayed long enough to make the one appearance, sharing the bill with the Rockin' Berries and compere Des O'Connor.

TV appearances
The London Palladium Show　　　　　1 January 1967

DEL SHANNON

January 1967		February 1967	
28　Chalk Farm　　Roundhouse		5-11　Newcastle　　La Dolce Vita	
		Middlesbrough　Marimba	
		19　London　　　　Saville	
Promoter unknown			

This was primarily a promotional visit for Del Shannon who was anxious to plug his new single, 'She'. As well as the usual round of media interviews, he travelled to Cannes at the beginning of February in the company of Paul Jones, to attend the music industry's *MIDEM Festival*. He then returned for a week in cabaret, doubling each night at Newcastle and Middlesbrough.

One evening, a pretty blonde approached him at the Newcastle gig. Del thought she was seeking an autograph, only to discover that she was from the Inland Revenue and had come to present him with a £500 income tax bill!

In mid-February, he travelled to Germany for an engagement in Hamburg, but returned in time to play the main

Sunday
19th February 1967

in order of appearance

HAMILTON and THE MOVEMENT

DEL SHANNON

intermission

CHUCK BERRY

Resident compere : Rick Dane

FOR YOU

supporting role to Chuck Berry at his first Saville Theatre concert. The evening eventually deteriorated into chaos during Chuck's set, but happily Shannon enjoyed a more peaceful time, his mixture of pop and rock'n'roll being readily accepted by the capacity audience, who especially enjoyed 'Swiss Maid', 'Runaway' and 'Keep Searchin' (We'll Follow The Sun)'.

TV appearances
Top Of The Pops   2 February 1967
The Rolf Harris Show   4 February 1967

CHUCK BERRY

February 1967					
			23	Streatham	Locarno
17	Manchester	Princess		London	Blaises
	Manchester	Domino	24	Durham	University
18	Manchester	New Century Hall		Newcastle	University
	Manchester	Technical College	25	Brighton	University
19	London	Saville		Camberley	Agincourt
20	Wolverhampton	Queen's	26	London	Saville
	Cardiff	Top Rank	27	Liverpool	Cavern
22	Stevenage	Locarno			
	Birmingham	Cedar			

Promoter — Roy Tempest

Chuck Berry at the Saville Theatre is one of the most vivid memories of live rock'n'roll in Britain during the mid-Sixties. Unfortunately, however, it is remembered for all the wrong reasons. The threat of violence which had been evident on several earlier occasions finally erupted on 19 February, when Chuck's act was cut short and the safety curtain brought down.

The evening had started in routine fashion with the hapless opening act, Hamilton & The Movement, being greeted with the usual boos and catcalls. Del Shannon fared much better, but it was Chuck who the thousand-strong audience had come to see, and as he fired his way through 'Rock & Roll Music', 'Nadine' and' Sweet Little Sixteen' everything seemed to be on schedule for a great night of rock'n'roll. However, as he swung into 'Roll Over Beethoven', a small number of teddy boys fought their way onto the stage and tried to dance, only to be rebuffed by an overzealous team of heavy-handed security men. The situation rapidly deteriorated when the theatre manager panicked, and made what in hindsight was the wrong decision.

The safety curtain was brought down with Chuck still singing away behind it and all hell broke loose. Light fittings were ripped off the walls, rows of seats were torn down, and one very large ted, swinging an upturned microphone stand like an axe, attempted to chop his way through the safety curtain. The rioting continued in the streets outside and several arrests were made before the police were finally able to disperse the crowd. Theatre owner Brian Epstein, who was watching the show in the company of Beatles John Lennon and Ringo Starr, was appalled by the premature actions of the manager and promptly fired the poor man, although later press reports did indicate that he was having second thoughts and was considering reinstating him.

Seven days later, Chuck Berry was back at the Saville again. A second concert was hastily convened to try and make up for the earlier debacle. Mama Cass Elliott and Graham Nash were among the celebrities who turned up, as much out of curiosity as anything. Compere Rick Dane took no chances and made all announcements smartly attired in a borrowed drape jacket. Hamilton & The Movement received their customary booing and were joined by the Truth and Herbie Goins & The Night-Timers as the support acts.

Fun with Chuck at the Princess Club, Manchester.

Generally, however, the audience were relatively subdued leading up to Berry's appearance. Possibly some were still in police custody from the week before. Chuck, who was backed throughout the tour by the Canadians, wore a coffee-coloured jacket and brown slacks and opened to a rousing welcome with 'School Day', before accelerating into 'Sweet Little Sixteen', during which he duckwalked back and forth across the stage. Happily, this time the show ran its course without any undue audience participation, and Chuck worked through his normal repertoire of rockers, interspersing two blues numbers, Muddy Waters' 'Hoochie Coochie Man' and his own 'Wee Wee Hours' before rounding off with a storming 'Johnny B. Goode'.

The remainder of the tour comprised the usual Roy Tempest hotchpotch of ballrooms and clubs, sometimes doubling up to squeeze the maximum revenue from the enterprise. Attendances were excellent throughout and Chuck was generally in top form. The playlist varied only slightly from night to night, but did include a few surprises — Elmore James' 'Dust My Broom' at Manchester Technical College being one.

At Streatham, he performed an incredibly energetic 'Roll Over Beethoven' on a revolving stage while doing the splits, his guitar thrust out provocatively from between his legs.

At Manchester's Princess Club, the lyrics to 'Reelin' And Rockin' ' were reported to have been X-Certificate, while he also included 'South Of The Border' and — some six years before Mary Whitehouse got to hear about it — 'My Ding-A-Ling', before closing with a wild version of 'Promised Land'. Later that night at the Domino, Chuck sang the whole of 'My Ding-A-Ling' with an over-excited female hanging onto his trouser leg for dear life.

At Cardiff, the proceedings were marred by a poor sound system, but he still managed a magical version of 'Memphis Tennessee'.

Berry's third British tour was another great success. The violence at the Saville was regrettable, but even that had resulted in a heavy dose of welcome publicity at a time when rock'n'roll was struggling to retain a foothold in the consciousness of the general public. As on his previous visits, Chuck made no appearances at all on British television.

DUANE EDDY

February 1967					
24	Manchester	Princess	4	Sheffield	University
	Manchester	Domino	5	Bayswater	Douglas House (USAF)
25	Liverpool	University		Camberley	Agincourt
26	Birmingham	Plaza	7	Streatham	Locarno
28	Leicester	Palais de Danse	8	Purley	Orchid
March 1967			9	London	Whiskey A Go Go
1	Stevenage	Locarno	10	Ruislip	USAF
2	Bristol	Locarno	11	Manchester	New Century Hall
3	Morecambe	Central Pier	12	London	Saville
Promoter — Roy Tempest					

The third Duane Eddy tour was an altogether quieter affair than his earlier theatre shows in the UK. Backed by the Senate, he was largely confined to ballroom dates on this occasion, leading up to a headlining night at the Saville Theatre. He had a new single, 'Monsoon', to promote, but it was his old hits that the audiences wanted to hear.

The gig at the Agincourt in Camberley was probably typical. Publicity for the show was limited, and only a small crowd turned out to see him. However, what they lacked in numbers was more than compensated for by their enthusiasm. As soon as he was announced, everybody moved down close to the stage, leaving the rear of the hall completely empty. Duane twanged his way through a succession of his hits and, although his set was only twenty minutes long, it was very well-received, while at Streatham the high point of the evening was an ear-splitting 'Some Kinda Earthquake' which had the fans screaming for more.

Likewise at the Saville, he went down well despite failing to draw a capacity crowd. Instrumental music was no longer fashionable and it was probably even tougher for Duane than for the rock'n'roll vocalists. Support was provided by Liverpool's Lomax Alliance and soul singer Edwin Starr, but an exceptionally cold night in London — and even inside the theatre itself — did not help the proceedings. Even so, Eddy provided the full works, his act complete with rebel yells and raunchy saxophone. One of the best moments came with a thoughtful '3.30 Blues', but it was 'Peter Gunn' and 'Cannonball' that earned him three curtain calls.

ROY ORBISON

March 1967					
3	Finsbury Park	Astoria	22	Carlisle	ABC
4	Exeter	ABC	23	Leeds	Odeon
5	Plymouth	ABC	24	Doncaster	Gaumont
7	Hadleigh	Kingsway	25	Lincoln	ABC
8	Birmingham	Odeon	26	Coventry	Theatre
9	Bolton	Odeon	27	Blackpool	Odeon
10	Manchester	Odeon	29	Cardiff	Capitol
11	Chesterfield	ABC	30	Bristol	Colston Hall
12	Liverpool	Empire	31	Cheltenham	Odeon
15	Luton	Ritz	**April 1967**		
16	Southampton	Gaumont	1	Bournemouth	Winter Gardens
17	Tooting	Granada	2	Leicester	De Montfort Hall
18	Wolverhampton	Gaumont	5	Ipswich	Gaumont
19	Newcastle	City Hall	6	Slough	Adelphi
20	Edinburgh	ABC	7	Aldershot	ABC
21	Glasgow	Odeon	9	Romford	ABC

Promoters — Harold Davison and Tito Burns

Roy Orbison returned for his annual tour of the UK fresh from a successful series of shows in Australia. He headlined on an old-style package along with the Small Faces, Paul & Barry Ryan, the Jeff Beck Group, the Settlers, Sonny Childe & The TNT, the Robb Storme Group and compere Ray Cameron. The opening night at Finsbury Park put paid to Jeff Beck's contribution. His newly-formed group, which included Rod Stewart and Ronnie Wood, were so unrehearsed and went over so badly that they dropped out and were replaced by P.P. Arnold. The Ryans left the show after Slough and were replaced on the last two nights by the Searchers.

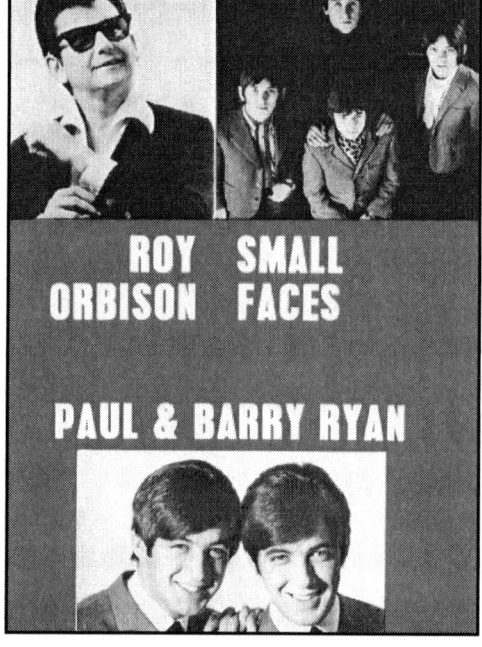

This was a routine tour for Roy, revisiting the scenes of many earlier triumphs. Backed on this occasion by his own group, the Candy Men, his familiar act included 'Only The Lonely', 'Lana', 'It's Too Soon To Know', 'So Good', 'Mean Woman Blues', 'It's Over' and 'Oh, Pretty Woman'. His popularity seemed as strong as ever, although — perhaps ominously — the prestigious show that had been scheduled for 8 April at the Hammersmith Odeon was axed at short notice and the theatre re-booked for Otis Redding. Even Roy's period of stardom was coming to an end. While in England, he took the opportunity to employ some staff, and a lucky couple from

Gateshead eventually flew out to Nashville clutching their P45's ready to take up their new positions as chauffeur and nanny to the Orbison family.

TV appearances
Top Of The Pops	2 March 1967
Crackerjack	17 March 1967

THE DRIFTERS

The popularity of the Drifters around the ballrooms cannot be overstated, and with three financially-successful tours by the Original Drifters of Pinkney, Thrasher, Hollis and Hendricks during 1966, it had become apparent that there were plenty more golden eggs to be laid by that particular goose. The public knew the Drifters' songs but had no strong impression of the group members — hardly surprising given that the personnel had altered so much over the years. For three weeks in March and April, the 'Drifters' were out on ballroom circuit again — but this time with a completely different line-up which was totally bogus and had no authenticity at all.

Eventually *Record Mirror* took notice and carried an exposé of the impostors. A photo had even been shown to former Drifter Ben E. King who failed to recognise them. They were finally unmasked as Herman Coefield, Bobby Rivers, Gary Gant and Bobby Morris — collectively better known as soul group the Invitations. This hoax demonstrated the fact that there were rich pickings to be had for an unscrupulous promoter if he was prepared to proliferate such a fraud. The Drifters may have been the first victims among rock'n'roll acts in the UK, but others would follow as we shall find out.

FATS DOMINO

March 1967			April 1967		
27-31	London	Saville	1	London	Saville
			2	Manchester	Palace
Promoter — Brian Epstein					

Fats Domino had already sold a reported fifty-five million records around the world by the time he made his British stage debut. His career, which stretched back to 1949, was littered with hits including some twenty-two million-sellers. He was a rock'n'roll heavyweight in every sense of the word, but along with Elvis Presley and Rick Nelson had still never performed in the UK. There had been numerous attempts to lure him to Britain but each successive promoter had eventually withdrawn from negotiations, the expense of transporting his sizeable entourage invariably proving to be the stumbling block. Ironically, it was Brian Epstein who finally underwrote the enormous cost of bringing Domino to Britain — a fact that produced mixed emotions in many hardcore rock'n'roll fans who loathed the Beatles and ordinarily didn't have a civil word to say about their manager.

With hindsight, Epstein ought be given a lot of credit. His Sunday evening concerts at the Saville Theatre were vitally important to rock'n'roll in

Fats and band on stage at the Saville Theatre.

1967. They provided the music with publicity and profile at a time when both were desperately needed. The bold decision to book Fats Domino for six nights at the Saville was the high point of the year for rock'n'roll, and only Epstein could have made it possible.

Domino flew into London on Easter Sunday accompanied by his nine-piece band: Walter Kimble (tenor sax), Robert Hagans (tenor sax), Clarence Ford (baritone sax), Nat Perrilliat (tenor sax), Herb Hardesty (trumpet and tenor sax), Wallace Davenport (trumpet), Roy Montrell (guitar), James Davis (bass) and Clarence Brown (drums). They were a formidable outfit, containing some of the cream of New Orleans musicians — Hardesty in particular having been with Fats right through from his first-ever recording session in 1949.

They opened at the Saville the following evening, with enthusiasts travelling from all over the country to catch one or other of the shows. Some fanatics even block-booked their seats for the week. This was perhaps the first occasion that rock'n'roll fans travelled long distances in this way — a regular occurrence by the Eighties when many artists would be brought in for one-off exclusive appearances at festivals or weekenders.

The thankless task of opening the proceedings fell upon an Australian band, newly arrived in Britain with hopes of furthering their antipodean success. They wisely stuck mainly with numbers like 'Dizzy Miss Lizzy' and 'Be-Bop-A-Lula', but although their day had yet to come, the Bee Gees performed well enough in difficult circumstances to show themselves as a cut above the normal opening act. Gerry & The Pacemakers closed the first half of the show, commencing with 'Long Tall Sally' and surviving the hostile calls from the audience, albeit more on the strength of Gerry Marsden's self-effacing wit than their musical ability.

Fats and his band performed for the whole of the second half of the show, which was unusual in itself to an audience brought up on the traditional package show featuring six or even more acts, each of them rarely performing for more than twenty minutes. The curtain opened to a darkened stage, and one by one a spotlight picked out each of the nine musicians strung out in a line as they burst into 'Peanut Vendor', during which Domino walked on to an enthusiastic welcome before taking his place at the piano to finish the tune. The main body of the act varied from night to night as different songs were introduced, but the overall impression was constant: namely, a top-class band, well-rehearsed and confident, behind one of the greatest rock'n'roll performers of all time.

A typical show opened with a pounding 'Whole Lotta Lovin' ', and, having grabbed the audience's attention right from the start, continued with 'I'm Walkin' ', 'Blueberry Hill' and 'Red Sails In The Sunset'. All the band members were highly-competent musicians in their own right, and were given the opportunity to shine individually as well as a part of the unit. 'Blue Monday' contained a fiery solo by Clarence Ford on baritone sax, while Herb Hardesty blew long and hard during 'Ain't That A Shame'. On 'I'm Gonna Be A Wheel Someday', it was the turn of Nat Perrilliat to take the solo with his tenor sax, while Hagans and Ford swapped instruments for 'Let The Four Winds Blow', the latter blowing a great tenor solo while Hagans waved and danced around the stage seemingly in a private world of his own.

Through it all, Domino sat hunched over his piano, garishly attired in a lime green jacket, blue trousers and a white shirt, his fingers and wrists decked with diamond cufflinks, a diamond wristwatch and numerous chunky diamond rings. Singing in his unique style, Fats could do no wrong as he worked through a selection from his many great recordings.

The evening finally reached a climax with 'Valley Of Tears', with all five saxmen blowing like crazy and swaying backwards and forwards in unison. Then, after a stomping 'Hello Josephine', they broke into a largely instrumental rendition of 'When The Saints Go Marching In', in which the band marched on and off the stage in procession — a trifle corny perhaps, but still a great visual effect. Finally, Fats himself rose to his feet, still playing but now also pushing the piano across the stage. The audience were cheering and applauding as one, and for an encore he travelled all the way back to 1949 for a tremendous version of 'The Fat Man' — his very first hit. Then he waved to the crowd and was gone. Fats at the Saville was a truly magical occasion.

BEN E. KING

March 1967		
31	Dunstable	California
April 1967		
1	Boston	Gliderdrome
	Nottingham	Dungeon *(all nighter)*
2	Greenford	Starlite
3	Birmingham	Cedar
?	London	Scotch of St. James
6	Sheffield	Locarno
7	Manchester	Domino
	Manchester	Princess
8	Manchester	Twisted Wheel
9	Liverpool	Cavern
10	Birmingham	Cedar
12	Windsor	Ricky Tick
14	Manchester	Domino
	Manchester	Princess
16	London	Saville
	London	Speakeasy

Promoter — Roy Tempest

Ben E. King was now one of the most consistently-popular acts on the ballroom circuit. On this, his fifth British visit, he toured again with the Senate plus his own guitarist, Jim Bowie, and again drew big crowds. He played two Manchester clubs, the Princess and the Domino, on a bill that also included Marty Wilde, and went over so well that he was re-booked for a week later. While in London, he stopped off at the Speakeasy to watch Mary Wells perform, and on another occasion at the same venue, sat in on drums for an impromptu jam session with Georgie Fame on organ and Jimi Hendrix on bass.

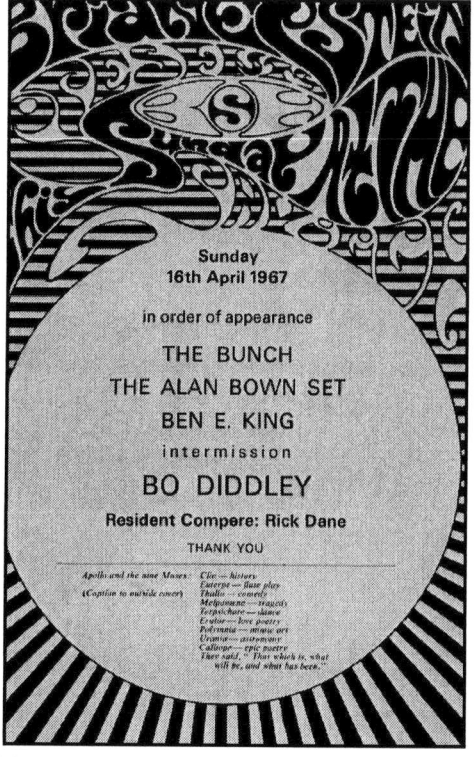

Sunday
16th April 1967

in order of appearance

THE BUNCH
THE ALAN BOWN SET
BEN E. KING
intermission
BO DIDDLEY

Resident Compere: Rick Dane

THANK YOU

The main gig of the tour was at the Saville Theatre. Ben was booked as support for Bo Diddley along with the Alan Bown Set and the Bunch. Ben's show was enthusiastically received — in sharp contrast to the Alan Bown Set, who unwisely attempted to send up rock'n'roll and probably regretted this when organist Jeff Bannister ended up needing hospital treatment after one of his teeth was broken by a flying penny (the big, heavy, pre-decimal variety). Meanwhile, vocalist Jess Roden was obliged to seek shelter behind a large amplifier while compere Rick Dane tried to calm the mob and was savagely booed for his trouble.

For his part, King judged his act perfectly, performing favourites like 'On Broadway', 'Spanish Harlem' and 'Save The Last Dance For Me', which the hardened rockers wanted to hear. The climax of the set was 'Will You Love Me Tomorrow', which left the audience cheering for more — adequate proof that the cool Mr. King had won them over.

BO DIDDLEY

April 1967			17	Cardiff	Top Rank
14	Dunstable	California	18	London	Cromwellian
15	Nelson	Imperial	19	London	Blaises
16	London	Saville		London	Sybilla's
Promoter — Roy Tempest					

Bo Diddley did not seem to be having a lot of good fortune in Britain. His 1965 tour had ended prematurely after a squabble over money, and his latest excursion around the ballroom circuit was sadly destined to follow the same pattern. Publicity for his visit was woefully inadequate and only his appearance at Brian Epstein's Saville Theatre received any sensible press coverage. Bo topped the bill at the Saville and went down a storm, providing precisely the excitement and raw jungle beat that the audience craved. They had already gorged themselves on the carcass of the Alan Bown Set — the evening's human sacrifices — and were now able to enjoy Bo, calling for requests and roaring him on with unrestrained enthusiasm. The pick of his fifty-minute show were long versions of 'Road Runner' and 'Hey Bo Diddley'. Backing throughout the tour was provided by the Canadians.

It would be gratifying to report that the remainder of the dates reached the same heights, but sadly this was not the case. At Cardiff, where Creation were the support act, all was clearly not well and a sullen Bo gave a less-than-satisfactory performance. The excrement hit the extrusion device a few days later. A brief announcement in the *Manchester Evening News* stated that: *'Bo Diddley cancelled for this evening. A telegram was received this morning. Bo collapsed at Sybilla's Club, Knightsbridge, London. Tour now cancelled.'*

That put paid to the double booking at Manchester's Domino and Princess clubs as well as other projected gigs in Birmingham, Chelmsford and London. The Little Richard fan club newsletter, *Penniman News*, reported that Bo had refused to play the remaining dates of the tour because the promoter was not paying him, but this allegation was hotly disputed by Roy Tempest's office. In any event, Bo was now back in USA, and once again his British fans were frustrated, while Diddley's reputation could not fail to be harmed by the debacle.

CLYDE McPHATTER

May 1967			25	Tunstall	Golden Torch
19	London	Flamingo	26	Stepney	New All Star
20	Nottingham	Dungeon		London	Roaring 20's
21	Manchester	Domino	27	Boston	Gliderdrome
	Manchester	Princess	28	Sheffield	King Mojo
23	London	Whiskey A Go Go	29	Nottingham	Dungeon
Promoter — Roy Tempest					

The arrival of Clyde McPhatter for a handful of dates in the UK was one of the big surprises of 1967. Clyde had toured with Duane Eddy and Bobby Darin in the spring of 1960 but had since made little impact with

Looking back: Clyde on *Saturday Spectacular* in April 1960.

record-buyers in Britain. In fact, his name was rarely mentioned. Perhaps it was the influx of Drifters — real and fabricated — that stirred the memory and brought about the UK return of their first and arguably greatest lead vocalist.

McPhatter opened at the Flamingo, playing two sets — one during the Friday evening of 19 May, and the other as part of an all-nighter which took place at the same venue and stretched from midnight through to five o'clock on the Saturday morning.

On the Sunday evening in Manchester, he appeared on the same bill as Hedgehoppers Anonymous, yet another bizarre coupling of two acts who were extremely unlikely to appeal to the same fans — a fact that should surely have been obvious to even the dimmest club manager.

The following Saturday at the Boston Gliderdrome, Clyde gave a confident and assured performance that was also a good deal more rocking than some would have expected. Backed by a competent British combo of three guitars, drums and saxophone (probably Sounds Force Five), he opened with a lively rendition of 'A Lover's Question'. His voice was in excellent shape, as he demonstrated on 'Treasure Of Love' and a fantastic rocking 'Money Honey', during which his legs buckled and swayed until the instrumental break, when he suddenly started bopping around the stage to the bewilderment of the largely mod audience. He continued with 'Lover Please' before dropping the pace for 'Without Love'. After that, it was furious rock'n'roll all the way: 'Little Bitty Pretty One' led into 'Money' and then 'What'd

I Say', during which the audience willingly participated with the 'oohs' and 'ahs'. Clyde McPhatter was an unexpected pleasure and, unlike some of the other acts on the circuit, entirely authentic.

DEL SHANNON

May 1967		June 1967		
27 Chalk Farm Roundhouse		11	Paignton	Festival Hall
		18-23	Stockton	Fiesta
			Sunderland	Porama
Promoter unknown				

Del Shannon's second visit of 1967 commenced with a well-publicised show at London's Roundhouse, along with Terry Reid and Peter Jay's Jaywalkers. He then departed for gigs in Ireland, before recording some material for an album in London with Andrew Loog Oldham. His visit was rounded off with appearances in cabaret, doubling at Stockton and Sunderland. The northern cabaret clubs were trying hard to compete with the Vegas-style entertainment on offer in the States, but their credibility remained a little suspect when the Porama proudly announced itself as *'Sunderland's latest nightclub'*, but added that it was to be found *'above Jackson's the Tailors'*. Shannon flew out to Canada on 26 June.

TV appearances
Dee Time   15 June 1967
Juke Box Jury   24 June 1967

THE CHIFFONS

June 1967			17	Nelson	Imperial
2	Dunstable	California	19	Tunstall	Golden Torch
3	Paddington	Cue	23	London	Tiles
4	London	Saville	24	Paddington	Cue
13	West Hampstead	Klook's Kleek		Brixton	Ram Jam
?	Birmingham	*unknown venue*	25	Greenford	Starlite
Promoter unknown					

By 1967, the craze for girl groups had largely evaporated — which was a pity, because Barbara Lee, Pat Stelley, Judy Mann and Sylvia Peterson, collectively known as the Chiffons, would probably have had a much greater impact had they toured two or three years earlier. Their UK dates were interrupted by a short German tour, but at Klook's Kleek they went over well enough with a fine selection of R&B-slanted material. 'One Fine Day' and 'He's So Fine' were well-received, as was their interpretation of 'Baby I Need Your Lovin' ', but it was the fast-moving 'Sweet Talkin' Guy' which they performed in a seemingly deadpan style that earned the greatest applause.   They were well-served by Pete Kelly's Rhythm & Blues Incorporated, who backed them up throughout the tour.
    The Chiffons did play the Saville Theatre, but were only allowed a

short set on a bill headed by the Jimi Hendrix Experience that also featured Procol Harum, Denny Laine, the Stormsville Shakers and the Electric String Band — hardly a line-up to attract the rock'n'roll fraternity. They closed the first half on a night which was plagued by technical difficulties.

THE ORIGINAL DRIFTERS

June 1967			July 1967		
9	Doncaster	Top Rank	1	Manchester	New Century Hall
10	Forest Gate	Upper Cut	2	Warrington	Co-op
	London	Flamingo		Middlewich	Warmington
13	Nottingham	Beachcomber	5	Salford	Riverboat
15	London	Whiskey A Go Go		Manchester	Oceans 11
16	Southampton	Top Rank	6	Tunstall	Golden Torch
17	Nottingham	Dungeon	8	Boston	Gliderdrome
18	Greenford	Starlite	11	London	Whiskey A Go Go
22	Sheffield	City Hall	12	Hulme	New Russell
23	Hull	Skyline		Pendleton	Gainsborough
26	Cardiff	Top Rank	15	Salford	Whiskey A Go Go
27	Nottingham	Dungeon	16	Sheffield	King Mojo
30	Derby	Clouds	19	Hanley	The Place
Promoter — Roy Tempest					

And still they kept coming... The Original Drifters returned to Britain with yet another line-up to add to the confusion. Bill Pinkney reported that Gerhart Thrasher and Bobby Lee Hollis had retired from the road, while Bobby Hendricks was having another stab at a solo career and had in fact just completed a tour of Ireland. Pinkney himself had recently joined forces with Benny Anderson, Albert Fortsom and Wallace Ezard (a trio who had recorded for King as the Tears) and guitarist Mark Williams to form a group called the Originals. They had even cut a record for United Artists but, rather than pursuing future stardom, were apparently content to slot back into the UK's ballroom circuit and masquerade as the Drifters.

Their stage shows received mixed reviews. At London's Flamingo Club, they opened with 'This Magic Moment' and a solid version of 'Ruby Baby', which was marred by the bizarre inclusion of a trombone amidst the accompaniment. The group were smartly dressed in white suits with gold waistcoats, while Pinkney proved himself a competent lead singer even though his vocal range was lower than is customary, giving some of the familiar Drifters songs an altogether unfamiliar sound. Perhaps the highlight of the show was Benny Anderson's 'Danny Boy', which utilised an identical arrangement to Jackie Wilson's show-stopping version of the same song. The set closed with a boisterous 'I Got A Woman', complete with gospel shouting and frantic dancing.

At the Boston Gliderdrome, the act was a good deal less effective. They only performed six songs in a half hour set, dragging each song out to the point where boredom set in. The final number, 'Stand By Me', in particular seemed endless and drove many of the audience off in search of the bar.

JERRY NAYLOR

Jerry had toured Britain in 1962 as vocalist with the Crickets and would have returned with them two years later but for serious health problems. He was now operating as a solo artist and plans were afoot for him to play shows in Germany, France and Britain during June 1967. Nothing materialised.

THE ORIGINAL DRIFTERS

September 1967					
15	Derby	Clouds	14	Manchester	New Century Hall
	Doncaster	Co-op		Manchester	University
16	Handsworth	Plaza	16	Tunstall	Golden Torch
	Birmingham	Penthouse	18	Manchester	Top Ten
17	Greenford	Starlite		Middlewich	Warmington
	Stonebridge Park	West Indies	20	Dunstable	California
19	London	Whiskey A Go Go	22	Kings Heath	Ritz
20	Nottingham	Dungeon		Handsworth	Plaza
22	Manchester	Domino	24	West Hampstead	Klook's Kleek
	Manchester	Princess		London	Whiskey A Go Go
23	Wigan	Paradise	27	Acton	White Hart
	Manchester	New Century Hall	28	Boston	Gliderdrome
24	Barnsley	The Hub	31	Hanley	The Place
27	Hanley	The Place	**November 1967**		
30	Boston	Gliderdrome	4	Manchester	St. Bernadette's
	Leicester	Nite Owl		Leicester	Nite Owl *(all nighter)*
October 1967			5	Manchester	Vaudeville
1	Nottingham	Dungeon		Manchester	Georgian
13	Manchester	Domino	6	Sheffield	City Hall
	Manchester	Princess			
Promoter — Roy Tempest					

Bill Pinkney, Benny Anderson, Wallace Ezard, Albert Fortsom and guitarist Mark Williams returned after a brief vacation back home to resume their 'Original Drifters' tour. They made quite an impact in the Manchester area and at one stage looked likely to take up permanent residence there.

However, the old question regarding the authenticity of the group continued to rumble on and eventually *Disc* managed to corner promoter Roy Tempest, who justified his actions by saying: 'I know it's a bit misleading, but most fans realise they're not the real Drifters. They're quite content to see a very good, polished, American vocal group. Promoters know only too well that they're not getting the real group. As far as I know, there are five sets of Drifters in America.'

DUANE EDDY

October 1967			14	Liverpool	Paradise
6	Manchester	Domino		Manchester	Domino
	Manchester	Princess		Manchester	Princess
7	Boston	Gliderdrome	17	Aylesbury	Assembly Hall
8	Birmingham	Cedar	21	Manchester	Technical College
?	Bristol	Locarno		Salford	Whiskey A Go Go
Promoter — Roy Tempest					

The return of Duane Eddy after eight months indicated a paucity of bookings back home rather than an overwhelming demand from the British public. Nevertheless, his dwindling UK fan base was delighted to see him again so soon, and his appearances at the Manchester Domino and Princess were so successful that he was immediately re-booked, the adverts proclaiming *'overwhelming demand'*.

Eddy was backed by the Gates Of Eden and the Senate at different points on the tour, although it was the latter who performed with him at Salford's Whiskey A Go Go — a routine booking, but one which rather unkindly highlighted the reduced circumstances of the rock'n'roll stars from the Fifties. The show was an all-nighter spearheaded by three American acts, Eddy, Clyde McPhatter and an apparently bogus trio of Isley Brothers.

It was the pairing of Eddy and McPhatter which tugged a little at the heartstrings. The two men had starred along with Bobby Darin on the controversial theatre tour of Britain in March 1960, when Eddy at least was at the peak of his popularity. Such memories must have come flooding back to provide a sobering contrast to the twilight tour of ballrooms that both men were now undertaking.

DEL SHANNON

October 1967			29-31	Stockton	Fiesta
7	Dunstable	California		Spennymoor	Top Hat
8-14	Batley	Variety	**November 1967**		
15-21	Sheffield	Cavendish	1-4	Stockton	Fiesta
22-28	Sunderland	Wetherell's		Spennymoor	Top Hat
	Newcastle	La Dolce Vita			
Promoter unknown					

Del Shannon had tasted British cabaret on his two previous visits during 1967, but now returned for a longer tour, having decided that this was the direction his career needed to take — at least for the immediate future. The itinerary included return bookings at Stockton and Newcastle, but other than an interview in *Record Mirror*, media interest was negligible.

CLYDE McPHATTER

October 1967					
13	Derby	Clouds	21	Manchester	Domino
14	Nottingham	Dungeon		Mancester	Princess
15	Handsworth	Plaza		Salford	Whiskey A Go Go
	Kings Heath	Ritz	26	London	Whiskey A Go Go
17	London	Whiskey A Go Go	27	Dunstable	California
			29	Nottingham	Dungeon
				Barnsley	The Hub
Promoter — Roy Tempest					

On his third visit to the UK, Clyde McPhatter mixed in some club and ballroom dates along with appearances at US military bases. His career was in decline back in the States and he was already thinking of making a permanent move to Britain. The music press took no interest at all in him. Engelbert Humperdinck was at the top of the British charts, but the majority of record buyers were unaware that a far more charismatic and talented vocalist was performing in their midst. Clyde worked with the Soul Survivors at Salford and possibly elsewhere, and the constantly-changing face of popular music was highlighted when he played the California ballroom in Dunstable. The following evening, Jimi Hendrix was booked to appear at the same venue.

BEN E. KING

October 1967			November 1967		
20	London	Tiles	2	Tunstall	Golden Torch
	London	Caribbean	3	Manchester	Domino
21	Forest Gate	Upper Cut		Manchester	Princess
	Stepney	New All Star	5	Greenford	Starlite
22	Bexley	Black Prince		London	Roaring 20's
23	Birmingham	Cedar	6	London	Bag O'Nails
	Wolverhampton	*unknown venue*		Brixton	Ram Jam
24	Hanley	The Place	8	Streatham	Locarno
26	Castleford	*unknown venue*	9	London	Scotch of St. James
29	Manchester	Domino	24	Warrington	Carlton
	Manchester	Princess	25	Manchester	Twisted Wheel
30	London	Marquee	26	Manchester	Domino
31	London	Scotch of St. James		Manchester	Princess
Promoter — Roy Tempest					

The continuing popularity of Ben E. King made an interesting contrast to Clyde McPhatter's lack of success. The two former Drifters both toured Britain in October 1967, and Ben — working once again with the Senate — packed the dance halls wherever he went. His act remained a mixture of soul material interspersed with Drifters classics. He interrupted his tour in mid-November for ten days of appearances in Germany.

BRENDA LEE

November 1967		9	Mildenhall	USAF
6 Birmingham	Castaways	12-18	Brighouse	Ritz
7 Southport	Kingsway Casino		Wakefield	Savoy
Southport	Grand Casino	19-25	Spennymoor	Top Hat
8 Leigh	Garrick		Stockton	Fiesta
Bolton	Casino			
Promoter unknown				

Brenda Lee was the latest rock'n'roller to ply her trade on the cabaret circuit. She had always been popular for her weepie ballads as well as her rockers, so it was probably a natural progression to develop in that direction. Ironically, her latest single, 'Where's The Melody', was a punchy number very much in her old style. After playing some dates in Germany, she arrived in the UK suffering with flu, which briefly threatened the tour. Happily, she recovered quickly and went over well with an act that still contained a sizeable smattering of rock'n'roll. Accompaniment was supplied by the Quotations and a vocal group called the Rag Dolls.

A proposed TV appearance on Simon Dee's *Dee Time* along with Gene Pitney was cancelled after a public row. Not surprisingly, Brenda wanted to perform 'Where's The Melody', whereas the BBC demanded one of her old hits. She refused to back down and was replaced by Kathy Kirby. She did, however, make a radio broadcast on *Saturday Club*, which also featured Long John Baldry. The music press highlighted the difference in their sizes with a photograph of the tiny Brenda standing on a chair and the six-foot seven-inch Baldry still towering over her.

TV appearances
The Eamonn Andrews Show   5 November 1967

CHAPTER THIRTEEN

1968

Get Rhythm

Rock music now took itself very seriously. New bands sneered at the singles charts and ridiculed acts who aimed their product at the teenage market. Underground music was the order of the day, and humourless musicians bored their audiences with long, tedious introspective songs that lacked the simple excitement of rock'n'roll. Disc-jockey John Peel eloquently described the situation as being 'like a woman who is endlessly pregnant but never has a baby'. Perhaps a dose of rock'n'roll was precisely what was needed to counter this eternal pregnancy, for — extraordinarily — 1968 saw a brief but highly welcome rock'n'roll revival, and for a few short weeks the media was full of stories about Elvis, Jerry Lee, Buddy Holly, and especially Bill Haley.

The first hint of the revival came in February. One of the new groups reported that, when they included a rock'n'roll number in their act, the audience (who were presumably bored stiff up to that point) crowded out onto the dance floor and both danced and applauded. This mind-blowing revelation spread like wildfire and before long, rock'n'roll nights were being introduced at clubs and ballrooms all over the country. Wee Willie Harris was booked into the trendy Cromwellian Club in London and went down a storm. Others, like pianist Roy Young and saxman Red Price, were soon gigging again alongside newer names, the most prominent of whom were Tommy Bishop, Freddie 'Fingers' Lee and Gerry Temple.

Nobody believed that the revival would last for long, as the fickle music press would soon move on to something else, but it was great fun while it lasted. John Fred & His Playboy Band took 'Judy In Disguise', a modern record with a heavy rock'n'roll flavour, into the British Top Ten, and then — amazingly — Bill Haley's original 'Rock Around The Clock' started to sell all over again to a new generation of record-buyers. In fact, during April, records by Haley, Buddy Holly and Eddie Cochran were all back in the charts. Just about every living rock'n'roll singer claimed to have a tour pending, although in the end it was Haley and Duane Eddy who were the main beneficiaries of the renewed enthusiasm for rock'n'roll.

Elsewhere, soul music was well catered for, and Aretha Franklin, Lou Rawls, Edwin Starr and Lee Dorsey were among the acts who toured during the year. Two Johnny Cash tours during 1968 again underlined the potential for country music, but although Eddy Arnold, Bobbie Gentry and Jeannie C. Riley made promotional visits, there was still no real live scene outside of the Irish clubs in Liverpool, Manchester and London.

CHUCK BERRY

February 1968	
2 Leeds	Queen's Hall
Promoter unknown	

Chuck made a brief and somewhat unexpected return to the UK to participate in what was billed as a '*Massive All-Nite Festival*', a ten-hour non-stop 'happening' at the Queen's Hall in Leeds running from 8.00 pm until 6.00 am. The show starred the Herd and the Move and also featured Chris Farlowe, Julie Driscoll, the Brian Auger Trinity and compere Jimmy Savile.

Berry and soul singer Edwin Starr were listed as 'special guest stars'. Although there was some talk of a ten-day club tour, no other dates in the UK materialised for him.

CLYDE McPHATTER

February 1968					
6	Great Yarmouth	Night Prowler	13	London	Whiskey A Go Go
7	Liverpool	Victoriana	15	London	Whiskey A Go Go
8	London	Whiskey A Go Go	17	Castleford	Tinned Chicken
9	Manchester	Vaudeville	18	Manchester	Domino
				Manchester	Princess
Promoter unknown					

Clyde's attempts to settle in the UK were not proving straightforward. He was refused entry in January, and several dates had to be cancelled after he failed to secure a work permit. His first scheduled appearance at the magnificently-named Tinned Chicken in Castleford had to be canned, with Edwin Starr standing in at the last minute. By the first week of February, the appropriate paperwork was in place and Clyde could get started on the difficult task of reviving his career in front of a new generation of fans who had little or no knowledge of his earlier triumphs.

THE G-CLEFS

March 1968		April 1968		
30 Nottingham Britannia		4	Camberley	Agincourt
		12	Paddington	Cue
		13	Brixton	Ram Jam
Promoters — Danny O'Donovan and Henry Sellers				

The first British tour by the G-Clefs was a most unexpected occurrence. A black doo-wop group from Boston, they had first recorded in 1956 and enjoyed brief success in the States with 'Ka-Ding Dong'. Five years later, they re-emerged with 'I Understand (Just How You Feel)', which gave them their one and only British hit, but by the spring of 1968 they had been largely forgotten and their cause was hardly assisted by the fact that their tour was conducted under an almost total veil of secrecy. No dates were listed in the music papers, no interviews printed, nor features written. If Britain in 1968 was obsessed with underground music, then the G-Clefs were arguably the most underground of all the groups. Such advertising as did exist was placed in local papers, and the inaccurate but optimistic comments which appeared in the *Nottingham Evening Post* give a clue to just how little the clubs knew about them: *'Direct From Seattle, their opening show in this country, four-man, all-coloured singing and dancing team — a Drifters-style show'*.

The G-Clefs were not a 'four-man' group at all. There were no less than eight of them and two of them were Caucasians. Four of the original group — brothers Teddy, Chris and Timmy Scott and their foster brother, Ray Gipson — were augmented by a fourth brother, Arnold 'Ilanga' Scott, plus drummer Lennie Nelson, bass-player Gene Ragosta and organist Richard McInnis. Even assuming that work was probably found on US military bases to fill out their itinerary, it is hard to imagine that the mechanics of housing, feeding and transporting the eight men throughout their stay in Britain made very much financial sense. In any event, few rock'n'roll fans even knew that the G-Clefs were in the country at all and were therefore unable to assess an act which, although inevitably slanted towards the soul market, still included a proportion of their old recordings including 'I Understand (Just How You Feel)', 'A Girl Has To Know' and 'Ka-Ding Dong'.

THE FABULOUS PLATTERS

The trafficking in bogus vocal groups had now reached ludicrous proportions. During 1968 alone there were five tours by 'Platters', three each by 'Drifters' and 'Ronettes' and a veritable plethora of 'Coasters', 'Chiffons', 'Crystals' and 'Imperials' clogging up the ballrooms and clubs the length and breadth of Britain. As with so many Roy Tempest tours, the dates were chopped and changed — often at the last minute — leaving a constant cloud of confusion and uncertainty. In truth of course, most people neither knew nor cared whether the four black faces occupying the stage belonged to the original hit group as long as they delivered an acceptable evening's entertainment and, in fairness to Tempest, the quality of his acts *was* rarely in question, only their authenticity.

The 'Fabulous Platters' who performed around Britain during April and May 1968 bore no resemblance to the line-up of Platters including Tony Williams and Zola Taylor who had visited Britain in 1957 and 1960. They had been the original hit group, whereas these 'Platters' identified themselves as Mickey Goody, Earl Marcus, James Cherry and Gloria Gayden. Opportunists they clearly were, but at least they could put on a show, as patrons of the Eden Park Hotel in Beckenham discovered on 2 May.

Backed by the Trends, the group provided a well-balanced mix of contemporary soul music including 'Knock On Wood' and 'Get Ready' interspersed with the Platters' hits: 'Twilight Time', 'Only You' and 'My Prayer'. They threw in a wild screaming version of 'Shout' during which they entertained the audience with some lightning footwork, although Gloria's dancing was seriously hampered by an extremely tight dress. By the time the act was concluded on 'With This Ring', there was no disputing that the Fabulous Platters had given value for money. They just were not the real thing and for some at least that did still matter.

CLYDE McPHATTER

April 1968	May 1968
13 Nottingham Britannia	11 Nottingham Britannia
Promoter unknown	

Poor old Clyde was still having trouble getting it together. Gigs were few and far between, and interest was lukewarm at best. However, Deram Records did provide some encouragement, and on 8 June he cut a 'comeback' session for them in England, which produced some worthwhile product. 'Only A Fool' was issued as a single but sadly failed to make any impact whatsoever. He still retained his wonderful voice, but few people were listening to it.

DUANE EDDY

April 1968					
26	Pontypridd	Municipal Hall	19-25	Stockton	Fiesta
27	Ramsey, IOM	Gaiety		Spennymoor	Variety
28	Portsmouth	Guildhall	27	Barrow	99 Club
29	London	Hatchett's	28	Malvern	Winter Gardens
May 1968			29	Birmingham	Cedar
1	London	Royal Albert Hall	30	Barry	Municipal Hall
	London	Blaises	31	Ramsgate	Coronation
2	Cardiff	Sophia Gardens	**June 1968**		
3	Tottenham	Royal	2	Greenford	Starlite
	London	Cromwellian	3	Gateshead	Town Hall
4	Prestatyn	Royal Lido	4	Great Yarmouth	*unknown venue*
5	Redcar	Coatham Hotel	19	Tonbridge	Six In One
6	Purley	Orchid	22	Northampton	Maple
7	London	Whiskey A Go Go	23-24	Leigh	Garrick
8	Norwich	Industrial	25-26	Leigh	Garrick
9	Liverpool	Victoriana		Bolton	Casino
10	Manchester	Domino	27	Leigh	Garrick
	Manchester	Princess	28-29	Leigh	Garrick
11	Manchester	*unknown venue*		Bolton	Casino
	Nelson	Imperial	30	Burnley	Cabaret
12-18	Wakefield	Savoy	**July 1968**		
	Brighouse	Ritz	1-6	Burnley	Cabaret
Promoter — Lorna Wallis					

In contrast to 1967, when Duane Eddy's British tours had created little media interest, on this occasion his timing was impeccable and he arrived back in the UK precisely as the rock'n'roll revival was getting underway. Bill Haley & His Comets gained the lion's share of the media attention, but Duane benefited as well through increased attendances at his club gigs and a full date-book which eventually stretched the tour to ten weeks duration.

Even the fashionable London clubs were eager to book the guitar man, and his appearance at the Cromwellian attracted their biggest crowd for over a year. Backed throughout the tour by the Quotations, Eddy's show was augmented by two girl vocalists, the Go-Jo Girls, who handled the vocals on '(Dance With The) Guitar Man'. Inevitably however, it was not the club work

but the two theatre bookings at the Royal Albert Hall and in Cardiff, where he appeared with Bill Haley, that became the focal points of the tour.

The Albert Hall gig was a complete sellout and packed to the rafters with a very volatile audience. Duane was scheduled to close the first half, coming on after the South London rocker band, the Wild Angels. They were unbilled but were precisely the opening act required for a major rock'n'roll show. Dressed in leathers, they pounded their way through a set comprising nothing but rock'n'roll standards. It wasn't particularly subtle, but they were received with great enthusiasm — a stark contrast to the Quotations who were given a hard time when they came out to perform their own set. A mod group wearing kaftans and beads was *not* what the audience wanted to see, and they were greeted with the customary abuse. Coins were thrown at them and tiles were torn from the walls and hurled in the direction of the stage.

By the time Eddy came out on stage, the atmosphere was electric. Soon after he commenced his set, a bottle bounced off the head of John Banks, drummer with the Quotations and formerly one of the Merseybeats. Duane stopped playing and tried to calm the audience, but he faced an impossible task. The violence was not, of course, aimed at him, and his hits 'Rebel-Rouser', 'Forty Miles Of Bad Road' and a particularly primitive 'Peter Gunn' were greeted with wild enthusiasm. Duane seemed stunned by the uncontrolled audience and again stopped playing when a rocker girl got on stage and attacked one of the Go-Jos. Fortunately, he was able to restrain the mob sufficiently to complete his act, eventually leaving the stage to frantic applause but bearing a puzzled expression that was probably a mixture of pleasure at the unexpected fervour of the audience and relief that he had survived his ordeal.

TV appearances
Late Night Line Up   28 May 1968
Dee Time   1 June 1968

BILL HALEY & HIS COMETS

April 1968			21	Ilford	Palais
29	Nottingham	Sherwood Rooms		London	Hatchett's
	Chesterfield	Victoria		London	Sybllla's
30	High Wycombe	Town Hall	22	Stevenage	Locarno
	London	Blaises		Alconbury	USAF
May 1968			23	Bristol	Locarno
1	London	Royal Albert Hall	24	Manchester	Princess
2	Cardiff	Sophia Gardens		Manchester	Domino
3	Chester	Clockwork Orange	25	Folkstone	Toft's
	Warrington	Carlton	31	Belfast	Floral Hall
4	Dunstable	California	**June 1968**		
5	Manchester	Princess	3	Leeds	Queen's Hall
	Manchester	Domino		London	Cromwellian
6	Leeds	Mecca		Bagshot	Pantiles
19	Wakefield	Locarno	4	Dudley	Zoo
	Nottingham	Pigalle		West Bromwich	Adelphi
20	Streatham	Silver Blades			
	Beckenham	Mistrale			

Promoters — Johnny Jones and Paddy Malynn

Bill Haley & His Comets were grinding their way through an arduous tour of Canada when the phone calls started. The British rock'n'roll revival was underway and 'Rock Around The Clock' had re-entered the UK charts on 3 April, so suddenly Bill was in great demand again. He flew into London on 28 April accompanied by his third wife, Martha, and Comets Rudy Pompilli (saxophone), Nick Nastos (guitar), Al Rappa (double bass) and Johnny 'Bam Bam' Lane (drums). Media interest was intense, although rather too much coverage focused on teddy boys and rock'n'roll riots rather than the music.

There was no shortage of bookings, and at one stage Bill was confronted with the logistically impossible prospect of opening the tour with performances in Nottingham, Chesterfield and Liverpool all on the same night. Eventually, the proposed date at Liverpool's Cavern was scrapped, resulting in hundreds of angry fans turning up and demanding their money back when the Comets failed to appear.

The show at the Sherwood Rooms, Nottingham was typical of the whole tour. The club was packed solid with fans who were jammed tight in front of a low stage. The Comets ambled out at 8.45 pm smartly dressed in red jackets and black trousers, and as soon as Haley was introduced the place erupted with noise.

Emerging in a green and gold jacket with his Gibson guitar slung around his neck, he went straight into 'Shake, Rattle And Roll' without a word of introduction. The pace did not slacken for a second as they rocked their way through 'Rip It Up' and 'Razzle Dazzle' before launching into 'Rudy's Rock'. Al Rappa switched from electric to slap bass and proceeded to deliver the full range of tricks, climbing on and riding the bass, lying on his back and even pretending to throw it out into the crowd. All the while Rudy blew his sax like a man possessed. The applause for 'Rudy's Rock' was almost deafening. Rappa wore a Little Richard wig while he sang 'Jenny, Jenny' and then Bill introduced his enormous drummer,

Bill at Warrington.

Johnny 'Bam Bam' Lane, who must have sweated off pounds as he slammed his way through 'Caravan' while the other Comets left the stage for several minutes. Nick Nastos sang 'Johnny B. Goode' and then it was back to Haley for 'Rock A-Beatin' Boogie', ' See You Later, Alligator' and a wild version of 'The Saints Rock'n'Roll'. He closed — as everyone knew he would — with the anthem of rock'n'roll, 'Rock Around The Clock'.

The crowd was still screaming for more as the Comets scrambled into waiting cars for the journey to Chesterfield where another full house cheered like crazy as this time Rudy sang 'Kansas City', while Nick Nastos grabbed the opportunity to show his prowess on the guitar with 'Fingers On Fire', and 'Malagueña' replacing 'Caravan'. Otherwise Bill and the Comets delivered what was their standard show throughout the tour and were visibly shaken by the incredible response they received.

The following day, Haley attended a reception thrown by MCA Records at the Revolution Club in London during which British rocker Freddie 'Fingers' Lee presented him with a framed 78 of 'Rock Around The Clock'.

The early evening show at High Wycombe was notable for a storming 'Johnny B. Goode' by Nick and a fantastic ovation at the conclusion of the show. A serious fire at the Speakeasy necessitated a change of venue for the late performance to — ironically — Blaises, where the audience included Duane Eddy, Phil Everly, Cliff Richard, Paul McCartney and a couple of Stones. The sound system was dreadful but nobody seemed to mind as Bill and the Comets rocked the night away.

The most important gig of the tour was at the Royal Albert Hall. All seven thousand tickets had been sold and touts were charging extortionate prices outside. The audience were in a highly excitable state and the first half of the show was marred by trouble during Duane Eddy's act. The intermission did little to calm the crowd who wanted nothing but rock'n'roll, and support act Kookie Etan sensibly declined to face the baying mob, permitting the Wild Angels to play a brief second set of rock'n'roll standards before compere Rick Dane introduced the Comets one by one. By the time Bill ran onto the stage the place was in uproar, and there can have been few if any wilder rock'n'roll scenes than the following thirty minutes as the gigantic auditorium was literally shaken to its foundations.

The Comets tore through their show while the audience went completely crazy. Several hundred people were actually standing on their seats while the beleaguered security men fought to keep the baying mob away from the stage. As Haley neared the end of 'Rock Around The Clock', twenty or so finally broke through and threatened to engulf the Comets, who cut short the song and ran for the dressing room. One fan made a grab for Haley but was knocked unconscious by a sharp blow from Nick's guitar. Compere Rick Dane made a futile attempt to calm the situation, but was pushed off the stage and into the fourth row of the seats. The cheers and applause for Haley continued long after the house lights had come back on, and despite the trouble everybody — including the national press — agreed that the event represented a massive triumph for Haley.

The tour continued in similar style with attendance records smashed at almost every gig. Bill and the Comets appeared on BBC1's *Dee Time* along with the Everly Brothers, Bobby Goldsboro and soul singer J.J. Jackson. A further appearance on BBC2's *Roy Hudd Show* was recorded but not screened due to work permit restrictions.

On 7 May, the first segment of the tour came to an end and the entourage flew from Manchester to Sweden, where they continued to draw big crowds — eleven thousand turning out for one show at the Tivoli Gardens in Stockholm. They flew back to London on 19 May and travelled by car to shows that evening in Wakefield and Nottingham. The following day, they returned to London and were mobbed at the end of their appearance at the Silver Blades Ice Rink in Streatham. This delayed their scheduled arrival at Beckenham's Mistrale Club by over an hour, where a capacity crowd had sweated off pounds impatiently waiting in the hot and poorly-ventilated basement. When Bill and his Comets finally hit the stage, the near-comatose audience sprang back to life in an instant and roared them through another memorable show. On 26 May they flew to the Netherlands, and then on to Ireland.

There was no let-up in the programme when they came back to England again on 3 June. Three separate shows were booked for that day, the first being a *matinée* spot on a Pete Stringfellow-promoted *MoJo Festival* at the Queen's Hall, Leeds, which also featured the Small Faces, the Herd, Edwin Starr, Alan Bown and the Fantastics. By this time, Al Rappa's Little Richard wig and double bass had both been stolen, so 'Rudy's Rock' was replaced by 'Guitar Boogie Shuffle' featuring the fluent guitar of Nick Nastos.

Then, it was a race back to London for two more club dates at the Cromwellian and Pantiles. Attempts had been made to extend the tour beyond 4 June, but unfortunately the work permits could not be changed and this incredible renaissance for rock'n'roll finally came to an end when they flew out to Austria the following day.

A promotion scheduled to take place that night at Kingsway Casino, Southport collapsed because Haley was unable to appear. He had been due to co-star with Scott Walker, who had contracted measles and was also missing, leaving agent Ian Hamilton threatening legal action against Haley.

TV appearances

The Eamonn Andrews Show	28 April 1968
Dee Time	4 May 1968
The Roy Hudd Show	6 May 1968 (not screened)

JOHNNY CASH
CARL PERKINS

May 1968					
3	Alconbury	USAF	11	Walthamstow	Granada
4	Manchester	Free Trade Hall	12	Liverpool	Empire
5	Portsmouth	Guildhall	13	Birmingham	Town Hall
6	Chicksands	USAF	14	Bedford	Granada
7	Cardiff	Capitol	15	Bentwaters	USAF
8	Bristol	Colston Hall	16	Glasgow	Odeon
9	London	Royal Albert Hall	17	Edinburgh	Usher Hall
10	Kingston	Granada	18	Carlisle	ABC
			19	Newcastle	Odeon
Promoter — Mervyn Conn					

Johnny Cash had first appeared on British television as far back as September 1959. It had taken a long while for him to gain popularity on this side of the Atlantic, but finally his time had come. This tour was an enormous success and was the first tangible evidence that there was a real potential for country music in the UK. Of course, Cash held considerable appeal for the rock'n'rollers as well, and they turned out in great numbers — not least because Carl Perkins was part of the touring package which also included Cash's regular band, the Tennessee Three, his new wife, June Carter, plus James Royal & The Royal Set.

At the Cardiff show, Perkins opened his act with 'Matchbox' and then slowed the pace with 'Country Boy's Dream', 'Turn Around' and his latest single, 'Lake County Cotton Country', before rocking his way through 'Boppin' The Blues' and 'Blue Suede Shoes'. Audience response was magnificent and he encored with 'Honey Don't' and a vibrant 'Mean Woman Blues'. Perkins was well received throughout the tour and undoubtedly sold his share of the tickets.

At Bristol, his spot provoked a wild reception and had the teddy boys

dancing in the aisles, while at Kingston he encored with a fiery version of 'That's All Right'. The audience at Walthamstow was exceptionally lively and not for the first time James Royal's efforts were greeted with a torrent of boos. Carl included a narration, 'Tonight I'm 21', and a punchy 'Whole Lotta Shakin' Goin' On'.

Even June Carter was put under pressure to include some rock'n'roll in her set, and at Kingston she relented and performed an exciting interpretation of Chuck Berry's 'Thirty Days', complete with a wild dance during the break that sent one of her shoes flying right across the stage.

Popular as Carl Perkins was with the rockers, Johnny Cash was unquestionably the star of the show. He strode on stage at Cardiff, a tall, imposing and charismatic figure dressed in a black drape jacket, pinstripe trousers, his hair slicked back and combed up into a large quiff, and an acoustic guitar slung round his neck. Luther Perkins' familiar guitar led straight into 'Big River' and the audience were already going wild. It was on this tour that Cash demonstrated for the first time in Britain quite why he would soon be elevated to the category of 'superstar'. His act was varied, interesting and just full of great songs.

He moved effortlessly from the tender 'I Still Miss Someone' to the novelty of 'Five Feet High And Rising', to the rockabilly of 'Folsom Prison Blues' and 'Get Rhythm', to the screeching harmonicas of 'Orange Blossom Special'. Other high points of an incredible show were 'John Henry', the brooding 'Dark As A Dungeon' and 'I Walk The Line'. Carl was called back on stage to join him on 'Long Legged Guitar Pickin' Man' and was rewarded with a roar of approval from the audience. He stayed at Cash's side as the latter closed his act with an energetic 'Ring Of Fire'.

Almost every show was sold out and, although the basic format remained the same, at Bristol Cash and Perkins threw in an unexpected duet of 'Gotta Travel On', while at Walthamstow the rockers were rewarded when Johnny really let rip on a smouldering 'Get Rhythm', even throwing in a couple of verses from 'Rock & Roll Ruby'.

The tour was not without its problems, however. Bass-player Marshall Grant flew home on 11 May after his father was taken seriously ill, and when the package reached Bedford, the Tennessee Three were reduced still further to the Tennessee One: Luther Perkins played the first house but was running a fever and could not stop shaking, so Carl Perkins played guitar in the second show while Luther was packed off to Bedford General Hospital.

He did not manage to rejoin the tour, which limped to a close with Carl imitating his namesake's distinctive guitar style. As far as Britain was concerned, Johnny Cash had finally arrived, and the rock'n'roll enthusiasts were more than happy that Carl Perkins was sharing his old friend's success.

THE EVERLY BROTHERS

May 1968		
6-8	Birmingham	Rum Runner
10	Belfast	Romano's
Promoter — Harold Davison		

Don and Phil Everly made a short promotional trip to the UK, arriving from Germany at the end of April to plug their latest single, 'It's My Time'. They made three television appearances, including the same edition of *Dee Time* as Bill Haley. Adam Faith turned up in the audience at the Rum Runner Club, but despite the so-called 'rock'n'roll revival', the publicity for their visit was pretty limited.

TV appearances

Lulu's Back In Town	1 May 1968 (screened 11 June 1968)
Dee Time	4 May 1968
Top Of The Pops	16 May 1968

JOHN FRED & HIS PLAYBOY BAND

May 1968					
31	Morecambe	Central Pier	7	Kelso	Corn Exchange
June 1968				Bonnyrigg	Regal
2	Dunfermline	Kinema	8	Nelson	Imperial
5	Hemel Hempstead	Pavilion	9	Warrington	Co-op
				Hanley	The Place
Promoter unknown					

One of the factors that provoked the music press into manufacturing a rock'n'roll revival was the appearance in the British charts during January of a modern record with a distinctively rock'n'roll feel to it. 'Judy In Disguise' was a novelty item and, as it turned out, the only UK hit by John Fred & His Playboy Band. Rumours of a tour commenced as soon as the disc entered the Top Twenty, and various dates were announced first for February, then March, and finally three weeks of one-nighters with the Tremeloes in April. However. nothing actually happened until the end of May by which time 'Judy In Disguise' had dropped out of the charts and interest in Mr. Fred had substantially reduced.

The seven-man Playboy Band — Jimmy O'Rouche (guitar), Hal Cowart (bass), Joe Miceli (drums), Andrew Bernard (saxophone), Ronnie Goodson (trumpet), Charlie Spin (trumpet) and Tommy Dee (organ) — had been performing together with John Fred since high school in Baton Rouge, Louisiana. An ex-college basketball player, Fred himself had some pedigree as a rock'n'roller, having earlier taken 'Shirley' (cut with Fats Domino's band) into the US pop charts in 1959, but created no interest whatsoever among British rock'n'roll fans, who pointedly ignored his tour. His image was all wrong and bookings were scarce. John Fred faded as quickly as the rock'n'roll revival.

BOBBY VEE

June 1968			July 1968		
9-15	Barnsley	Ba Ba	1-6	Stockton	Fiesta
	Greasbrough	Social		Spennymoor	Top Hat
30	Stockton	Fiesta			
	Spennymoor	Top Hat			
Promoter unknown					

Bobby Vee had been absent from the UK since April 1965, but on 5 June flew into London to promote his latest US hit, 'My Girl — Hey Girl', and to show his face on the Northern cabaret circuit. Liberty Records held a reception for him, and there was quite an acceptable level of media interest — especially considering that his British hits had dried up more than five years earlier. He guested on several radio shows including those hosted by Pete Murray and Stuart Henry, before flying to Hamburg on 18 June for a German TV appearance. Upon his return, he spent two days in the recording studios at Liberty on 26 and 27 June but still found time to squeeze in three TV spots. Vee may not have been a fashionable name in 1968, but nobody could criticise him for lack of effort.

TV appearances
Time For Blackburn	28 June 1968 (screened 29 June 1968)
Here And Now	7 July 1968 (screened 15 July 1968)
Meet Joe Ferrer	10 July 1968

CHUCK BERRY

It is hard to believe that anyone was taking much notice of Roy Tempest's press releases by the summer of 1968. He announced a batch of club dates for Chuck covering the middle of June, but yet again they seem to have been no more than speculation. In any event, Berry never appeared and his fans were left frustrated. Episodes like this were doing considerable harm to rock'n'roll.

THE CRICKETS

June 1968			28	Manchester	Princess
21	Tottenham	Royal		Manchester	Domino
22	Middlewich	Warmington	29	Manchester	Penny Farthing
23	Manchester	Sloopy's		Manchester	New Century Hall
24	Purley	Orchid	**July 1968**		
25	Great Yarmouth	Towers	5	Norwich	St. Andrew's Hall
27	Camberley	Agincourt	6	Manchester	Sloopy's
Promoter — Roy Tempest					

This tour's probably due some kind of award for being the most chaotic and — at least as far as the public were concerned — the most poorly organised.

It was originally announced that the Crickets would play fourteen nights of club and ballroom dates, commencing 25 May. Later, a completely new itinerary was published in the music press with a start date of 21 June, while Roy Tempest switched the original bookings to either his fake Coasters outfit or the bogus Ruby & The Romantics who were in Britain at the time. Not surprisingly, the fans had little idea what was going on, and even the revised dates were chopped and changed until it was really only the healthy club scene in Manchester that kept the project afloat.

The reason given for the tour being delayed by a month was that this would enable Jerry Allison to get off the Vietnam reserve list. The 1968 Crickets consisted of Allison, Sonny Curtis and Glen D. Hardin. Jerry Naylor's name had been mentioned in the press but he did not make the trip.

What was so tragic about the whole affair was that only a month earlier the media had been gobbling up news about the return of Bill Haley. 'Rock Around The Clock' had re-entered the British charts, but so too had 'Peggy Sue', yet few people even realised that the Crickets were in the country, and a golden opportunity to resurrect interest among the general public was wasted.

At Manchester's New Century Hall, they opened confidently with 'Keep A-Knockin' ' and centred the majority of their show on songs from the Buddy Holly era. Jerry had compensated for his fast-receding hairline with a Mexican-styled moustache, and both he and Sonny were dressed in baggy shirts and hippy beads Only Glen D. Hardin was more soberly attired, and he had the unusual task of playing both bass-guitar and piano. He coped admirably except for 'Don't Ever Change', where he lost his way completely until he was advised by Sonny to 'catch us in the middle eight'.

The Crickets did not seem to be taking things too seriously — which was a shame, because the rock'n'roll revival was already fading fast and they had dismally failed to gain any advantage from it.

ROY ORBISON

July 1968			12-17	London	Talk Of The Town
21-27	Batley	Variety	19-24	London	Talk Of The Town
28-31	Stockton	Fiesta	26-31	London	Talk Of The Town
August 1968			**September 1968**		
1-3	Stockton	Fiesta	1	Great Yarmouth	ABC
4	Blackpool	ABC	9-14	Birmingham	Theatre
5-10	London	Talk Of The Town	15	Bournemouth	Pavilion
11	Great Yarmouth	ABC			
		Promoter unknown			

This was Roy Orbison's first excursion on the British cabaret scene, and four weeks at London's high-profile Talk Of The Town provided the necessary proof to anybody who may have doubted that he was still in considerable demand.

Working with a full orchestra containing both brass and string sections, Roy looked very nervous on the opening night as he walked on stage carrying his guitar, but the response of the audience was immediate and tumultuous. He rarely spoke throughout his act, in fact hardly even moved. He stood perfectly still, left leg bent, right leg rigid, and played and sang his way through his hits, letting that distinctive, haunting voice speak for itself.

His total lack of any sort of stage act was in itself a feature which distinguished him from anyone else. Orbison's charisma and the aura of sadness which hung over him had an emotional effect on his audience, plus there was a hypnotic quality to his singing that was quite unique.

The tour was a long one — nearly two months in all — but was very successful and was just nearing the end when news reached Roy of another enormous personal tragedy. Two days before he was due to return home, a fire broke out at his house on the shore of Old Hickory Lake near Nashville, Tennessee and claimed the lives of his sons Roy (11) and Tony (6). Thankfully, the youngest, Wesley (3), was pulled to safety by his grandfather.

Coming only a little over two years after the death of Claudette, Orbison was completely devastated and naturally flew straight back to the States. At such a terrible time in his life — at least with hindsight — there was one ray of sunshine amongst the clouds. During his sellout season at Batley Variety Club, Roy had met his future wife, Barbara, and in time this charming lady would help him to rebuild his life and somehow come to terms with the dual disasters that had struck him so unkindly and so hard.

TV appearances

Top Of The Pops	18 July 1968
Night Club	28 July 1968
Star Light Entertainment	17 August 1968
Saturday Spectacular	24 August 1968

BRUCE CHANNEL

July 1968			4	London	Hatchett's
30	Derby	Disc Jockey	5	Purley	Orchid
August 1968			7	Stevenage	Locarno
2	Bournemouth	Pavilion	9	Tottenham	Royal
3	Brentwood	St. Thomas' Hall	10	Herne Bay	New King's Hall
Promoter — Arthur Howes					

Bruce Channel's tour of Britain in 1962 had been made on the back of his hit record, 'Hey! Baby', and frankly he did not set the world alight. Few would have predicted a return visit almost exactly six years later, but after his recording of 'Keep On' entered the British charts in June 1968, Bruce flew in for a hurriedly-arranged promo visit and a small batch of ballroom dates. There was plenty of media interest as befits a man with a hit record, and a smiling Channel assured all and sundry just how pleased he was to be back in Britain.

For his live shows, Bruce was backed by the quaintly-named Doctor Marigold's Prescription, while he — not unreasonably — tried to project himself with a modern image, coming on stage at Tottenham clad in a light blue military-styled jacket with a mandarin collar from which dangled a sparkling medallion. He performed a mixture of material, apparently hedging his bets on exactly where his act was going, including some soul in the shape of 'In The Midnight Hour' and the more romantic 'Try A Little Tenderness', as well as his old hit, 'Hey! Baby'. There was little evidence of his youth spent as a rock'n'roller back in Texas, but in the end what the audience really wanted to hear was 'Keep On', which he duly delivered on cue.

TV appearances
Top Of The Pops   1 August 1968
Top Of The Pops   8 August 1968
Dee Time   10 August 1968

JERRY LEE LEWIS

August 1968		
9	Sunbury	Kempton Park
11	Elstree	ATV Studios
	Promoter unknown	

After his successes on British television during the Fifties with programmes like *Oh Boy!* and *Boy Meets Girls,* Jack Good had enjoyed similar acclaim in the States, where he produced the hit ABC-TV show *Shindig!* More recently, he had brought to the stage an updated musical interpretation of Shakespeare's *Othello,* which he titled *Catch My Soul.* Jerry Lee Lewis had starred in the role of Iago when the play was performed at the Ahmanson Theatre in Los Angeles, and now flew into Britain to work on another of Good's projects — an ambitious three-part television spectacular that would trace the history of popular music, *Innocence, Anarchy And Soul.*

Additionally, Lewis had been added to the bill for the *8th National Jazz & Blues Festival.* This event, which subsequently settled down as the *Reading Festival,* struggled to find a permanent home during its early years and on this occasion was held in the open at Kempton Park Racecourse in Sunbury. Jerry Lee had not appeared in Britain for two years and there was considerable interest in his involvement, with some fans travelling from as far away as Scotland specifically to catch his portion of the show.

Yorkshire Television invites you to a colour recording of **INNOCENCE, ANARCHY AND SOUL** (Three Chapters from the History of Rock) in Studio D ATV Elstree Studios on Sunday 11th August 1968 at 6.00 pm

Doors open 4.45 pm
Doors close 5.15 pm   Recording ends 7.45 pm

Once again, the organisers misjudged the situation. They did not anticipate anything like the level of support that Lewis attracted, nor the fact that his followers were unlikely to sit quietly through the rest of the show. British rock'n'roll fans had demonstrated time and again that what they wanted was rock'n'roll and nothing else. The first two acts, Taste and Timebox, got away relatively unscathed while the massed army of teddy boys and rockers refuelled in the refreshments marquee. Perhaps fearing the inevitable, the organisers had made a late change to the running order and Marmalade were brought on ahead of Jerry Lee. They were always going to be in serious trouble and must have been dismayed to see the bars emptying as the alcohol-fuelled masses moved to take up positions immediately in front of the stage. The group were greeted with abuse and sustained booing, and although they struggled on for a time, were obliged to cut short their act when the teddy boys persisted with a football-styled chant of 'Off! Off! Off!'

It had taken Jerry Lee Lewis ten long years to live down the scandal of his first British tour, and only now was he finally rebuilding his career in the States. He had brought with him his road manager, Dick Thompson, and guitarist Kenny Lovelace. Other backing was provided by Chas Hodges (bass) and Mickey Burt (drums).

His act at Kempton Park featured not only his recent country hit, 'Another Place, Another Time', but also gave his British followers their first opportunity to hear him perform his latest American single, 'What Made Milwaukee Famous'. Otherwise it was business as usual. The set opened with 'Memphis Tennessee' and included 'Hi-Heel Sneakers', 'Blue Suede Shoes' and 'What'd I Say'. Each act was permitted a strictly-enforced time slot of forty-five minutes, but as Marmalade had retired early, Jerry used up the extra time, playing for an hour and eventually concluding a somewhat restrained performance with 'Good Golly Miss Molly'.

The audience, on the other hand, were far from restrained and had kept the bouncers fully occupied throughout his act as they fought to get up on the stage. The trouble persisted, and bottles, stones and coins were thrown as the stage crew prepared for the arrival of the Herd, who were the final act of the evening. One steward was hit in the mouth by a bottle and a metal peg struck the Herd's drum kit, following which an announcement was made to the effect that they were declining to appear. It was an ugly end to an otherwise enjoyable evening, but if nothing else again demonstrated that the passion and enthusiasm for rock'n'roll was as strong as ever.

A smaller, less aggressive audience of perhaps a hundred or so mainly rock'n'roll fans was fortunate to obtain tickets for the filming of *Innocence, Anarchy And Soul* two days later at the ATV Studios in Elstree. The first segment of the show representing *'Innocence'* was intended to be an *Oh Boy!*-styled, fast-moving rock'n'roll sequence, but no sooner had they completed the preparation work than the television technicians called a strike and the whole proceedings ground to a halt. There followed several hours of waiting around while negotiations were attempted to settle the dispute.

As the audience were becoming restless, Jerry Lee strolled into the studio and to their delight offered to play for them. He performed an impromptu concert even taking requests, although he did appear stunned by the shouts for 'Milkshake Mademoiselle', which at that time was a still unissued but much talked-about Sun recording dating back to 1957. To his credit, he made an attempt at the song, although understandably he had some difficulty recalling all of the lyrics.

Eventually, when it became clear that the strike would not be settled that day, all of the acts performed for the small but privileged gathering. In addition to Jerry Lee, the cast comprised Lord Rockingham's XI, the

Breakaways, Ian Whitcomb, Julie Driscoll, the Brian Auger Trinity, Don Lang, Chris Farlowe, Lulu, the Flirtations, Alan Bown, Dominic Grant and Lonnie Donegan. When they were reassembled at a later date to tele-record the show, Jerry Lee was unfortunately unavailable due to other commitments and his place was taken by the largely unknown Lance LeGault from Louisiana.

BEN E. KING

August 1968					
16	Tottenham	Royal	28	Birmingham	Cedar
	London	Revolution		Stevenage	Locarno
17	Dunstable	California	29	Blackpool	Locarno
	Stepney	New All Star	30	Harlow	Birdcage
18	Warrington	Carlton		Tottenham	Royal
	Nantwich	Beau Brummell	31	Middlesbrough	*Tees Pop '68*
19	Purley	Orchid		Nottingham	Beachcomber
	London	Scotch of St. James		Boston	Gliderdrome
20	Guildford	Civic Hall	**September 1968**		
	London	Blaises	1	Leeds	Queen's Hall
21	Southampton	Top Rank	3	Ilford	Palais
	Portsmouth	Guildhall	4	Sevenoaks	Bligh's Hotel
22	Worthing	Assembly Hall	5	Bristol	Locarno
	London	Sybilla's		Birmingham	Locarno
23	Liverpool	Mardi Gras	6	Beckenham	Mistrale
	Liverpool	Victoriana		London	New Cue
24	Chester	Clockwork Orange	7	Ramsey, IOM	Gaiety
	Manchester	Twisted Wheel		Manchester	Twisted Wheel
25	Bayswater	Douglas House (USAF)	8	Manchester	Princess
	London	Bag O'Nails		Manchester	Domino
	Paddington	Cue	9	Purley	Orchid
26	Tunstall	Golden Torch	10	Bagshot	Pantiles
26-27	Birmingham	Cedar		London	Scotch of St. James
			11	London	Samantha's
Promoters — Henry Sellers and Danny O'Donovan					

Ben E. King returned to Britain on 15 August for a month of club dates, this time backed by the Chris Shakespeare Globe Show. His popularity on the ballroom circuit was underlined by a full date-book and a gruelling programme which involved two and occasionally even three different venues a night. King broke box office records at several clubs during this tour, including the popular Orchid Ballroom at Purley, which was filled to capacity. It was estimated that he performed for in excess of fifty thousand people on this tour — a staggering statistic — and, as always, it was his Drifters material that brought the greatest number of dancers out on to the floor.

On most occasions, King was the sole or at least the main attraction but at Leeds he co-starred with Clyde McPhatter, at the late show in Birmingham on 5 September he appeared with P.P. Arnold, while three days later at the Princess in Manchester he headlined over the Rockin' Berries. The ambitious *Tees Pop '68* festival also included Long John Baldry, Joe Cocker, Family, Traffic and the Bonzo Dog Doo Dah Band.

TV appearances
Late Night Line Up   28 August 1968

CLYDE McPHATTER

August 1968			October 1968		
31	Dunstable	Civic Hall	13	Nantwich	Beau Brummell
September 1968					
1	Leeds	Queen's Hall			
14	Manchester	Twisted Wheel			
Promoter unknown					

Clyde McPhatter had been more-or-less resident in the UK since February and had moved into a house in Water Gardens, off London's Edgware Road. He had dreams of self-financing his own TV spectacular which he could then sell to world-wide markets — especially if Ben E. King and Cliff Richard could be persuaded to participate. In reality, he was struggling on all levels. Bureaucracy was still giving him work permit problems and, although he could still work occasionally at military bases, he was not exactly inundated with offers. To make matters worse, he was drinking heavily and probably not in the best shape to take advantage of any opportunities that did arise. Deram Records financed another recording session in October, which sadly failed to produce anything of note.

For his appearance at Dunstable, Clyde was backed by a four-piece group called Thor, and was supported by American girl group the Flirtations. His act was a mixture of rockers and pop ballads including 'Money Honey', 'A Lover's Question' and 'Lavender Lace'. The audience, who were mainly teenagers, failed to respond until McPhatter worked in some more contemporary material and both 'Son Of Hickory Holler's Tramp' and 'Hold Me Tight', sung in his exquisite way, really grabbed their attention. On the faster numbers like 'Little Bitty Pretty One', he would push the microphone stand away from him and, standing upright with his feet close together, start to bop to the music while waving his arms around in frantic fashion. He brought his set to a close with the Drifters' 'Whatcha Gonna Do' and an extended 'What'd I Say' during which he made a couple of fake exits only to return and develop the song into a wild rave-up involving all the kids in the audience who by this time were packed tight in front of the stage.

The following night, Clyde shared billing with Ben E. King on an all-nighter at the Queen's Hall in Leeds promoted by Pete Stringfellow which also featured the Fantastics, the Flirtations, Tim Rose and Timebox.

BRUCE CHANNEL

September 1968			26	Bolton	Aspin
15-21	Stockton	Fiesta		Leigh	Garrick
	Middlesbrough	Excel	27	Bolton	Aspin
22	Bolton	Aspin		Manchester	Princess
	Nantwich	Beau Brummell		Manchester	Domino
23	Bolton	Aspin	28	Bolton	Aspin
	Chester	Quaintways		Manchester	Twisted Wheel
24	Bolton	Aspin	29	Edinburgh	Newton Grange
	Hanley	The Place			
25	Bolton	Aspin			
	Liverpool	Cavern			
Promoter — Barry Clayman					

Bruce Channel's visit in August had been hurriedly set up in response to the success of 'Keep On'. He now returned for a fortnight of cabaret and club dates in the North of England and remained in the UK for a further couple of weeks in October during which he was joined by American rock'n'roller Dale Hawkins. Bruce was putting the finishing touches to his album for Bell Records and Dale was in charge of arrangements and production. What a shame that Hawkins was not offered any live appearances while he was in the country!

JOHNNY CASH
CARL PERKINS

October 1968			November 1968		
25	Manchester	Odeon	1	Glasgow	Odeon
26	Liverpool	Empire	2	Walthamstow	Granada
27	London	Palladium	3	Birmingham	Theatre
Promoter — Mervyn Conn					

The overwhelming success of the Cash–Perkins tour in May ensured an early return. On this occasion, in addition to the Tennessee Three and June Carter they were accompanied by the Statler Brothers, compere Ray Cameron, and — unexpectedly — by June's sisters Helen and Anita, plus Mother Maybelle Carter. The Carter Family had not been scheduled to appear but at the last moment Maybelle overcame her fear of flying and so the whole family travelled to the UK for the first time.

There was one important omission however, which was explained during the Palladium show. During a quiet moment between numbers, a

Carl, June and Johnny backstage at the Manchester Odeon.

member of the audience called out: "Johnny, where's Luther?" Whereupon Cash halted the show and explained in a faltering voice that his old friend and guitarist, Luther Perkins had died in a fire at his home on 5 August.

Luther's distinctive playing had always been an integral part of the Johnny Cash sound, especially on those numbers such as 'Big River', 'Get Rhythm' and of course 'Luther Played The Boogie' that were favourites with the rock'n'roll fans. His replacement in the Tennessee Three was Bob Wootton, who joined W.S. Holland and Marshall Grant in providing the backing for both Cash and Perkins throughout the tour.

At the Palladium, Carl Perkins introduced his latest single, 'Restless', into his short set, and went over extremely well with some dynamic guitar-work and powerful performances of 'Matchbox', 'Mean Woman Blues' and 'Blue Suede Shoes'.

Cash was simply awesome and moved effortlessly between 'Ring Of Fire', 'Five Feet High And Rising' and 'I Still Miss Someone'. He also scored strongly with 'Folsom Prison Blues', 'Cocaine Blues' and 'I Walk The Line' before recalling Carl, the Statlers and the Carters onto the stage for a gospel-flavoured finale that culminated with everybody singing verses of Perkins' 'Daddy Sang Bass'. There was still a fair proportion of rockers at each show, and their influence was felt at Birmingham when Cash was again cajoled into performing 'Rock & Roll Ruby'.

BRUCE CHANNEL

November 1968			December 1968		
18	Purley	Orchid	1	London	Palladium
22	Mansfield	Palais de Danse	2	Bristol	Colston Hall
22	Birmingham	Cedar	4	Sheffield	City Hall
30	Sutton Coldfield	Belfry	5	Manchester	Odeon
			6	Birmingham	Odeon
			7	Cardiff	Capitol
			8	Finsbury Park	Astoria
			9	Glasgow	Odeon
Promoter — Arthur Howes					

Just weeks after his last tour, Bruce Channel was back in Britain again. He maintained a high profile and managed to be seen in all the right places. He and Dusty Springfield were reported to have led the applause at Hatchett's in London at a show by the soul singer, Freddie Mack, and one sensed that Channel was up for anything that would prolong his brief return to the spotlight.

He did manage to secure a supporting role on the Beach Boys' tour which commenced at the Palladium on 1 December, appearing alongside Vanity Fare, Barry Ryan, Sharon Tandy, Eclection and Les Fleur de Lys. He was again backed by Doctor Marigold's Prescription.

CHAPTER FOURTEEN

1969

Some Kinda Earthquake

The rock'n'roll revival of 1968 had quickly faded, and by the following year popular music was moving into the era of the supergroup. Bands split up and reformed again like a bunch of demented amoebas — as if anybody really cared. In truth however, rock'n'roll enthusiasts had long since ceased to show any interest in the passing fads and were slowly but surely creating their own parallel universe. Like green shoots in spring, the first rock'n'roll venues were appearing in run-down pubs and halls around the country giving the rockers and teddy boys somewhere to listen and dance to the music they loved. The circuit was small but it was lovingly nurtured and featured the likes of the Wild Angels, Shakin' Stevens & The Sunsets, the Impalas and Freddie 'Fingers' Lee. As the years progressed, rock'n'roll would eventually become a completely self-contained unit with specialist promoters, agents, magazines, photographers, record companies and venues. Nobody would ever need to listen to Radio One, watch *Top Of The Pops* or endure the Swinging Blue Jeans again — an intoxicating thought, but still only a dream in 1969.

For the time being, rock'n'roll was still dependent on the mainstream promoters for tours and the disorganised shambles continued. The choice was either to vegetate on the Northern cabaret circuit, where at least the venues were of a reasonable standard, or to work the clubs and ballrooms where anything could happen. More was promised than delivered in 1969, with tours by Little Richard, Screamin' Jay Hawkins, Bo Diddley and Jackie Wilson all failing to materialise.

The good news was that C&W music was finally taking off in Britain, and over the next decade many rock'n'rollers would be brought in under the banner of country tours. Promoter Mervyn Conn staged the first *International Festival Of Country & Western Music* at Wembley over Easter, while other visitors that year included Willie Nelson, Buck Owens, Connie Smith, Nat Stuckey and Bobby Bare — all of whom made live appearances in clubs or concert halls.

In fact, more and more American acts of all descriptions were coming to Britain, and in 1969 you could have taken your pick from Clifton Chenier, the Chambers Brothers, Tiny Tim, Howlin' Wolf, Nina Simone, the Flying Burrito Brothers and Liberace. There was something for everybody, but not nearly enough rock'n'roll.

CLYDE McPHATTER

January 1969			March 1969		
1-4	Manchester	Mr. Smith's	1	Liverpool	Wooky Hollow
5-11	Hanley	Mr. Smith's	23	Nottingham	Union Rowing
February 1969					
23-28	Liverpool	Wooky Hollow			
Promoter unknown					

Clyde's drinking and unreliability were becoming more pronounced, probably through frustration at lack of any headway in rebuilding his career in Britain. Bookings remained infrequent, although this brief spell in cabaret again demonstrated just what he had to offer. Audience response was generally positive, while the *Manchester Evening News* noted that he played to packed houses and had everybody screaming for more.

At Liverpool, he co-starred with none other than Skippy, the boxing kangaroo from Australia, but unlike Johnny Burnette who came off worst when he tussled with a similar marsupial immediately prior to his 1963 British tour, Clyde sensibly kept his distance.

TV appearances
Discothèque   12 February 1969

DUANE EDDY

Duane Eddy flew into the UK early in January with vague plans to establish London as his centre of operations. His career in the States was pretty flat at the time, so memories of his successful tour in the spring of 1968 had focused his thoughts on Britain. Aware that he needed to update his image if he was to reclaim hit status, he recorded 'Break My Mind' in London. It was a complete change of direction being a vocal record, but ultimately failed to make any real impact.

TV appearances
The Golden Shot   26 January 1969
Discothèque   26 February 1969

LITTLE RICHARD

An ambitious European tour was set up for Little Richard and it was originally announced that he would open in the UK on 20 January. This date was later moved back to the early part of February, with agent Arthur Howes organising four concerts including an appearance at the Royal Albert Hall on 4 February. The problem appeared to be that the Musicians' Union was unhappy with Richard's intention to bring a fifteen-piece band with him. No reciprocal exchange deal could be worked out and the UK gigs collapsed. Although Richard played shows in Munich, Berlin, Frankfurt and Geneva, attempts to organise appearances in Italy, Sweden and France were also unsuccessful.

FRANKIE AVALON

Frankie Avalon's popularity in Britain never came close to the adulation that he received in the States and by 1969 his name was rarely mentioned, although he did occasionally turn up on the cinema screen in rather limp beach movies. It was therefore a surprise when he made a promotional visit to Britain during the early part of February. Its impact was negligible.

TV appearances

The Leslie Crowther Show	2 February 1969
The Saturday Crowd	8 February 1969

SCREAMIN' JAY HAWKINS

A good, healthy dose of Screamin' Jay was just what Britain needed in February 1969. Roy Tempest announced an impressive string of one-nighters commencing in Bristol on 13 February, and for once it looked as if there was some sensible publicity to accompany the tour. The music papers printed the proposed dates and, after an absence of almost three years, Jay's return was eagerly anticipated by his loyal fans. The only problem was that he did not show up.

The initial response from Tempest was: 'He was supposed to arrive last week, I can't understand the guy,' while London's Flamingo Club explained his non-appearance as 'due to his being grounded through bad weather in New York'. Wild rumours circulated among the rock'n'roll fraternity including an unsubstantiated story that Jay had arrived at Heathrow smoking cannabis, was arrested and put on the next plane back to the States. Later, it was claimed that he never signed a contract with Roy Tempest and the whole tour was pure fantasy. During the period that he was scheduled to be in the UK, Jay was doing great business at the Avalon Ballroom, San Francisco.

BEN E. KING

February 1969			March 1969		
2	Tottenham	Royal	1	Chester	Clockwork Orange
	London	Bag O'Nails		Nantwich	Civic Hall
22	Margate	Dreamland		Manchester	Twisted Wheel
	Islington	Rock Steady	2	Doncaster	Attic
23	Retford	Broken Wheel		Derby	Clouds
	Manchester	Princess	3	Tunstall	Golden Torch
	Manchester	Domino		Birmingham	Cedar
24	Purley	Orchid	6	Portsmouth	Locarno
	London	Scotch of St. James	7	Canterbury	Bridge
26	Sevenoaks	Bligh's Hotel		Beckenham	Mistrale
	London	Samantha's	8	Nelson	Imperial
27	Worthing	Assembly Hall	9	Southampton	Top Rank
28	Leicester	University	10	Bishops Stortford	Rhodes Centre
	Sutton-in-Ashfield	Baths		London	Bag O'Nails

March 1969 (continued)					
			22	Dunstable	California
12	Wolverhampton	Lafayette		Birmingham	Cedar
	Birmingham	Cedar		Nottingham	Beachcomber
13	Bristol	Locarno	23-24	Middlesbrough	Showboat
	Birmingham	Cedar	25	Middlesbrough	Showboat
14	Birmingham	Odeon		Chester-le-Street	Garden Farm
	Sheffield	Shades	26	Middlesbrough	Showboat
15	Manchester	Princess		Whitley Bay	Sands
	Manchester	Domino	27-28	Middlesbrough	Showboat
16	Bolton	Casino		Middlesbrough	Town Hall
17	London	Scotch of St. James		Spennymoor	Top Hat
19	Leeds	Town Hall	29	Middlesbrough	Showboat
20	Stoke	Crystal		Manchester	Twisted Wheel
	Birmingham	Cedar	30	Crystal Palace	Hotel
21	Liverpool	Victoriana	31	Purley	Orchid
	Liverpool	Mardi Gras			
Promoters — Danny O'Donovan and Henry Sellers					

Ben E. King's UK tours got longer and longer, and no other comment on his continuing popularity should be necessary. On this occasion, he again worked with the Chris Shakespeare Globe Show and was seemingly in equal demand in the Northern clubs, the scampi-and-chips cabaret circuit and the trendy London nightspots. Tucked in among all his club dates was one concert at the Birmingham Odeon where he co-starred with Gene Pitney. (The reason for this booking was that Pitney was contracted to perform a free concert as compensation for missing an earlier one at the same venue due to heavy snow.) The following day, King was supported by Wayne Fontana at the Domino Club in Manchester.

TV appearances
Dee Time   24 February 1969

DUANE EDDY

March 1969			May 1969		
3-8	Greasbrough	Social	25	Manchester	Georgian
23	Middlesbrough	Excel	30	Farnworth	Monaco
24	Middlesbrough	Excel		Manchester	Princess
	Billingham	Social	31	Farnworth	Monaco
25-29	Middlesbrough	Excel		Manchester	Domino
April 1969					
2	Inverness	Caledonian Hotel			
5	Aberdeen	Douglas Hotel			
19	London	Queen Elizabeth Hall			
Promoter — Harold Davison					

Duane's dates in Britain were part of an extensive European trip and he was again backed by the Quotations and the Go-Jos. His guitar was stolen in Inverness, but happily the Scottish police recovered it in time for the show in Aberdeen to proceed on schedule.

Perhaps the most interesting booking was at the Queen Elizabeth Hall in London, which is part of the Royal Festival Hall complex and a venue more normally associated with classical concerts. Adverts for the show promised *'An evening with Duane Eddy, his group and strings'* and probably for the first time in Britain he was given the opportunity to demonstrate his versatility as a guitarist.

Eddy played for two hours and had the audience eating out of his hand. In a truly varied programme, he worked through his hits including 'Peter Gunn', 'Shazam!', 'Forty Miles Of Bad Road' and 'Rebel-Rouser', several movie themes ('Born Free', 'Pepe', 'Because They're Young' and 'High Noon'), plus Fats Domino's 'Blueberry Hill' and a jazzy treatment of '3.30 Blues'. He even performed the Irish ballad, 'Danny Boy', the Lovin' Spoonful's 'Daydream' and his own composition, 'Along Came Linda', as well as a truly original interpretation of Paganini's 'The Story of Three Loves'. He was brought back for two encores and departed to a thunderous standing ovation.

THE G-CLEFS

March 1969			22	Manchester	Twisted Wheel
7	Islington	Rock Steady	26	Hanley	The Place
	Paddington	Cue	28	Liverpool	Mardi Gras
9	Manchester	Georgian		Liverpool	Victoriana
17	Purley	Orchid	29	Nelson	Imperial
19	Birmingham	Cedar			
Promoters — Danny O'Donovan and Henry Sellers					

The G-Clefs spent the month of March in Europe but gained even less media coverage in Britain than for their first tour twelve months earlier. Any chance of really establishing themselves on this side of the Atlantic meant aiming at the soul market, as there was no real following for doo-wop among British rock'n'rollers at this time.

JERRY LEE LEWIS

One of the top television variety programmes in Britain during 1969 was *This Is Tom Jones,* which was screened by the ITV networks every Sunday evening. When the list of forthcoming guest appearances was announced at the beginning of February, it was no real surprise to find the Louisiana wildman scheduled to appear on 30 March, as he was a long-standing favourite of Jones'. Jerry Lee flew over purely for the one show in the company of his friend and sometime brother-in-law Cecil Harrelson. He performed his latest country hit, 'To Make Love Sweeter For You', and then duetted with the show's host on 'Whole Lotta Shakin' Goin' On', 'Lovin' Up A Storm', 'Great Balls Of Fire' and 'Long Tall Sally'.

TV appearances
This Is Tom Jones   30 March 1969

ROSE MADDOX

March 1969	
31 London	Nashville Room
Promoter unknown	

Country music was finally gaining popularity in Britain. *Opry*, the first specialist magazine and forerunner of *Country Music People*, had been launched in June 1968, while on 5 March a sizeable crowd had turned out to see guitar virtuoso Chet Atkins perform on opening night at the Nashville Room, London's new specialist country music venue.

The Maddox Brothers & Rose had recorded a whole range of hillbilly, bluegrass and country music during a long career that stretched back to the Forties. They had also dabbled in rockabilly, and Rose's rocking interpretation of material such as 'Wild, Wild Young Men' and 'My Little Baby' would delight British fans when reissues of the American singles became available in the UK during the Seventies.

In 1969 however, Rose Maddox was largely unknown in Britain and was engaged upon a tour of US military bases. On the date in question, she turned up at the Nashville Room where the American country star, Hank Locklin was performing with support from Johnny & The Tumbleweeds, Little Ginny, the Muskrats and the Jonny Young Four, and duetted with Locklin on 'Y'All Come' at the end of the evening.

CONWAY TWITTY

April 1969	
5 Wembley	Empire Pool
6 London	Nashville Room
Promoter — Mervyn Conn	

The success of his tours with Johnny Cash had inspired Mervyn Conn to launch the *International Festival Of Country & Western Music*. It was a very ambitious project, the success of which was by no means a foregone conclusion, and Conn must be given a lot of credit for his contribution towards finally breaking country music in Britain. In the end — and despite negative comments from many quarters within the music business — the first show was a great success, selling out the Empire Pool at Wembley with a crowd that was reported as being ten thousand, although Conn himself, with his natural promoter's flamboyance, claimed twelve.

Conway Twitty had last appeared in Britain during May 1960, when he had toured with Johnny Preston and Freddy Cannon. Since that time his career had experienced many ups and downs, but with three Top Ten C&W hits in America within the last twelve months, he was at last establishing himself as a major player in the field of country music.

He flew into London on the morning of Good Friday, 4 April accompanied by his manager, Bob Neal, and his backing band, the Lonely Blue Boys: Joe E. Lewis (bass guitar), Tommy 'Porkchop' Markham (drums) and John Hughey (pedal steel guitar). He was rushed to the BBC studios, and during the afternoon recorded 'It's Only Make Believe' and 'The Image Of Me' for later transmission on BBC2's *Late Night Line Up* — in colour for those few who had access to the latest technology.

The main show took place on Easter Saturday, and Twitty was the last of fourteen acts to perform, opening with his 1966 US hit, 'Look Into My Teardrops'. He was smartly dressed in a dark suit, white shirt and tie but — strangely — at no time spoke to the audience. Every number was announced by Joe Lewis, while Twitty played lead guitar and sang in his distinctive style, working his way through 'Sing Me Back Home', 'Jambalaya', 'I Started Lovin' You Again' and 'Dim Lights, Thick Smoke'.

There had been major problems with the sound system throughout the show and, unfortunately, Conway's performance was badly affected at times, his voice being overpowered by the volume of the backing. Nevertheless, after struggling through his 1968 hit, 'The Image Of Me', he managed to win the audience over with a driving 'Folsom Prison Blues' and his recent Number One, 'Next In Line'. He continued with an exquisitely-performed medley of Hank Williams songs that for many was the highlight of his show, before turning back the clock for a run-through of his rock'n'roll hits.

With Joe and Porkchop doing a valiant job on the backing vocals, he performed 'What Am I Living For', merging it into 'Halfway To Heaven', and received a very positive response. He then sang 'Unchained Melody' in its entirety. Such was the reaction to the old songs that Conway continued with 'I'll Try', 'Is A Blue Bird Blue' and a rocking 'Got My Mojo Working'. He received so much applause for the rock'n'roll numbers that his latest country hit, 'Darling, You Know I Wouldn't Lie', was left out of the set, and there only remained time for a superb 'It's Only Make Believe' before the festival came to a close.

The following day, he enjoyed some sightseeing in London before turning up at the Nashville Room to catch Charlie Walker's spot. The audience were then informed that a surprise guest would be making an appearance. Conway and the Lonely Blue Boys then repeated the Hank Williams medley that had proved so popular at Wembley. Unfortunately, time did not permit them to perform any longer, as the club was due to close. They flew back to the States the following day.

TV appearances
Late Night Line Up   4 April 1969 (screened 1 May 1969)

THIS IS MERRILL MOORE

MERRILL MOORE PLAYS ROCK

If you don't like rock, then you certainly won't like this colour picture of vintage piano-pounder Moore. In fact, Rockers and non-Rockers are welcome to write in to tell us what they think of rock colour portraits. Merrill, rediscovered by helmsman Max Needham, needs to be listened to carefully — his rock-country boogie style and solid vocals grow on you and he has been tipped to play on future Presley singles. Presley at present is spearheading the rock revival with his "Guitar Man", while Merrill's second LP on Ember called "Rough-house 88" is scheduled for release shortly. (Pic. courtesy Q.F.M.M.).

MERRILL E. MOORE

April 1969
5   Wembley   Empire Pool

Promoter — Mervyn Conn

In order to sell tickets in sufficient quantities to ensure the success of the *International Festival Of Country & Western Music*, Mervyn Conn needed to attract rock'n'roll fans to Wembley. He succeeded in his aim by booking Conway Twitty and also an obscure singer/pianist from San Diego, California named Merrill E. Moore, who had never enjoyed a hit record but who had recently been the subject of a sustained and highly successful publicity campaign.

The emergence of Moore was due entirely to the somewhat wacky efforts of a teddy boy named Max 'Waxie Maxie' Needham. He had single-handedly bombarded the media with information about his protégé and had cajoled Ember Records into issuing two albums containing the material recorded by Moore in the mid-fifties for Capitol. Merrill sang and played in a country boogie style with a voice not dissimilar to Bill Haley and a piano technique which contained at least the seeds of the style adopted by Jerry Lee Lewis only a little later.

Moore's appearance at Wembley was the crowning glory for Maxie's *'Quest for Merrill Moore'* campaign, and he organised a welcoming reception of teds to greet his hero when he arrived in Britain. This provided a highly amusing incident when the plane containing the American performers landed and the entourage first appeared at the Arrivals terminal. Established country stars like Loretta Lynn and Bill Anderson — still virtually unknown in the UK — were pointedly ignored as the reception committee mobbed Merrill Moore, the veteran rocker who could not get himself arrested back home.

The festival itself was not as star-studded as had been promised. Names such as Johnny Cash and Jeannie C. Riley had been talked about, but the fact that even the likes of Conway Twitty were appearing for expenses only, precluded Conn from landing any of the very big fish. In fairness to him, the operation was immensely costly and he was taking on a significant financial gamble. In addition to Moore, the show featured Conway Twitty & The Lonely Blue Boys, Bill Anderson & The Po' Boys, Jan Howard, Loretta Lynn, George Hamilton IV, Charlie Walker, John Wesley Ryles, Wes Buchanan, Larry Cunningham, the Kentuckians, the Orange Blossom Sound, Phil Brady & The Ranchers, the Hillsiders, plus comperes Murray Kash, David Allan and Stephen West.

Merrill was the fourth act to appear and was only allocated three numbers. Backed by the Kentuckians, he performed 'House Of Blue Lights' and both sides of his newly-recorded B&C label release, Roger Miller's 'Little Green Apples' and a pounding 'Sweet Mama Tree Top Tall'. The sound was atrocious during his short spot, and with the piano stranded in a far corner of the stage, it was difficult for him to make full use of his opportunity to shine in front of a British audience. The enduring memory for those close enough to the stage was the sight of his hands moving across the keyboard at a simply electrifying pace during the two rockers.

During his stay in London, Moore resided at the Royal Garden Hotel.

By coincidence, another American singer, Janis Joplin — darling to a wholly different generation of music lovers — was staying there at the same time. Whether the two ever met in the lift or over breakfast has never been documented, but the whiskey-swilling Joplin and the God-fearing Moore would have made an interesting contrast as popular music continued to stretch out into different directions.

Plans had been made for Merrill to stay on in the UK, and a firm booking was set up for London's 100 Club on 10 April. More dates and a possible recording session were also in the pipeline, only for the old problem of work permits to resurface. Moore was forced to return home prematurely with the bulk of the Wembley contingent on 9 April, and fans who turned up at the 100 Club to see him were disappointed to discover that he had been replaced by the Wild Angels.

TV appearances
Late Night Line Up   4 April 1969 (screened 1 May 1969)

ROY ORBISON

April 1969			17	Bolton	Casino
20-26	Stockton	Fiesta	18	Hammersmith	Odeon
27-30	Batley	Variety	19-20	Glasgow	Odeon
May 1969			21	Birmingham	Odeon
1-10	Batley	Variety	22	Cardiff	Capitol
11-14	Bolton	Casino	24-26	Blackpool	ABC
15-16	Wigan	Casino			
Promoter unknown					

Nobody could ever criticise Roy Orbison's treatment of his British fans, and at the beginning of April he arrived in the UK for his ninth UK visit. This time, however, the first part of his stay was also doubling as a honeymoon, as he was accompanied by his new wife, German-born Barbara Wellhörner. Upon his arrival, Roy slipped and fell downstairs at the airport, and for the early part of the month suffered considerable back pain.

The first segment of the tour comprised almost a month in Northern cabaret. Even that was less than straightforward. Driving to Stockton for the opening night of his engagement at the Fiesta, Roy's hire car seized up on the M1 at Luton and he was obliged to charter a private plane to get him to the venue in time.

Backed by the Art Movement, his act remained largely as before, although now including 'My Friend' — his latest single — which later nibbled briefly at the lower reaches of the UK charts in June. From 18 May, the tour transferred to theatre dates, and there were some protests from Orbison's followers when it transpired that his support act was the ultra-square Scottish singer, Moira Anderson. For the two nights in Glasgow he was additionally joined by Marmalade.

TV appearances
Sez Les   14 May 1969

BOBBY VEE

May 1969			8-14	Birmingham	La Dolce Vita
11-17	Newcastle	La Dolce Vita		Yardley	Cavendish
18-24	Stockton	Tito's	29	Failsworth	Broadway
	Billingham	La Ronde	**July 1969**		
June 1969			2-3	Failsworth	Broadway
1-7	Bolton	Casino	5	Failsworth	Broadway
Promoter unknown					

Back in the USA, Bobby Vee was still racking up hit records in 1969, although on this side of the Atlantic his new material was largely ignored. Working on the theory that a different format was needed to appeal to British record buyers, he travelled to the UK with producer Snuff Garrett and cut a new record, 'I'm Gonna Make It Up To You', which he promoted for all he was worth.

Sadly, Vee was by now perceived as a name from a bygone era and the new disc had little chance of success, receiving almost no airplay or media exposure. Rockers like Chuck Berry or Jerry Lee Lewis were better able to survive without hit records as their successes had been built on dynamic and exciting stage acts. Bobby's career, on the other hand, was based on his popularity with the girls, who bought his records in vast quantities, but this made him extra vulnerable now that the hits had dried up. Still, he did not give up without a fight, and to pay the bills he plied his trade around the Northern cabaret clubs.

TOMMY ROE

Just as a new hit record had given the career of Bruce Channel an unexpected boost in 1968, so did the success of 'Dizzy' for Tommy Roe a year later. During the first week of June, 'Dizzy' knocked the Beatles off the top of the British charts and Roe flew into London to accept the plaudits from the music press who were suddenly interested in him all over again. He conducted the usual round of interviews and talked of a proposed movie project in the summer and a full British tour for October. By 6 June, Tommy had concluded his whirlwind visit and flew home to the States.

TV appearances
Top Of The Pops   5 June 1969

SAM THE SHAM

June 1969					
6	Liverpool	Mardi Gras	13	Tottenham	Royal
	Liverpool	Victoriana	14	Nelson	Imperial
7	Dunstable	California	15	Nottingham	Britannia
8	Burton	76 Club	16	Wolverhampton	Park
9	Sunderland	Annabelle's		Birmingham	Cedar
11	Eastbourne	Winter Gardens	17	Manchester	Sloopy's
Promoter — Roy Tempest					

The music of Sam The Sham descends along with Chan Romero, Eddie Quinteros and Chris Montez through a line which can be traced back to the Chicano rock'n'roll of Ritchie Valens — or Richard Valenzuela to give him his correct name. Valens died in the same 1959 plane crash as Buddy Holly, but before doing so bequeathed to the world such greasy classics as 'La Bamba', 'Donna' and 'Ooh, My Head'. Sam The Sham turned up in 1965, disguised in a turban and, with a suitably-attired group dubbed the Pharaohs, and hit No.2 in the *Billboard* 'Hot 100' with 'Wooly Bully'. Later successes were harder to find, but records like 'Yakety Yak', 'Haunted House' and 'I Found A Love' at least showed where he was coming from. His real name by the way, was Domingo Samudio — a Chicano rocker trying to make a career for himself in the Beatles-obsessed mid-Sixties.

In June 1969, Roy Tempest announced that Sam The Sham would be touring the UK and the music press dutifully printed the dates without any additional comment. He came and he went. The world took no notice at all. We are left with one unanswered question: was it Domingo Samudio who toured Britain in 1969, or was it really Sam The Sham?

CHUCK BERRY

July 1969		
4-5	London	Royal Albert Hall
6	Liverpool	Empire
Promoters — Roy Guest and Vic Lewis		

It must have seemed like a great idea at the time: a week-long series of concerts would be staged at the Royal Albert Hall under the banner *'Pop Proms'*. Major acts including Led Zeppelin, Fleetwood Mac and Amen Corner were signed up. On the final two nights, Chuck Berry would headline, appearing on Friday alongside the Chicken Shack and Alan Bown, while on the Saturday he would co-star with the Who.

In retrospect, it is difficult to imagine a more ill-advised project, coming as it did in the wake of the Haley riots at the Albert Hall, Jerry Lee's gig at Kempton Park and Chuck's own spot of bother at the Saville. The Who were the darlings of the mods, and by billing them and Berry on the same evening, the promoters were almost inviting the inevitable trouble. The *naïveté* which led to this decision almost beggars belief.

It was therefore no great surprise when rockers stormed the stage,

and the post-show reports concentrated almost exclusively on the trouble. Co-promoter Roy Guest commented: 'It would seem that Chuck Berry attracts a minority fringe who have to wreck it for everyone else. You can dig someone without smashing your way into a place.'

Subsequently, the *Pop Proms* were banished to the less prestigious Chalk Farm Roundhouse, but never really caught on. They eventually sank without trace, and nobody ever again booked Chuck Berry and the Who together.

Chuck did play one further gig up at the Liverpool Empire, where he was reunited with his old adversaries, the Swinging Blue Jeans, along with Jon Hiseman's Colosseum.

CLYDE McPHATTER

July 1969		
10	Sheffield	Penthouse
18-19	Sunderland	Annabelle's
20	Retford	Broken Wheel
Promoter unknown		

Time was running out for Clyde McPhatter. His last single, 'Denver', was released by B&C Records during July, but from then on his only publicity arose from a rather unseemly incident when he was arrested for loitering with intent. The case against him went into court but then collapsed, though not before embarrassing revelations had been made as to the pitiful state of his finances.

These cabaret engagements in Sheffield and Sunderland, plus his appearance along with Jimmy James & The Vagabonds at a mini-soul festival in Retford, were Clyde's final shows in Britain. He returned home to the United States in 1970, and died in his sleep in Manhattan on 12 June 1972 from a heart attack brought about by chronic alcohol abuse — a tragic demise for a truly great entertainer.

BILL HALEY & HIS COMETS

July 1969			August 1969		
21-23	Stockton	Fiesta	1-2	Failsworth	Broadway
	Middlesbrough	Excel		Whalley	Ace Of Spades
24	Stockton	Fiesta	3-9	Stockport	Poco Poco
25-26	Stockton	Fiesta		Eccles	Talk Of The North
	Sunderland	Annabelle's	10-13	Leigh	Garrick
27	Failsworth	Broadway		Bolton	Casino
28-31	Failsworth	Broadway	14	Leigh	Garrick
	Whalley	Ace Of Spades		Wigan	Casino
			15-16	Leigh	Garrick
				Bolton	Casino
Promoter — Paddy Malynn					

The rock'n'roll revival of 1968 was a distant memory when Bill Haley & His Comets returned to the UK following a successful tour of Scandinavia. They arrived in Britain on 20 July for almost a month of cabaret appearances in the North, with not a single date in London or the South — a surprising omission in view of the success of the Royal Albert Hall show on the previous tour. Bill and his wife, Martha, were accompanied by Rudy Pompilli (saxophone), Nick Nastos (guitar) and two new Comets, Ray Cawley (bass) and Bill Nolte (drums). Also travelling with them was Nick's wife, Carol, and their young son, E.J. The hysterical excitement that accompanied the 1968 tour had by now dissolved completely, but Haley and his group still proved a good draw at the box office wherever they played.

Their act had not changed dramatically, and the set list remained more-or-less constant throughout the tour. Bill opened with 'Shake, Rattle And Roll' and the ever-popular 'Rudy's Rock', during which horn-man Pompilli gave his usual exuberant display while Ray Cawley — a less extrovert character than his predecessor Al Rappa — climbed onto the double bass, much to the delight of the audience. A spirited 'See You Later, Alligator' was followed by the country ballad, 'There Goes My Everything', on which drummer Bill Nolte handled the vocal duties, and a couple of instrumentals — 'Fingers On Fire' and 'Malagueña' — featuring the blistering guitar-playing of Nick Nastos. Haley stepped back to the microphone for 'Razzle Dazzle' before giving way to Ray Cawley with 'Hey Mama'. Another instrumental, 'Wipe Out', featured an extended drum solo. Rudy then led on 'Kansas City' and Nick on 'Johnny B. Goode' before Bill wrapped up the proceedings with the one and only 'Rock Around The Clock'.

There were few variations to this set, although on a couple of occasions Bill Nolte also sang 'Danny Boy' or 'Almost Persuaded', while at Bolton 'Rudy's Rock' was replaced by 'Yakety Sax' on at least one night. At Stockton, there were specially printed beermats announcing '*Direct from America for six nights — Bill Haley & His Comets*', and a 'yard of ale' drinking contest took place. Ray Cawley smashed the double bass while climbing on top of it at Middlesbrough, and at the same venue a '*Miss Astronaut*' contest was held as an acknowledgement that Buzz Aldrin and Neil Armstrong had landed on the Moon.

The Comets had always been more than a backing group and were all individually-talented musicians, but such criticism as was forthcoming centred on the fact that Haley himself only sang four songs in each show, which for many fans was not nearly enough.

A concert on 10 August at the Hibernian Football Club in Edinburgh was advertised extensively in the preceding weeks. However, no contract had been signed, and both Bill and his management took exception to the fact that he was billed below the Tremeloes and Marmalade. He refused to appear, and the show turned out to be a complete flop without him. There was also talk of the Comets participating in an open-air concert at London's Regents Park during late August along with Chuck Berry, but this project never got off the ground due to objections from the local authority.

Haley returned to the States on 20 August, where he had business to conclude in connection with some property investments.

THE FLAMINGOS

Attempts were made to set up a club and ballroom tour for the Flamingos commencing 25 July. It was later announced that they would be included on a Jackie Wilson tour in September. Neither project got far off the drawing board.

JACKIE WILSON

Clayman Management in conjunction with Danny Betesh made enthusiastic noises about a Jackie Wilson theatre tour with support by the Bandwagon and co-starring the Flamingos. At one stage, Clyde McPhatter was to be added to the bill as well, but, despite a start date of 4 September being announced, the project stalled. A later attempt to bring Wilson to the UK in December with Eddie Floyd also failed.

CHUCK BERRY

On either side of Chuck's appearances at the ill-fated *Pop Proms* in July, attempts were made to bring him over to the UK for a full-blown tour. Roy Tempest dribbled out a proposed set of dates for May in his usual style, but nobody was particularly surprised when they came to nothing.

A more serious attempt was made by Jim Dawson with a theatre tour scheduled to commence on 27 September on which Berry would co-star with the Foundations. The proposed itinerary was to have included a high-profile appearance at the Royal Albert Hall, but their management would have none of it. The *Pop Proms* debacle was still fresh in everyone's minds, as was the 1968 Haley concert riot. Dawson duly received a cancellation letter stating: *'We regret we cannot accept Chuck Berry's booking, nor indeed that of any other rock and roll artist.'*

After the Albert Hall banned Chuck, several other theatres also stated their disapproval and the promoter started to back off. An attempt was made to replace Berry with Creedence Clearwater Revival, but they were unavailable at short notice and eventually the whole scheme just fizzled out.

BEN E. KING

October 1969					
2	London	Hatchett's	19-25	Stockton	Fiesta
3	Tottenham	Royal	30	Birmingham	Rebecca's
	Paddington	Cue		Birmingham	Cedar
4	Dunstable	California	31	Manchester	Domino
5	Birmingham	Top Rank		Manchester	Princess
6	Purley	Orchid	**November 1969**		
8	Wellington	Town House	1	Dunstable	California
9	Worthing	*unknown venue*	2	Paddington	Cue
	London	Hatchett's	3	Birmingham	Rebecca's
16	Birmingham	Rebecca's	6	Birmingham	Rebecca's
17	Liverpool	Mardi Gras	8	Manchester	Domino
	Liverpool	Victoriana		Manchester	Princess
18	Oswestry	Copa-Mo	11	Birmingham	Rebecca's
	Crewe	Up The Junction	13	Birmingham	Rebecca's
	Manchester	Twisted Wheel			

Promoter — Danny O'Donovan

Ben E. King returned in the autumn for his second tour of 1969, backed once again by the Chris Shakespeare Globe Show. He remained just about the most consistently popular draw on the ballroom circuit — as was evidenced by the return bookings at the same venues each time he visited Britain. If a club owner wanted a sure-fire successful night, he would book Ben E. King.

THE EVERLY BROTHERS

A booking was announced for Don and Phil to play two weeks at the Golden Garter Theatre Club in Wythenshawe, Greater Manchester, opening on 13 October. A few days later, a club date in Scarborough was added to the proposed itinerary. The tour was eventually cancelled, with just a vague promise that the popular duo would be coming in the spring of 1970 instead.

LITTLE RICHARD

Little Richard flew into Britain from Canada on 28 October to tape a guest spot on Tom Jones' TV show. Recording took place at ATV's Elstree Studios, where he made a dramatic entrance, emerging exotically attired in a bright orange pair of slacks complete with matching cloak and his long black hair piled high up on his head. After some initial microphone problems had been rectified, he thrilled the invited studio audience with a dynamic version of 'Lucille', his voice and piano pyrotechnics as amazing as ever. He was then joined by the show's host and the two men performed a medley of 'Tutti Frutti', 'Jenny, Jenny' and 'Rip It Up'. They also sang complete versions of 'Good Golly Miss Molly' and 'Send Me Some Lovin' '.

Later in the show, Richard was featured in a bar-room scene — this time wearing a beige suit and a red bow tie. After a few lines of dialogue, he played a piano blues and — unexpectedly — a restrained 'As Time Goes By'. The latter number gave them difficulties and needed many takes before everyone was happy with it.

The ebullient Mr. Penniman finished by running around the studio shaking hands in turn with each of the crew. Also guesting on the same episode was French singer Claudine Longet.

TV appearances
This Is Tom Jones   2 November 1969 (screened 21 December 1969)

THE SHIRELLES

A group purporting to be the Shirelles appeared in clubs around Britain during November, but were just the latest batch of imposters. They were in good company, as all the usual suspects were still to be found working the clubs: various 'Platters' and 'Drifters' operated throughout the year, being joined at different times by the 'Crystals', 'Ronettes' and 'Coasters'. Cornered by *NME* in February while announcing his latest tour projects, Roy Tempest had promised: 'I guarantee that these are all genuine and original artists. I am through with presenting imitators.'

GENE VINCENT

November 1969			18	Orpington	Civic Halls
8	Ryde, IOW	Royal York Hotel	20	London	Speakeasy
10	Mildenhall	USAF	23	London	Palladium
11	Southall	Northcote Arms	24	Nottingham	Sherwood Rooms
12	Sevenoaks	Bligh's Hotel	26	Belfast	Floral Hall
16	Hampstead	Country Club			
Promoter — Henry Henroid					

More than four years had passed since Gene Vincent last performed in Britain and during that time his fortunes had dipped still further, both professionally and in his personal life. With little happening for him back in the States, he had recently recorded a comeback album — *I'm Back And I'm Proud* — for British disc-jockey John Peel's Dandelion label.

An unbelievably chaotic tour of France immediately preceded his British visit, but when Gene's flight from Orly touched down at Heathrow shortly before eleven on the morning of 5 November there was an enthusiastic crowd of fans waiting to greet the prodigal son including a motorcade of bikers who escorted his white Rolls-Royce limo into town. An independent film crew had been hired to make a documentary of the tour for BBC television, and with them in tow Vincent headed for the nearest hostelry to renew his acquaintance with Watney's Red Barrel, his favoured brand of British beer.

It soon became clear that Gene's life was in turmoil. His English wife, Margie, was pursuing him for unpaid maintenance, while his previous management were also seeking monies allegedly owed to them. Vincent's personality was such that any sort of friendly compromise was out of the question, and the opening night of the tour was always going to be interesting — especially when a team of enforcers arrived on the Isle of Wight to discuss his outstanding management dispute.

287

Gene gives it his all at the Hampstead Country Club.

The show took place in the ballroom of a large holiday hotel in Ryde and Gene's presence had ensured a capacity crowd. Backed throughout the tour by the Wild Angels, he commenced his act with 'Say Mama'. Gene was noticeably heavier and less mobile than previously but dressed all in black with a medallion hanging round his neck. It soon became clear that his wonderfully distinctive voice was as strong as ever.

As he worked his way through 'Baby Blue' and the Delaney & Bonnie song 'Get Ourselves Together', the film crew crawled around the stage, nearly colliding with Gene as he prowled from side to side. The pace slowed for 'Lonesome Whistle' before accelerating through 'Pistol Packin' Mama' and 'Rocky Road Blues'. During the latter, Gene tried to swing the microphone around his head only for it to come apart in his hand. None of the stage equipment seemed suitable for the rocking treatment that was being dished out by both Vincent and the Wild Angels, and there was some concern that it might not survive the experience — especially when they tore into a tempestuous version of 'Good Golly Miss Molly' that brought cheers and applause from all around the hall. The set closed with 'Be-Bop-A-Lula', and for an encore a frenzied 'Long Tall Sally'. Even after he had left the stage for the last time, the chanting and applause carried on for a full five minutes.

The night's entertainment had not yet finished. Gene and a small group of privileged fans stayed in the hotel — which was otherwise devoid of guests in out-of-season November — and later the startled film crew joined them in Gene's bedroom when his ex-management representatives called in to forcefully resolve their business differences. The subsequent scenes were filmed but largely edited from the documentary, although enough remained for the viewer to get the general drift as Gene screamed 'I want my money!' over and over again.

After this rather dramatic start, the tour settled down and at Southall the teddy boys turned out in force. London rock'n'rollers Lee Tracey & The Tributes opened the show, and by the time the Wild Angels had completed their spot the place was packed and the atmosphere electric. Gene received a hero's welcome and was on top form, despite the fact that earlier in the day his damaged leg had been so painful that a doctor had prescribed morphine, forbidden him to perform and ordered thirty-six hours bed rest.

Somethin' Else were the opening act at Sevenoaks. That show had been poorly advertised but still drew a large crowd. Gene's leg was playing up again, so he cut his set to only eight numbers but still went down a storm despite a rather intrusive psychedelic lightshow.

The following day, he filmed an appearance for *Top Of The Pops* to promote his new single, 'Be-Bop-A-Lula '69'. Unfortunately, this was never screened due to a union dispute.

The Orpington gig was a mess. There was inadequate security, an appalling PA system, and the Wild Angels had an off night and played out of tune for much of the evening.

The prestigious date at London's Speakeasy went over much better. The club's attendance record was smashed by an audience that included John Lennon and Yoko Ono, George Harrison and Nic Simper of Deep Purple. Gene's performance was very well received and he encored by repeating 'Be-Bop-A-Lula' with Georgie Fame sitting in on piano and Tony Sheridan on guitar.

Support acts at the London Palladium were Lee Tracey & The Tributes, the Impalas and the Nashville Teens. Emperor Rosko compered the show. Gene scored strongly with an outstanding version of 'Lonesome Whistle' and a torrid 'Rocky Road Blues' which ended with him down on one knee and the microphone stand swinging upside down in the air.

Even a less than fit and healthy Gene Vincent was a tremendous boost for rock'n'roll, and it was great to have him back in Britain after so long.

TV appearances

The Rock'n'Roll Singer	6-8 November 1969 (screened 7 May 1970)
Today	7 November 1969
Top Of The Pops	13 November 1969 (not screened)

BO DIDDLEY

The Lorna Wallis Agency announced a string of dates for Bo covering most of November. It was proposed that he would bring one of his own musicians and work with a British drummer and bass player. It did not happen and Diddley's poor touring record in the UK continued.

TOMMY ROE

Tommy had followed up his smash, 'Dizzy', with another, if smaller chart record, 'Heather Honey'. Although there had been persistent rumours of a tour it never materialised, but instead he came to the UK on 10 December for a short promotional visit.

TV appearances
Top Of The Pops   11 December 1969

BIG AL DOWNING

Oklahoma-born rock'n'roller Big Al Downing visited Britain on two occasions during 1969 and 1970 to play military bases in the company of his guitarist, Vernon Sandusky. When interviewed in 1980 by *New Kommotion*, he did recall playing a few 'civilian clubs' as well as the USAF bases at Mildenhall and Lakenheath, although to date no evidence or confirmation has come to light. Surely somebody can remember stumbling into Downing and Sandusky at their local club and rocking the night away to 'Down On The Farm' and 'Miss Lucy'?

CHAPTER FIFTEEN

1970

Let's Have A Party

1970 was a disappointing year for rock'n'roll. None of the major acts like Chuck Berry or Jerry Lee Lewis toured Britain and media interest in the subject was probably at an all-time low. Once again, several interesting tours were promised, only for the fans to be frustrated when they failed to materialise. Around this time it was not a great career move to declare to the world that you were a rock'n'roll singer. Far better to classify yourself as a soul, R&B, country or rock artist. Prejudice against rock'n'roll had always been there of course. Originally it came from older musicians who felt threatened by something which they could not understand, but later a form of rock snobbery had crept in, whereby writers for journals like *New Musical Express* and *Melody Maker* were rarely slow in ridiculing the early sounds which they dismissed as old-fashioned and trivial.

With hindsight, the short British tour by Buddy Knox during May would prove the most significant event of the year. It was another example of fan power and would surely never have taken place at all had it been left to the full-time promoters. There was significantly more money to be made in peddling groups of fake Drifters than in bringing over a comparatively unknown but authentic rock'n'roller like Knox who would only ever appeal to a minority of enthusiasts.

Despite this rather gloomy scenario, British rock'n'roll was showing some signs of life. A sizeable crowd turned up at the Roundhouse in London's Chalk Farm during February for a concert compered by Emperor Rosko which featured Marty Wilde, Joe Brown, Roy Young, Tommy Bruce and Bert Weedon along with contemporary rock'n'rollers the Wild Angels, Dave Travis & Bad River and Legend. The lion's share of publicity, however, went to the irrepressible Lord Sutch. He had the music press at fever pitch with reports that he had chatted with Elvis at a private party and was able to exclusively reveal that the King would be coming to the UK at last... definitely... although he couldn't say exactly when...

Outside the field of rock'n'roll the number of American acts touring Britain continued to increase. Visitors worthy of mention included pop singers Lou Christie, Gene Pitney and former rock'n'rollers Paul Anka and Bobby Darin, while the contemporary rock fraternity was catered for by Johnny Winter, Canned Heat and Dr. John. Soul enthusiasts were able to take their pick from Joe Tex, Marv Johnson, Jimmy Ruffin and Arthur Conley, while the developing country music scene provided the opportunity for entertainment by the likes of Buck Owens, Kenny Rogers, Jerry Reed and Slim Whitman. Through it all, rock'n'roll just kept hanging in there.

RONNIE HAWKINS

Canadian-based rocker Ronnie Hawkins arrived in Britain on 11 February as part of the John Lennon-inspired *World Peace* tour. It was strictly a promotional visit, and he holed up at the Playboy Club in London's Park Lane for the duration of his stay. This was Ronnie's first time in the UK since his television appearance on *Boy Meets Girls* back in January 1960. Atlantic Records threw a reception for him, but the highlight of his visit was a private party hosted by Hawkins himself at the Playboy Club, which has since taken on mythical proportions. It was a strictly 'X Certificate' affair and well in line with Ronnie's reputation as a rock'n'roll hellraiser.

TOMMY ROE

February 1970			March 1970		
14	Sutton Coldfield	Belfry	3-6	Newcastle	La Dolce Vita
17-18	Newcastle	La Dolce Vita	8-14	Blackburn	Cavendish
20	Newcastle	La Dolce Vita	18	Birmingham	Rebecca's
22-28	Birmingham	La Dolce Vita			
	Yardley	Cavendish			
Promoter unknown					

Some ten months after 'Dizzy' brought Tommy Roe back into the British Top Ten, he finally arrived accompanied by his wife for a month on the UK cabaret circuit. Unfortunately, press interest had completely evaporated by this time and he made little impact outside of his long-time fans. 'Dizzy' had been such a big record that Roe should really have made more of his second chance, but timing was all-important, and to be frank, he blew it. To make matters worse, shows at the beginning of March had to be cancelled when he contracted a nasty bout of laryngitis.

TV appearances
The Engelbert Humperdinck Show   18 February 1970

JERRY LEE LEWIS

Theatre managers, like elephants, never forget. Plans for a package tour by Lewis in March were scuppered by the news that he was still blacklisted by the Rank Organisation and banned from all of their theatre outlets as a result of the scandal of 1958. Rock'n'roll had indeed cast very long shadows.

RICK NELSON

Apart from Elvis, Rick Nelson was just about the most important rock'n'roller who had yet to appear live in Britain. He had recently returned to the US charts with a Bob Dylan song, 'She Belongs To Me', and was enthusiastically cultivating a new image complete with long hair, jeans and cowboy boots. A tour was announced for April 1970, with Nelson due to fly into Britain over the Easter weekend for a series of ballroom and college dates. A new single, 'I Shall Be Released', was scheduled to coincide with his visit and television appearances lined up on *Top Of The Pops* and BBC2's *Disco 2*.

It did seem that arrangements were being made at very short notice, and only two dates (in Hampstead and Birmingham) had been announced when the tour was cancelled again. Rick was reportedly suffering with a throat infection, but what the general public did not appreciate was that he and his Stone Canyon Band — Allen Kemp (guitar), Randy Meisner (bass), Pat Shanahan (drums) and Tom Brumley (steel guitar) — flew into Britain after all.

They arrived on 11 March, and when interviewed at the Cumberland Hotel, Rick revealed that he had never been properly consulted about the proposed shows and had in fact only been contracted to perform at US military bases in Britain and Europe. Two such appearances at Upper Heyford and Alconbury were all that remained of his tour and even his television appearances were cancelled.

CARL PERKINS

Mervyn Conn's *Second International Festival Of Country & Western Music* took place at the Empire Pool, Wembley on Easter Saturday, 28 March. Rock'n'roll enthusiasts were pleased to see the great Carl Perkins among the artists billed to appear, but sadly his name had disappeared by the final days leading up to the show, to be replaced by that of singer-songwriter Don Gibson. The festival proved to be another resounding success for Conn, who had assembled a stronger line-up than the first year including David Houston, Roy Acuff, Skeeter Davis and Loretta Lynn. Unfortunately, the rock'n'roll content of the show was negligible.

CREEDENCE CLEARWATER REVIVAL

April 1970		
14-15	London	Royal Albert Hall
	Promoter — Robert Paterson	

Creedence had burst into the British charts during 1969 with two pure nuggets of rock'n'roll gold, 'Proud Mary' and 'Bad Moon Rising'. However, this was a rock'n'roll revival of a very different kind: they were a four-piece group, modern in dress and appearance, but steeped in the traditions of the Fifties.

CREEDENCE CLEARWATER REVIVAL

In John Fogerty they had a massive talent who not only sang and played, but also wrote much of their material. Some of the purists were suspicious of the long hair and critical of the heavier guitar style which sometimes intruded on their records, but in the spring of 1970 any doubts about their credibility were blown away when they shook up the British charts with 'Travellin' Band', a wild slab of rock'n'roll that was so good you wondered why Little Richard hadn't thought of it first.

Creedence Clearwater Revival spent most of April 1970 in Europe playing gigs at major venues commensurate with their status as one of the hottest bands in the world. John Fogerty (vocals, guitar and piano), Tom Fogerty (rhythm guitar), Doug Clifford (drums) and Stuart Cook (bass) all hailed from California. They sold out both nights at the Royal Albert Hall with ease, performing for a little over an hour and receiving sensational response, which culminated with a standing ovation the like of which had not been seen in years.

The show opened with 'Born On The Bayou' which eased them into another hit song, 'Green River'. The band's own favourite tune, 'Tombstone Shadow', was a prelude to an explosive 'Travellin' Band', which got the dancers out of their seats and jiving in the aisles. Another high spot of the act was 'Midnight Special', which inspired much audience participation before the temperature was pushed up to boiling point by 'Bad Moon Rising' and 'Proud Mary'. A heavy version of 'Night Time Is The Right Time' was followed by a frantic 'Good Golly Miss Molly' containing all the impact and excitement that Little Richard intended. The show closed with John playing mouth-harp on 'Keep On Chooglin' ' while the other three jammed away behind him like crazy. The doubters were silenced. This was most emphatically rock'n'roll at its very best.

Earlier in the evening there had been support from Quintessence, and — of more interest to the rockers — R&B singer Wilbert Harrison. He performed a one-man band act, but was more than a little lost in the vast concert hall. Nevertheless, he still scored strongly with 'Kansas City', 'Let's Work Together' (a recent hit for Canned Heat) and a good version of 'Stand By Me', though he would probably have been more effective in a small, intimate club atmosphere.

TV appearances
Creedence Clearwater Revival In Concert 14-15 April 1970 (screened 7 August 1971)

WANDA JACKSON

April 1970			24	Glasgow	City Hall
19	Liverpool	Empire	26	London	Palladium
23	Belfast	Usher Hall			
Promoter – Mervyn Conn					

With two successful Wembley country shows under his belt, Mervyn Conn launched a promotional tour for Capitol Records titled *Country Music Caravan*, featuring the cream of their country roster: Buck Owens & His Buckaroos, Tex Ritter, Wanda Jackson, Billie Jo Spears, the Hagers, Buddy Alan and compere Murray Kash. For two weeks in April they roared across Europe playing twelve cities in nine different countries and, owing to the inclusion of Wanda on the package, attracted a fair proportion of rock'n'roll enthusiasts who remembered her classic recordings 'Let's Have A Party' and 'Mean Mean Man', which had been minor British hits almost a decade earlier.

A warm Sunday evening resulted in a near-capacity audience at the London Palladium, and Wanda looked quite stunning when she walked out on stage in a silver mini-dress. Backing was provided by Tex Ritter's band, the Bo Weevils, and Wanda's own guitarist, Mike Post.

To the delight of the rockers in the audience, she opened with 'There's A Party Goin' On', immediately demonstrating that her powerful voice had lost none of its edge. After a lengthy chat she slowed the tempo for a flawless interpretation of her biggest country song, 'Right Or Wrong', following which Mike Post joined her for a duet on 'Jackson'. 'If I Had A Hammer' was marred by an unfunny comedy routine that completely missed the mark, but just as some of the audience was starting to get restless, Wanda opened her lungs and tore into 'Let's Have A Party' — an all-time classic rocker that was greeted with a roar of approval. For the final number of her short spot, she even tried some yodelling on 'Bet You My Heart I Love You'.

For the fans it was a wonderful opportunity to glimpse for the first time one of the greatest female rock'n'roll vocalists, but it was also frustrating not to hear a full rock'n'roll show. Songs like 'Honey Bop', 'Fujiyama Mama' and 'Mean, Mean Man' would remain unheard by British audiences until Wanda came back to rock'n'roll again in the late Eighties.

LONDON PALLADIUM
Telephone: 01-437 7373
6.0 — SUNDAY, 26th APRIL — 8.30
TWO PERFORMANCES ONLY

COUNTRY MUSIC CARAVAN
PRESENTED BY MERVYN CONN IN ASSOCIATION WITH CAPITOL RECORDS

★★★★★★
THE HAGERS
WANDA JACKSON
BUCK OWENS
TEX RITTER
BILLIE JO SPEARS
★★★★★★

COMPERE :
MURRAY KASH

Capitol.

STALLS 40/-, 30/-, 20/-. CIRCLE 40/-, 30/-, 20/-.
UPPER CIRCLE 15/-, 10/6. BOXES 160/-, 120/-, 60/-, 15/-.
All seats may be booked in advance. Box Office open 10 a.m. to 9.30 p.m.

ROY ORBISON

April 1970			June 1970		
24	Paignton	Festival Theatre	1-6	Wythenshawe	Golden Garter
26-30	Stockton	Fiesta	7	Birmingham	Odeon
May 1970			8-13	Wythenshawe	Golden Garter
1-9	Stockton	Fiesta	14-19	Batley	Variety
10-16	Batley	Variety	22	Walthamstow	Granada
17	Bournemouth	Winter Gardens			
22-24	Blackpool	ABC			
28	Bristol	Colston Hall			
31	Wythenshawe	Golden Garter			
		Promoter unknown			

Roy Orbison

Roy's annual visit to Britain was a combination of cabaret engagements and theatre one-nighters. Backed throughout the tour by the Art Movement, he remained a massive draw for live shows. His initial week at Batley Variety Club was a complete sellout and created the demand for a second booking only a month later. Similarly, at the Golden Garter in the Wythenshawe area of Manchester, Roy's residency broke all attendance records. While there, he surprised his regular fans by performing a wild version of 'Ooby Dooby' — his first rock'n'roll hit — and was rewarded by sustained applause and the sight of jivers hurrying out on to the floor. Arrival were the main supporting act on the one-nighters, but Roy also worked with the Kaye Sisters at Blackpool and Karen Young in Walthamstow.

On 18 May, Roy attended the British Country Music Association Awards Dinner at the Royal Lancaster Hotel in London, where Conway Twitty was among the guests of honour, and he presented to Loretta Lynn the CMA (GB) Award for *Female Vocalist Of The Year*. His wife Barbara was pregnant at the time of this tour, and would give birth to Roy Orbison Jr. on 10 October. Perhaps by way of celebration, Roy treated himself to a Rolls-Royce whilst shopping in Bond Street. He finally departed on 26 June for a ten-day tour of Ireland.

TV appearances
The Golden Shot   7 June 1970
Mike & Bernie's Scene   8 June 1970

BEN E. KING

May 1970					
1	Liverpool	Mardi Gras	17	Hanley	The Place
	Liverpool	Victoriana	18	Nottingham	Palais
2	Middlewich	Civic Hall		Birmingham	Rebecca's
	Crewe	Up The Junction	20	Chicksands	USAF
	Manchester	Twisted Wheel	21	Birmingham	Rebecca's
3	Kennington	Surrey Rooms	23	Oswestry	Plaza
4	Purley	Orchid		Oakengates	Town Hall
	London	Valbonne		Manchester	Twisted Wheel
5	London	Samantha's	24	East Sheen	Bull
	London	Scotch of St. James	27	Birmingham	Rebecca's
6-7	Birmingham	Rebecca's	29	Manchester	Princess
9	Dunstable	California		Manchester	Domino
11-16	Middlesbrough	Variety Showboat	30	Dunstable	California
			31	Retford	Broken Wheel Scene
Unknown promoter					

Another routine ballroom tour by Ben E. King included return bookings at many of the venues that he had played on earlier visits — a sure indication that he was still hot stuff at the box office. On the final night of the tour, Ben co-starred with Inez & Charlie Foxx at the Broken Wheel Scene in Retford. Backing once again was provided by the Globe Show.

GARY 'US' BONDS

The visit of Gary 'US' Bonds to play a club and ballroom tour for promoter Roy Tempest in May 1970 seemed like a routine job of work for Tez Stokes, who, as a member of the one-time hit group the Cherokees, was employed to back Bonds. He rehearsed the hit records such as 'Quarter To Three' and 'School Is Out' assuming that they would be the major part of the act, only to find that Bonds did not intend to perform any of these songs and instead would be singing the likes of 'Proud Mary' and 'Yesterday'. The other surprise was that, instead of being a slim Puerto Rican American, he had mysteriously transformed into a chubby black man with an English accent. The 'Gary 'US' Bonds' touring the UK was in fact Jamaican singer Horace Faith who would go on to score a hit of his own in September 1970 with the song 'Black Pearl'.

For several nights the illusion was maintained. As with so many of Tempest's fake tours, the audience enjoyed a quality performance from a competent singer and band. The lack of any resemblance to the real Gary 'US' Bonds in either appearance or music seemed to escape the attention of successive audiences until finally at one Northern club, the president of Bonds' fan club arrived with a bunch of records to be autographed by his hero. The game was up: the manager called and the show was abruptly cancelled. The tour ground to a halt at that point and no further dates were undertaken. Horace Faith was free to concentrate on his own fledgling career while Tez Stokes limped back home, wiser but poorer, never having received any payment for his efforts.

BUDDY KNOX

May 1970			13	London	Nashville Room
9	Greenwich	Mitre	14-16	Birmingham	Watersplash
10	Hampstead	Country	19	Coventry	Locarno
12	London	100 Club	22	Wethersfield	USAF
Promoters — Graham Wood and Mal Derrick					

      This short tour was a deeply significant one for the future of rock'n'roll in that it was the first time that a fan rather than a professional promoter had brought an American rocker over to England. Buddy Knox was not unknown. He had enjoyed million-selling records and movie roles in the States during the Fifties but had never attained anything like the same level of recognition on this side of the Atlantic where 'Party Doll', his most popular record, had made no more than a cameo appearance in the charts back in 1957.

      Thirteen years later, Knox was forgotten in Britain by all but the keenest rock'n'roll enthusiasts and no big-time promoter was ever going to chance his arm with such an uncommercial proposition. It took the enthusiasm of rock'n'roll fan Graham Wood, working with a small-time fringe promoter, Mal Derrick, to set up this unlikely tour on which Buddy would work with the British band, Dave Travis & Bad River. In fact it nearly failed to happen at all. Forty-eight hours before Knox was due to travel, the promoters had still not managed to come up with his plane ticket and the project was only salvaged when Travis agreed to loan the money to them. Buddy and his manager, former Canadian rock'n'roller Les Vogt, eventually landed at London Heathrow Airport on 8 May.

THE NASHVILLE ROOM

Northend Road   W.12

WEDNESDAY, 13th MAY, at 7.30 p.m.

U.S. Country Rock Star

BUDDY KNOX

with

DAVE TRAVIS & BAD RIVER

plus Guest Artists

DOUBLE   *17/6*

      The opening show at the Mitre, a run-down pub immediately outside the southern entrance to the Blackwall Tunnel in Greenwich was a nightmare for all concerned. It was shabby and depressing, and the sound system so bad that the band may as well have been playing inside the tunnel itself. Knox was unprepared for the aggressive British rock'n'roll audiences and performed a set that contained a mixture of his early hits, 'Party Doll', 'Hula Love' and 'Rock Your Little Baby To Sleep' plus contemporary country rock material such as Waylon Jennings' 'Good Hearted Woman'. The audience wanted rock'n'roll — as frantic as possible, and definitely not country music of any sort. To make matters worse, the lead guitarist had not bothered to learn the breaks in Knox's songs. It was not a good night.

      Happily, by the time the tour reached the Nashville Room four days later, things had improved beyond all recognition. Knox had adapted his set for the British audiences and executed each song superbly in his highly-distinctive and melodic rockabilly style.

The wider audience got an opportunity to enjoy Buddy Knox when he appeared on *Disco 2* performing both 'Party Doll' and 'I Washed My Hands In Muddy Water', while the show at London's 100 Club was filmed by broadcaster and writer Charlie Gillett. The resultant short film, *Buddy Knox At The 100 Club*, was given a public viewing during the mid-Seventies but has since disappeared from sight. Knox returned home on 23 May.

Although nobody realised it at the time, this style of tour, operated largely by the fans themselves, would eventually become common practice.

Buddy at the Nashville Room.

TV appearances
Disco 2   14 May 1970

CONWAY TWITTY

May 1970		
15	Birmingham	Town Hall
16	Liverpool	Empire
17	London	Palladium
20	Belfast	Ulster Hall
Promoter — Mervyn Conn		

Hot on the heels of the Capitol *Country Music Caravan*, Mervyn Conn repeated the process with a promotional package of artists signed to MCA Records called the *Country Roundabout Show*. It featured Conway Twitty, Loretta Lynn, Bill Anderson & The Po' Boys, Sonny Wright, Jan Howard, Peggy Sue and compere Doyle Wilburn. This was a quick return to the UK for Conway and his band, now known as the Twitty Birds. The line-up of Joe E. Lewis (electric bass), John Hughey (steel guitar) and Porkchop Markham (drums) had not changed, but three No. 1 country hits in the preceding twelve

LONDON PALLADIUM

Telephone - 01-437 7373

■ — SUNDAY, 17th MAY — ■

6.0   TWO PERFORMANCES ONLY   8.30

mca ► MERVYN CONN

(IN ASSOCIATION WITH M.C.A RECORDS) PRESENTS THE

COUNTRY ROUNDABOUT SHOW

BILL ANDERSON ★
★ JAN HOWARD
LORETTA LYNN ★
★ CONWAY TWITTY
HARLAN COUNTY

All seats may be booked in advance. Box Office open 10 a.m. to 9.30 p.m.

STALLS 40/-, 30/-, 20/-. CIRCLE 40/-, 30/-, 20/-.
UPPER CIRCLE 15/-, 10/6. BOXES 160/-, 120/-, 60/-, 15/-.

months had reinforced his status as a major act.

At the London Palladium, Twitty opened with a punchy version of 'Proud Mary' and a stirring interpretation of Merle Haggard's 'The Bottle Let Me Down', but it was 'Jambalaya' featuring some fine steel guitar-work from John Hughey that really brought the show alive. A trio of his hits, 'The Image Of Me', 'I Love You More Today' and 'Hello Darlin'', and a ten-minute Hank Williams medley had the audience softened up for a rocking 'Johnny B. Goode' and the inevitable 'It's Only Make Believe'.

The package played to only average attendances in the UK, but also visited Germany, Holland and Scandinavia. Conway and the others were guests of honour at the British Country Music Association Awards Dinner in London but still found some spare time for sightseeing in London. Incredibly, during a shopping expedition in London's West End, Twitty bumped into Texan rocker Buddy Knox. How's that for a coincidence?

JOHNNY CASH

Announcements in the press indicated that Mervyn Conn was bringing the entire Johnny Cash Show — including Carl Perkins — back for concerts at Wembley, Glasgow, Manchester and Liverpool at the end of May. This would have been the fourth major country event in only about eight weeks, and probably more than the UK could support financially in such a short period of time. In any case, the project did not proceed and a statement was made that Cash would not be available to tour Britain again until early 1971.

BO DIDDLEY

Bo was billed to appear on 3 June at London's Olympia for a major show titled *Extravaganza '70* which would be an eight-day festival of music featuring acts as diverse as Status Quo, Black Sabbath, Tyrannosaurus Rex and the Wild Angels. He would also play the *Hampden Park Festival* in Glasgow and sundry other dates including the Chalk Farm Roundhouse and

Beckenham's Mistrale club. As Bo was badly in need of just such a high-profile tour to remove memories of the 1967 debacle, this seemed just about too good to be true. So it turned out. Work permit problems were blamed when the whole exercise collapsed just a few days before his scheduled arrival.

CHUCK BERRY

Arthur Howes was the latest promoter to try and put together a tour for the elusive Mr. Berry. There had already been two other abortive attempts earlier in the year, but this time it seemed that something was really going to happen. Chuck would fly into Glasgow in time to perform at the *Hampden Park Festival* on 6 June, and then make theatre appearances at Croydon, Cardiff, Bristol, Manchester, Finsbury Park and Birmingham. The Wild Angels and Shakin' Stevens were both lined up as support acts, but with box office interest below par, the tour was scrapped. Howes blamed the lack of response on football: 'The World Cup is on and people are staying home. The theatres are empty,' he lamented.

THE EVERLY BROTHERS

Don and Phil Everly flew into London for a brief stay during which they recorded a guest spot for a Petula Clark US television special at Elstree on 22 June. Later in the year, they were advertised to appear on the massive *Isle of Wight Festival* which was being held on several hundred acres of natural grassland at East Afton Farm, near Freshwater. Right up to the week before the festival their names appeared on the bill for Sunday, 30 August along with Jimi Hendrix, Joan Baez, Jethro Tull, Donovan and Richie Havens. Contemporary reports of the festival merely observed that the Everlys did not turn up. No reasons were given.

BILL HALEY & HIS COMETS

Rock'n'roll seemed to have run into a depressing period with tour after tour being announced, hopes raised and then dashed again. This time it was promoter Paddy Malynn who dreamed up the exciting prospect of Bill Haley & His Comets, Jackie Wilson and Chuck Berry supported by the Wild Angels playing concerts in Cardiff, Birmingham, Glasgow and London. Of course, sometimes promoters were merely testing public reaction with such announcements, so it wasn't altogether a surprise when in the blink of an eye the whole tour disappeared.

CLARENCE 'FROGMAN' HENRY

Clarence Henry's career seemed to operate on a different astral plane to the rest of showbusiness. Since his participation on the Bobby Vee tour of 1962, he had become a shadowy figure often mentioned briefly in the music press and usually with British tours pending or at least under consideration. From time to time, dates had been announced and it was even rumoured for a while that a bogus Frogman was operating in the North of England. However, other than the organised chaos of his 1966 tour, there had been no confirmed sightings. Promoter John Edwards did announce a handful of dates in Uxbridge, Chester, Ipswich and Manchester for November 1970, but like so many other similar projects there appears to have been no end result.

BEN E. KING

November 1970					
13	Crewe	Up The Junction	23-24	Whitley Bay	Sands
	Birmingham	Rebecca's		Stockton	Fiesta
14	Old Hill	Plaza	25-26	Spennymoor	Top Hat
	Birmingham	Cedar		Stockton	Fiesta
15	Wealdstone	Railway	27-28	Manchester	Princess
16	Chester	Quaintways		Manchester	Domino
20	Draycott	Blue Orchid	29	Hanley	The Place
21	Dalston	Four Aces		Manchester	Twisted Wheel
Promoter unknown					

After so much attention to his British fans, Ben E. King was at last picking up some good-quality cabaret bookings. Whether this was a good thing or not is arguable, but nine years after his last British hit, he was finding it increasingly difficult to move away from his roots. It was the Drifters' hits that the public wanted to hear and that usually gained the greatest response. Backing was provided by a nine-piece band called Orange Rainbow.

CHAPTER SIXTEEN

1971

Baby, That Is Rock'n'Roll

The sad demise of Gene Vincent overshadowed just about every other rock'n'roll event in 1971. The black leather rebel will always be remembered as one of the true greats, thanks to those magnificent and timeless classics that he cut for Capitol Records during the Fifties. However, when his contribution to rock'n'roll is considered from the perspective of his live appearances it becomes even more immense, for it was Gene who toured the UK over and over again during the early Sixties, maintaining a frighteningly high standard of performance at every conceivable type of venue, both large and small. He often appeared contrary to doctor's orders while suffering intense pain from his leg, rather than disappoint his audience.

The fact that Gene was a messed-up human being and temperamentally unsuited for fame in some ways made his achievements all the greater. Many of his problems were admittedly of his own making, but as the wives, girlfriends, Inland Revenue and management heavies began to close in on him and his frail body finally signalled that the end of the rocky road was in sight, Vincent just kept dragging himself out on stage. What else could he do? Rock'n'roll was his whole life and we should be forever thankful for it.

Elsewhere, there was a welcome increase both in the number of US acts visiting Britain, and equally importantly in the quality of the tours. At last the shambles of the past few years was being replaced by properly-publicised events, although regrettably there were still some notable exceptions. Rock'n'roll needed something big to push it back into the public consciousness and to shake off the stigmas and embarrassment that were still attached to the name. Something big would happen soon, but not just yet.

Country music was going from strength to strength thanks largely to Mervyn Conn's annual Wembley festival — now in its third year — in addition to which Hank Snow, Stonewall Jackson, Merle Travis and Slim Whitman all came over for live appearances. Soul music was represented by Stevie Wonder, Eddie Floyd, Curtis Mayfield and James Brown, while a number of veteran bluesmen including Arthur 'Big Boy' Crudup, Memphis Slim and John Lee Hooker also trod British stages during 1971. A former member of Ronnie Hawkins' Hawks, Richard Newell *aka* King Biscuit Boy, picked up rave reviews while performing his harmonica blues around the clubs, and major rock and pop acts including the Byrds, Gordon Lightfoot, the Band and the Four Seasons all added to the diversity of live music available — but we still needed more rock'n'roll!

BRUCE CHANNEL

January 1971			8	Newcastle	La Dolce Vita
18-23	Sheffield	Cavendish		South Shields	Tavern
24-30	Barnsley	Monk Bretton	9-10	Newcastle	La Dolce Vita
31	Liverpool	Wooky Hollow	11-14	South Shields	Latino
	Liverpool	Allinson's	15-21	Yardley	Cavendish
February 1971				Birmingham	La Dolce Vita
1-6	Liverpool	Wooky Hollow	22-28	Manchester	Mersey Hotel
	Liverpool	Allinson's			
Promoter unknown					

Bruce had originally been lined up for cabaret dates in August 1970 and, with little happening for him back home, was now making noises about moving to Britain semi-permanently. Unfortunately, the resurgence of interest in his career arising from his 1968 hit, 'Keep On', had completely dissolved and when he finally arrived in mid-January, nobody got very excited. Still, six weeks performing on the scampi-and-chips circuit doubtless helped to pay the mortgage and also enabled him to promote his new single, 'Drivin' '.

GENE VINCENT

January 1971			February 1971		
22	Liverpool	College of Technology	4	Swansea	University
23	Bangor	University	5	Kingston	Coronation Hall
24	Norwich	Three C's	6	Chelmsford	Magnet
30	Wood Green	Fishmonger's Arms	9	Southall	Seagull Hotel
Promoter — Earl Sheridan					

The decline of the great Gene Vincent started to become apparent when he returned for a short and chaotic tour of clubs, pubs and colleges. His drinking had intensified and his behaviour was more erratic than ever, although he was still able to perform to an acceptable level.

He flew into Heathrow on 20 January with his girlfriend, Marcia Avron, and after a rehearsal in South London with his backing band, the Houseshakers, travelled up to Liverpool for the opening show which took place at the Polytechnic College in front of a packed audience, most of whom were students rather than his long-time fans. Supporting Gene on this show and again at Wood Green was Screaming Lord Sutch, and by the time His Lordship had entertained the bewildered students with his full routine, including the infamous 'Jack The Ripper' sequence, they were most definitely ready to rock'n'roll.

Gene came on stage wearing a white shirt, black leather waistcoat and trousers, his hair combed back and longer than on his last visit. He opened with 'Say Mama', his voice as distinctive as ever, and within seconds the audience were going wild. By the time he had worked through 'Baby Blue' and 'Rocky Road Blues' it was apparent that the Houseshakers, who included former Downliners Sect guitarist Terry Clemson, were achieving a very tight sound. 'Maybelline' was performed at a terrific pace and when Gene tried to speak at the end of the song, his words were drowned out by the noise from

First gig of the tour at Liverpool. In the background, Lord Sutch watches from the wings.

the audience. During 'Whole Lotta Shakin' Goin' On' he appeared quite overcome by the extent of his welcome as fans tried to clamber on to the stage and the act had to be halted briefly while the security regained control. 'Good Golly Miss Molly' led into 'Be-Bop-A-Lula', after which Gene encored with a frantic 'Long Tall Sally' and the title track of his latest album, *The Day The World Turned Blue*. The students had never seen anything like it and responded with great enthusiasm.

Not all the shows maintained the promise of the opening night. There was only a small crowd for the all-dayer at Norwich, where the Houseshakers were desperately tired, having hardly slept for two days owing to mechanical problems with their van. Gene went on so late that many of the audience had already gone home, and he struggled to follow the young Welsh band, Shakin' Stevens & The Sunsets, who were the main support act. Support on other shows was provided by the Magic Rock Band and the Impalas, while at Swansea Crazy Cavan & The Rhythm Rockers were the opening act.

At Kingston, an enthusiastic teddy boy crowd ensured a rowdy evening which culminated in a heavy bank of speakers being knocked down at the end of 'Be-Bop-A-Lula', slightly injuring musicologist Bob Dunham, who had been bopping away immediately in front of the stage.

In contrast, the gig at Southall was a good deal less than capacity owing to poor pre-show publicity, and Gene stopped midway through his set to harangue promoter Earl Sheridan over some imagined financial irregularities. He received a roar of support from the audience who failed to appreciate that the alleged problem was drink-related and that Gene had actually been fully paid in cash for the show before he walked on stage.

Rock and Roll Sensation!

THE SEAGULL HOTEL
Lady Margaret Road, Southall, Middx., presents

The Living Legend Himself

Gene Vincent

plus the fabulous HOUSESHAKERS

and D.J.'s Tongue Tied Danny and Rocking Roy

TUESDAY, 9th FEBRUARY, 1971 from 7.30 p.m.—10.30 p.m.

ADMISSION BY TICKET — £1.00

The Wood Green show was an outstanding success. They packed in far more people than the legal limit and were later fined for breaking Health & Safety regulations, but the atmosphere in the hall was electric and Gene delivered one of his best performances of the tour.

By now, Gene's behaviour was becoming increasingly erratic and unpredictable. Forever short of cash, he was talked into an ill-advised recording session for B&C Records and on 30 January cut two songs for them — 'Say Mama' and Hank Snow's 'I'm Movin' On' — at the Morgan Studios in North London. His voice was in poor shape and the band under-rehearsed. The resultant product was a sad reminder that one of rock'n'roll's greatest exponents was far from holding things together. A short way off his 36th birthday, he seemed a good deal older, his lifetime on the road beginning to take its toll. Vincent flew home to Los Angeles on 10 February.

MARVIN RAINWATER

February 1971
28 Southwick   Ponderosa
Promoter unknown

Thirteen years after he topped the bill at the London Palladium, Marvin Rainwater returned to Britain for a very different reception to that which he had received in 1958 when he had a No. 1 hit record. This time, his visit passed unnoticed by all but a small minority and indeed, all his UK bookings except for one were on US military camps and unavailable to the general public.

The only exception found Marvin and his backing band, Country Fever, travelling down into Hampshire for a club appearance at the Ponderosa, a relatively new country music venue. Rainwater had stopped performing rock'n'roll some years earlier and never dreamed that in the future he would be in demand again as a rock'n'roller. The high points of his act at the Ponderosa were 'Gonna Find Me A Bluebird' and a Hank Williams medley, but he also slipped in a lively rendition of 'Whole Lotta Woman' for the few who still remembered.

BRIAN HYLAND

The song 'Gypsy Woman' had brought Brian Hyland back to chart prominence in the USA, and during the second week in March he made a short promotional visit to Britain where the record had made little impact.

Del Shannon had recently produced a new album for him which included an updated version of Charlie Rich's 'Lonely Weekends', and this was issued by MCA on 2 April.

TV appearances
Top Of The Pops   11 March 1971

THE CRICKETS
BUDDY KNOX

Liberty Records had album releases on both Knox and the Crickets in their *Rock Reflections* series and a story did the rounds that both acts would be touring the UK together during April. An announcement confirming the rumours appeared in *New Musical Express* but nothing further materialised.

WAYLON JENNINGS

April 1971
11   Wembley   Empire Pool
Promoter — Mervyn Conn

Nobody would pretend that Waylon Jennings was a rock'n'roll singer, but the indulgence of including him in this book can at least be partly justified because of his early career association with Buddy Holly.   Jennings was Holly's bass-player at the time of his death in February 1959, and because of this connection there were many rock'n'roll enthusiasts among the sizeable crowd at Wembley for Mervyn Conn's *Third International Festival Of Country Music* specifically to witness his British stage debut.

The festival had been expanded to two days and Waylon performed on the Sunday along with Hank Williams Jr, Merle Kilgore, John Hartford (a late

THIRD INTERNATIONAL FESTIVAL OF COUNTRY MUSIC EMPIRE POOL WEMBLEY

APRIL 10   APRIL 11

1971

OFFICIAL SOUVENIR
A MERVYN CONN PROMOTION

replacement for Bobby Bare), George Hamilton IV, Roy Acuff, Tompall & The Glaser Brothers, Ray Lynam and Patsy Powell. Smartly attired in a white suit, black shirt and cowboy boots, his hair combed back with a greasy quiff and sideburns, Jennings was accompanied by his own band, the Waylors, comprising Ralph Mooney (steel guitar), Billy Reynolds (guitar), Al Cunningham (bass), Eddie Fox (drums) and Bobby Harrell (piano).

He certainly looked like a rocker, but his repertoire was strictly country, including 'Only Daddy That'll Walk The Line', 'Me And Bobby McGee', and 'Kentucky Woman'. His wife, Jessi Colter — formerly Mrs. Duane Eddy — was not billed to appear, but joined her husband to duet on 'Suspicious Minds'. In truth, however, the whole performance was something of a fiasco. Waylon's quiet, almost mumbling vocals were completely drowned out by a perfectly appalling sound system. From certain parts of the auditorium, the audience were unable to even work out what songs he was singing.

If Waylon Jennings proved a disappointment, at least there was an unexpected surprise in store for the rock'n'roll contingent. Hank Williams Jr. closed the show with a dynamic and visual act containing a selection of his father's songs interspersed with out-and-out rock'n'roll. On 'Memphis Tennessee' he showed off his versatility by switching from lead guitar to bass, drums and finally piano, and the act closed with him hammering the piano keys and roaring through 'Great Balls Of Fire'. The rock'n'roll fans went home happy after all.

ROY ORBISON

April 1971					
15	Belfast	Ulster Hall	30	Craughton	USAF
16	Hilltown	*unknown venue*		Upper Heyford	USAF
25-30	Batley	Variety	31	Stockton	Fiesta
May 1971			**June 1971**		
1-8	Batley	Variety	1-6	Stockton	Fiesta
10-15	Birmingham	La Dolce Vita	7-13	Sheffield	Fiesta
Promoter unknown					

The Big O was now spending six months of every year on the road, and a gruelling thirty-day tour of Australia was immediately followed by dates in Germany, two in Northern Ireland and several more in the Irish Republic.

On 25 April, the English leg of his marathon opened at the Batley Variety Club. Roy was again backed by the Art Movement, this time augmented by a brass section. Now featuring seventeen numbers in his act, he performed all of his hits as well as versions of Neil Diamond's 'Sweet Caroline' and the Simon & Garfunkel favourite, 'Bridge Over Troubled Water'. It was pleasing to note that his revised programme now included a higher proportion of rock'n'roll material than at any time in the recent past. 'Down The Line', 'Mean Woman Blues', 'Ooby Dooby' and 'Land Of A Thousand Dances' were all well received, although at least on the opening night at Batley, it was a haunting version of 'Leah' that made the greatest impact.

During one performance at Batley, some thirty over-excited women broke through the stage barriers at the conclusion of 'Oh, Pretty Woman', at the sight of which Orbison grabbed his guitar and fled to the dressing room.

The two-week residency at Batley was a great success, and when the show moved on to La Dolce Vita in Birmingham that venue too was packed to capacity. Here Roy seemed in excellent spirits, laughing and chatting with the audience between songs. Unfortunately, as the week progressed he developed a throat infection which caused him to miss one show completely on 12 May. He was replaced at short notice by the Barnsley comic, Bobby Peters. He did struggle on to complete the rest of the week, but by the end was telling his fans: 'I have three million units of penicillin inside me and I can't go on for much longer.'

A two-week booking at Manchester's Golden Garter during the second half of May was cancelled completely, and Orbison spent the time recuperating in London with his wife, Barbara and Roy Jr. Happily, he recovered sufficiently to complete the remaining tour dates, although several of the later performances were slightly shortened to protect his voice.

TV appearances
The Golden Shot   9 May 1971

BOBBY VEE

A cabaret tour for Bobby Vee was set up for June 1971 to include a week at the Batley Variety Club. Unfortunately, some two weeks before he was due to arrive, it was reported that he had suffered a breakdown in Germany and had returned direct to the States to recover.

SHA NA NA

June 1971			July 1971		
18	London	Speakeasy	1	Southend	Kursaal
21	Wolverhampton	Civic Hall	2	Birmingham	Town Hall
22	Sunderland	Empire	3	Liverpool	Stadium
23	Falkirk	Town Hall	4	Hanley	Victoria Hall
24	East Kilbride	Town Hall	5	Portsmouth	Guildhall
27	Plymouth	Guildhall	7	Middlesbrough	Town Hall
29	Leeds	Mecca	8	Manchester	Free Trade Hall
30	Sheffield	University	9	Nottingham	Albert Hall
			10	Bury	Memorial Hall
			11	Chalk Farm	Roundhouse
Promoter unknown					

Rock'n'roll fans were quite ambivalent on the subject of Sha Na Na. Some looked on them as fakes who were trying to snatch a quick buck by ridiculing the music of the Fifties, while others were prepared to laugh at themselves and be entertained by a slick, fast-moving and well-choreographed act which, while openly satirising rock'n'roll, did so with considerable accuracy and affection. Sha Na Na had been formed in 1969 by undergraduates of New York's Columbia University and achieved international

The one and only Sha Na Na.

acclaim when they appeared later that year at the original *Woodstock Festival*, since when they had become favourites of the hippy generation, working extensively on the US college circuit.

They opened their first British tour at the Speakeasy, one of London's trendier nightspots and went down a storm, provoking an amazing reaction from what was normally one of the coolest audiences imaginable. For much of their time in Britain they went out as part of a package which also featured Paladin and Uriah Heap. Sha Na Na carried a twelve-man line-up, and although the music press gave reasonable coverage to their visit, the precise identities of the members were never revealed. Nine who definitely toured the UK were Scott Powell, Johnny Contardo, Denny Greene, Screamin' Scott Simon (piano), Lennie Baker (saxophone), Rich Jaffe, Jon 'Bowzer' Bauman, Donny York and Eliot 'Gino' Cahn, while the remaining three were probably Jocko Marcellino (drums), Rob Leonard and Alan Cooper.

Their appearance at the Liverpool Stadium was reasonably typical, the show opening with nine greasy punks running on to the stage, combing their hair, chewing gum and eventually bursting into their opening number as the other three — vocalists Powell, Contardo and Greene — made a spectacular entrance elegantly dressed in gold lamé suits. The whole act was a whirl of activity and extremely visual. Musically, Sha Na Na were up to par as well, and worked through a programme of rock'n'roll classics that included a storming 'Jailhouse Rock', some great harmonies on 'Blue Moon', fine sax-playing on 'Yakety Yak', a tongue-in-cheek 'Teenager In Love' and the song which gave them their name, 'Get A Job'.

Not every performance was deemed a success however. At Middlesbrough, the young audience were unfamiliar with the material and walked out in droves, prompting Donny York to comment: 'In Britain there seems too much intolerance, which doesn't allow a person to enjoy all types of music.'

The final leg of the tour was a charity gig in North London at the Roundhouse, where they appeared with Manfred Mann on one of the hottest days of the year. The venue was packed-out and poorly ventilated, with the audience squashed tightly together, sitting on the floor in a vast pool of beer and perspiration. Nevertheless, the atmosphere was electric and numbers like 'Teen Angel' and 'Yakety Yak' demonstrated that rock'n'roll could sometimes still appeal to a wider audience despite the prejudices of Seventies' rock music fans.

BEN E. KING

July 1971					
16	Greenham Common	RAF	26	Chester	Quaintways
	Paddington	Cue		Wolverhampton	Pink Elephant
17	St. Albans	Civic Hall	27	Droitwich	Winter Gardens
	Kettering	North Park		London	Countdown
18	Upper Heyford	USAF	29	Hanley	The Place
19-24	Birmingham	Rebecca's	30	Liverpool	Mardi Gras
	Birmingham	Barbarella's		Liverpool	Victoriana
25	Crewe	Up The Junction	31	Kettering	Tin Hat
	Birmingham	Cedar		London	Bumpers
			August 1971		
			1	Chalk Farm	Roundhouse
Promoter unknown					

In an interview with *Sounds*, Ben E. King explained how life on the road could still be tolerable after so many years of travelling: 'The thing is, man, you have to love what you are doing, and I love my work. I don't mind all the travelling. I haven't got any hang-ups — unlike some people in this business — which makes it easy for me. People still come up and say: "Man, you shouldn't have ever left the Drifters." I don't mind them saying that. After all, my time with the Drifters did an awful lot of good for me.'

Ben, who was backed on this occasion by the John McFlair Band, flew off on 6 August to commence a tour of Germany. They say that the road stretches out forever...

DION

July 1971	
26 Bardney	Tupholme Park
Promoter — Freddy Bannister	

It is unlikely that there were many of the rock'n'roll fraternity among the thirty thousand who congregated in a field near to the village of Bardney on Saturday 26 July. The attraction was the star-studded *Lincoln Folk*

Festival which featured James Taylor, Tom Paxton, Ralph McTell, the Byrds, Buffy Sainte-Marie, Tim Hardin, the Incredible String Band, Steeleye Span and bluesmen Sonny Terry & Brownie McGhee. There was extensive press coverage in advance of the event, but none of it bothered to mention the fact that New York rocker Dion di Mucci would also be participating — his first appearance in Britain since 1963.

Dion was going through his 'string vest' period at the time, and had changed out of all recognition from the slick tuxedo-clad entertainer who had performed with the Ken Thorne Orchestra on his last visit. He had grown his hair long, was allegedly messing with drugs and had developed a folksy, acoustic act far removed from his early work. He appeared at the start of the day before many of the crowd had settled down for the show, but was politely received as he worked through the likes of 'Sunshine Lady', 'Abraham, Martin and John' and a surprisingly effective treatment of Chuck Berry's 'Too Much Monkey Business'.

THE DRIFTERS

August 1971			September 1971		
27	Wigan	Casino	2	Portsmouth	Locarno
	Liverpool	Mardi Gras		Southampton	Adam & Eve
28	Margate	Dreamland	3	Birmingham	Rebecca's
	Willesden	Apollo		Birmingham	Barbarella's
29	Ruislip	USAF	4	Birmingham	Plaza
	Stevenage	Locarno		Birmingham	Barbarella's
30	St. Albans	Civic Hall	5	Mildenhall	USAF
	Peckham	Mr. Bee's	9	Purley	Orchid
31	Chicksands	USAF		Paddington	Cue
			10	Birmingham	Barbarella's
				Birmingham	Rebecca's
			11	Whitchurch	Civic Hall
				Nantwich	Windmill Farm
Promoter — Henry Sellers					

By the summer of 1971 it seemed as if the Drifters, in one form or another, had been touring Britain continuously for the past five years. In reality, the legitimate Drifters who recorded for Atlantic Records had only made the one short tour in the spring of 1965, but, with their career stagnating in the States, their latest line-up of Johnny Moore, Bill Fredericks, Butch Leake, Grant Kitchings and guitarist Butch Mann arrived on 24 August accompanied by their manager, Faye Treadwell. (It was Faye's late husband, George Treadwell, who had set up a corporation called 'Drifters Inc.' and who had copyrighted the group name back in 1954. When he died during the Sixties, rights to the Drifters' name passed to his widow, and she had already fought several court battles in her attempts to prevent former group members cashing in on it.) Significantly, the bogus groups disappeared completely from the British club scene for some time after the Johnny Moore-led Drifters arrived — doubtless due at least in part to Mrs. Treadwell's litigiousness, as well as the increased media attention that had made both club owners and the public more aware of the group's identity.

The tour was the usual mixture of ballrooms, clubs and military bases — with the difference that promoter Henry Sellers did an outstanding job on the publicity. Interviews, photographs and date lists were carried by all the music press, so the public could at last get to grips with what was happening. Attendances were excellent throughout, the John McFlair Band provided some solid backing, and the group went down so well that Faye Treadwell was persuaded that the future of the Drifters lay in British clubland. They flew home for a season of cabaret at Lake Tahoe with plans already being made for a quick return in the New Year.

CREEDENCE CLEARWATER REVIVAL

September 1971		
1	Manchester	Free Trade Hall
27-28	London	Royal Albert Hall
Promoter — Jay Vickers		

The second Creedence tour of Europe took place during September, with gigs in Britain fitted in at both the beginning and end of the month. Their act had not altered greatly in style or substance since their first visit, although they included several different songs: 'Fortunate Son', 'Lodi', 'It Came Out Of The Sky' and their latest UK single, 'Sweet Hitch-Hiker'. Not surprisingly, however, it was still the classics — 'Proud Mary', 'Travellin' Band' and 'Bad Moon Rising' — that provoked the greatest audience reaction. They were ably supported at the Royal Albert Hall by the 'Polk Salad Annie' man, Tony Joe White.

The biggest change had come about within Creedence themselves. Tom, the elder of the Fogerty brothers, had left the group in February to try his luck with a solo career and had not been replaced. So, Stu Cook, Doug Clifford and John Fogerty were now operating as a trio. In truth Tom's absence made little apparent difference to their sound and the three remaining musicians still cooked up a powerful rocking act. Sadly, Tom Fogerty never achieved any significant degree of success as a solo artist and died prematurely of respiratory failure in Arizona during 1990.

THE EVERLY BROTHERS

September 1971			October 1971		
12-25	Batley	Variety	2-3	Birmingham	Barbarella's
27	Birmingham	Barbarella's	12	London	Royal Albert Hall
Promoter — Harold Davison					

This was the first major European tour undertaken by Don and Phil for six years, and they arrived from Amsterdam to a welcome barrage of pre-tour publicity. Travelling with them were their parents, Ike and Margaret. Phil expressed fears that their old fans may have deserted them, but was quickly reassured by the news that the Royal Albert Hall gig sold out both houses within forty-eight hours of the tickets going on sale.

The set list did not vary much throughout the tour and they opened each night at Batley with 'Bowling Green' — far from one of their biggest hits and really a rather surprising choice. After a slow-motion version of 'Walk Right Back', they launched into the Rolling Stones' 'Honky Tonk Women', by which stage the audience started becoming a little restless. From that point on, however, they brought out the big guns and moved effortlessly through 'Wake Up Little Susie', 'Cathy's Clown' and '('Til) I Kissed You'. With so many hits to choose from, it was really more a case of what to leave out. 'Bye Bye Love' and 'Bird Dog' led into 'All I Have To Do Is Dream', during which cloud effects were projected onto the backdrop. After a superb rendition of Merle Haggard's 'Mama Tried', Ike Everly joined his sons on stage and performed a short segment of country material which was enthusiastically received. The act was wrapped up with a moving 'Let It Be Me' and the tuneful 'Kentucky'. The support act was Shane Fenton & The Fentones.

Inevitably, the Albert Hall show was the high point of the tour and the fans were more than ready to greet the Everlys, having already suffered the opening act, a hippy called Loudon Wainwright III, who droned on about dead skunks in the road and drove a significant portion of the audience out to the bar. Don and Phil soon rescued the situation and had the rockers dancing in the aisles, especially during 'Bye Bye Love'. They included a melodic 'Sing Me Back Home', but Don declined shouted requests for 'Ebony Eyes' with a brief comment: 'We fly everywhere.' A highly-successful visit was rounded off with a storming 'Lucille', on which their four-man backing group (led by guitarist Bob Waddell) excelled themselves.

TV appearances
The Old Grey Whistle Test   ? October 1971

BRUCE CHANNEL

September 1971			October 1971		
13-19	Middlesbrough	Excel	1-3	Birmingham	Rebecca's
20-26	Darwen	Uncle Tom's Cabin	4-10	Cardiff	Queen's
27-30	Birmingham	Rebecca's			
Promoter — Barry Clayman					

Bruce Channel had done well enough on his January cabaret tour to earn a second visit within the year, but this time attracted almost no media attention whatsoever. Many people looked upon the cabaret circuit as being a graveyard for clapped-out performers, and maybe there was some truth in this theory, but the constantly changing face of popular music often left little alternative for entertainers who did not want to return to washing cars or driving a truck.

JOHNNY CASH
CARL PERKINS

September 1971		
16	Glasgow	Green's Playhouse
17	Manchester	Belle Vue
18	London	Queen Elizabeth Hall
19	Birmingham	Odeon
Promoter — NEMS Enterprises		

The two tours in 1968 had established Johnny Cash as a major attraction in the UK. Three years later, following a successful television series and huge album sales throughout the world, he was an international star. His four concerts in Britain sold out immediately, the ticket office at London's Queen Elizabeth Hall (part of the Royal Festival Hall complex) claiming to have been under siege with all seats disposed of in an hour. Simultaneous to his live shows, the documentary film *Johnny Cash — The Man, His World, His Music* was being screened at cinemas all across the country, giving added exposure to the tour.

Cash flew in from Scandinavia on 15 September accompanied by his wife June, their young son John Carter Cash, Carl Perkins, the Carter Family, the Statler Brothers and the Tennessee Three – Marshall Grant (bass), Bob Wootton (guitar) and W.S. Holland (drums). At one stage it also seemed likely

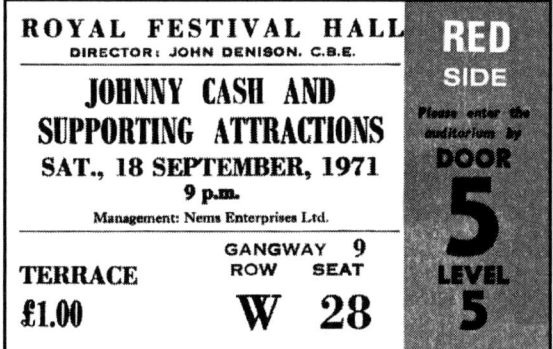

that singer-songwriter Glen Sherley would also make the trip, but the conditions of his parole from Folsom Prison would not permit him to travel overseas.

Cash was amazing. At the Queen Elizabeth Hall, his personality and charisma filled the auditorium and he had the audience eating out of his hand from the opening lines of 'A Boy Named Sue'. He weaved his way through 'Sunday Morning Coming Down', 'Me And Bobby McGee' and 'Man In Black', interspersing the classic 'Wreck Of The Old 97' and a harmonica-enhanced 'Orange Blossom Special'. Every song in his hour-long show was greeted with enthusiastic applause. After 'Forty Shades Of Green' and the ever-popular 'Big River', he duetted with Anita Carter on 'No Setting Sun'. Other highlights were an amusing 'Five Feet High And Rising', 'Folsom Prison Blues' and the evergreen 'I Walk The Line' on which Carl Perkins contributed lead guitar. June Carter joined her husband for 'Jackson', 'If I Were A Carpenter' and John Sebastian's 'Darling Companion' before the whole cast reassembled for the gospel-flavoured 'Two By Two'.

The only sad aspect of a tremendous night was the fact that Carl's contribution to the show had now diminished to being no more than the opening act. Restricted to just four numbers, he performed 'Matchbox', a new song called 'Goin' To Memphis', a bluesy 'Turn Around' and the inevitable 'Blue Suede Shoes'. However, it was just not long enough, and the rockers in the audience were left with a feeling of frustration. Carl did return to the stage briefly at the start and close of Cash's act, but it still seemed wholly unsatisfactory that such a talented and popular entertainer had not been given a more prominent position in the proceedings.

The Queen Elizabeth Hall show, and indeed the whole tour was an unqualified success for Cash, who flew home to the States to link up with evangelist Billy Graham for a week-long religious crusade in Dallas, Texas.

GENE VINCENT

September 1971	October 1971
19-21 Leigh Garrick	3-4 Liverpool Wooky Hollow
Promoter — George Cooper	

Gene arrived in Britain for the final time on 16 September. Since February, his life had continued to unravel and his alcoholism had intensified, fuelling bouts of depression and paranoia. Furthermore, he was now financially desperate and really in no condition to perform, but despite all his problems, his reputation — although somewhat tarnished — still enabled work to be found for him. He was accompanied by his guitarist/manager Richard Cole and backed by Kansas Hook from Birmingham.

The tour opened with a week's residency at the Garrick Theatre Club in Leigh, near Manchester. However, it didn't take long for the trouble to start. Suffering from a bad cold on top of all his other troubles, Gene was slow-handclapped on the second night and fired by the club manager after the third. Other gigs, including a proposed appearance at London's Marquee Club, were also cancelled.

On 23 September, Gene appeared on Granada TV's *Newsday* programme. He performed the Kris Kristofferson song, 'Sunday Morning Coming Down', and engaged in a studio discussion with Roy Jackson — the owner of the Garrick — as to the reasons for the cancellation of his booking. As the debate became heated, Gene insulted Jackson, calling him a 'big, fat, cigar-smoking bum'. By now anyone who was paying attention could see that the end was near.

A Radio One session for the *Johnny Walker Show* at the BBC studios in Maida Vale on 1 October produced five songs including a rough though engaging version of the Jim Reeves hit, 'Distant Drums', and two days later Gene commenced a week-long booking at Liverpool's Wooky Hollow Club. This time he only lasted two nights before his voice gave out completely and he was fired again.

Throughout this troubled period there was a pending court case hanging over Gene involving non-payment of alimony and child support to his English wife, Margie. He was supposed to travel down from Liverpool to appear in the High Court at the Strand on 4 October but failed to appear before Justice Robin Dunn, who promptly adjourned the hearing and issued a warrant for Vincent's arrest. Early editions of the London *Evening News* carried the front page headline, *'Judge orders pop star Gene Vincent's arrest'.* Gene did eventually turn up and the warrant was withdrawn, but he made a hopeless defendant, rambling on incoherently until the judge finally lost patience and ordered him to make a payment of £600 to the court within two weeks or go to prison.

Gene flew back to California on 8 October with both his career and his personal life in tatters. When he arrived, he found that his girlfriend, Marcia Avron, had deserted him as well. His physical condition was also deteriorating rapidly, and he died four days later in the emergency room of the Inter-Valley Community Hospital, Saugus, California due to sudden liver failure resulting from chronic alcoholism.

For many people in Britain, this was truly the end of an era. Despite all his well-chronicled failings, Gene had lived his life 100% for rock'n'roll and left behind him memories for those fortunate enough to have seen him at the peak of his powers that will remain with them forever.

TV appearances
Newsday   23 September 1971

THE SHIRELLES

It was reported that the Shirelles had signed a new recording contract with RCA and that their first album would be completed in time for a September release. The girls, now a trio comprising original members Shirley Alston, Beverly Lee and Micki Harris, were to embark on an ambitious European tour including club, ballroom and possibly even a couple of concert appearances as part of the promotion for the album. Nothing happened.

TONY ORLANDO & DAWN

September 1971		October 1971	
24 Halifax	Scene Three	8 Spennymoor	Top Hat
25 Scarborough	Scene Two	9 Boston	Gliderdrome
		12 Purley	Orchid
Promoter — MAM Agency			

A familiar voice had reappeared in the British Top Ten during January. 'Candida' by Dawn was a vehicle for the rasping vocals of Tony Orlando, who had first toured the UK in 1962 on the Bobby Vee–Clarence 'Frogman' Henry package and last been seen around the British clubs in 1964. In the intervening years he had been employed by a New York music publisher and only cut 'Candida' as a favour to an old friend, Hank Medress (a member of the Tokens of 'The Lion Sleeps Tonight' fame). The song was very much in the pop-rock style that had proved so successful for the Drifters in the early Sixties. By the time Orlando followed up 'Candida' with an even bigger hit, 'Knock Three Times', there were no less than five groups calling themselves 'Dawn' and making personal appearances around the States.

One such group of impostors were lined up to tour the UK for six weeks commencing 11 September, and it took legal threats from Orlando to prevent this fraud. He duly arrived along with two black girls, Thelma Hopkins and Joyce Vincent, but much confusion still existed as to precisely who Dawn were and where they could be heard. For this reason the tour was pretty messy and far less successful than their chart status had promised. At the Orchid Ballroom, Purley only a handful of people turned up. Despite the sparse crowd, Orlando gave it his best shot and Dawn delivered a very professional act.

TV appearances

Top Of The Pops	7 October 1971
Lift Off!	? October 1971 (screened 1 December 1971)

ROY ORBISON

September 1971			October 1971		
27-30	Wythenshawe	Golden Garter	1-9	Wythenshawe	Golden Garter
Promoter unknown					

Roy Orbison interrupted a tour of Germany to play a two-week engagement at the Golden Garter as compensation for the booking which had been lost in May due to his throat ailment. He arrived in high spirits direct from a concert in Giessen with Carla Thomas. His usual backing group, the Art Movement, had disbanded but its former members comprised the nucleus of the seven-man band he played with at the club. In another break with tradition, Roy also discarded his black clothes in favour of a royal blue jumpsuit. His act had not changed at all, however, and he ran through the usual mix of rockers like 'Down The Line' and 'Ooby Dooby' interspersed with his powerful rock ballads. At the conclusion of the engagement, he returned for further dates in Germany.

CHUCK BERRY
JERRY LEE LEWIS
LITTLE RICHARD
BO DIDDLEY

Over the past couple of years, New York promoter Richard Nader had masterminded a series of rock'n'roll revival shows which had brought back to prominence many of the principal acts of the Fifties. These concerts had proved highly successful, and there had been speculation for some months that something similar might be attempted in Britain.

An announcement was made in August to the effect that Phil Lubman was planning a mammoth concert on 17 October at the Empire Pool, Wembley. Chuck Berry, Jerry Lee Lewis, Little Richard and Bo Diddley were just some of the acts under consideration. It was later claimed that Little Richard had signed a contract, and that the concert was to be recorded for a live album. In the end Lubman postponed the whole project stating: 'It hasn't been possible to get it together in time, but I shall be staging it before the year is out.'

The idea of a massive rock'n'roll show had been launched, however, and rumours along these lines would persist for some time to come.

DEL SHANNON

October 1971			15-21	Stockton	Fiesta
31	Liverpool	Wooky Hollow		Middlesbrough	Excel
	Liverpool	Allinson's	22-27	Darwen	Uncle Tom's Cabin
November 1971			28	Maidstone	Tudor House
1-6	Liverpool	Wooky Hollow	29-30	Sheffield	Fiesta
	Liverpool	Allinson's	December 1971		
7-14	Spennymoor	Top Hat	1	Sheffield	Fiesta
Promoter — Barry Clayman					

Del Shannon was the latest visitor to hit the cabaret trail. Despite a string of hit records in the early Sixties, he no longer received much attention from the contemporary music press although he still had a sufficiently large fanbase to do well in the Northern clubs.

At Allinson's in Liverpool he looked fit and well dressed in a leather waistcoat, open-necked shirt and blue trousers. The show commenced with 'Hats Off To Larry' and a sparkling 'Handy Man' that was ideally suited to his falsetto style. He continued with 'Under My Thumb' and then a succession of his hits including 'Swiss Maid' and 'Keep Searchin' (We'll Follow The Sun)', plus a moving version of Roy Orbison's 'Crying'. A member of the audience called out for 'The Answer To Everything' and he had a stab at it, despite it being unrehearsed. Backing was provided by the John McFlair Band, whose two tenor saxes helped to provide a full-bodied sound. Del closed the show with his biggest hit, 'Runaway'.

LITTLE RICHARD

Henry Douglas Promotions announced a ten-day tour for Little Richard commencing in Bournemouth on 12 November and including two nights at London's new Rainbow Theatre. Even as late as 30 October, *New Musical Express* ran a piece confirming the arrangements and promising a television appearance on *Top Of The Pops*, but yet again nothing happened and the tour was quickly forgotten.

Left to right: Earl Carroll and Billy Guy.

THE COASTERS

December 1971					
17	Hull	Phoenix	27	Tunstall	Golden Torch
	Hull	Malcolm's		Leek	Samantha's
18	Cambridge	Dorothy	30	Birmingham	Rebecca's
	London	Bumpers		Birmingham	Barbarella's
19	Gillingham	Central Hotel	31	Old Hill	Plaza
	Paddington	Cue		Birmingham	Barbarella's
22	Thornaby	Lancaster	**January 1972**		
	Spennymoor	Variety	1	Leicester	Il Rondo
23	Stevenage	Locarno		Birmingham	Barbarella's
24	Whitchurch	Civic Hall	2	Retford	Broken Wheel Scene
	Oakengates	Town Hall		Ruislip	USAF
26	Camberley	Samantha's	4	London	Samantha's
	Peckham	Mr. Bee's			
Promoter — Henry Sellers					

Cornel Gunter's Original Coasters had visited Britain in 1966 and various other groups purporting to be Coasters had worked the ballroom circuit more recently, but this was the first occasion when the authentic Coasters in the form of Carl Gardner, Billy Guy, Earl Carroll, Ronnie Bright and guitarist Curley Palmer toured the UK. Again, credit must be given to promoter Henry Sellers for delivering the real thing, and doing so with a high level of pre-tour publicity that enabled fans to attend shows without the usual uncertainty. It would be pleasing to report that this increased level of organisation resulted in capacity attendances, but in truth this was not always the case.

At Stevenage, a small but enthusiastic crowd were charmed by a stylish and well-choreographed act. The vitality and humour of the Coasters' songs was immediately apparent as they burst into 'Poison Ivy' and 'Searchin' '. The material was familiar to everybody, if only because their repertoire had been savagely plundered by the British beat groups during the early Sixties, but this time the audience was hearing the original versions. 'Young Blood' led into 'I'm A Hog For You', after which they introduced their latest recording, a reworking of the Clovers' 'Love Potion Number 9'.

With three outstanding vocalists in Gardner, Carroll and Guy, plus the deep bass voice of Ronnie Bright, the Coasters were a cut above most vocal groups, but what made them so different was the humorous way in which each song was delivered. Billy Guy in particular was a natural clown and highly believable as 'Charlie Brown'. 'Yakety Yak' was taken at a frantic pace, while in contrast 'Zing Went The Strings Of My Heart' was torturously slow, Bright painfully extracting every last bass note from the song. This wonderfully engaging show climaxed with a theatrical 'Little Egypt', only for the group to be brought back for 'Along Came Jones' during which Guy (as the villain) appeared disguised in a long white beard.

The repertoire did vary a little from night to night. At Bumpers, Earl Carroll finally woke up an uncommunicative audience when he rocked the joint with 'Speedo's Back In Town', while late on Boxing Day, a tough and well-lubricated crowd at Mr. Bee's in Peckham, South London enjoyed a glorious 'T'ain't Nothin' To Me' which lasted for nearly ten minutes and was performed like a musical play. It concluded with Billy Guy, the central character, being shot dead by Carl Gardner — a dramatic climax that nearly sparked a riot. 'Yakety Yak' really got the fans jumping about as all four Coasters' vocalists raced around the stage in manic fashion.

The first Coasters tour was immensely entertaining, and if at times the attendances were disappointing, it was perhaps the unwise decision to run the tour over the Christmas period that was partly responsible.

Left to right: Carl Gardner, Earl Carroll and Billy Guy.

CHAPTER SEVENTEEN

1972

Rock'n'Roll Is Here To Stay, It Will Never Die

British jazz drummer turned rock'n'roller Tony Crombie had started it all off on 11 September 1956 at the Theatre Royal, Portsmouth when his Rock'n'Roll Rockets became the first live rock'n'roll act to appear on a British stage. Of course Crombie was largely an opportunist who soon turned his back on rock'n'roll when more lucrative pickings were to be had elsewhere, but it is true to say that few people in 1956 gave this new music, this unwanted cuckoo in the nest, as much as six months, while many longed for the day when it would be no more than an unpleasant memory. The BBC did not want to broadcast rock'n'roll. Record company executives hated it, as did teachers, preachers and parents. Nobody in their wildest nightmares imagined that rock'n'roll would still be going strong in 1972. Yet, despite the mods, the hippies and the eternally negative press, it would still emerge battered and bruised into the sunshine of a summer's afternoon at Wembley Stadium to conclusively prove the prophetic words of Danny & The Juniors: 'I don't care what people say, rock'n'roll is here to stay.'

In the final analysis, rock'n'roll survived the changing trends of popular music because enough people cared. All of the greatest exponents of the music such as Bill Haley, Chuck Berry, Little Richard and Gene Vincent were larger-than-life personalities with dynamic, exciting and often unpredictable stage acts. When Jerry Lee Lewis walks out on to a stage, nobody knows what precisely is going to happen. By 1972 rock'n'roll was separate from the mainstream of rock music, but it was healthy, it was surviving and was at last being viewed as a permanent branch of popular music.

More Americans toured in 1972 than in any previous year. Admittedly, many of the venues were still to be found on the cabaret circuit and not everyone was yet pulling in the same direction, but in the future things would improve. The live scene would become more specialist and even less mainstream, but if you wanted to hear live rock'n'roll you could find it out there in venues large and small where feet would be tapping and fingers popping to the most exciting music in the world.

Outside of rock'n'roll there was plenty of live music for everybody. Country music had the two-day Wembley Festival, tours by the likes of Charley Pride and Glen Campbell as well as country rock acts such as the

Flying Burrito Brothers and Poco. Veteran blues performers Muddy Waters, Big Mama Thornton and Lightnin' Slim jostled for bookings alongside soul singers Edwin Starr and the Temptations. Rock and pop acts as diverse as the Beach Boys, Edgar Winter's White Trash, the Steve Miller Band, Arlo Guthrie and Don McLean all visited Britain, but in truth there was one show which eclipsed all others. On 5 August 1972 there was only one place to be...

CHUCK BERRY

February 1972		
3	Coventry	Locarno
Promoters — Phil Lubman and Alan Lubin		

After countless failed attempts, Chuck Berry returned to Britain for the *Lanchester Arts Festival*. Two separate shows took place on the same night, one starring Chuck and the other Pink Floyd. He was backed by the Roy Young Band, while the other support acts were Billy Preston, Slade and a comedian called Uncle Dirty. The ballroom was jam-packed with a mass of sweating bodies producing an atmosphere that was as thick as a Midlands smog. Chess Records had hired the Pye Mobile Recording Unit with a view to turning Berry's set into a live album and their presence added to the tension of the occasion.

Chuck hit the stage in a dazzling multi-coloured satin shirt, white trousers and red, white and black patent leather shoes. He was clutching his famous cherry-red Gibson and with no more than a flick of his fingers burst into 'Roll Over Beethoven'. The mass of bodies in front of the stage roared the lyrics back to him and immediately it became clear that this was going to be audience participation night. Quite how a crowd, comprising two thousand young people, most of whom were students, knew all the words to every Chuck Berry song was never properly addressed in the extensive press coverage, which followed the concert. Perhaps rock'n'roll was not so far out of things as we were all being led to believe.

Berry worked his way through his standard repertoire including 'School Day', 'Around and Around' and 'Back In The USA'. He even slipped in a version of Joe Turner's 'Roll 'Em Pete', then slowed the proceedings with 'It Hurts Me Too' before accelerating forward into 'Sweet Little Sixteen' and 'Nadine'. His guitar sounded pretty rough in places, but it hardly mattered. The crowd went crazy from start to finish, and with the time already overrunning, Chuck embarked upon a hilarious if strictly X-Certificate interpretation of 'Reelin' And Rockin' '. By now the place was in uproar, but rather than wind up the show, he chose that moment to share with his audience what he described as 'My fourth grade ditty' — the now-infamous 'My Ding-A-Ling'.

He had first recorded the song as long ago as 1966 as 'My Tambourine' and had performed it live on a regular basis for the past five years. It was no more than a smutty, adolescent nursery rhyme but Berry knew how to milk the audience with it to maximum effect, and the version at Lanchester which was recorded for posterity ran to close on twelve minutes.

The song had found its time and place. Already high on rock'n'roll, the crowd loved it, and when he finally closed the proceedings with what started out as 'Bye Bye Johnny', but which the audience sang as 'Johnny B. Goode', his triumph was complete. Chuck had scored a memorable victory and proved that his music was just as exciting for the teenagers of the Seventies as it had been for previous generations.

Sadly, the quality of the live recording made it impossible for more than the final three numbers to be used, so on 5 February Berry recorded a further five tracks including 'Let's Boogie' and 'Mean Old World' at the Pye studio in Cumberland Place, London. Backing was provided by top British musicians Ian McLagan and Kenny Jones of the Faces, Derek Griffiths of the Alan Bown Group and Rick Grech of Traffic. Ron Wood should also have participated but arrived without his guitar and so could only watch the proceedings. The resultant album, *The London Chuck Berry Sessions*, was a smash hit on both sides of the Atlantic.

Not everybody was delighted with Chuck's newly acquired fame, however. The *Lanchester Arts Festival* had incurred a reported loss of some £12,000 and the organisers felt — not unreasonably — that their shortfall could be made up by royalties from the *London Sessions* album, one complete side being live from their festival. Unfortunately, they had omitted to make any formal arrangements with Chess, who hotly disputed their entitlement to any of the proceeds from the record sales.

THE DRIFTERS

February 1972						
			26	Whitchurch	Civic Hall	
11	Hull	Malcolm's		Crewe	Up The Junction	
	Doncaster	Top Rank	27	Birmingham	Cedar	
12	Lincoln	Aquarius	28-29	Spennymoor	Variety	
13	Camberley	Samantha's		Middlesbrough	South Bank	
	Peckham	Mr. Bee's	**March 1972**			
14	Chester	Quaintways	1	Peterlee	Senate	
15	Smethwick	Baths	2	Portsmouth	Locarno	
	Walsall	George	3	Bolton	Nevada	
16	Liverpool	Pyramid		Liverpool	Mardi Gras	
17-18	Birmingham	Barbarella's	4	St. Albans	Civic Hall	
	Birmingham	Rebecca's		Willesden	Apollo	
19	Birmingham	Barbarella's	5	Wolverhampton	Cavendish	
	Old Hill	Plaza		Retford	Broken Wheel	
20	Leek	Samantha's	7	Bristol	Top Rank	
	Tunstall	Golden Torch		Cardiff	Top Rank	
22	Stevenage	Locarno	15	Harrogate	Intercon	
	London	Speakeasy	16	Paddington	Cue	
24	Purley	Orchid	17	Banbury	Winter Gardens	
	London	Bumpers		Dudley	College	
25	Birmingham	Barbarella's	18	Dunstable	California	
	Birmingham	Rebecca's	19	Reading	Top Rank	
Promoter — Henry Sellers						

Faye Treadwell had got herself organised. The Drifters' manager, having identified Britain as a lucrative market for her boys, sprang into action. The fake groups had been chased away, at least for the time being, so Johnny Moore, Bill Fredericks, Butch Leake and Grant Kitchings set out on a mammoth tour of clubs and ballrooms. The enduring popularity of the group led to Atlantic

Records re-releasing 'At The Club' and 'Saturday Night At The Movies', and by the end of March the single was climbing the charts in Britain, eventually peaking at No. 3. Clearly there was still a lot of life left in the Drifters.

They threw themselves into this latest tour with considerable energy and enthusiasm. Fredericks in particular, was a very strong live performer, controlling the audience with a mixture of humour and musicianship plus the strength of his personality. This was a highly successful period for the group and there was as much work as they could handle. Backing throughout the tour came courtesy of John McFlair's band.

TV appearances
Sounding Out   14 February 1971

RICK NELSON

February 1972		
25	Birmingham	Odeon
27	Liverpool	Empire
28	London	Royal Albert Hall
Promoter unknown		

If Rick Nelson had toured Britain a decade or so earlier it would have been a very big deal indeed. He was, of course, one of rock'n'roll's brightest stars, and for years his many British fans had waited in vain for his UK debut. By the time that he finally crossed the Atlantic, his career was in decline and he was suffering something of a mid-life crisis. The hits had dried up and his efforts to modernise his image were meeting resistance from long-time fans who still wanted to hear the old songs in preference to newer material penned by the likes of Bob Dylan and the Rolling Stones. In October 1971, Rick had played a rock'n'roll revival show for promoter Richard Nader at Madison Square Gardens, New York, appearing alongside Chuck Berry, Bo Diddley and the Shirelles. His long hair and attempts to present a modern sound had not won over the audience and it was reported that he was booed from the stage, although Nader himself later explained that the booing had not been directed at Nelson but at a group of policemen who were trying to control some rowdies in the gallery.

Nevertheless, it was against this backdrop of uncertainty as to his image and direction that Rick and his wife, Kris, flew into Britain with his Stone Canyon Band — Allen Kemp (guitar), Steve Love (bass), Pat Shanahan (drums) and Tom Brumley (steel guitar).

They arrived a week before the first show, so that some promotion could be carried out. His album *Rudy The Fifth* had been given a UK release on 18 February, and for his appearance on BBC-TV's *Old Grey Whistle Test*, Rick performed the Dylan song, 'Love Minus Zero'. It was an inauspicious start, as he sang live and screwed things up by forgetting the lyrics halfway through, plus he seemed nervous and unsure of himself during the subsequent interview. Furthermore, he found Britain in the midst of a power workers' dispute which was causing considerable disruption to normal life and which directly led to cancellation of a show at the Manchester Odeon scheduled for 26 February.

The weekly music paper, *Sounds*, reported that Nelson showed distinct touches of schizophrenia during the opening show at Birmingham, and a seeming lack of conviction that the new image could make it on its own. They seemed unimpressed by his faded Levis and bright yellow flowered satin shirt. He wanted to present a new image to an audience who had never before had the opportunity to observe the old one — at least not in the context of a live show. To add to the unsatisfactory nature of the proceedings, the lights kept coming on after each number so that the audience knew when to applaud. He was finally cajoled into playing a fine version of 'I'm Walkin' ' which at least gave some comfort to long-time fans trying to mask their disappointment.

The Albert Hall gig went over rather better, although the audience were shouting for 'Hello Mary Lou' before he had even plugged in his guitar. He made that his second number after a bluesy opening with 'Feel So Good'. He then worked through his newer material, 'Gypsy Pilot', 'She Belongs To Me' and 'California' before slipping in an old rocker in the shape of 'My Babe'. The Stone Canyon Band did not seem very inspiring on the old songs, although Tom Brumley's steel was outstanding throughout.

Rick continued with 'Life', 'The Last Time Around' and 'Love Minus Zero', before an enormous cheer greeted 'Travellin' Man'. There was no doubt what the audience wanted to hear and no doubt what Rick wanted to sing. His strongest number proved to be a rousing version of Chuck Berry's 'I'm Talking About You' which really stirred the crowd, but just when a powerful 'Believe What You Say' or 'Stood Up' would have raised the roof, Rick chose 'Anytime' and 'Honky Tonk Women' to close the show. It was a classic case of an artist trying to lead his fans into places where the majority did not want to go. Only ten weeks later Nelson would pen 'Garden Party' — the last major hit of his career and a song inspired by his experiences at Madison Square Gardens and possibly in England as well.

Support on the tour was provided by Seals & Crofts, both former members of the instrumental group, the Champs. Like Nelson, they were in the process of reinventing themselves and had been transformed into a pair of hippies. With no prospect whatsoever that 'Tequila' would be on the set list, many of the rockers remained in the bar until after the intermission.

TV appearances
The Old Grey Whistle Test   22 February 1972

THE EVERLY BROTHERS

Engelbert Humperdinck was signed by BBC1 to front a thirteen-week variety show with a whole range of top-line guests. The programme scheduled for 2 April would include Jack Jones and the Everly Brothers. It was later announced that Don and Phil would also record a session for BBC2's new *Sounds For Saturday* as well. In the end, the brothers pulled the plug on the whole venture citing the unusual excuse that they didn't want to do an unscripted show.

BEN E. KING

March 1972					
2	Purley	Orchid	19	Birmingham	Barbarella's
	London	Revolution		Wolverhampton	Cavendish
3	Wigan	Casino	21	Bristol	Top Rank
	Manchester	Carib		Cardiff	Top Rank
4	Dunstable	California	22	Llandudno	Café Royal
	Paddington	Cue	23	Camberley	Samantha's
5	Gillingham	Central Hotel		London	Ronnie Scott's
	Peckham	Mr. Bee's	24	Tunstall	Golden Torch
7	Hastings	Aquarius		Leek	Samantha's
8	Watford	Top Rank	25	Bristol	Bamboo
	London	Samantha's	26	Reading	Top Rank
9	Hanley	The Place		Peckham	Mr. Bee's
10	Warrington	Carlton	29	Croydon	Top Rank
	Manchester	Princess	30	Hammersmith	Palais
11	Scampton	RAF		London	Hatchett's
	Lincoln	Aquarius	**April 1972**		
14	York	Hypnotique	1	Whitchurch	Civic Hall
15	Carlisle	Pink Panther		Oakengates	Town Hall
16-18	Birmingham	Barbarella's	2	Coventry	Theatre
	Birmingham	Rebecca's	3	Birmingham	Cedar
				Birmingham	Top Rank
Promoter — Danny O'Donovan					

This was another mammoth tour for the inexhaustible Ben E. King. He had not impacted on the British charts since October 1961, but was reaping the rewards for all the time and energy invested in his British fans. 'I've made so many friends here — I've even been to their weddings and have lost count of all my godchildren. Yeah, some of the people who used to come and see me have their own kids now,' he told *NME*.

Carla Thomas and the Fantastics were among the audience when Ben played Hatchett's. They witnessed his usual assured performance and participated in a veritable orgy of cheering. He was not allowed to depart without a stream of encores. At Coventry, late in the tour, he provided support for Slade — one of the top chart acts of the period.

CHUCK BERRY

March 1972					
22	Lancaster	University	26	Birmingham	Barbarella's
25	Liverpool	Stadium	27	Stevenage	Locarno
			28	Leeds	Locarno
Promoter — Henry Sellers					

Chuck's triumph at the *Lanchester Arts Festival* in February created demand for a quick return, and promoter Phil Lubman initially announced plans for him to tour with Bo Diddley. Dates were announced to include an appearance at London's Rainbow Theatre on 24 March, but when the venue unexpectedly closed pending extensive refurbishment, Lubman pulled the tour. Fortunately rival promoter Henry Sellers stepped in to take over at short notice, although Diddley became an immediate casualty. Sellers failed to secure a central London gig for Chuck, and another scheduled for Stoke on 23 March also fell by the wayside, but in the limited time available he did a fine job in publicising the project. His cause was greatly assisted by the fact that Berry was hot and his music right back in fashion, appealing not only to the hardcore of rock'n'rollers but also to the college set as well.

Backed on the tour by Rockin' Horse, which included former Merseybeat Billy Kinsley on bass, Chuck delivered the goods in his inimitable style. There had just been a few days to publicise the show at Liverpool Stadium and the vast arena was only half full. Nevertheless, a crowd in excess of a thousand swarmed around the boxing ring which had been converted into a stage, as Chuck walked out already playing the introduction to 'Roll Over Beethoven'. His forty-five minute set only contained eight numbers but included 'School Day', 'Carol', 'Rock & Roll Music', 'Memphis Tennessee' and the risqué version of 'Reelin' And Rockin' '. He put a lot of energy into his performance, moving around the stage and duckwalking to the delight of his fans. He concluded his act with a fifteen-minute 'Johnny B. Goode' which ended abruptly as he left the stadium to roars of appreciation. There was no encore and an appalling PA system did not help matters, but Chuck was riding high at this point in his career and this show like the others on the tour was a triumph for him. He, more than any of the other rock'n'rollers, seemed able to transcend the generations and appeal to all age groups.

TV appearances
Sounds For Saturday   29 March 1972 (screened 17 June 1972)

CONWAY TWITTY

April 1972		
1 Wembley	Empire Pool	
Promoter — Mervyn Conn		

The *Fourth International Festival Of Country Music* took place at Wembley on the Saturday and Sunday of the Easter weekend. Conway Twitty was among the star names who participated and was again accompanied by the Twitty Birds — Joe Lewis (bass), Porkchop Markham (drums) and John Hughey (steel guitar). They flew into Heathrow early on Good Friday, and that evening Conway was a guest of broadcaster Bob Powel on his *London Country* show on Radio London.

In addition to Twitty, the Saturday line-up for Wembley comprised Loretta Lynn, Dottie West, George Hamilton IV, the Stoneman Family, Del Reeves, Tex Withers, Ray Lynam & The Hillbillies, Margo, Country Fever and compere Murray Kash.

The Twitty Birds commenced playing shortly after 10.00 pm. George Hamilton IV introduced each of the musicians in turn, finally announcing Conway as the 'No. 1 Twitty Bird'. They were all greeted with a roar of encouragement from the capacity crowd. Twitty was dazzlingly attired in a bright green suit edged in white, and burst straight into 'Proud Mary'. His second song, 'What Am I Living For', took the audience back to his days as a rock'n'roller, but from then on it was a succession of his country hits, including 'I Can't See Me Without You', '15 Years Ago' and 'Wonder What She'll Think About Me Leavin' '.

On his other recent visits to the UK, Conway had left his bass-player, Joe Lewis, to make all the announcements between songs. Now finally he spoke in his deep Southern drawl, first thanking the audience and then introducing his latest record, a vocal version of Floyd Cramer's 1959 instrumental hit, 'Last Date'. This was followed by an immensely popular medley of Hank Williams' songs that sent shivers up the spine. He concluded his performance with his biggest country hit, 'Hello Darlin' ' and the ever-popular 'It's Only Make Believe'. The show was already overrunning, so there was no time for an encore, but Conway later returned during Loretta Lynn's set and the two of them duetted on 'Lead Me On' and 'Picking Wild Mountain Berries'.

Sadly, this was the last occasion that Joe Lewis played to a British audience. He had started out in Arkansas with rockabilly singer Sonny Burgess as one of his group, the Pacers, before joining Twitty in 1957. Joe died in a car wreck in Nashville on 15 April 1976.

CHRIS MONTEZ

April 1972		
9-14 Luton	Caesar's Palace	
Promoter unknown		

An unexpected visitor to Britain for ten days in April was Chris Montez, almost a decade after his previous tour with Tommy Roe. On that occasion he had been caught up in the midst of Beatlemania, but this time life was altogether more peaceful. Like so many rock'n'rollers in the early Seventies, Chris was undergoing something of an identity crisis. He had thrown himself wholeheartedly into his role as a cabaret singer and concentrated his act on easy listening-styled versions of 'Call Me', 'The More I See You and his latest effort, 'Loco Por Ti'. He even told his audience that 'Let's Dance' was no longer his style and he did not sing it anymore. Nevertheless, Montez seemed uncomfortable throughout his act and looked as though he would really have been happier with his jacket off belting out a rocker. Eventually, he did relent and the audience were treated to an exciting version of 'Let's Dance'. He would soon wake up to the fact that he was pulling in the wrong direction, when a reissue of his biggest hit brought him back to the British singles charts in October 1972.

TV appearances
Top Of The Pops   13 April 1972

BOBBY RYDELL

April 1972		
18-19	Birmingham	Barbarella's
23-29	Batley	Variety
Promoter unknown		

If the appearance of Chris Montez back in Britain had been a surprise, then that of Bobby Rydell was even more so. He had last played live in Britain in December 1963 on a package with Helen Shapiro, but had never really developed much of a following in the UK even when 'Wild One' made the Top Ten in 1960. His efforts in cabaret passed completely unnoticed among the rock'n'roll set.

JERRY LEE LEWIS
LINDA GAIL LEWIS

April 1972			May 1972		
22	Stockton	ABC	1	Chatham	Central Hall
23	London	Palladium	2	Manchester	Free Trade Hall
24	Glasgow	Kelvin Hall	3	Stoke	*Festival*
26	Gloucester	ABC	4	Hull	ABC
27	Birmingham	Theatre	5-6	Liverpool	Empire
28	Ipswich	ABC	7	Coventry	Theatre
29	Peterborough	ABC	19	Walthamstow	Granada
			20	Slough	Adelphi
Promoter — Mervyn Conn					

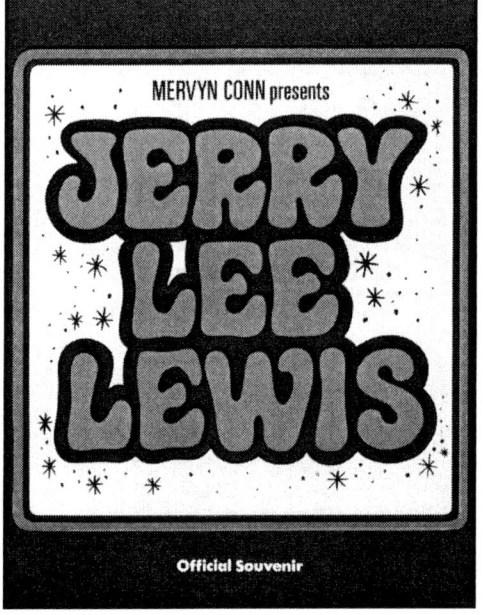

MERVYN CONN presents

JERRY LEE LEWIS

Official Souvenir

Nearly four years had elapsed since Jerry Lee Lewis had last played live in Britain. During that time, he had clocked up a string of hits on the American country charts. His career had finally recovered from the child bride scandal of 1958, and this incredibly talented performer was back on the top of the pile where he rightfully belonged.

Interestingly, Mervyn Conn slanted his tour towards the country market with a support bill comprising James Royal, Country Fever, Liz Christian and compere Murray Kash, whereas the bulk of Jerry's follows were far more interested in seeing a no-holds-barred rock'n'roll show than a

A hirsute JLL performing on the *Old Grey Whistle Test.*

country act. This always seemed likely to provide friction, and so it transpired, although it was pleasing that Lewis was at last back playing top-quality venues again in Britain.

He was accompanied on the tour by a sizeable entourage that included his bodyguard Dick West, road manager Jean Abinader, promotions manager Jud Phillips and general factotum Cecil Harrelson. He was backed throughout his stay in Britain by his own band, the Memphis Beats — Ken Lovelace (guitar and fiddle), Buddy Church (guitar), Herman Hawkins (bass), Jo-Jo Tate (drums), Bill Strom (organ) and Charlie Owen (steel guitar).

The tour opened at Stockton on a very cold night. Jerry Lee emerged sporting a full beard and casually dressed. He performed a mixture of rock'n'roll and country including 'Down The Line', 'Great Balls Of Fire', 'Would You Take Another Chance On Me' and even 'The Old Rugged Cross'. The focus of his act had clearly changed. No longer was it an out-and-out rock'n'roll show. Jerry would sing just whatever his mood dictated, but much of the animal wildness was missing. He would move away from the piano during songs and stroll around the stage with just a hand mike. There was no set list and neither the audience nor the band had any idea what was coming next, so the hapless Ken Lovelace was obliged to jump between guitar and fiddle trying to second-guess whether the next song would be a ballad or a rocker.

Nevertheless, the tour gained masses of publicity and the show at the Palladium was the focal point. Jerry Lee opened the first house slowly with

'Before The Next Teardrop Falls', before pumping the throttle for 'Lewis Boogie'. He then alternated slow and fast numbers and was just reaching the climax of the act when an enthusiastic fan side-stepped the ring of security and leapt on to the stage to join him in an impromptu rendition of 'Whole Lotta Shakin' Goin' On'.

Never one to miss a trick, Mervyn Conn maximised the effects of this incident and later that week the *Daily Mirror* reported enthusiastically that Roy 'Cuddles' Osborn, a £10-a-week gardener would be given a spot on the tour, a recording test and a chance to hit the big time. Needless to say Cuddles' career in showbusiness was very short, and it is only to be hoped that he did not give up his gardening job. Back in the dressing room, such luminaries as Elton John, Ringo Starr and visiting American rocker Ronnie Hawkins hung out with Jerry — everybody was trying to get in on the act. Like Chuck Berry, Jerry Lee had become fashionable again.

At Stoke, Lewis opened with a string of country ballads, following which he slapped down some hecklers before kicking away the piano stool and launching into one wild rocker after another.

The first house at Liverpool found him in a less amiable mood. The audience were quiet and unresponsive, so halfway through his set Jerry walked off stage commenting: 'You cats don't dig me and I don't dig you.' The second show, however, was a great success as he launched into 'Mean Woman Blues' and later praised the fans: 'I love you all. You ain't like that first bunch of bums.' Every performance was excitingly different and not in the least predictable.

After the show at Coventry, Jerry and his party flew to Paris for ten days in Europe. One member of his entourage who had been missing was his youngest sister, Linda Gail Lewis. She had given birth to her daughter Mary Jean on 4 April but now flew to join her brother for the remainder of the tour. She made her British debut at the Walthamstow Granada and also appeared on the final night at Slough — an exciting farewell show consisting almost entirely of rock'n'roll from Jerry including outstanding versions of 'Lewis Boogie' and 'Great Balls Of Fire'.

TV appearances
The Old Grey Whistle Test   25 April 1972 (repeated 26 December 1972)

RONNIE HAWKINS

The Arkansas rock'n'roller had recently signed a recording deal with Monument Records and flew into London for a promotional visit in the company of label boss, Fred Foster. Ronnie's idea of promotion involved much drinking and story-telling, although he did venture as far as the Palladium to hang out for a time with Jerry Lee on 23 April. Yet again, neither his record company nor any credible promoter took advantage of his presence by arranging any live shows for him.

DEL SHANNON

May 1972			14-20	Whitley Bay	Sands
3-6	Darwen	Uncle Tom's Cabin	21-27	Liverpool	Allinson's
7-13	Spennymoor	Top Hat		Liverpool	Wooky Hollow
Promoter — Barry Clayman					

Del Shannon remained a popular visitor. He still enjoyed a positive image and even though the hits had dried up for him there was plenty of goodwill, plus a feeling that it just needed a change of direction or perhaps a move towards the country market for him to get back on track. In the meantime, it was the old hits that the cabaret audiences wanted to hear and Del delivered the goods right on cue.

DION

Rock music was still in the midst of the Grand Festival era. Ever since Woodstock, successive promoters had tried for the big killing although most had come to financial grief. The latest disaster waiting to happen was the *Bickershaw Festival* near Wigan on the weekend of 5–7 May. The site was 150 acres in size and the organisers were preparing themselves for a crowd in excess of 100,000 people. Dion was announced as one of the star acts along with a host of others including the Grateful Dead, Donovan, Dr. John and Country Joe McDonald.

It did not stop raining for the entire weekend and the attendances were way below expectation. Dion did not even show up, which was probably quite a shrewd move in the circumstances.

BIG JOE TURNER

An interesting venture was announced for the second week in May. A package comprising the Count Basie Orchestra, Eddie 'Cleanhead' Vinson, Joe Williams, Roy Eldridge, Eddie 'Lockjaw' Davis and Joe Turner would play concerts in Oxford, Bolton, Sheffield and Hammersmith. The tour went ahead, but without Turner who dropped out at the last minute: 'I was all set to go, but a few weeks back I was having trouble with my leg. It was arthritis and I decided to go to the doctor for a check-up. I mentioned to him that I'd been going to the bathroom an awful lot and he thought he'd better test me for sugar in my blood. He told me that I've got diabetes. It really shook me up. He advised me not to make the English gigs while I'm taking the medication and needing to see him regularly,' he explained.

ROY ORBISON

May 1972					
17	London	Royal Albert Hall	18	Taunton	Odeon
18	Southport	Floral Hall	19	Portsmouth	Guildhall
19	Norwich	Melody Rooms	20	Hanley	Victoria Hall
20	Chatham	Central Hall	21	Birmingham	Top Rank
21-27	Derby	Talk Of The Midlands	22	Margate	Dreamland
28-31	Luton	Caesar's Palace	23-29	Liverpool	Shakespeare
June 1972			30-31	Batley	Variety
1-3	Luton	Caesar's Palace	**August 1972**		
4	Bournemouth	Winter Gardens	1-12	Batley	Variety
5-10	Wythenshawe	Golden Garter	13-19	Weston-super-Mare	Webbington
11	Croydon	Fairfield Halls	20	London	Palladium
12-17	Wythenshawe	Golden Garter	21-26	Southend	Talk Of The South
18-24	Wakefield	Theatre Club	27	Scarborough	Floral Hall
25-30	Stockton	Fiesta	28	Glasgow	Kelvin Hall
July 1972			31	Morecambe	Miami Bowl
1	Stockton	Fiesta	**September 1972**		
2-15	Sheffield	Fiesta	3	Blackpool	ABC
16	Newcastle	City Hall	4-9	Birmingham	Cresta
17	Cheltenham	Odeon	10-16	Solihull	New Cresta

Promoter — Arthur Howes

Roy spent four months in the UK on this occasion, undertaking a mixture of cabaret residencies and one nighters. The Art Movement were back providing the accompaniment, while on many of the gigs Friday Brown was the support.

Surprisingly, he picked up some hostile press when the tour opened at the Royal Albert Hall. Both *NME* and *Melody Maker* laid into him with great relish, claiming that he was rattling off the same old tired songs parrot-fashion. There was no new material at all, and he was frequently drowned out by the over-loud backing band and orchestra. They did, however, grudgingly mention that the audience were highly enthusiastic.

This was certainly the case at Chatham three days later. Roy had the crowd in the palm of his hand. He closed as usual with 'Oh, Pretty Woman' and made countless curtain calls before the fans would let him leave.

NEIL SEDAKA

May 1972			June 1972	
21-26	Liverpool	Wooky Hollow	1-3 Batley Variety	
28-31	Batley	Variety		

Promoter — Henry Sellers

Singer-songwriter Neil Sedaka had enjoyed more than his share of hit records and had toured Britain back in April 1962. When the British groups took over the charts in the mid-Sixties, he gave up performing live and for several years concentrated his energies on songwriting alone. His return to Britain was very well-received and he turned in a quality performance at Liverpool's Wooky Hollow, alternating his old rock'n'roll hits 'I Go Ape', 'Calendar Girl', 'Happy Birthday Sweet Sixteen' and 'Oh Carol' with newer material from his *Emergence* album including the tuneful 'If I Could Write A Song' and the ballad 'Superbird'. He closed his set with the hit song 'Is This The Way To Amarillo', which he had written for Tony Christie.

DOCTOR ROSS

May 1972			28	Boston	Jazz Club
23	London	100 Club	30	Moseley	Fighting Cocks
24	Birmingham	University	31	Birmingham	Digbeth Civic Hall
25	Birmingham	Cedar	**June 1972**		
26	Bardney	Great Western Express Festival	1	London	100 Club
			2	London	Marquee
27	Keele	University	13-14	Birmingham	Cedar
28	Peterborough	Halcyon Inn			

Promoter — Jim Simpson

Blues veteran John Lee Granderson withdrew at short notice from his European tour and was replaced by Doctor Ross, who picked up the whole itinerary. It would still be several more years before the good Doctor became the darling of the rockabilly crowd and his audience for this tour was strictly from the blues set. For opening night at the 100 Club, he gave a long and memorable performance scoring strongly with 'Good Morning Little Schoolgirl', 'You Gotta Step Back' and 'Let's Boogie'. His act revealed the considerable influence of Sonny Boy Williamson, and the audience were entranced by his one-man band, combining vocal duties, left-handed guitar, harmonica and drums.

For his visit to Digbeth Hall and the return booking at the 100 Club he provided the support for the Muddy Waters Band with ace pianist Pinetop Perkins. Muddy's show was sensational and included 'Hoochie Coochie Man', 'Got My Mojo Working' and 'Pinetop's Boogie Woogie', while the Doctor pitched in with outstanding renditions of 'Chicago Breakdown' and 'Sugar Mama'. The 100 Club was so crowded that from the stage only the tops of heads were visible.

SHA NA NA

May 1972			19	Southsea	South Parade Pier
19	Bardney	*Great Western*	21	Cardiff	University
		Express Festival	22	Plymouth	Guildhall
June 1972			23	Exeter	University
3	Crystal Palace	Bowl	24	Cambridge	Corn Exchange
9	Newcastle	Mayfair	25	Chalk Farm	Roundhouse
10	Hull	University	**July 1972**		
11	Kenilworth	Kinetic	7	Birmingham	Kinetic Circus
12	Manchester	Belle Vue	8	Farnborough	Technical College
16	Sheffield	University	9	Croydon	Greyhound
17	Liverpool	Stadium			
Promoter — William Morris					

Sha Na Na returned to the UK with the same twelve-man line-up as in 1971, arriving in time to participate in the final day of the *Great Western Express Festival*, a very grand event taking place near Lincoln. They shared the stage with Joe Cocker, Humble Pie, Don McLean, Vinegar Joe, Status Quo, the Sutherland Brothers and Genesis, going over extremely well and returning for three encores with 'Rock & Roll Is Here To Stay' and 'Heartbreak Hotel'. No further gigs could be undertaken over the next few days as two of the group had to briefly return home to sit their final exams at Columbia University.

They were back to full strength for the big open-air concert at Crystal Palace on 3 June. They went on first around lunchtime and played to a disappointingly small crowd which later swelled to some fourteen thousand. Also on the bill were the Beach Boys, Melanie, Richie Havens and compere Keith Moon. The whole event was plagued with technical difficulties and problems with the sound system, and by the end was running close to five hours behind schedule.

Fortunately, the remainder of the tour went off reasonably smoothly. Paladin opened for them at several venues, while they also shared billing with Slade and the Pretty Things at Exeter, Thin Lizzy at Plymouth and the Houseshakers at the Roundhouse.

BILL HALEY & HIS COMETS

The recurring rumours of a big rock'n'roll show in Britain seemed to be moving closer to reality. Early in the year, promoter Mervyn Conn announced that he was putting together a major event to be called the *'1950s Rock & Roll Revival Show'*. It would take place over two nights on 2 and 3 June at Belle Vue, Manchester and the Empire Pool, Wembley. By the middle of March, Conn had confirmed the line-up as Bill Haley & His Comets, Chuck Berry, Bo Diddley, the Shirelles, Gary 'US' Bonds and the Spirit Of John Morgan. He stressed that all the American acts were under contract and ticket sales were underway.

Before too long, first Chuck Berry and then Bill Haley denied all knowledge of the venture. Conn responded quite reasonably by stating that he had purchased the whole package from US promoter, Richard Nader, but evidently something was amiss because this ambitious project was scrapped during May.

THE CHIFFONS

During March, a reissued single of 'Sweet Talkin' Guy' gave the Chiffons their biggest ever UK hit and the Clayman Agency formulated plans for the girls to tour Britain and cash in on their latest success. Lead vocalist Judy Mann had left the group by this time, with Barbara Lee, Pat Stelley and Sylvia Peterson continuing to work as a trio. A seven-week tour commencing on 7 July was confirmed, but they never showed up and no explanation was ever given in the music press, who soon forgot about them again once 'Sweet Talkin' Guy' had dropped out of the charts.

BOBBY VEE

July 1972			August 1972		
16-22	Farnworth	Blighty's	1-5	Birmingham	Barbarella's
	Manchester	Fagin's	6-12	Spennymoor	Variety
23-29	Liverpool	Wooky Hollow		Middlesbrough	South Bank
	Liverpool	Allinson's			
30-31	Birmingham	Barbarella's			
Promoter — Henry Sellers					

Backed by Body & Soul, Bobby Vee worked hard on the cabaret circuit, mixing old songs like 'More Than I Can Say', 'Take Good Care Of My Baby' and 'Run To Him' with a few new ones like 'Rawhide Medicine Show', 'My Brother Matthew' and a revamped 'My Old Kentucky Home'.

In interviews, Vee would later enthuse about the early Sun records out of Memphis and claim that he had been brought up on Holly, Cochran, Perkins and even Ronnie Hawkins, while at the same time acknowledging that his own musical output had been very much pop with just a little bit of rock'n'roll. When asked by author Dave Nicolson to name the songs that he wished he had recorded first, he came up with Eddie Cochran's 'Summertime Blues' and Ricky Nelson's 'Believe What You Say' — an interesting thought!

THE JOHNNY OTIS SHOW

July 1972			August 1972		
25	London	100 Club	1	Hastings	Aquarius
26	Ruislip	USAF	2	Doncaster	Top Rank
27	East Sheen	Bull	3	Liverpool	Top Rank
	London	Speakeasy	10	Cardiff	Top Rank
28	Edinburgh	Baron Suite	11	Bournemouth	Chelsea Village
29	Northwich	Victory Memorial Hall	12	Reading	*11th National Jazz,*
	Manchester	Carib			*Blues, Folk &*
30	Birmingham	Barbarella's			*Rock Festival*
31	Great Yarmouth	Tiffany's			
Promoter unknown					

Johnny Otis & His Orchestra, with Marie Adams & The Three Tons Of Joy, had scored a massive British hit in 1957 with 'Ma, He's Making Eyes At Me'. Since that time, rock'n'roll fans had come to realise the importance of Otis' contribution to black music on the West Coast, where he had consistently championed the cause of many worthwhile talents including Ivory Joe Hunter, Joe Turner and Esther Phillips. His touring show comprised an old-style revue and was quite different to anything previously encountered by UK audiences. It is hard to comprehend how the financial aspects of the experience made very much sense, especially as venues such as the Bull at East Sheen could hardly be expected to pay top dollars, but when first night queues formed outside the 100 Club as early as four in the afternoon, it became clear that interest in the tour was considerable.

Like all great generals, Otis led from the front, both singing and playing piano and vibes. He surrounded himself with the multi-talented Johnny Otis Band — Willie 'Jitter' Webb (guitar), Jimmy Reed Jr. (bass), Thomas Norman (drums), Clifford Solomon (tenor sax), Big Jim Wynn (baritone sax) and Gene 'Mighty Flea' Connors (trombone and trumpet).

At the 100 Club, they kicked off the proceedings with a storming instrumental before being joined on stage by Big Daddy Rucker for an energetic display of blues shouting which included 'Lawdy Miss Clawdy' and 'Turn On Your Lovelight'. Then the stage of the 100 Club was strained close to breaking point by the arrival of the Three Tons Of Joy. Marie Adams (266 pounds), Millicent Calhoun (224 pounds) and Sadie Mae McKinley (an incredible 392 pounds) grabbed the attention and then held it as Marie led them through 'Little Bitty Pretty One', 'Shake A Hand', Jimmy Reed's 'You Don't Have To Go' and of course 'Ma, He's Making Eyes At Me', following which Mighty Flea enjoyed his chance in the spotlight, contributing some wild trombone-playing during 'Preacher Blues'.

Throughout the proceedings, Otis, smartly attired in a buckskin jacket, presided over this mini-history of jazz, blues, soul and rock'n'roll. When it was his turn to take the microphone, he launched into 'Linda Lu' and the song which gained the biggest roar of the night, his own 'Willie And The Hand Jive'.

The atmosphere throughout the show was incredible. So many people crammed together in a confined space (both performers and audience) meant that personal hygiene could become a problem. The atmosphere eventually became so humid that droplets of water began falling like rain from the ceiling.

The show continued with the introduction of four leggy black girls, the Otisettes — namely Donna Jenkins, Barbara Cooks and twins Tiresia and Alesia Butler. They sang and shimmied their way through 'Proud Mary' and 'Dedicated To The One I Love' until they in turn were replaced by Otis' nineteen year old son Shuggie, who was probably the one disappointment of the evening. His blues guitar-playing was very self indulgent, although he did serve up an exciting 'Little Red Rooster' before disappearing into a freaky Hendrix display which was out of context with the rest of the revue. Mercifully, his contribution was not too lengthy and the momentum was regained with a storming 'Honky Tonk', featuring Clifford Solomon on tenor sax, after which the whole ensemble re-grouped for the finale, a rip-roaring 'Boogie Woogie Bye Bye'.

It must have been a logistical nightmare moving this extensive entourage around the country. Thirteen year old Nicky Otis, himself a budding drummer, was also travelling with his father, and the sheer cost of transporting and finding accommodation for everyone must have been prohibitive, especially as two seats reportedly had to be booked for each of the Three Tons Of Joy when they all flew out to Benidorm for four gigs between their appearances at Liverpool and Cardiff.

The final night of the tour found the Johnny Otis Show participating in the *11th National Jazz, Blues, Folk & Rock Festival* which had finally settled down to a permanent home by the Thames and would soon change its name to the *Reading Festival*. Also appearing were the Faces, the Electric Light Orchestra, Focus, If, Linda Lewis and the Edgar Broughton Band.

CHUCK BERRY
LITTLE RICHARD
JERRY LEE LEWIS
BILL HALEY & HIS COMETS
BO DIDDLEY
LINDA GAIL LEWIS

August 1972	
5 Wembley Stadium	
Promoters — Ron and Ray Faulk	

Mervyn Conn's plan to stage two enormous Richard Nader-style concerts in Britain had foundered, and rock'n'roll fans had barely got over the disappointment when an even bigger and less probable project was announced by former estate agent Ron Faulk and his ex-printer brother Ray.

The two men had already organised a series of high-profile festivals, notably 1969's *Isle of Wight Festival* starring Bob Dylan and the Band, and had now obtained permission to stage a music concert at Wembley Stadium for the first time in the famous venue's near-fifty year history. Obtaining a

suitable site for the event was of course only the first of many problems confronting the brothers, who now had to secure the services of the major players if the scheme was to have any prospect of success. Ray Faulk travelled to Las Vegas where he signed up Chuck Berry and then on to New Mexico for Bo Diddley. He caught up with Jerry Lee Lewis in Memphis before being led a merry dance by Little Richard, who kept him waiting for a week while he completed a recording session before finally agreeing to participate. The only big name to decline was Fats Domino, who was already contracted to perform elsewhere and was therefore unavailable. A little later, Bill Haley was added to the bill and the brothers had all their headliners in place.

The show was extensively advertised and the full line-up promised Berry, Richard, Lewis, Haley and Diddley plus the Drifters, the Coasters, the Platters, Screaming Lord Sutch, Billy Fury, the Move, the MC5, Gary Glitter, the Houseshakers, and comperes Emperor Rosko and Tony Prince. Problems arose almost immediately when it became obvious that the three most counterfeited groups in the world were again to have their identities called into question. Rival promoter Henry Sellers had the authentic Coasters, Drifters and Platters under contract elsewhere, and heavy threats of legal intervention were made when it came to light that the *London Rock'n'Roll Festival* had signed up original member Zola Taylor's version of the Platters, a bunch of Coasters fronted by either Will 'Dub' Jones or Cornel Gunter (depending upon which report you read) and goodness knows which set of bogus Drifters. The Faulk brothers backed off, and all three groups were withdrawn and replaced by British veterans Joe Brown, Heinz and Emile Ford.

In the days leading up to the show, the whole experience seemed unreal. Additional trains were being laid on from various parts of Britain and British Rail were selling tickets which included the price of admission, while marauding hordes of French teddy boys were preparing to invade aboard specially chartered airplanes.

The media knew precisely where to go for the pre-show hype. Lord Sutch, the king of self-publicity, went into overdrive promising that his usual flamboyant act would be enhanced by the inclusion of a couple of strippers. When this pronouncement had the desired effect, he expanded the theme by arriving at Downing Street with five well-endowed girls who stripped naked before handing out leaflets publicising the show. They were all duly arrested and re-convened at Bow Street Magistrates Court; Sutch this time dressed in football kit, including shorts and boots with a top hat and his hair dyed bright green. They were all charged with insulting behaviour and with provoking a breach of the peace. The girls pleaded guilty and were duly fined while His Lordship opted for the full trial experience and a larger fine at a later date. They were probably pleased to see the back of him, freed on bail of £10.

On the eve of the show, and with the American acts now in town there was the inevitable clash of egos. Little Richard appeared distinctly underwhelmed by the prospect of performing immediately before his great rival Chuck Berry and stated his views forcibly at the press conference. 'No-one, and I mean no-one, should have the nerve to be over me,' he ranted. "I'm gonna play with Chuck's ding-a-ling. Ooee, if he is being paid more than I am, then I am gonna scream and scream like a black lady!' Richard had brought his lawyer with him: 'He is here to help me get my money out of the country,' he explained. '$43,000 they are paying me.'

In fairness to him, Richard often adopted a Muhammad Ali style of boasting as a means of publicity for a gig, and he may have been less than serious as he raged on about being the King Of Rock'n'Roll, but sadly these boasts would come back to haunt him over the next few days.

5 August was warm and sunny, and long-time rock'n'roll fans could

scarcely believe their eyes as thousands of people surged out of the underground stations and hurried along Empire Way towards the stadium. Numerically, it was like watching a football crowd, but instead of scarves and rosettes the uniform of the day was drape suits or leather jackets and either winkle-pickers or blue suede shoes. A vast stage had been erected on the terraces at one end of the ground and the audience would eventually cover both the pitch itself and a large part of the stands both in front and to the side of the stage area. There were already many thousands present when the show got underway, and streams of people would continue drifting into the stadium right through until the evening.

The difficult job of opening the proceedings fell to the Houseshakers from South London — Graham Fenton (vocals), Terry Clemson (lead guitar), Jimmy Walls (bass), Tommy Husky (tenor sax) and Vic Searle (drums). They were the only one of the newer breed of rock'n'roll acts to appear and they had a heavy workload, for in addition to their own set they would later be backing both Bo Diddley and Chuck Berry. They created a good impression with an act consisting entirely of Gene Vincent material, including 'Say Mama', 'Rocky Road Blues', 'Wild Cat', 'Baby Blue' and 'Be-Bop-A-Lula'. At times, Fenton's voice sounded uncannily like Vincent, whom the group had of course backed on his British tour in January 1971.

Next on stage was Joe Brown, who tore into 'Let The Good Times Roll' and also featured the novelty 'I'm Henery The Eighth I Am' and an instrumental, 'Hava Nagila '72', along with the Coasters' 'I'm A Hog For You' and his own hit, 'A Picture Of You'.

A surprise late inclusion on the show was Emile Ford who had been living in Sweden for several years and was rarely seen in Britain. He burst into 'Run, Boy, Run', but for the bulk of his act concentrated on Buddy Holly material, performing 'Peggy Sue', 'That'll Be The Day' and 'Oh Boy!'. He concluded his spot with his own smash, 'What Do You Want To Make Those Eyes At Me For'.

Heinz, backed by Dr. Feelgood, played safe with a set comprised almost entirely of Presley and Cochran songs. He opened with 'C'mon Everybody' and also featured 'Hound Dog', 'My Baby Left Me' and his own 'Just Like Eddie' before closing with 'Summertime Blues'.

One British artist who deserved greater prominence on the show was Billy Fury. He was only permitted five numbers but still made a strong impression with a brooding 'That's All Right', and animated takes of 'I'd Never Find Another You' and 'Halfway To Paradise'.

No sooner had Fury left the stage than the whole proceedings descended into chaos. Screaming Lord Sutch & The New Savages, pantomimed their way through ' 'Til The Following Night' and 'Gotta Keep A-Rocking', but most people were more intrigued by the arrival of four go-go dancers who weaved furiously around the stage in tiny bikinis, including one Carla England. Sutch had been warned that the show could be stopped if the laws of decency were shattered, so journalists from the Sunday papers hovered attentively as close as possible to the gyrating figures.

The *News Of The World* provided their usual detailed report of the event: '*As curvaceous Carla's bra slipped to the floor and her hands slithered seductively to the clasp of her tiny G-string, officials leapt on to the stage at Wembley Stadium'*, they reported with unconcealed glee. The seductive Ms. England subsequently confirmed that not quite all of her 35-24-35 figure had been visible to the hordes in front of the stage. 'Normally I take off my bra and then strip off my G-string under a cloak, but after I had taken off my bra I was told not to go any further,' she lamented. With the stage in a state of total disarray, Sutch hammered out 'Good Golly Miss Molly' and a totally over-the-top 'Jack The Ripper' before retiring to the dressing room leaving a trail of confusion behind him.

The MC5 from Chicago were a band in the wrong place at the wrong time. Their afro haircuts and heavy rock style made them a total irrelevancy to a rock'n'roll show and the crowd, who were now fired up by Sutch's antics, gave them a tough time. They sensibly restricted their contribution to four songs, struggling with the likes of 'Gloria' and 'Kick Out The Jams' amidst a torrent of abuse and beer cans.

However, their reception was nothing compared with that which was reserved for Gary Glitter. Rock'n'roll fans had correctly identified him as a creep many years before the rest of Britain came to the same conclusion. He minced onto the stage and proceeded to bait the audience with exaggerated and poorly-delivered versions of 'Money Honey' and 'Donna'. As he danced around like a whirling dervish he was showered with missiles, several of which found their target. Only the height of the stage protected him from physical attack, which was a strong possibility as he closed with his hit, 'Rock & Roll (Part 2)'.

Roy Wood's new band Wizzard, replacements for the recently-disbanded Move, followed Glitter and were given an uncomfortable debut although they did manage a half-decent 'The Girl Can't Help It' and at least avoided provoking the same degree of hatred as their predecessor.

Finally, it was time for the first of the heavyweights. The Houseshakers had been rehearsing with Bo Diddley in the dressing room and Terry Clemson remembers how laid-back and easygoing he was. 'A nice, friendly guy to work with,' was his description. Bo had vocalist and tambourine-player Cookie Vee with him and was smartly turned-out in a white suit and black hat. His familiar guitar style heralded a set which moved effortlessly from 'Bo Diddley' to a combined version of 'I'm A Man' and 'Shut

Bo and Cookie strut their stuff.

Up, Woman' during which he traded vocals with Cookie, and then on through 'Diddley Daddy' and 'Road Runner'. Other highlights were a hypnotic 'Bring It To Jerome' and a superb rendition of 'Mona'. Bo was not the star of the night, but he did at least get the show back on track.

Next up was Jerry Lee Lewis, but first his band (the Memphis Beats, fronted by Kenny Lovelace) got things warmed up with a routine rock'n'roll medley. When their leader was not forthcoming, they ploughed on with a dire attempt at 'Hey Jude', then into Honeycomb' and a second medley. The crowd was becoming restless. After two further songs, Jerry's sister Linda Gail appeared on stage and kicked into 'Lovin' Up A Storm' and cabaret-styled renditions of 'Personality' and 'Shout'. By the time she was into her fourth number, 'Johnny B. Goode', minor panic was beginning to set in as the crowd speculated as to what had happened to their hero.

Then suddenly without warning Jerry Lee strolled out on to the stage and with no explanation for his extended absence, tore into 'Down The Line' and 'Mean Woman Blues'. There were no country numbers in the set, nor indeed any slow songs at all. Outstanding versions of 'Don't Put No Headstone On My Grave' and 'You Can Have Her' were interspersed with his classic songs. It was a workmanlike performance, though perhaps lacking some of the uncontrolled abandon of days gone by. Jerry finished up on top of the piano tearing up 'Be-Bop-A-Lula' and 'Sweet Little Sixteen'. As he swaggered away, he couldn't help noticing Mick Jagger crouched low taking photographs from the side of the stage.

By now the stadium was heaving, but happily there was no undue delay before the next act. Bill Haley walked on stage along with Comets Rudy Pompilli (saxophone), Johnny Kay (guitar), Ray Cawley (bass) and Buddy Dee (drums). With the minimum of fuss he went straight into 'Shake, Rattle And Roll' and 'Razzle Dazzle'. This was first-class rock'n'roll containing

A glittering Little Richard salutes the crowd.

masses of energy and excitement, and the audience reacted accordingly. Johnny Kay took the limelight for an exuberant 'Guitar Boogie Shuffle' before Bill piled on the pressure with 'See You Later, Alligator'. In no time at all they were into 'Rock Around The Clock' and the entire stadium erupted in a sea of noise. A casual passer-by would have imagined that a winning cup final goal had been scored. Without doubt Haley's act was the pick of the whole day, although Chuck Berry was yet to run him close. He encored with another brief reprise of 'Rock Around The Clock', a few bars of 'Rock The Joint' and then he was gone. The whole set lasted no more than twenty minutes —time restrictions presumably having been imposed due to Jerry Lee's tardy arrival which had left the show running seriously behind schedule.

The most eagerly-awaited of all the acts on show at Wembley was Little Richard. This was his first time live in Britain since 1966 and his return was long overdue. He made a glorious entrance, resplendent in a golden suit covered in tiny mirrors and with his jet-black hair piled high up on his head. He tore straight into 'Lucille' and then onto 'Rip It Up', his voice as powerful and unique as ever.

Only those close to the stage were in a position to observe that he was experiencing difficulties with his microphone while at the same time his band seemed to be far from together. Everything did seem to be coming right during a long boogie-woogie piano instrumental which he followed with a manic interpretation of 'Good Golly Miss Molly' and if he had stopped at that point, Richard would have been acclaimed as the star of the show.

Sadly 'Tutti Frutti' was where it all started to go wrong. A teddy boy had scaled the battlements in front of the stage and was bopping away as

The climax of a truly memorable day.

Richard again found his microphone to be malfunctioning, while at the same time his drummer was losing his way and the band were struggling to stay with him. At this point he climbed on to the piano and removed the top portion of his mirror suit, tearing it into small pieces and throwing each section out to the crowd while behind him the band repeated the riffs to 'When The Saints Go Marching In' over and over again. His striptease lasted for several minutes as the remainder of his suit and even his boots were tossed out to the baying mob in front of the stage. They were cheering enthusiastically, but were soon drowned out by the sound of slow handclapping and eventually booing from the fans too far away to understand what was going on. Richard had stopped singing, and in doing so lost all the momentum of an act which had started so well. He did regain a measure of control with an earthy 'Long Tall Sally', but the damage had been done and the newshounds scribbling furiously had only to decide whether Richard's debacle or Sutch's stripper were to make the headlines the following day.

Only Chuck Berry remained to perform and there was a feeling of anti-climax in the air following Little Richard's extraordinary display. During the day Chuck had been his usual cantankerous self. He had made a fuss and refused to share a dressing room with Bo Diddley, while during a run-through with the Houseshakers he chastised Terry Clemson for playing too loudly, warning him that if he did so during the act, he would be asked to leave the stage. However, this was to be Berry's night.

He strode out confidently, wearing a paisley shirt and white trousers and jumped straight into 'Roll Over Beethoven'. In no time the audience were with him, anxious to forget the earlier fiasco. They swayed and sang along to

'Maybellene', 'Sweet Little Sixteen' and 'Memphis Tennessee'. Chuck slipped in 'Mean Ol' Frisco' and a slow 'Wee Wee Hours', but otherwise it was pumping, adrenalin-filled rock'n'roll all the way. Sensibly, he kept his ding-a-ling firmly zipped up and stuck with 'Carol', 'Let It Rock' and 'Little Queenie'.

Three quarters of the way through, Berry broke a string on his guitar and Terry Clemson, having had the threat of a red card hanging over him, now handed over his Gibson Firebird, so that Chuck could finish the set without any loss of momentum. It was Berry's showmanship which rescued the night, and as the marathon eleven hours of rock'n'roll drew finally to a close, he had the audience holding up cigarettes and lighters in the darkness — a dramatic and memorable effect — as he roared through 'Johnny B. Goode' to bring to an end the biggest rock'n'roll show that would ever be seen in Britain.

TV appearances (Little Richard)
Late Night Line Up   3 August 1972 (screened 4 August 1972)

LITTLE RICHARD

August 1972		
10 Nottingham	Intercon	
Promoter unknown		

Little Richard's reputation had taken a battering following his Wembley fiasco, but five days later he had the opportunity to repair at least some of the damage via a club date in Nottingham. Emperor Rosko was compering and kindly provided his own PA equipment, but first the fans had to suffer another seemingly endless set from the woeful Gary Glitter.

Richard's band had come in for a fair amount of criticism at Wembley, but as he was travelling with an extensive entourage, there really was no excuse. His party comprised Bumps Blackwell (personal manager), Stevie Woods (attorney), his brother Peyton Penniman (sound man), a road manager known only as Jesse, and a young man called Candy Hunter who was Richard's valet. The musicians were George Davis (guitar), Eddie Fletcher (bass), Lee Allen (saxophone) and Robin Russell (drums). At Wembley, the efforts of the drummer had left plenty of room for improvement, while even the legendary Lee Allen had not been free from censure.

Richard came on stage at 11.50 pm, by which time the club was packed. He was wearing a dazzling white mirror suit and, after making peace signs to the audience, walked straight over to the piano and launched into 'Lucille'. He then apologised for the fact that his band were drunk and played unaccompanied through a magnificent piano boogie. A couple were invited up on stage to dance at this point and he hammered his way through 'Keep A-Knockin' ' wearing a borrowed bright red drape jacket while they jived alongside him.

It became clear that the band were barely adequate, and at one stage Richard ordered the drummer to stop playing completely. He seemed in good spirits however, and included several unexpected numbers including 'Rock & Roll Music', 'Dock Of The Bay' and a slow version of 'Baby Face'. Audience reaction was on the frenzied side of positive, and he closed strongly with 'Miss Ann', 'The Girl Can't Help It' and a mesmerising 'Long Tall Sally'.

Other proposed European shows had disintegrated, so Little Richard returned home with his reputation distinctly tarnished despite demonstrating at Nottingham that he could still deliver the goods when he was in the right frame of mind.

NEIL SEDAKA

August 1972			3-9	Liverpool	Wooky Hollow
27-31	Batley	Variety	10-16	Sheffield	Fiesta
September 1972			17-23	Stockton	Fiesta
1-2	Batley	Variety	29	London	Royal Albert Hall
Promoter — Henry Sellers					

Neil Sedaka's career was back in full swing by the time he made his second UK visit of 1972. His easy, laid-back style made him a natural for the cabaret circuit. RCA re-issued 'Oh Carol' to coincide with the tour and it crept silently into the Top Twenty during October giving Neil his first British hit for nine years. At the Royal Albert Hall he was supported by Thelma Houston but the fans stayed away and they only achieved one-third capacity. Nevertheless his act went over well enough, consisting mainly of songs from his *Emergence* and *Solitaire* albums interspersed with the old hits 'Happy Birthday Sweet Sixteen', 'Next Door To An Angel' and 'Breaking Up Is Hard To Do'. At one point drummer Mike Giles stopped playing to remove his jacket, but that was about as wild as it got.

LINK WRAY

Link Wray had created some of the toughest and most primitive guitar sounds in rock'n'roll and was infamous around Washington DC even before his incredible 'Rumble' charted in the States during 1958. At a time when British audiences were struggling to accept the raw talent of Jerry Lee Lewis, it was probably just as well that Wray did not also find his way across the Atlantic, as his presence alongside Lewis may possibly have heralded the end of civilisation as we know it.

After some time out of the public eye, Link was being lined up for a two or three week British tour in September. The problem appeared to be that he was living in the desert some twelve miles out from Tucson, Arizona and the lines of communication to his representatives at Polydor Records were proving sadly inadequate. Civilisation would be safe for a little while longer.

THE EVERLY BROTHERS

September 1972			October 1972		
3-16	Batley	Variety	1	Oxford	New
20	Manchester	Free Trade Hall	2-3	Birmingham	Barbarella's
22	Liverpool	Stadium	4	Bournemouth	Winter Gardens
23	Grangemouth	*Festival*	7	Newcastle	City Hall
24	London	Palladium	23-28	Southend	Talk Of The South
25	Croydon	Fairfield Halls			
27	Chatham	Central Hall			
30	Scarborough	Spa Hall			
Promoter — MAM Agency					

The Everlys returned for what would prove to be their last British tour for more than a decade. This was not a happy period for the brothers, who seemed frustrated partly through the lack of success with their last album, *Stories We Could Tell*, and partly through personal differences which had been exacerbated by so many years on the road and so much time spent in each other's company. Unfortunately, the fans added to the problem by always wanting to hear the old hits and leaving little opportunity for them to develop fresh songs.

They arrived in England at the beginning of September, Phil accompanied by his new wife, Pat and Don by his girlfriend, Karen. The Everly Trio now comprised Sammy McCue (guitar), Ron Coleman (bass) and Gene Gunnels (drums). Support throughout their stay was provided by singer-songwriter Dave Loggins, although the Searchers also appeared at the Palladium and Raymond Froggatt at Birmingham.

A fortnight at Batley Variety Club got the proceedings underway, and along with their usual hits they regularly included 'Up In Mabel's Room' and a Waylon Jennings song, 'Good Hearted Woman'. Their set lasted close to an hour, and for most of this residency attendances were excellent.

At Manchester, both brothers had difficulty keeping their guitars in tune but despite this turned in a stunning 'So Sad'. There was a full house at Chatham, where they really let rip on 'Lucille', while at Oxford they both seemed tired and somewhat below par. The songs did vary from night to night, and at Croydon both 'Bowling Green' and 'Brand New Tennessee Waltz' worked well.

The first show at the Palladium was pretty messy, with both Don and Phil playing out of tune, but they improved enormously on the second show and 'Walk Right Back' in particular was superb.

After Newcastle, the entourage departed to play shows in the Netherlands and Germany before returning for a week of cabaret at Southend, but by now their boredom and frustration were becoming more apparent. The big hits were being performed with no apparent enthusiasm and some were being messed up by altering the speed or the arrangements. Don still managed to retain at least some of his sense of humour and compared the muddy-looking sea on Southend beach to the Mississippi River. Despite everything, they smashed the attendance records at the Talk Of The South and it was reported that two thousand punters without tickets were turned away on the final night.

Nine months later, on 14 July 1973, Phil Everly stormed off stage during an appearance at Knotts Berry Farm, California proclaiming the end of the Everly Brothers. They had been imprisoned by their own past and would not perform together live again until September 1983.

TV appearances
The Old Grey Whistle Test   19 September 1972

THE DRIFTERS

September 1972					
15	Doncaster	Mayfair	8	Castleford	Civic Hall
	Nottingham	Intercon		Batley	Variety
16	Chicksands	USAF	9	Reading	Top Rank
	Dunstable	California	10	Stevenage	Locarno
17-23	Farnworth	Blighty's		London	Sundown
	Manchester	Fagin's	12	Chester	ABC
24-30	Liverpool	Allinson's		Bury	Basement
	Liverpool	Wooky Hollow	13	Doncaster	Top Rank
October 1972				Hull	Malcolm's
1	Mildenhall	USAF	14	Whitchurch	Civic Hall
3	Bristol	Yate Centre		Tunstall	Golden Torch
	Cardiff	Top Rank	15	Watford	Top Rank
5	Spennymoor	Variety	20	Stafford	Top Of The World
	Middlesbrough	South Bank		Wolverhampton	Lafayette
6-7	Birmingham	Barbarella's	21	Brixton	Sundown

Promoter — Henry Sellers

Johnny Moore, Butch Leake, Grant Kitchings and Bill Fredericks undertook the second Drifters tour of 1972 during September and October, and once again it was an unqualified success. 'Come On Over To My Place', another of their vintage Atlantic recordings, had been reissued and swept into the Top Ten during their visit. Meanwhile, the group had signed a new recording deal with Bell Records and during October put the finishing touches to their first session under the supervision of songwriters Roger Cook and Roger Greenaway, the rhythm tracks having already been laid down in Muscle Shoals, Alabama. The first Bell single, 'Every Night', was released in November.

Yet again, the contrasting styles of Fredericks and Moore gave depth and quality to the act. Bill's sensitive treatments of 'Some Kind Of Wonderful', 'On Broadway' and 'Tears On My Pillow' were often showstoppers, while Johnny's personality and consistency as a performer kept the proceedings at a constant high. *New Musical Express* compared his voice to that of the late Sam Cooke, which was praise indeed. The John McFlair Band provided backing throughout the tour, while at Chester support was provided by Shakin' Stevens & The Sunsets. So popular were the Drifters in Britain that the original schedule was extended by ditching some planned dates in Spain, so that they could return after a few days in Dublin. The proceedings were rounded off with a sellout gig at the new Sundown Ballroom in Brixton, following which they flew off to a season in Las Vegas.

TV appearances
Top Of The Pops   21 September 1972

LITTLE EVA

'The Loco-motion' returned to the British charts during August and this sparked the inevitable scramble to set up a quick charge around the UK ballrooms while there was some fresh mileage to be had from the record. Promoter Terry King contacted Eva's US Manager and they quickly reached agreement for a September tour. The only problem appeared to be Eva herself who had disappeared off to South Carolina on holiday and could not be located before the moment had passed.

JACKIE WILSON

September 1972			October 1972	
22	Nottingham	Intercon	2 Chester	Silhouette
23	Ruislip	USAF	3 Southend	Zero 6
24	Gillingham	Central Hotel	5 Spennymoor	Top Hat
25	Stafford	Top Of The World	6 Manchester	Princess
	Wolverhampton	Lafayette	Manchester	Domino
26	Stoke	Tiffany's	7 Norwich	Melody Rooms
29	Finsbury Park	Rainbow	8 Carlisle	Cosmo
30	Dunstable	California		
	Peckham	Mr. Bee's		
Promoter – Contempo Artists				

Jackie Wilson was always one of those entertainers whose music was difficult to classify, his repertoire containing an eclectic mix of soul, R&B and rock'n'roll, plus the ability to slip into a tuxedo and perform for a nightclub audience at the poshest cabaret venues. His rock'n'roll fans knew him best for his 1957 Top Ten hit, 'Reet Petite', but it was the soul number 'I Get The Sweetest Feeling' which grabbed the attention of British record buyers and was directly responsible for Wilson finally appearing in Britain for the first time. He arrived in the company of his girlfriend, Lynn Crochet, and with his own musicians, Sonny Forrest (guitar), Ron 'Young Blood' Jenkins (bass) and James Lawton (drums).

The tour opened at Nottingham before an assorted audience of boppers and soul fans and Jackie was able to satisfy both factions with a set that included many highlights from throughout his long career. 'Higher And Higher', 'Night' and an amazing 'Reet Petite' were each received with great enthusiasm, but it was the rendition of his million-selling 'Lonely Teardrops' that won the day.

Jackie's appearance at Stafford was no less than sensational, and he later described it as one of the best of his whole career. Unfortunately, the main gig of the tour at the Rainbow in London failed to reach the same heights. Inexplicably only about six hundred people turned up. The main support act, Love Unlimited, failed to materialise and when Jackie arrived at the theatre nobody could find the key to open up his dressing room. By the time he went on stage, the audience were becoming understandably restless but he won them over with the sheer power and range of his wonderful voice and the clarity of his delivery. He again mixed together old and new material and for fifty minutes picked his way through 'Whispers', 'Stormy Monday', 'Lonely Teardrops', 'To Be Loved' and the rest. The lack of a brass section probably affected the soul material more than the rock'n'roll songs, but his energy levels were incredible and he rarely stopped moving for a second throughout his entire act.

Jackie Wilson should have toured Britain years earlier, and had he participated on one of Don Arden's package tours in the early Sixties, he would surely have become a major draw in Britain.

JOHNNY CASH
CARL PERKINS

September 1972		
26-28 London	Royal Albert Hall	
Promoter — NEMS Enterprises		

The *Johnny Cash Show* returned to the UK and effortlessly sold out three nights at the Royal Albert Hall. Johnny and wife June were accompanied by Carl Perkins, the Carter Family, the Statler Brothers, and the Tennessee Three — Marshall Grant (bass), Bob Wootton (guitar) and W.S. Holland (drums) — augmented by pianist and musical director Larry Butler. It had been hoped that singer-songwriter Glen Sherley would make the trip this year but he was still obliged to remain in the States as a condition of his parole.

The total show lasted for two and a half hours of which Cash performed for all but one hour, and once again Carl was restricted to a brief opening spot during which he sang 'Matchbox', 'Me And Jesus' and the inevitable 'Blue Suede Shoes'. The rockers in the audience could have done with a lot more of Perkins and less of the Statlers, who merely repeated the identical act that they had delivered in 1971.

Cash's show was divided into three parts. He opened with 'A Boy Named Sue' and 'Sunday Morning Coming Down', then eased his way through favourites like 'I Still Miss Someone', 'San Quentin' and even 'Silver Haired Daddy Of Mine'.

Carl was on stage trading

ROYAL ALBERT HALL

General Manager: FRANK J. MUNDY

Thursday, 28 September, 1972
at 7.30 p.m.   Doors open at 7

Nems Enterprises Ltd. present
The JOHNNY CASH Show
starring Johnny Cash
An Artist Consultants Production

BALCONY **W**   £1.50

ROW **5**

SEAT **162**   Enter by Door No. **8**

TO BE RETAINED   Official Programme on sale only inside the Royal Albert Hall guitar licks with Bob Wootton right from the start, and for the middle portion of the set Cash performed a series of duets. The first of these was with an unseen Anita Carter, whose beautiful soprano voice floated around the Albert Hall from offstage on 'Uncloudy Day'. Then June Carter, dressed all in white, joined her husband, and they sang four songs together including a lively 'Jackson'.

For the final half hour, the Carters and Statlers regrouped on stage for a stirring climax of gospel music including a moving 'Children, Go Where I Send Thee' and a rousing 'Will The Circle Be Unbroken'. Another triumph for Johnny Cash concluded with well-deserved encores of 'Ring Of Fire' and 'A Thing Called Love'.

BRENDA LEE

Cabaret dates were announced for Brenda Lee in Southend, Sheffield, Stockton, Glasgow and Batley covering a five week period commencing 16 October. However the tour was cancelled when she was taken ill in New Orleans. The press did not reveal the nature of her illness but it was deemed sufficiently serious to require a spell in hospital followed by a period of three months convalescing at home.

DOCTOR ROSS

October 1972			28	London	100 Club
24	London	100 Club	29	Leeds	University
25	Birmingham	University	30	Leicester	Rosie's Blues
26	Lancaster	Duke's Playhouse	**December 1972**		
November 1972			1	London	British Council
2	London	South Bank Poly			Students' Centre
3	Southampton	Concorde	2	Liverpool	Polytechnic
4	High Wycombe	Blues Loft	3	Totnes	Cider House
25	Bedford	College of Education	5	Plymouth	Polytechnic
26	Birmingham	Barbarella's	7	Cambridge	University
27	Corby	Civic Centre	9	London	School of Economics
Promoter unknown					

A second UK tour in 1972 found Doctor Ross playing a mixture of colleges and blues clubs, interspersed with gigs in Europe. His presence was not a big event for rock'n'roll fans although the fascination with Sun Records was now intensifying, and his own 1954 recording of 'The Boogie Disease' for Sun would later become a favourite of the rockabilly enthusiasts. At the London School of Economics he shared billing with MC5 while his appearance at Barbarella's in Birmingham was a part of an American blues festival which also starred Lightnin' Slim.

DEL SHANNON

October 1972			26	Carlisle	Cosmo
29-31	Liverpool	Allinson's	27	Goole	Viking
	Liverpool	Wooky Hollow	28	Bradford	Thornton
November 1972				Bradford	Father Time
1-4	Liverpool	Allinson's	29	Leigh	Garrick
	Liverpool	Wooky Hollow	30	Doncaster	Side Saddle
5	Spennymoor	Top Hat		Lincoln	Aquarius
	Peterlee	Senate	**December 1972**		
6-11	Peterlee	Senate	1	Manchester	Georgian
12-18	Birmingham	Barbarella's		Manchester	Princess
19	Bolton	Copperfield	2	Manchester	Princess
20-25	Southend	Talk Of The South			
Promoter — Henry Sellers					

By October 1972, promoter Henry Sellers had sorted out a worthwhile circuit of clubs and cabaret venues, most of which were located in the north of England. Del Shannon had been added to the roster of artists whom he represented and returned for a five week visit, which like all of Sellers' projects was at least given reasonable pre-tour news coverage in the music press.

However, Sellers could not control the weather and during Shannon's residency at Southend it turned extremely cold and icy. Those who did brave the elements were treated to a confident and well-performed display of his hits, of which 'Little Town Flirt', 'Hats Off To Larry', 'Hey Little Girl', a great version of 'Two Kinds of Teardrops' and (of course) 'Runaway' were the high points of the act. Del's voice appeared to have acquired a deeper, richer tone, and when he steered it up into the higher range, his trademark falsetto did seem a little more ragged than usual, as if he were struggling to reach it.

A live album titled *Live In England* was recorded at the Princess Club in Manchester, preserving this tour for posterity. Backing on the album (and indeed the entire tour) was provided by the ever-reliable John McFlair Band.

DANNY & THE JUNIORS

With so many old records finding a new lease of life in the charts again, every record company was scrutinising its back catalogue for potential chartbusters. Probe Records held the UK rights to 'At The Hop', the 1958 rock'n'roll hit by Danny & The Juniors and, spotting this as a contender for renewed glory, a promotional visit for the group was announced for the end of October. Moreover, it was confidently stated that the original line-up was still intact. However, no more was ever heard of this scheme. Danny & The Juniors remained in the States and 'At The Hop' made little or no impact on the sales graphs.

LITTLE RICHARD

Little Richard was scheduled for three London appearances in mid-November exclusive to the 'Sundown' circuit of venues. Dates were announced and it was hinted that a possible television appearance was in the pipeline as well. Right at the last minute the whole deal collapsed. A spokesman for Sundown claimed that dates and fees had all been agreed, but when their representative flew to the States to meet Richard he flatly refused to sign the contract.

THE CRICKETS

November 1972			3-9	Liverpool	Wooky Hollow
30	Birmingham	Barbarella's		Liverpool	Allinson's
	Birmingham	Rebecca's	10	Carlisle	Cosmo
December 1972			13	Sheffield	Bailey's
1	London	Sundown	14-16	Peterlee	Senate
2	Whitchurch	Civic Hall		Spennymoor	Top Hat
	Shrewsbury	Silhouette	17-23	Stockton	Fiesta
			26-31	Southend	Talk Of The South
Promoter — Henry Sellers					

Over four years had elapsed since the last, rather chaotic Crickets tour, so their many fans were pleased to welcome back Sonny Curtis, Jerry Allison and Glen D. Hardin for a month of ballroom and cabaret dates. The line-up was augmented by the inclusion of bass player, Rick Grech, born in France but brought up in Leicester and a former member of Family, Blind Faith and Traffic. Glen D. had run into Grech at a crap game in Las Vegas and they had both worked together on a Gram Parsons album session. Their road manager, Steve Krikorian had also travelled over from the States for the tour, while another figure of interest to Buddy Holly fans was record producer Bob Montgomery, who hung out with the group but was primarily in Britain to work on their new album.

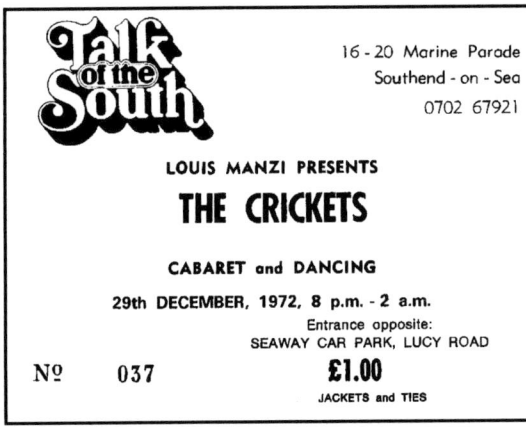

16 - 20 Marine Parade
Southend - on - Sea
0702 67921

LOUIS MANZI PRESENTS

THE CRICKETS

CABARET and DANCING

29th DECEMBER, 1972, 8 p.m. - 2 a.m.
Entrance opposite:
SEAWAY CAR PARK, LUCY ROAD

No 037 **£1.00**
JACKETS and TIES

The shows went over well. At Liverpool's Wooky Hollow Club they opened with 'Oh Boy!' and then performed 'Peggy Sue' — an ideal showcase for Jerry Allison's inimitable drumming. Their new single, 'Lovesick Blues', was well received and led into the melodic 'Raining In My Heart'. Glen D. Hardin's fine piano-playing was a feature of 'Rockin' Pneumonia And The Boogie Woogie Flu', while other highlights were a gentle 'It's So Easy' and an aggressive take on Little Richard's 'Keep A-Knockin' '. They closed with

'That'll Be The Day', but were brought back and repeated 'Oh Boy!' and finally left with a rousing 'Don't Ever Change'.

The Crickets remained in Britain during the early part of January recording their new album, which was released by Philips with the title *Bubblegum, Bop, Ballads And Boogies*. They also made a rare television appearance earlier in the tour when they guested on BBC2's *Old Grey Whistle Test*, performing 'That'll Be The Day', 'Lovesick Blues' and 'My Rockin' Days'.

TV appearances
The Old Grey Whistle Test   1 December 1972 (screened 12 December 1972)

BEN E. KING

December 1972					
1	Manchester	Princess	5	Leicester	Incognito
	Manchester	Georgian	8	Worksop	Intercon
2	Bristol	Yate Centre		Nottingham	Intercon
	Bristol	Bamboo	9	Whitchurch	Civic Hall
3	Carlisle	Cosmo		Cannock	Sloopy's
			10	Sheffield	Fiesta
Promoter — Danny O'Donovan					

Ben E. King's second British tour of 1972 was considerably more low-key than his previous excursions. Publicity in the music press was virtually non-existent, but then after so many visits there was very little new to be written. Popular music is continually on the lookout for something fresh and different. King was always reassuringly the same, which did not make him very newsworthy but pleased his loyal followers as well as the club owners who judged success based on the size of the ticket sales. At the two Manchester clubs he appeared alongside Del Shannon.

BUCK RAM'S PLATTERS

December 1972					
24-30	Sheffield	Fiesta	10	Chester-le-Street	Garden Farm
31	Stockton	Fiesta	11-13	Spennymoor	Top Hat
January 1973				Peterlee	Senate
1-6	Stockton	Fiesta	15-21	Southend	Talk Of The South
7	Spennymoor	Top Hat	22-28	Leicester	Cavendish
8-9	Whitley Bay	Sands	**February 1973**		
			1-3	Birmingham	Barbarella's
Promoter — Danny O'Donovan					

A busy and productive year for live rock'n'roll was concluded with the start of a six-week cabaret tour by the Platters, who flew into Britain on 23 December. This reopened the old debate about authenticity which had at least now been resolved as far as the Drifters and the Coasters were concerned.

The situation regarding the Platters was less straightforward. The group's identity was the property of their long-time manager, Buck Ram, and he had registered it as a corporation called 'Five Platters Inc.', which gave him alone the legal right to use the name. Unfortunately, his group (Monroe Powell, Sherman James, Gene Williams, Lita Fonza and Hal Howard) did not include even one of the individuals who had been responsible for the success of the Platters in the Fifties, or had participated on any of their hit records. So, legally they may have been Platters, but perhaps some of the bogus groups operating in the States with an original member in their line-up could at least claim the moral high ground.

At Southend, Buck Ram's Platters (as they were billed) proved to be a superbly slick and professional outfit. Lead singer Monroe Powell showed perfect pitch and an impressively powerful voice that was ideally suited to their big ballads like 'My Prayer' and 'Smoke Gets In Your Eyes'. Although he sang lead on the majority of the songs, the other group members all contributed as well. Sherman James had a husky voice much better suited to the soul numbers, while it was the deep bass of Gene Williams which brought Paul Robeson's 'Ol' Man River' to life. Hal Howard proved to be the comedian of the group, while Lita Fonza in a tight figure-hugging dress provided a very pleasing physical presence as she danced and shimmied across the stage. 'The Great Pretender', 'Only You', 'With This Ring' and even Mario Lanza's 'Come Prima', were devoured in a well-choreographed set which closed with a frantic 'Land Of A Thousand Dances'.

Postscript

Nobody could agree on precisely how many attended the Wembley rock'n'roll show. Figures as high as 90,000 were claimed, although the Faulk Brothers — who had taxes to pay — seemed anxious to play down the estimates. 56,000 became accepted as the official figure but probably the truth was somewhere in between. Not in dispute was the fact that this was the biggest live rock'n'roll show to ever be held in Britain and, although we have now reached the end of our story, clearly rock'n'roll was far from finished.

In fact, the future could not have been brighter. During the Seventies, British fans hooked on to rockabilly music, restored rock'n'roll to the charts and, with more old recordings being legally or illegally made available, the floodgates finally burst open so that by the Eighties even less prominent names like Mac Curtis, Ray Campi, Charlie Feathers, Sleepy LaBeef and Frankie Ford were regularly to be found touring Britain, while stalwarts such as Charlie Gracie, Freddie Bell and Marvin Rainwater returned again to relive their earlier triumphs.

To close on a personal note, I am already conducting the necessary research to carry *American Rock'n'Roll — The UK Tours* on through the Eighties and, who knows, perhaps it will end up as a trilogy.

I should appreciate any feedback, corrections, additions or comments — even negative ones — about the period 1956–72 and would also like to hear from anybody with detailed knowledge or memorabilia applicable to the later years. I can be reached through: Dixie Fried Music, 111 Worlds End Lane, Orpington, Kent BR6 6AW.

BIBLIOGRAPHY

In addition to all the magazines and newspapers mentioned in the Acknowledgments, the following books were consulted and proved helpful:

Tony Allan, *Save The Last Dance For Me* (Popular Culture, Michigan) 1993.
Derek Henderson, *Gene Vincent – A Discography*
          (Spent Brothers, Southampton) 1998.
John Ingman, *Crickets Fact File* (Ingman Music Research, Brimington) 1998.
Myra Lewis with Murray Silver, *Great Balls Of Fire* (Virgin Books, London) 1982.
Steven Mandich, *Sweet Gene Vincent* (Orange Syringe, London) 2002.
Bill Millar, *The Coasters* (W.H. Allen & Co, London) 1975.
Bill Millar, *The Drifters* (Studio Vista, London) 1971.
Julie Mundy & Darrel Higham, *Don't Forget Me*
          (Mainstream, Edinburgh) 2000.
Dave Nicolson, *On The Road* (Music Mentor Books, York) 2002.
Fred Rothwell, *Long Distance Information* (Music Mentor Books, York) 2001.
Joel Selvin, *Ricky Nelson – Idol For A Generation*
          (Contemporary Books, Chicago) 1990.
Alan Vince, *I Remember Gene Vincent* (Now Dig This, Hendon) 1985.
Ian Wallis, *The Hawk* (Quarry Books, Kingston, Ontario) 1996.
Charles White, *The Life & Times Of Little Richard* (Pan Books, London) 1985.
George R. White, *Bo Diddley – Living Legend*
          (Castle Communications, Chessington) 1995.

SUMMARY OF VISITS BY ARTIST

☐ = TV appearance, recording session or promotional visit only.

Alexander, Arthur
April 1966 215

Anka, Paul
December 1957 30
March 1958 38
☐ January 1959 52
May-June 1959 58
☐ August 1961 93
☐ February 1962 100

Avalon, Frankie
☐ February 1969 273

Bell, Freddie, & The Bellboys
May-June 1957 27

Berry, Chuck
May 1964 *(with Carl Perkins)* 164
January 1965 186
February 1967 233
February 1968 250
July 1969 *(Pop Proms)* 282
February 1972 *(Lanchester Arts Festival)*..324
March 1972 328
August 1972 *(London Rock'n'Roll Show)*.. 340

Black's Combo, Bill
September-October 1964 *(with the Ronettes)*... 173

Bonds, Gary 'US'
April-May 1962 *(with Johnny Burnette)* 103
November 1963 *(with Duane Eddy, the Shirelles and Gene Vincent)*...................... 152
December 1963 152

Boone, Pat
December 1956-January 1957 16
April 1958 39
November 1958 50
☐ February 1960 72
☐ April 1962 104
October 1962 117

Bumble, B., & The Stingers
October-November 1962 116

Burnette, Johnny
April-May 1962 *(with Gary 'US' Bonds)* 103
November 1963 146

Montez, Chris
March 1963 *(with Tommy Roe)* 125
April 1963 127
April 1972 330

Moore, Merrill E.
April 1969 279

Nelson, Rick
February 1972 326

Orbison, Roy
May-June 1963 130
September-October 1963 *(with Bob Luman)* 137
April-May 1964 161
October 1964 175
February-March 1965 192
July 1965 202
March-May 1966 212
January 1967 232
March-April 1967 236
July-September 1968 262
April-May 1969 280
April-June 1970 296
April-June 1971 308
September-October 1971 318
May-September 1972 335

Original Coasters
November 1966 224
See also Coasters

Original Drifters
January 1966 210
May-June 1966 217
December 1966 229
June-July 1967 244
September-November 1967 245
See also 'Drifters'

Orlando, Tony
February 1962 *(with Clarence 'Frogman' Henry and Bobby Vee)* 98
February-March 1962 100
May 1964 167
September-October 1971 *(Dawn)* 317

Otis Show, Johnny
July-August 1972 338

Perkins, Carl
May 1964 *(with Chuck Berry)* 164
June 1964 168
October-November 1964 177
May 1968 *(with Johnny Cash)* 257
October-November 1968 *(with Johnny Cash)* 268
September 1971 *(with Johnny Cash)* 315
September 1972 *(with Johnny Cash)* 352

Platters
See also Fabulous Platters *and* Ram's Platters, Buck

Pomus, Doc, & Mort Shuman

Poni-Tails

Preston, Johnny

Rainwater, Marvin

Ram's Platters, Buck
See also Fabulous Platters *and* Platters

Rivers, Johnny

Roe, Tommy

Ronettes

Doctor Ross

Rydell, Bobby

Sam The Sham & The Pharaohs

Sedaka, Neil

INDEX OF VENUES

Page numbers of venues listed in tour itineraries are shown in normal type.
Page numbers of show reports are shown in **boldface**.

INDEX OF PEOPLE'S NAMES

INDEX OF SONGS & ALBUM TITLES

■ = LP Title

409

INDEX OF FILM & SHOW TITLES

Nothing But The Blues *(TV show)* 220
Off The Record *(TV show)* 38
Oh Boy! *(TV show)* 34, 51, 53, 54, 55, 57, 264, 265
Old Grey Whistle Test *(TV show)* 314, 326, 327, 333, 350, 356
One O'Clock Gang, The *(TV show)* 93
On The Scene *(TV show)* 126
Open House *(TV show)* 167, 170, 179, 180
Othello *(stage play)* 264
People And Places *(TV show)* 119
Play It Cool *(film)* 98
Pop Inn *(radio show)* 187
Pop Proms *(concert)* 282-3, 285
Private Lives Of Adam And Eve, The *(film)* 56
Reading Festival *(concert)* 264, 340
Ready Steady Go *(TV show)* 136, 138, 142, 144, 145, 146, 155, 156, 158, 161, 162, 163, 164,
167, 169, 170, 171, 173, 174, 176, 177, 178, 179, 180, 182, 187,
188, 189, 193, 194, 196, 197, 203, 205, 206, 216, 217, 219, 225,
227, 228
Ready Steady Goes Live *(TV show)* 199
Ready Steady Win *(TV show)* 171, 173
Rock Across The Channel *(concert)* 92
Rock All Night *(film)* 24
Rock Around The Clock *(film)* 13
Rockerscope '62 *(concert)* 106
Rock'n'Roll Singer, The *(TV show)* 289
Rock'n'Trad *(tour)* 87
Rock'n'Trad 2 *(tour)* 87, 90
Rock-Twist-Jive Across The Channel *(concert)* 132-3
Rolf Harris Show *(TV show)* 233
Roy Hudd Show *(TV show)* 256, 257
Roy Orbison Show *(TV show)* 175
Royal Command Performance *(TV show)* 179
Royal Variety Performance *(concert)* 50
Saturday Club *(radio show)* 52, 59, 160, 248
Saturday Crowd, The *(TV show)* 273
Saturday Spectacular *(TV show)* 40, 42, 48, 49, 53, 75, 83, 85, 262
Scene, The *(TV show)* 228
Scene At 6.30 *(TV show)* 124, 127, 128, 130, 131, 136, 142, 147, 158, 160, 161, 167, 169, 173,
174, 179, 182, 187, 191, 196, 199, 202, 206, 216
(S)cool For Cats *(tour)* 18
Scottish Royal Variety Show *(concert)* 135
See You, Soho *(TV show)* 38
Sez Les *(TV show)* 280
Sheriff Of Fractured Jaw, The *(film)* 48
She Stoops To Conquer *(stage play)* 61
Shindig! *(TV show)* 264
Sing, Boy, Sing *(film)* 34
Sounding Out *(TV show)* 326
Sounds For Saturday *(TV show)* 327, 329
Spin Along *(TV show)* 93
Star Light Entertainment *(TV show)* 262
Star Scene 65 *(tour)* 204
Star Time *(TV show)* - *See* Val Parnell's Star Time
Stramash *(TV show)* 211
Sunday Break *(TV show)* 56
Sunday Night At The London Palladium *(TV show)*
13, 16, 22, 23, 24, 27, 31, 34, 37, 38, 39-40, 42, 49, 53, 65, 72, 75, 77, 78, 80-1, 85,
90, 91, 93, 98, 99, 101, 104, 116, 117, 151, 174, 175, 193
See also London Palladium Show
Sunday Night At The Prince Of Wales *(TV show)* 43

ILLUSTRATIONS & PHOTO CREDITS

Back cover photos (left to right) by Colin Phillips, courtesy Granada-TV/George R. White collection, courtesy ABC-TV/Brian Smith collection and courtesy Dr. Rock collection.

Front cover photo and photos on pages 20, 44, 45, 63, 64, 169 courtesy Ian Wallis collection; photos on pages 21, 24, 131, 344 and 346 courtesy George R. White collection; photo on page 26 by Al Ferdman (courtesy Bill Millar collection); photo on page 36 courtesy BBC-TV/ John Goldman/Chris Rees collection; photos on pages 54, 58, 71, 104 and 190 courtesy ABC-TV/ Brian Smith collection; photo on page 68 courtesy ABC-TV/Ian Wallis collection; photo on page 73 courtesy *New Musical Express*/Terry Kay collection; photos on pages 75, 101 and 242 courtesy ATV/Brian Smith collection; photo on page 77 courtesy ATV/Bob Naylor collection; photos on pages 107, 182 and 345 courtesy Dr. Rock collection; photo on page 114 by Jean-Louis Rancurel (courtesy John Garodkin collection); photo on page 141 courtesy of ABC-TV/ George R. White collection; photos on pages 144, 148, 149, 163, 165, 166, 191, 198, 214, 234, 255 and 269 by Brian Smith; photos on pages 156, 263 and 267 courtesy *Melody Maker*/Bill Millar collection; photo on page 160 courtesy Granada-TV/Brian Smith collection; photo on page 170 courtesy of Associated Rediffusion/John Firminger collection; photo on page 193 courtesy of ABC-TV/Terry Kay collection; photos on pages 207, 210, 215, 216, 224 and 226 by Steve Richards (courtesy Bill Millar collection); photos on pages 222, 238 and 288 by Colin Phillips; photo on page 283 courtesy Morten Reff collection; photo on page 299 by Willie Jeffery; photos on pages 305, 320 and 321 by Ian Wallis; photo on page 310 courtesy of Showtime Archive, Stouffville, Ontario; photo on page 332 courtesy of BBC-TV/George R. White collection

Cutting on page 278 courtesy of *Sounds*/Terry Kay collection.

OTHER TITLES FROM MUSIC MENTOR BOOKS

(35 Years of) British Hit EPs
George R. White
ISBN 0-9519888-1-6 *(pbk, 256 pages)* 2001 RRP £16.99

At last, a chart book dedicated to British hit EPs! Includes a history of the format, an artist-by-artist listing of every 7-inch EP hit from 1955 to 1989 (with full track details for each record), analyses of chart performance, and — for the first time ever — the official UK EP charts reproduced in their entirety. Profusely illustrated with *over 600* sleeve shots. A collector's dream!

Long Distance Information: Chuck Berry's Recorded Legacy
Fred Rothwell
ISBN 0-9519888-2-4 *(pbk, 352 pages)* 2001 RRP £18.99

Detailed analysis of every recording Chuck Berry has ever made. Includes an overview of his life and career, his influences, the stories behind his most famous compositions, full session details, listings of all his key US/UK vinyl and CD releases (including track details), TV and film appearances, and much, much more. Over 100 illustrations including label shots, vintage ads and previously unpublished photos.

On The Road
Dave Nicolson
ISBN 0-9519888-4-0 *(pbk, 256 pages)* 2002 RRP £16.99

Gary 'US' Bonds, Pat Boone, Freddy Cannon, Crickets Jerry Allison, Sonny Curtis and Joe B. Mauldin, Bo Diddley, Dion, Fats Domino, Duane Eddy, Frankie Ford, Charlie Gracie, Brian Hyland, Marv Johnson, Ben E. King, Brenda Lee, Little Eva, Chris Montez, Johnny Moore (Drifters), Gene Pitney, Johnny Preston, Tommy Roe, Del Shannon, Edwin Starr, Johnny Tillotson and Bobby Vee tell the fascinating stories of their careers as hitmakers and beyond. Over 150 illustrations.

Elvis & Buddy — Linked Lives
Alan Mann
ISBN 0-9519888-5-9 *(pbk, 160 pages)* 2002 RRP £12.99

The achievements of Elvis Presley and Buddy Holly have been extensively documented, but until now little if anything has been known about the many ways in which their lives were interconnected. For the first time anywhere, rock & roll expert Alan Mann, author of *The A–Z Of Buddy Holly*, takes a detailed look at each artist's early years, comparing their backgrounds and influences, chronicling all their meetings and examining the many amazing parallels in their lives, careers and tragic deaths. Over 50 illustrations including many rare/previously unpublished.

**Music Mentor books
are available from all good bookshops
or by mail order from:**

Music Mentor Books
69 Station Road
Upper Poppleton
YORK YO26 6PZ
England

Telephone/Fax: 01904 330308
International Telephone/Fax: +44 1904 330308
email: music.mentor@lineone.net
website: http://musicmentor0.tripod.com